MW01257280

Financial Accounting
in
SAP S/4HANA
Finance Simplified

Questions & Answers

2nd Edition

Narayanan Veeriah

www.bpbonline.com

Second Edition 2025

Copyright © BPB Publications, India

ISBN: 978-93-65898-675

The first edition of this book was published in 2008, with the name, *SAP FI/CO Questions & Answers*, ISBN: 978-81-83332-316

All Rights Reserved. No part of this publication may be reproduced, distributed or transmitted in any form or by any means or stored in a database or retrieval system, without the prior written permission of the publisher with the exception to the program listings which may be entered, stored and executed in a computer system, but they can not be reproduced by the means of publication, photocopy, recording, or by any electronic and mechanical means.

LIMITS OF LIABILITY AND DISCLAIMER OF WARRANTY

The information contained in this book is true to correct and the best of author's and publisher's knowledge. The author has made every effort to ensure the accuracy of these publications, but publisher cannot be held responsible for any loss or damage arising from any information in this book.

All trademarks referred to in the book are acknowledged as properties of their respective owners but BPB Publications cannot guarantee the accuracy of this information.

To View Complete
BPB Publications Catalogue
Scan the QR Code:

www.bpbonline.com

Dedicated to

My Wife and My Sons

About the Author

A postgraduate in Sciences, a **Chartered Financial Analyst (CFA)**, and a **Project Management Professional (PMP)**, **Narayanan Veeriah** has over 30 years of work experience in accounting, banking, finance, and Information Technology. Trained in SAP FICO, he is a practicing SAP Finance Consultant-cum-Project Manager. Experienced in various versions of SAP (SAP R/3, SAP ERP, and SAP S/4HANA), he has been instrumental in managing SAP implementations (new, rollouts, upgrades, etc.) for several multinational clients.

Until recently, he was an Executive Project Management Professional (Thought Leader) at IBM and an SAP Practice Area Leader. After retiring from IBM, he currently works as a freelancer in SAP consulting. Trained by Thames Valley University of UK, he is also a professional trainer and a visiting faculty member in the areas of ERP, SAP, Banking, etc.

Armed with an excellent understanding of SAP Financial Accounting and Controlling and with good cross-module expertise, he has authored several best-selling books on SAP Finance.

Acknowledgement

A book like this requires a lot of input. We have been fortunate enough to have several SAP experts, as my friends and well-wishers, who were more than willing to provide me with helpful inputs in the form of tips, clarifications, and reviews to shape the questions presented in this book. We have consciously avoided listing all of them here for the simple reason that it may be possible that we inadvertently leave one or more names, and that may look inappropriate. Instead, we extend a loud 'thanks' to all of them.

We thank BPB Publishers for suggesting the publication of this title, which is a revision of an earlier book published in 2006. We acknowledge and thank the content development and technical editors for their input and feedback that helped refine the contents of this book, which reflects the latest in SAP, the 'SAP S/4HANA Finance'. We also appreciate and acknowledge the excellent work done by the layout experts who helped have a world-class book as the end product with pleasing aesthetics.

We want to thank our readers, who have shown tremendous interest in our previous book, which was similar to this and hope that they will continue to support this revised and updated book as well.

Preface

This is the revised version of my earlier book '*SAP FICO Demystified: Questions & Answers*' published in 2006. The book was related to SAP R/3. Over time, SAP has evolved so much that it would not be possible to just 'revise' the earlier book without re-writing to cover the latest in SAP. That is what you have in your hands: a book fully revised to cover SAP S/4HANA Finance. Accordingly, the book has also been renamed '*Financial Accounting in SAP S/4HANA Finance Simplified: Questions & Answers.*'

The book unravels the complexity of SAP S/4HANA Finance through numerous 'Questions & Answers' in the crucial application and sub-application areas. The questions are collated and explained logically so that you progress seamlessly from the basic to the advanced topics. Still, should you find it difficult to visualize what is dealt with in a particular question, there is help through numerous illustrations in the form of screenshots, diagrams, etc., throughout the book. The screenshots (from SAP S/4HANA Finance OP 2023 version), in particular, will help you to comprehend as if you are in front of a computer running the application!

This book comprises of **19 chapters**:

While the first chapter focuses on the basics of SAP and its evolution over the years, the second chapter discusses the technical side of SAP, providing insight into ABAP, Basis, and NetWeaver. The third and fourth chapters discuss SAP HANA and SAP S/4HANA, respectively. Chapter five is all about SAP Fiori. The sixth one is on SAP project management, dealing with the various aspects you need to know while implementing SAP. The seventh chapter deals with SAP S/4HANA Finance, outlining the different solution areas. Chapters eight and nine provide you with the basics of Financial Accounting (FI) in SAP, paving the way for further understanding.

Chapters 10, 11 and *12* deal with the SAP FI global settings, with *Chapter 10* dealing with ledgers, *Chapter 11* on documents, and *Chapter 12* on tax on sales/purchases. *Chapter 13* discusses withholding tax, including extended withholding tax (EWT). *Chapter 14* is all about inflation accounting in SAP. *Chapters 15* to *19* deal with the various application areas within SAP S/4HANA Finance, in detail: General Ledger, Accounts Receivable & Payable, Bank Accounting, and Asset Accounting.

Within these chapters, you will see questions covering the concepts, customizing aspects, tips & tricks, pitfalls, and suggestions to overcome them with numerous screenshots & illustrations, examples, etc.

In all, this book provides you with answers to about 650 questions. You can use the book the way you want: you can start reading from the first chapter, or you can pick up any chapter or question at random and read that. Either way, the answers to the questions will provide you with the required conceptual background of the aspect being discussed, together with the examples and screenshots, including specific customizing inputs that may be required to work with the system.

I am sure that this book will be useful and handy to all, irrespective of the fact whether you are an experienced SAP consultant, a beginner, an end-user, or just someone who is about to learn about SAP, SAP Finance, or SAP S/4HANA Finance.

Chapter 1: SAP Basics: This chapter discusses the basics of SAP, including its evolution from small accounting software to its current stature as the most preferred enterprise resource planning, computing, and management application.

Chapter 2: ABAP, Basis and NetWeaver: Though a functional consultant may not need to know all about the technical side of SAP, it is often helpful to have some idea of this area to appreciate how the application works and comprehend some of the technical jargon you will come across. That is why this chapter discusses SAP ABAP (the programming language in SAP), SAP Basis, and SAP NetWeaver, in addition to SAP BAPI, ALE, OLE, SAP XI, etc.

Chapter 3: SAP HANA: This chapter provides a brief introduction to SAP HANA. You will learn about an in-memory database, how it is different from other databases, its history and evolution, its benefits, its architecture, and how to migrate to SAP HANA.

Chapter 4: SAP S/4HANA: Here, in this chapter, you will get answers to questions like how different SAP S/4HANA is from SAP ERP, the deployment options should you decide to go in for SAP S/4HANA, how the on-premises edition of SAP S/4HANA is different from the cloud edition, SAP S/4HANA Public Cloud vs SAP S/4HANA Private Cloud, the **lines of business (LOB)** that are covered in SAP S/4HANA Private Cloud, GROW with SAP, RISE with SAP, the release cycle of SAP S/4HANA and how to migrate to SAP S/4HANA.

Chapter 5: SAP Fiori: This chapter teaches you all about SAP Fiori. It comprehensively discusses the various aspects of SAP Fiori, including its meaning, evolution, SAP UI, SAP Fiori Launchpad, deployment options, SAP Fiori Mobile Start, SAP Companion, SAP Fiori apps reference library, SAP Fiori Lighthouse, types of SAP Fiori apps, etc.

Chapter 6: Project Implementation: SAP implementation is a complex piece of work, but in this chapter, you will get to know the various project implementation methodologies (SAP Activate, ASAP, and SAP Launch) employed in SAP projects, the various roadmaps in SAP Activate, the different phases of SAP Activate, etc. Besides learning about the SAP Solution Manager in detail, you will understand the different ways of customizing SAP applications to meet your exact business requirements.

Chapter 7: SAP S/4HANA Finance: This chapter provides details about SAP S/4HANA Finance's capabilities, the advantages of implementing it, and the different solution areas that are supported within it.

Chapter 8: FI: General: This chapter explains SAP FI briefly and provides all the necessary information on each functional area, which forms the basis for the forthcoming chapters.

Chapter 9: FI: Enterprise Structure: This chapter introduces you to the enterprise structure in SAP FI. You will learn about the various organizational units, including Company, Company Code, business area, etc., that make up the FI enterprise structure, which is the basis for further discussion in the rest of the chapters.

Chapter 10: FI Global Settings: Ledgers: In this chapter, you will learn all about ledgers and the associated settings: standard and custom fields, the field status, **field status variant (FSV)** and **field status groups (FSG)**, the accounting principles and parallel accounting in SAP, the different types of ledgers, ledger groups and universal journal, the usage of currencies in SAP S/4HANA Finance, the fiscal year, **fiscal year variant (FYV)**, posting period & special period, **posting period variant (PPV)**, the opening and closing of posting periods, the retained earnings account, the special purpose ledger, etc.

Chapter 11: FI Global Settings: Document: This chapter deals with all about documents in SAP: document principle, components of a document, document types, document numbering, reference methods, tolerance and tolerance groups, clearing, partial and residual payments in payment processing, packing and holding a document, document archiving and the like.

Chapter 12: FI Global Settings: Tax on Sales/Purchase: This chapter focuses on the FI global settings relating to taxation in SAP. It discusses the concept of taxation in SAP, the various taxes that are supported, the system configuration relating to tax on sales/ purchases, and the mechanics of tax calculation in SAP, including calculation using an external tax calculation interface.

Chapter 13: FI Global Settings: Withholding Tax: This chapter discusses withholding tax, including **extended withholding tax (EWT)**, in SAP S/4HANA Finance. You will understand all about withholding tax, the framework, the country-specific requirements, the difference between classic and EWT, the configuration of EWT, and the procedure to migrate from classic withholding tax to EWT.

Chapter 14: FI Global Settings: Inflation Accounting: This chapter is the final set of FI global settings that focusses on the inflation accounting. You will learn about inflation index, inflation key, inflation method, etc.

Chapter 15: FI: General Ledger: This chapter provides a detailed view of SAP **General Ledger (G/L)** Accounting in SAP S/4HANA Finance. It highlights the salient features of SAP G/L and outlines the system configuration settings. The chapter discusses the chart of accounts, G/L account master data, G/L account group, sample and reference accounts, financial statement version, document splitting, document clearing, balance interest calculation, etc.

Chapter 16: FI: Accounts Receivable & Accounts Payable – I: In this chapter, you will learn about the overview of FI-A/R and FI-A/P, the customer and vendor master records, the one-time accounts, the configuration settings required for the payment program, the payment processing, the payment proposal, the payment run, etc.

Chapter 17: FI: Accounts Receivable & Accounts Payable – II: In this second installment of FI -A/R and FI-A/P, you will learn all about the dunning in SAP: the concept, the process, and the configuration. Besides the dunning key, the dunning procedure, the dunning level, the dunning area, etc., the chapter also discusses the special G/L transactions, the item interest calculation, the sales and purchase cycles in SAP, and the integration of SD and MM with SAP FI.

Chapter 18: FI: Bank Accounting: Dealing with bank accounting in SAP S/4HANA Finance, the chapter discusses the bank directory, the bank master data, the house bank, SWIFT and IBAN, the bank chains, the manual and electronic bank statements, the lockbox, the cash journal, and the Orbian Payment System.

Chapter 19: FI: Asset Accounting: This final chapter of the book discusses asset accounting in SAP S/4HANA Finance in detail. It deals with asset types, asset numbering, chart of depreciation, depreciation areas, asset class, asset master, the concept of depreciation, depreciation calculation methods, and the different asset transactions, including asset acquisition, asset transfer, asset retirement, etc. The chapter also deals with the depreciation run, depreciation calculation and posting, and scrapping of an asset.

Coloured Images

Please follow the link to download the
Coloured Images of the book:

https://rebrand.ly/4b1e75

We have code bundles from our rich catalogue of books and videos available at **https://github.com/bpbpublications**. Check them out!

Errata

We take immense pride in our work at BPB Publications and follow best practices to ensure the accuracy of our content to provide with an indulging reading experience to our subscribers. Our readers are our mirrors, and we use their inputs to reflect and improve upon human errors, if any, that may have occurred during the publishing processes involved. To let us maintain the quality and help us reach out to any readers who might be having difficulties due to any unforeseen errors, please write to us at :

errata@bpbonline.com

Your support, suggestions and feedbacks are highly appreciated by the BPB Publications' Family.

Did you know that BPB offers eBook versions of every book published, with PDF and ePub files available? You can upgrade to the eBook version at www.bpbonline.com and as a print book customer, you are entitled to a discount on the eBook copy. Get in touch with us at :

business@bpbonline.com for more details.

At **www.bpbonline.com**, you can also read a collection of free technical articles, sign up for a range of free newsletters, and receive exclusive discounts and offers on BPB books and eBooks.

Piracy

If you come across any illegal copies of our works in any form on the internet, we would be grateful if you would provide us with the location address or website name. Please contact us at **business@bpbonline.com** with a link to the material.

If you are interested in becoming an author

If there is a topic that you have expertise in, and you are interested in either writing or contributing to a book, please visit **www.bpbonline.com**. We have worked with thousands of developers and tech professionals, just like you, to help them share their insights with the global tech community. You can make a general application, apply for a specific hot topic that we are recruiting an author for, or submit your own idea.

Reviews

Please leave a review. Once you have read and used this book, why not leave a review on the site that you purchased it from? Potential readers can then see and use your unbiased opinion to make purchase decisions. We at BPB can understand what you think about our products, and our authors can see your feedback on their book. Thank you!

For more information about BPB, please visit **www.bpbonline.com**.

Join our book's Discord space

Join the book's Discord Workspace for Latest updates, Offers, Tech happenings around the world, New Release and Sessions with the Authors:

https://discord.bpbonline.com

Table of Contents

CHAPTER 1
SAP Basics

Introduction

In this chapter, you will be introduced to **Systems, Applications, and Products in Data Processing (SAP)** and its history. You will also gain in-depth knowledge of the different generations of the application while understanding the products and functions available.

1. What is an ERP software application?

Enterprise resource planning (ERP) is a software application that contains programs for running and managing all the core areas of a business, like finance and accounting, human resources, procurement, materials management, manufacturing, and sales and marketing. SAP has been the leading ERP application for several decades.

2. What is 'SAP'?

SAP is an acronym for '*Systeme, Anwendungen, Produkte der Dataenverarbeitung*' in German, meaning 'Systems, Applications and Products in Data Processing.' Founded in 1972, SAP, headquartered in Walldorf, Germany, is the global market leader in enterprise applications software for enterprise resource planning and management, procurement applications, supply chain management, and travel and expense management. SAP has more than 105,000 employees worldwide across 157+ countries. There are 26 industry-specific

Industry Solutions (IS) (IS-Oil, IS-Retail, IS-IS-Bank, etc.); besides the solutions for 16 Lines-of-Business (LOB), SAP solutions can be deployed either on-premises, in-cloud, or as a hybrid. The Cloud user base alone is more than 295 million worldwide.

3. Tell me more about (the history of) SAP.

SAP has evolved over a period from a simple business application to its current form of multiple ERP and other business application offerings, including the cloud-based solutions listed as follows:

- SAP was founded by five former IBM employees (*Dietmar Hopp, Hasso Plattner, Claus Wellenreuther, Klaus Tschira,* and *Hans-Werner Hector*) in 1972 to develop standard business application software with the idea of processing business information in real-time. The company was known as (in German) *Systemanalyse Programmentwicklung*, meaning *System Analysis Program Development*. The Company was set in Weinheim, Germany. By the end of 1972, they introduced a software application called *MIAS* to take care of Materials, Information, and Accounting.

- In *1973*, the company brought out the first financial accounting software (on a mainframe) called *RF*, with the letter 'R' standing for '*Real-Time Processing.*' It was later known as **SAP R/1**. *Knoll Pharmaceuticals* and the furniture producer *3K*, in Germany, were the early adopters running the software application in their companies.

- By 1975, SAP developed a new materials management system called *RM* that integrated purchasing, inventory management, and invoice verification, aiming at a larger market.

- Near the end of the seventies, **SAP R/2** was rolled out with IBM's database as a dialog-oriented business application.

- R/2 was further stabilized during the early years of the eighties: by 1982, there were 250+ companies (in Austria, Germany, and Switzerland) that deployed SAP. It was during this time that the company came out with a version capable of processing business transactions in *multi-language* and *multi-currency* to meet its international clientele. In 1987, SAP established *SAP Consulting* to support new customers, and the company started developing a new generation of software known as SAP R/3, which was multiplatform-enabled.

- SAP GmbH became SAP AG in *1988*. Later, the company established subsidiaries in countries like the US, Sweden, Denmark, and Italy. It also opened an **International Training Center (ITC)** in Walldorf.

- 1989 saw the beginning of the shaping up of **SAP R/3**. The first **Industry Solution (IS)** for utilities was piloted in Germany.

- The nineties saw the introduction of **SAP R/3**, with its *client-server architecture* and *GUI*, which would run on almost any database and most operating systems. SAP

R/3 heralded a new era in enterprise computing, moving from *main frame* to *3-tier architecture* (**Database** | **Application** | **User interface**), and this has become the industry-standard from then on.

- By 1997, more than two million people were working with SAP applications.

- By the end of the nineties, SAP had released the e-commerce-enabled 'mySAP' suite of products, which combined e-commerce solutions with SAP's ERP applications, leveraging cutting-edge web technology.

- SAP's 21st century started with the Enterprise Portal and role-based access to business information. SAP made mySAP ERP, the most comprehensive yet flexible and extensible ERP offering, available as part of the mySAP Business Suite.

- The year 2004 saw the release of the first version of **SAP NetWeaver**.

- In 2006, SAP announced the release of **SAP ERP**, the general release of SAP's flagship application

- 2011 heralded a new era of in-memory computing for SAP. The **SAP HANA** platform enabled its customers to analyze their data in seconds, which would otherwise take days or even weeks.

- SAP's journey into cloud-based solutions began with the acquisition of **Ariba** in 2012 and was further bolstered by the addition of **Fieldglass** in 2014 and later by **Concur**. All these acquisitions allowed SAP to offer a comprehensive suite of services in procurement processes and expense management.

- In 2015, SAP unveiled its next-generation business suite on HANA called **SAP S/4HANA**. This year also saw the launch of the **SAP HANA Cloud Platform** expanding SAP's portfolio of **Internet of Things (IoT)** solutions.

- SAP launched **SAP Leonardo** in 2017 as a digital innovation platform that combines the capabilities of machine learning, IoT, Big Data, blockchain, and analytics on the SAP Cloud Platform with SAP's deep process and industry knowledge.

- SAP C/4HANA was launched in 2018 as a new suite of integrated applications for **Customer Relationship Management (CRM)**.

- In 2021, SAP announced **RISE with SAP**, a 360-degree offering of cloud solutions, infrastructure, and services that enables the migration of SAP ERP to the cloud at one's own pace via a guided journey from SAP.

- The year 2022 brought **SAP AI Solutions,** delivering AI-powered innovations to optimize business processes end to end, including lead-to-cash, design-to-operate, recruit-to-retire, and source-to-pay. SAP also announced **SAP Build**, a low-code solution and a key component of **SAP Business Technology Platform (SAP BTP)**, as well as other innovations. SAP Build, with its easy drag-and-drop interface, allows users (with limited technical expertise) to create enterprise apps, automate processes, and design business sites.

- SAP continues to evolve and innovate, bringing cutting-edge technologies for business information processing.

4. What is SAP ECC?

SAP ERP Central Component (**SAP ECC**) is the predecessor to SAP HANA. Modular by design, SAP ECC is highly customizable to meet any business need, from sales to marketing, materials to production, finance to accounting, human resources to research, etc. It can work with any third-party application, making it both versatile and complex at the same time.

SAP started releasing its ECC versions in 2004 with the release of SAP ERP (ECC) 5.0. The next version, SAP ERP (ECC) 6.0, was released in 2005. Several enhancement packages (EHP) were released, starting with EHP1 in 2006 and ending with EHP8 in 2016. With the introduction of SAP S/4HANA in 2015, SAP announced that it would no longer maintain SAP ERP (ECC) post-2027, necessitating the companies to migrate from ECC to SAP S/4HANA.

5. What is SAP HANA?

Historically, transactional and analytical data were stored separately in two different databases. Often, data needs to be moved from operational systems to data warehouses and retrieved later for data analysis, resulting in considerable delay in the availability of processed data, which leads to difficulties in intra-day decision-making. To address this issue, SAP developed **SAP HANA** (Hasso's New Architecture), which is an in-memory, column-oriented, **relational database management system** (**RDBMS**) with its primary function (as a database server) of storing or retrieving data as requested by the applications and performing analytics as an application server. You will learn more about SAP HANA in a later chapter.

6. What is SAP S/4HANA?

Launched in 2015, **SAP S/4HANA** is the short name for **SAP Business Suite 4 SAP HANA**. It is the fourth generation of SAP Business Suite and runs only on the SAP HANA database. A simplified yet versatile business suite, it is the digital core of your company that combines all the functionalities of ERP, CRM, SRM, and other enterprise applications into a single HANA system. You will learn more about SAP S/4HANA in a later chapter.

7. What are all the 'Products' currently available from SAP?

As of now, the **SAP Products** are available for the following categories:

- Business network
- CRM and customer experience

- Enterprise resource planning
- Financial management
- Human capital management
- Spend management
- Supply chain management
- Sustainability management

8. What SAP Products are available for Enterprise Resource Planning?

Under **Enterprise Resource Planning** (**ERP**), SAP provides SAP S/4HANA that you can deploy on-premises, in the cloud, or as a hybrid mode (a combination of on-premises and cloud deployments). The solutions within SAP S/4HANA include:

- Finance
- Sales
- Procurement
- Manufacturing and supply chain
- Professional services automation

9. Outline the Supply Chain Management Solutions of SAP.

SAP enables a sustainable supply chain with minimal risk and cost through its various **Supply Chain Management** (**SCM**) solutions and products that include:

- Supply Chain Planning:
  - SAP Integrated Business Planning for Supply Chain
  - SAP Business Network Supply Chain Collaboration
  - SAP S/4HANA Supply Chain for extended service parts planning
  - SAP S/4HANA for advanced ATP
  - SAP S/4HANA Manufacturing for planning and scheduling
- Supply Chain Logistics:
  - SAP Extended Warehouse Management
  - SAP Transportation Management
  - SAP Business Network Global Track and Trace
  - SAP Yard Logistics

- o   SAP Business Network Freight Collaboration
- Manufacturing:
  - o   SAP Digital Manufacturing
  - o   SAP S/4HANA for EHS workplace safety
  - o   SAP S/4HANA Manufacturing for production engineering and operations
  - o   SAP S/4HANA for EHS environment management
  - o   SAP Quality Issue Resolution
- Product Lifecycle Management:
  - o   SAP Enterprise Portfolio and Project Management
  - o   SAP Product Lifecycle Costing
  - o   SAP S/4HANA for product compliance
  - o   SAP Engineering Control Center
  - o   SAP S/4HANA Cloud for projects, collaborative project management
  - o   SAP Enterprise Product Development
- Enterprise Asset Management:
  - o   SAP Asset Performance Management
  - o   SAP Business Network Asset Collaboration
  - o   SAP Service and Asset Manager
  - o   SAP Field Service Management
  - o   SAP Crowd Service
  - o   Asset management with SAP S/4HANA Cloud

10. What are the components of SAP's Financial Management solution?

SAP's Financial Management enables the following:

- **Financial planning and analysis (FP&A)**
- Accounting and financial close
- Tax management
- Treasury management
- Quote-to-cash management
- **Governance, risk, and compliance (GRC)** and cybersecurity

11. What are the different products under SAP's Financial Management?

SAP's Financial Management products include the following:

- Financial planning and analysis:
  - o SAP Analytics Cloud
  - o SAP Profitability and Performance Management
- Accounting and financial close:
  - o SAP S/4HANA Finance for group reporting
  - o SAP S/4HANA Cloud for advanced financial closing
  - o SAP S/4HANA for central finance
  - o SAP Document and Reporting Compliance
  - o SAP Tax Compliance
  - o SAP Account Substantiation and Automation by BlackLine
  - o SAP Intercompany Financial Hub by BlackLine
- Tax management:
  - o SAP Document and Reporting Compliance
  - o SAP Tax Compliance
  - o SAP Responsible Design and Production
  - o SAP Profitability and Performance Management
- Treasury management:
  - o SAP Cash Management
  - o SAP S/4HANA Finance
  - o SAP Treasury and Risk Management
- Quote-to-cash management:
  - o SAP Billing and Revenue Innovation Management
  - o SAP CPQ
  - o SAP S/4HANA for receivables management
  - o SAP Cash Application
- Cybersecurity and governance, risk, and compliance:
  - o SAP Risk Management
  - o SAP Process Control
  - o SAP Audit Management

- o SAP Business Integrity Screening
- o SAP Financial Compliance Management
- o SAP Watch List Screening
- o SAP Global Trade Services
- o SAP Enterprise Threat Detection
- o SAP Privacy Governance
- o SAP Access Control
- o SAP Cloud Identity Access Governance

12. What is 'SAP Spend Management'?

SAP Spend Management is all about automating spending processes, thereby actively managing spending for better control that will result in more savings and better value. The solution, via **SAP Ariba, SAP Fieldglass,** and **SAP Concur**, helps develop a deeper understanding of a company's spending and aims at streamlined end-to-end spend process integration with business partners, back-end systems, and pay processes of the company.

13. What are all the components and products in 'SAP Spend Management' solution?

The SAP Spend Management component and products are as follows:

SAP Spend Management component	Products
Sourcing and contracts	• SAP Ariba Spend Analysis • SAP Ariba Sourcing • SAP Ariba Contracts • SAP Ariba Category Management • SAP Ariba Source-to-Contract Suite • SAP Ariba Strategic Sourcing Suite • Product sourcing solutions from SAP • SAP Business Network Discovery
Procurement	• SAP Ariba Buying and Invoicing • SAP Ariba Catalog • SAP Ariba Buying • SAP Ariba Central Procurement, private cloud edition

SAP Spend Management component	Products
Invoice and payment	• SAP Ariba Invoice Management • SAP Ariba Central Invoice Management
Supplier management	• SAP Ariba Supplier Lifecycle and Performance • SAP Ariba Supplier Risk
External workforce and services	• SAP Fieldglass Contingent Workforce Management • SAP Fieldglass Worker Profile Management • SAP Fieldglass Services Procurement • SAP Fieldglass Assignment Management
Travel and expense	• Concur Expense • Concur Travel • Concur Invoice

Table 1.1: SAP Spend Management Components and Products

14. What is SAP Business Network?

SAP Business Network is a comprehensive B2B collaboration platform that connects people, processes, and systems across multiple enterprises. Its purpose is to digitize transactions and create transparent, resilient, and sustainable supply chains. This is considered a better way to collaborate with a company's trading partners in a networked economy.

The products include the following:

- SAP Business Network Commerce Automation and SAP Business Network Discovery for procurement collaboration
- SAP Business Network Planning Collaboration and SAP Business Network Supply Chain Collaboration, for supply chain collaboration
- SAP Business Network Freight Collaboration, SAP Business Network Global Track and Trace, and SAP Business Network Material Traceability for logistics collaboration
- SAP Business Network Asset Collaboration, for asset collaboration
- Taulia Dynamic Discounting, Taulia Virtual Cards, Taulia Supply Chain Finance, Taulia Accounts Receivable Financing and Taulia Inventory Management, for finance collaboration
- SAP Business Network for suppliers for customer collaboration

15. What is 'SAP Success Factors'?

SAP Success Factors helps manage an enterprise's **Human Resource Capital (HCM)**. Traditional HCM software applications fall short of expectations for managing today's digital economy. SAP SuccessFactors **Human Experience Management (HXM)** Suite puts the company's human resources at the center and creates AI-powered solutions for competitive advantage.

16. What about the CRM and Customer Experience solutions from SAP?

SAP CRM and Customer Experience (CX) are intelligent and tailor-made solutions for meeting any company's critical business needs for an intelligent customer experience. They support end-to-end processes that leverage the SAP application. They take care of every company's e-commerce, customer data, marketing, customer service, and sales automation via a plethora of products.

17. How does SAP handle sustainability management for enterprises?

SAP's sustainability solutions help record, report, and act on a company's sustainability goals with its product called **SAP Cloud for Sustainable Enterprises**. The solutions deliver company-wide functionality and industry-specific features enabling sustainability in business, embedding operations, experience, and financial insights into the company's core business processes. The product portfolio is made up of the following:

- SAP Sustainability Control Tower
- SAP Sustainability Footprint Management
- SAP S/4HANA Cloud for EHS environment management
- SAP Responsible Design and Production
- SAP Green Token

18. What are all the offerings from SAP for small and midsize businesses?

Several business solutions from SAP provide ready-to-run processes and industry best practices for managing finance, HR, operations, procurement, sales, etc., for small and medium enterprises. While the solution **SAP Business One** is for small businesses, one can use **SAP Business ByDesign** for midsize business enterprises.

19. Explain 'SAP Business One'?

SAP Business One is an affordable ERP application for a small business. The application helps to manage the whole gamut of business functions and processes, from accounting, financials, purchase, inventory, production, sales, marketing, and customer service. The solution can be integrated with SAP HANA and deployed on-premises or in the cloud. It is flexible, modular, quick, and easy to implement; the application can be up and running within days.

20. What is SAP's 'Business ByDesign'?

A single cloud-based ERP, **SAP Business ByDesign** can take care of the business needs of any mid-size enterprise. The solution helps scale and grow without the complexities of a regular ERP and is affordable. A single unified solution, it comes with pre-built processes that you can use to manage the enterprise's finance, sales, product management, purchasing, human resources, etc. It can connect every function across the company with best practices. It also provides in-depth analytics for quicker decision-making.

21. What is 'SAP Build Code'?

SAP Build code is a generative AI-based code development with *Joule copilot*. Optimized for Java and JavaScript application development, it provides a readily available development environment for coding, testing, integrations, and application lifecycle management.

22. What are the 'Industry Solutions' that are made available by SAP?

SAP's **Industry Solutions** (**IS**) helps solve complex business challenges in various industries, besides enabling digital transformation in the modern day. SAP provides packaged solutions for the following industries:

- Aerospace and defense
- Agribusiness
- Automotive
- Banking
- Building materials
- Cargo, transportation, and logistics
- Chemicals
- Consumer products
- Defence and security

- Engineering, construction, and operations
- Fashion
- Government
- Healthcare
- High tech
- Higher education and research
- Industrial manufacturing
- Insurance
- Life sciences
- Media and entertainment
- Mill products
- Mining
- Oil, gas, and energy
- Passenger travel and leisure
- Professional services
- Real estate
- Retail
- Sports
- Telecommunications
- Utilities
- Wholesale distribution
- Sports
- Telecommunications
- Utilities

Join our book's Discord space

Join the book's Discord Workspace for Latest updates, Offers, Tech happenings around the world, New Release and Sessions with the Authors:

https://discord.bpbonline.com

CHAPTER 2
ABAP, Basis and NetWeaver

Introduction

The chapter gives you a brief idea about the technical side of SAP. Here, you will learn about ABAP, BASIS, and NetWeaver. You will also learn about technical terms like Client and Instance, besides understanding SAP BAPI, ALE, OLE, SAP XI, Internal Tables, Logical Database, Screen Painter and Menu Painter, Transport and CTS, Enhancements and Authorizations, Drill-down Reports, SAP Query and the like.

23. What is 'SAP BASIS'?

SAP Business Application Software Integration Solution (BASIS) is a collection of SAP programs that provide the run-time environment for ABAP. SAP BASIS can be thought of as the essential link between the ABAP program code and the computer's operating system. It functions as a specialized interpreter, reading the ABAP code and translating it into instructions that the operating system can understand and execute. This layer of abstraction not only ensures that ABAP programs run smoothly across different operating systems but also provides a protective environment to prevent accidental alterations or external interference with the program code; without BASIS, you will not be able to execute any of your ABAP programs in SAP.

With tools designed for system monitoring, administration, and performance optimization, BASIS is crucial for maintaining system health and enabling businesses to adapt their systems to evolving needs. The SAP BASIS administrator is usually called the 'SAP BASIS *Consultant'*.

SAP BASIS was the technology platform for all SAP releases based on client-server technology. While all R/3 releases of SAP used SAP BASIS, the later versions of SAP, that is, ECC, were on NetWeaver technology, with NetWeaver being the web application server.

24. So, what is 'SAP NetWeaver'?

SAP NetWeaver (NW) is the integrated web application technology platform or software stack that supports various SAP ECC applications like ERP, CRM, BW, SRM, PI/XI, etc. Previously, SAP BASIS remained the technology platform for all SAP R/3 applications. Since then, SAP has moved to this latest technology, even though the SAP BASIS and SAP NetWeaver terms are used interchangeably.

SAP NetWeaver is an open web-based application platform that provides an extensive range of technologies for integrating all business applications and overcoming any technological barrier. As it uses open standards, it can facilitate integration with data/programs from almost any technology or source. SAP NetWeaver Application Server is also called **WebAS**.

SAP NetWeaver is a versatile platform that supports a **service-oriented architecture (SOA)** for **enterprise resource planning (ERP)** application integration. It enables custom development and facilitates integration with various applications and systems, enhancing operational efficiency and data consistency across the business. While ABAP is the primary programming language for SAP NetWeaver, it also provides the flexibility to develop using other languages such as C, C++, and Java, allowing for a wide range of programming skills to be utilized in creating robust business solutions. SAP NetWeaver can run both Java (J2EE Services) and ABAP independently or, in some cases, together, such as SAP Solution Manager and PI. As with any other SAP application, SAP NetWeaver has its release strategy.

25. Explain the SAP NetWeaver versions.

The Israeli business *'TopTier Software'* brought out the NetWeaver platform originally in 1997. SAP acquired this Company in early 2000, and the first SAP NetWeaver was released in 2005 as SAP NW 7.0. Since then, there have been several releases, the current being SAP NW 7.54 AS ABAP. The alignment of SAP NetWeaver 7.5's maintenance strategy with that of SAP Business Suite 7 is a strategic move to ensure a smooth transition to SAP S/4HANA. This approach provides businesses with the assurance of continued support for SAP NetWeaver 7.5 in mainstream maintenance until the end of 2027, with an option for extended maintenance until 2030. This extended support period is crucial for organizations planning their migration to SAP S/4HANA, allowing them ample time to manage the transition effectively and with minimal disruption to their operations.

26. What are the components of SAP NetWeaver?

SAP NetWeaver, the central foundation for the SAP software stack, provides a flexible platform for other NetWeaver components like **Process Integrator** (**PI**), **Business Intelligence** (**BI**), **Enterprise Portal** (**EP**), and ABAP and Java applications. The SAP NetWeaver components are built on the SAP **Web Application Server** (**WebAS**) and programmed in J2EE or ABAP.

The SAP NW consists of three integration layers (people, information, and process) and one application platform, the SAP WebAS. This platform supports both the ABAP and JAVA runtime environments: the **Application Server ABAP** (**AS ABAP**) and the **Application Server Java** (**AS JAVA**).

27. Explain SAP R/3 system (classic) architecture.

An SAP R/3 system consists of a 3-tier architecture made up of the following, as shown in *Figure 2.1*:

- Database Layer
- Application Layer
- Presentation Layer

The **Database Layer**, an integral component of the three-tier architecture, is responsible for data storage and management. It utilizes a **Relational Database Management System** (**RDBMS**) to handle requests from the Application Layer, ensuring data integrity and security. Additionally, this layer may contain other data storage mechanisms, providing a robust and scalable environment for handling diverse data requirements and facilitating seamless data retrieval and manipulation for the Application Layer.

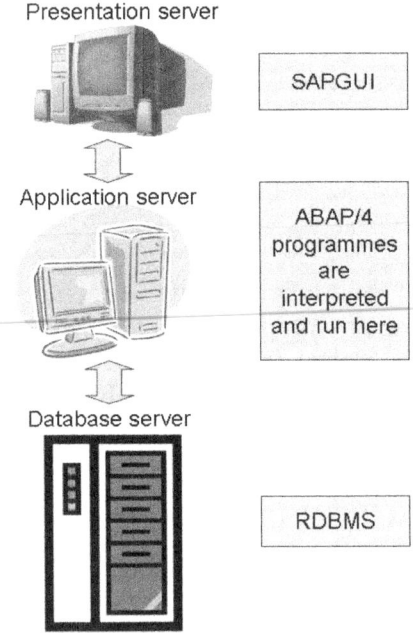

Figure 2.1: *SAP R/3 system architecture*

The **Application Layer** comprises one or more application servers besides a message server. The application server interprets the ABAP or Java programs, getting input from them and providing processed output back to them. Irrespective of the number of application servers, there will be only one message server, which facilitates communication between the application servers.

The *Presentation Server*, commonly called the **Presentation Layer**, is an essential component of the three-tier architecture of SAP systems. It is installed on the user's workstation and includes interfaces such as SAPGUI or Web GUI, and is often called the front-end. These interfaces are responsible for collecting user inputs, forwarding them to the Application Server for processing, and then displaying the processed outputs. The Application Server may also interact with the Database Layer if needed, ensuring a seamless data flow across the system and providing the user with a coherent and responsive experience.

28. What is a 'Client' in an SAP system?

The '**Client**' in an SAP system is a technical, structural feature that has an independent status both in legal and organizational terms. Denoted by a three-character alphanumeric code, you can define a Client while Customizing the SAP application (more details later). As a default, an SAP application is normally set up with two Clients: Client 000 and Client 001.

Client 000 is known as the 'SAP standard Client,' and the original SAP system is held there. This Client consists of default values for all the SAP tables and gets updated with every system upgrade/release from SAP. You will not be able to work with this Client.

The Client 001 is an exact replica of Client 000. You can work with this Client while Customizing the SAP standard system to meet your specific business requirements.

29. What is an 'Instance' in SAP?

In the context of SAP systems, an '**instance**' is a crucial administrative unit that encapsulates components and work processes of an application server. Multiple instances can be grouped under a single client, each operating independently yet contributing to the system's collective functionality. The term *'central instance'* specifically denotes the primary database server, which plays a pivotal role in managing and maintaining the integrity of the data across the entire SAP landscape. Understanding these definitions is key to navigating the complex architecture of SAP systems.

30. What do you mean by 'SAP System Landscape'?

In the context of SAP, the **system landscape** is a critical aspect of managing and deploying SAP solutions effectively. It typically consists of multiple servers or systems, each with a specific role in the development lifecycle. The *Development System* (aka 'Development Client') is where new applications and changes are created, and the *Test System* (aka 'Test Client') is used to evaluate new developments in an environment that simulates the *Production System* (aka 'Production Client'), which is the live environment where all business processes are executed. This structured approach allows for thorough testing and development before changes affect the live business operations.

31. What is 'SAP Data Dictionary'?

The **SAP Data Dictionary**, or DDIC, is the central repository for metadata related to database objects. Facilitating efficient management of data definitions and ensuring consistency and integrity across the system, the DDIC supports various object types, including tables, views, and structures, which are essential for application development. It is also seamlessly integrated with the underlying RDBMS. This integration allows for a harmonious mapping between the logical structures used within SAP and their physical counterparts in the database, streamlining data operations and maintenance.

32. What is called an 'SAP Business Object'?

SAP Business Objects serve as virtual representations of real-world business entities within SAP systems, encapsulating data and processes while abstracting the complexities of the underlying structures. They are integral to the *SAP BusinessObjects Business Intelligence suite*, which provides a centralized platform for data reporting, visualization, and sharing, enabling informed decision-making based on real-time insights. The **Business Object Repository** (**BOR**) acts as a centralized database to manage these objects, ensuring consistency and accessibility across the business's operations (*Figure 2.2*):

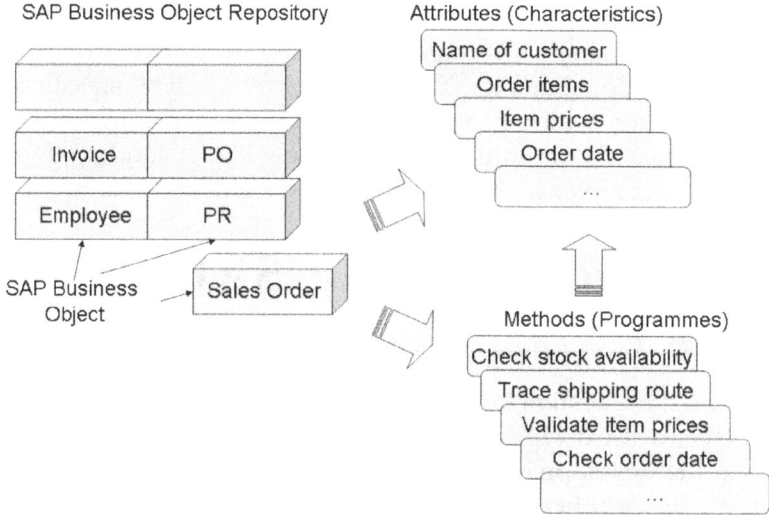

Figure 2.2: SAP Business Object

Attributes are essential in defining the properties and specifications of a business object. In the context of a Sales Order', for example, attributes such as the date, items, and prices provide a detailed snapshot of the transaction. They not only facilitate the tracking and processing of orders but also enable businesses to analyze sales patterns and customer behavior. Accurate and comprehensive attributes are crucial for effective business operations and customer relationship management.

In the SAP context, *methods* are integral to the system's functionality, allowing for a wide range of business processes to be automated and optimized. These methods can be tailored to perform specific tasks such as verifying stock levels, tracking delivery routes, monitoring item pricing, and confirming order dates. By leveraging these methods, businesses can enhance efficiency, reduce errors, and improve overall operational workflow.

33. Explain the 'Client-dependent' and 'Client-independent' elements in SAP.

While the '**Client-independent**' elements are objects used in all Clients, the '**Client-dependent**' (or *Client-specific*) elements are used only in a specific Client. Hence, the Client-dependent data is limited to the Client for which you create them and is not accessible to any other Client. However, Client-independent data is available for all clients of an SAP system.

The data structures (such as field definitions, table structures, and file set-ups), tables (such as T000, MARA, KNA1, LFA1 etc.), SAP transactions, SAP programs, SAP standard reports, SAP authorization objects, and SAP Library are all Client-independent.

The Client-specific tables that you have copied from Client 000, HR and user master records, authorization profiles, and customer-specific programs that you have created are all examples of Client-dependent objects that are available only in the Client wherein you created them.

In database management, particularly within SAP systems, client-dependency is crucial. Client-dependent tables contain a MANDT field (data type 'CLNT') that specifies the Client ID, ensuring that data is segregated between clients. Conversely, client-independent tables lack this field, allowing data to be shared across all Clients. This distinction is vital for maintaining data integrity and ensuring that the system's multi-tenancy architecture functions correctly.

34. What is 'ABAP'?

ABAP, or *Advanced Business Application Programming*, is a high-level programming language created by SAP for developing **enterprise resource planning** (**ERP**) applications. It is known for its robustness and ability to handle complex business applications, making it a cornerstone of SAP software development. ABAP's evolution into ABAP/4 highlights its fourth-generation language features, emphasizing database interaction and a descriptive approach to programming. This language has played a significant role in business software, offering a specialized toolset for SAP application development. It has a very easy syntax, like COBOL, and is simple to program. Depending on the ABAP Platform, you need to use different versions of the ABAP language.

35. So, what is an 'ABAP Platform'?

The ABAP Platform is a technical platform for products such as SAP S/4HANA or SAP **Business Technology Platform** (**BTP**) used to develop and execute ABAP-based application programs.

The ABAP Platform provides an **ABAP development environment (ABAP DE)** that mainly consists of ABAP programming language, development tools (like ABAP Editor and ABAP Workbench) for developing ABAP applications, and the possibility to access APIs made up by other repository objects.

There are two types of ABAP Platforms according to the programming paradigm:

- ABAP Platform for ABAP Cloud
- ABAP Platform for Classic ABAP

Note: The evolution of SAP's backend technology terminology reflects its ongoing innovation and development. The ABAP Platform (replacing the earlier terminology 'Application Server ABAP'), as it is known today, serves as the comprehensive, modern foundation for SAP applications written in the ABAP language, much like its predecessor, SAP BASIS (now known as 'SAP NetWeaver'), did in the past. This platform provides the services and framework necessary for the effective execution and operation of SAP systems, ensuring robust performance and compatibility with the latest technologies and standards in enterprise software.

36. Explain 'ABAP Platform for ABAP Cloud.'

The ABAP Platform for ABAP Cloud, or simply the 'ABAP Cloud,' represents a modern approach to developing ABAP-based applications optimized for the cloud environment. You will use a subset of ABAP Platform, with special rules, for programming in ABAP Cloud. Compared to classic ABAP, you will notice restrictions regarding ABAP language versions, development tools, and access to released APIs.

The examples of ABAP Platforms used for ABAP Cloud include the following:

- SAP BTP ABAP Environment (a standalone ABAP Platform for cloud applications, also known as "**Steampunk**".
- ABAP Platform Cloud (delivered as the ABAP Platform of SAP S/4HANA Cloud, also known as **embedded Steampunk**).

37. Describe the 'Classic ABAP Platform' for SAP.

The ABAP Platform for classic ABAP, or simply the "classic ABAP," is the ABAP programming environment for legacy solutions. Here, you can use the complete ABAP Platform for ABAP developments. There is no restriction on ABAP language versions, development tools, or access to repository objects. Such an unrestricted ABAP Platform is used by SAP S/4HANA.

Offering an unrestricted ABAP development environment, the classic ABAP Platform has the following features:

- You can freely choose the ABAP language version for your ABAP programs, even though the default is Standard ABAP.
- You can use both the **ABAP development tools for Eclipse** (**ADT**) and the ABAP Workbench as development tools.
- You can access all repository objects from other repository objects. Though a package concept is available, it is not enforced.

38. What is 'ABAP Dictionary'?

ABAP Dictionary is a persistent repository of metadata. SAP uses this dictionary to describe data types, database tables, views, etc., used in development objects such as ABAP programs or CDS (core data services) entities.

39. What are the different 'Types' of 'ABAP Programs'?

There are eleven types of ABAP Programs in SAP, as shown in *Figure 2.3*:

- **1**: Executable Programs (ABAP Reports)
- **I**: INCLUDE Program
- **M**: Module Pool
- **S**: Sub-Routine Pool
- **J:** Interface Pool
- **K:** Class Pool
- **T:** Type Pool
- **F:** Function Group
- **X**: Transformation (XSLT or ST Program)
- **Q:** Database Procedure Proxy
- **B:** Behavior Definition

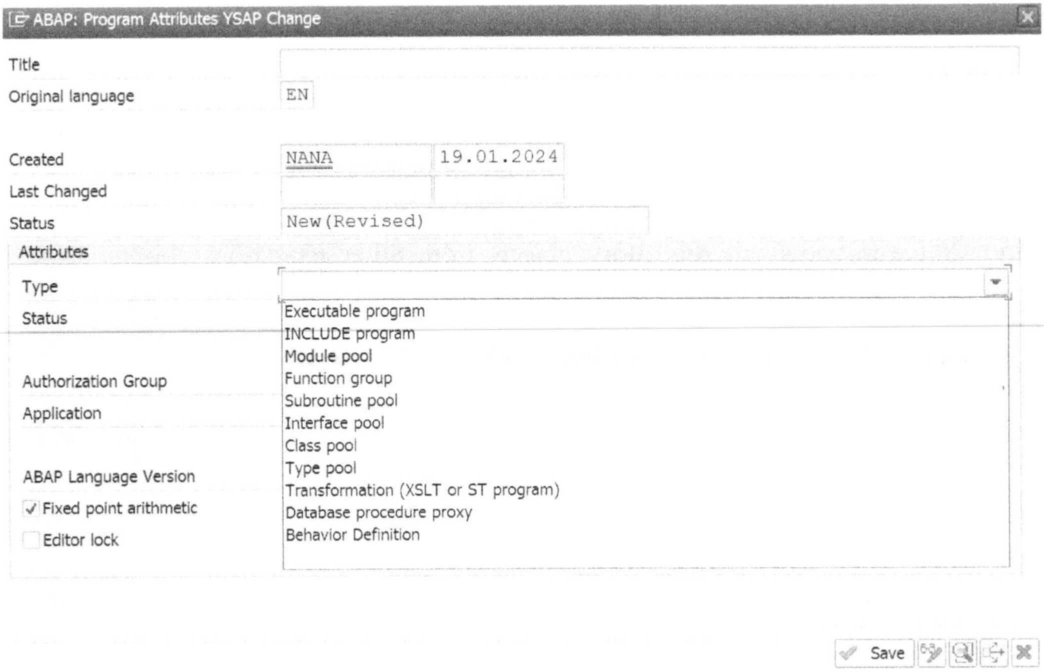

Figure 2.3: ABAP program types

40. What are 'Internal Tables'?

Internal tables in ABAP/4 are pivotal for handling data during the runtime of a program. Present only during the program's runtime, they offer a flexible way to work with subsets of database tables, allowing for calculations and data reorganization to meet user requirements. The three types of internal tables, Standard, Sorted, and Hashed, each serve distinct purposes, from maintaining non-unique keys in a linear index to managing unique keys in a non-linear structure. This versatility makes internal tables a fundamental aspect of ABAP/4 programming, providing functionality similar to arrays in other programming languages.

41. What is a 'Logical Database'?

SAP's **logical databases** provide a streamlined approach to data retrieval, focusing on coding the processing logic, such as GET and CHECK statements, rather than the underlying data access methods. This architecture allows for a 'read' program that mirrors the structure of the local database, complete with a dynamic selection screen. The benefits of this system are multifaceted, including check functions that ensure user inputs are both complete and correct, enhancing data integrity. Additionally, it facilitates meaningful data selection by allowing users to retrieve relevant data to their specific context. Central authorization checks are also a key feature, providing a secure environment for database access. Moreover, the system is designed for excellent read access performance, which does not compromise the hierarchical data view that is essential for the application logic. This balance of efficiency and structure makes logical databases an invaluable tool in data management within SAP environments.

Figure 2.4

42. How do you modify SAP 'Standard Tables'?

In SAP, standard tables can be modified to meet specific business requirements, in two ways:

- *"Append Structures"* allows you to add custom fields to standard tables without modifying the original structure.
- *"INCLUDES"*, on the other hand, are used to include custom fields in the standard table structures.

Both methods ensure that modifications are preserved during system upgrades, maintaining the integrity of the original SAP system while providing the flexibility needed for customization.

43. What is 'BDC' Programming in SAP?

Batch Data Conversion (BDC) is a critical process in SAP for migrating large amounts of data from external or legacy systems. It utilizes batch input programming to ensure data integrity and system stability during the transfer.

The three primary methods for BDC are as follows:

- **Call Transaction Method**: This is suitable for small to medium datasets and allows error handling on a transaction basis.
- **Session Method**: This is ideal for large data volumes and provides a comprehensive error log.
- **Direct Input Method**: This is the fastest approach and is used for standard data structures.

Each method has its own set of advantages and is chosen based on the specific requirements of the data migration project. Whatever the BDC method, they all involve identifying the transaction screens, programming a BDC table to hold the data, and then submitting this data to SAP either in batch mode or as a single transaction (using 'CALL TRANSACTION' command). However, note that you cannot use 'CALL TRANSACTION' if there is a requirement to process multiple transactions; in such a case, you should, instead, use the 'BDC INSERT' function.

44. What is 'BAPI'?

Business Application Programming Interfaces (BAPIs) are essential components of the SAP system, enabling seamless integration between SAP and third-party applications. They play a crucial role in extending the capabilities of SAP's robust business processes and data management systems. By utilizing BAPIs, developers can create or modify business objects within the SAP environment, ensuring that each BAPI is uniquely assigned to one business object, reflecting a one-to-one relationship. Some common use cases for BAPIs in SAP systems include data exchange (that allows for the transfer of information between SAP and non-SAP systems) and process triggering (that results in, for example, creating sales orders or posting financial documents).

The *BAPI Explorer* (*Figure 2.5*) is an invaluable tool for navigating the extensive library of BAPIs. It organizes BAPIs in a user-friendly manner, both hierarchically and alphabetically, and provides detailed information, documentation, and tools for each BAPI. This facilitates developers in their efforts to enhance the SAP system's functionality, whether through the creation of new BAPIs or the modification of existing ones. The structured approach of the BAPI Explorer aids in maintaining the integrity and efficiency of business processes, making it an indispensable asset for SAP users and developers.

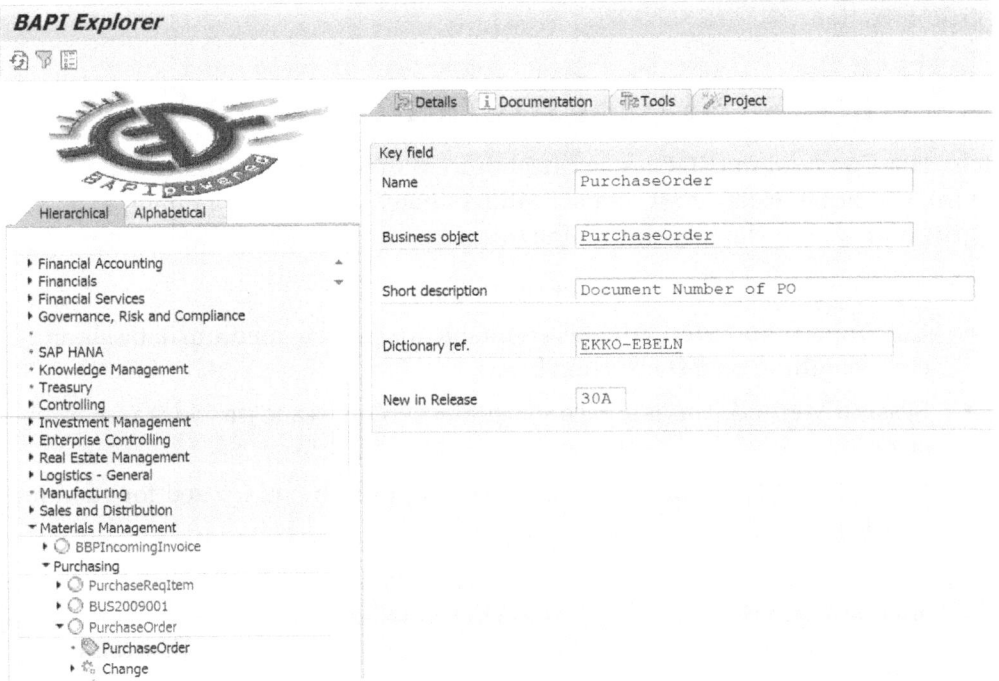

Figure 2.5: BAPI explorer

Figure 2.6

45. What is 'ALE'?

Application Link Enabling (ALE) is a robust framework that facilitates communication and data distribution between different SAP systems, ensuring consistency and integration across a distributed environment. It operates on three core layers: application services, distribution services, and communication services. ALE's architecture allows for both synchronous and asynchronous data transfer without relying on a central database, making it a flexible solution for various business scenarios.

The introduction of *SAP* **Exchange Infrastructure (XI)**, which later evolved into **Process Integration (PI)** and then into **Process Orchestration (PO)**, was aimed at broadening the scope of integration capabilities beyond what ALE could offer. SAP XI/PI/PO is a middleware solution connecting SAP and non-SAP systems, facilitating a more extensive enterprise-wide integration. This is particularly beneficial for complex system landscapes where multiple systems from different vendors must be integrated. While ALE specializes in SAP-to-SAP communication via IDocs, SAP XI/PI/PO extends this functionality to include non-SAP systems.

46. Is 'SAP XI' intended to replace 'ALE'?

While ALE has been a cornerstone in SAP's integration strategy, particularly for SAP-to-SAP communication, SAP XI/PI/PO is intended to provide a more comprehensive and scalable integration solution. It is not a replacement but an evolution that addresses the growing need for integration in increasingly complex IT environments. The decision to use ALE or SAP XI/PI/PO would depend on the specific requirements of the business scenario, the complexity of the system landscape, and the need for integration with non-SAP systems.

47. What is 'RFC'?

Remote Function Call (RFC) is a powerful communication interface in multi-tiered environments, enabling the seamless execution of functions across different systems. In the context of SAP systems, RFC enables interoperability by allowing distinct systems to call function modules located in remote systems. This mechanism is not only pivotal for system-to-system communication but also for client-server interactions where an SAP system may act as either the client or the server. By facilitating these communications, RFC ensures that businesses can maintain a distributed yet interconnected system architecture, which is essential for modern ERP environments. The ability to perform remote calls within the same system also adds a layer of flexibility, allowing for more dynamic and scalable configurations.

48. What is 'OLE'?

SAP's integration with Microsoft's **Object Linking and Embedding (OLE)** Automation allows for seamless embedding of objects such as MS Excel files into the Windows front-end. This functionality is particularly useful for customizing front-end communication, enabling options like storing from the front-end, displaying stored documents, and closing display windows.

49. What is a 'Match Code' in SAP?

Match Codes, updated to *Search Help* from SAP 4.6, are essential for retrieving data when you do not know the exact record key. Creating a *Search Help Object* and defining a match code ID are the initial steps in this process. Users can easily access this feature by pressing 'F4' while the cursor is in the field, selecting 'possible entries' with a right-click, or simply clicking the magnifying glass icon. These intuitive methods streamline the data retrieval process, enhancing user experience and efficiency within the SAP system.

50. What is a 'Drill-down' Report?

Drill-down reports are a powerful feature in SAP reporting, providing a hierarchical view of data from the most general to the most specific. They allow users to start with a summary (the *basic list*) and delve deeper into more detailed views (the *secondary lists*) of the data, such as the components of fixed assets, for example (*Figure 2.7*). This interactive approach makes it easier to understand a report better besides pinpointing line items that may require further investigation. By enabling a granular examination of statements, drill-down reports are invaluable tools for accountants, auditors, and business analysts alike. You will be able to create a 'drill-down' report with a maximum 'drill' level of 20. That is, including the basic list, you can have a total of 21 levels in a single 'drill-down' report.

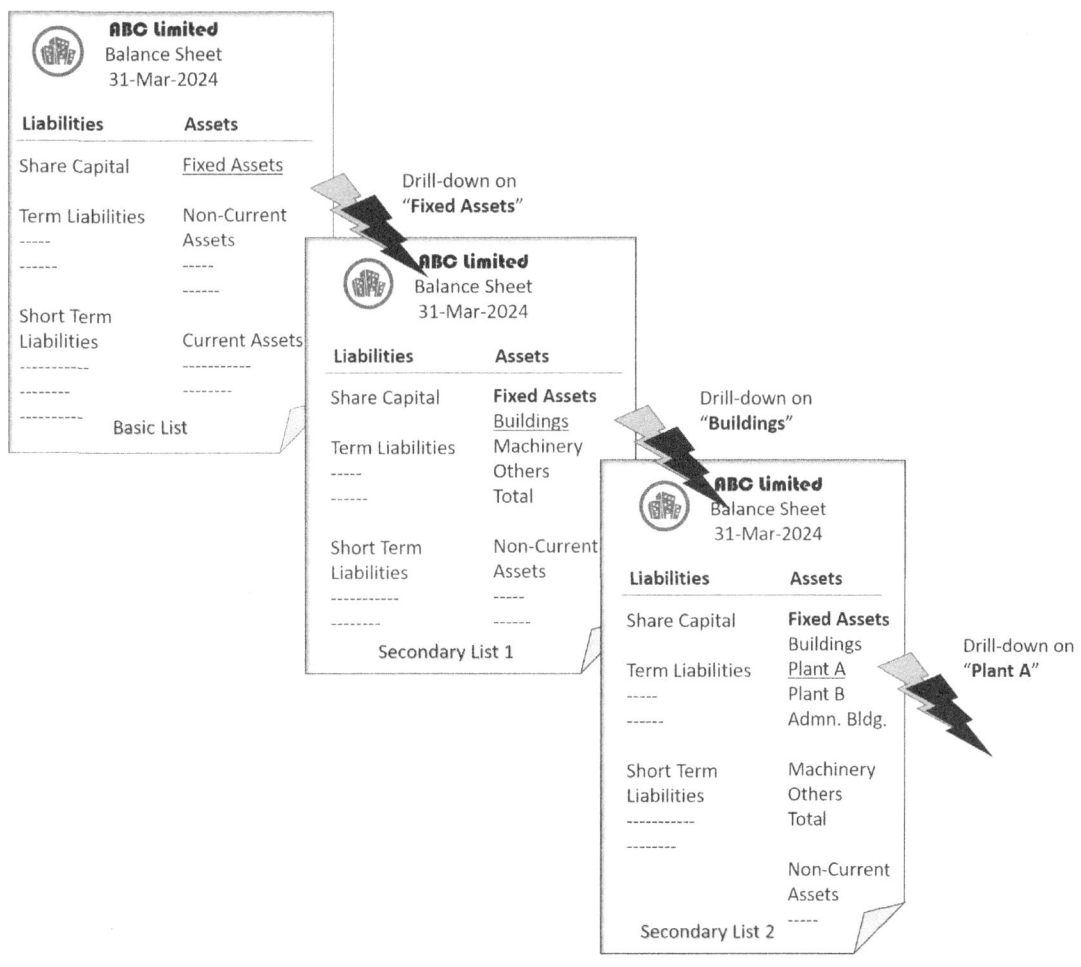

Figure 2.7: Drill-down report

51. What is 'ALV' programming in ABAP?

The **ABAP List Viewer** (**ALV**) provided by SAP is a powerful toolset designed to enhance the presentation and management of report outputs. It offers a suite of function modules that allow users to effectively manage and display data, especially when dealing with extensive columns that exceed 255 characters. The ALV functions enable users to select, arrange, and save various display variants of report outputs, streamlining the process of sorting and organizing data.

With the advent of SAP HANA, SAP has introduced a specialized version of the ALV optimized for high-speed data processing. This innovation is part of the SAP List Viewer object model, seamlessly integrated into the ABAP Objects programming environment. It provides developers with three distinct tools for displaying data, facilitating a more efficient and flexible approach to data visualization in enterprise applications. The tools are as follows:

- Simple two-dimensional tables
- Hierarchical-sequential list
- Tree structures

52. What is 'DynPro'?

In SAP, '**DynPro**' stands for *Dynamic Programming*, a key concept involving the creation and management of screens, also known as '*DynPros*'. These screens are integral to user interactions, providing a graphical interface for users to input data and execute functions. The 'flow logic' behind these screens orchestrates the processing and display, ensuring a seamless and efficient user experience.

53. What is an 'ABAP Query'?

ABAP Query, also known as **SAP Query**, is a versatile tool that simplifies report generation in SAP. It allows you to create reports without extensive programming knowledge, making it accessible to a wider range of users. By defining 'user groups' and 'functional groups,' one can tailor the data sources and authorization levels to suit specific reporting needs.

The three types of reports that you generate with ABAP Query, Basic List, Statistics, and Ranked Lists, offer a range of functionalities from simple data representation to complex analytical outputs. While the 'Basic Lists' provide straightforward, uncalculated data views, the 'Statistics' reports allow for incorporating aggregate functions such as averages and percentages. The 'Ranked Lists,' on the other hand, are particularly useful for sorting and analyzing data based on certain criteria, providing valuable insights for decision-making processes. Overall, ABAP Query is a powerful feature for creating customized reports efficiently within the SAP environment.

54. What are the components of 'SAPscript'?

SAPscript is a robust text-processing system within the SAP environment. It is designed to efficiently handle a variety of text-related tasks. It is an integral part of the SAP system, ensuring that standard styles and layout sets are consistently maintained across client interfaces.

The layout sets, which are pivotal for the page layout of SAPscript documents, comprise several elements that work in tandem to produce well-structured documents:

- **Header** data stores essential development-related information and layout set specifics, including the mandatory start page.

- **Paragraph** formats bring structure to the document, allowing for consistent text elements throughout.

- **Character** formats offer a more granular level of text formatting within paragraphs, enhancing the readability and presentation of the text.

- **Windows** serves as placeholders for content, which is then precisely positioned on pages through defined measurements.

- **Pages** establish the flow of the document, marking the beginning and end of text formatting, while page windows merge the concept of windows and pages, detailing the exact size and location of content blocks within the document.

55. Why do we need 'Enhancements'?

SAP's enhancement framework is a versatile tool that allows businesses to tailor SAP standard applications to their specific needs without disrupting the core software. This customization is crucial for companies with unique processes that are not covered by SAP's standard functionality.

The enhancement framework includes the following:

- **Customer exits** are points within SAP where custom code can be inserted. These exits ensure that personalized modifications are preserved during upgrades, providing continuity and stability for business operations. Enhancements can range from simple user interface adjustments with menu and screen exits to more complex functional enhancements using function module exits or keyword exits.

- **ABAP Dictionary Elements** allow for structural enhancements like adding fields to existing tables. This framework empowers businesses to maintain a competitive edge by enabling them to adapt quickly to changing market demands while ensuring the integrity and upgradability of their SAP system.

56. Differentiate 'Screen Painter' from 'Menu Painter'.

The **Screen Painter** (*Figure 2.8*) in ABAP Workbench is a vital tool for SAP developers. It facilitates the creation and modification of user interface screens for transaction modules. With its intuitive design, developers can easily adjust screen attributes, manage the flow logic, and customize the layout to enhance user experience. This tool is essential for tailoring SAP applications to meet specific business requirements and workflows, ensuring a seamless and efficient interaction for end-users:

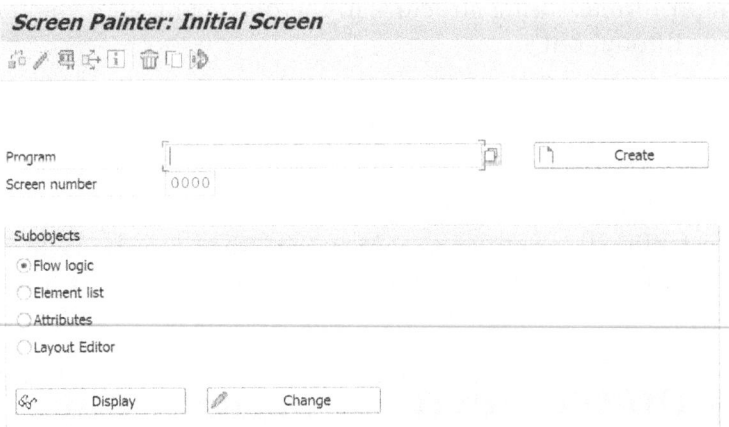

Figure 2.8: *Screen painter*

Figure 2.9

The **Menu Painter**, on the other hand, is an essential tool for designing user interfaces in ABAP programs (*Figure 2.10*). It allows developers to create and manage various interface components such as status bars, menu lists, function key settings, and titles. With this tool, one can define the functionality and appearance of an application's interface, ensuring a user-friendly experience. The Menu Painter is particularly useful for setting up the GUI status and GUI title, which dictate how the interface will look and behave within the ABAP program.

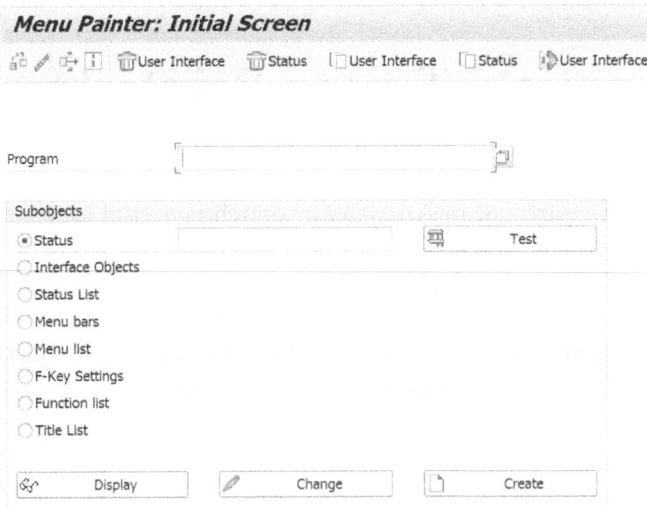

Figure 2.10: *Menu Painter*

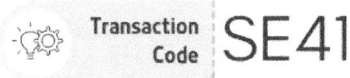

Figure 2.11

57. What is a 'Modification Assistant' in ABAP?

The **ABAP Modification Assistant** is an important tool for developers working with SAP systems. It streamlines the process of altering standard SAP applications by safeguarding the original code and providing a structured approach to modifications. The 'special modification mode' ensures that changes are made consciously and with full awareness of their implications. The logging feature of the Modification Assistant is particularly beneficial as it meticulously records every change, simplifying future upgrades and maintenance. This tool not only enhances productivity but also contributes to maintaining the integrity and stability of the SAP system during customizations. Its user-friendly interface, equipped with 'pushbuttons,' allows for an intuitive and controlled modification process, making it an indispensable asset for developers in the SAP ecosystem.

The modification assistant assists in various areas, including:

- ABAP Dictionary
- ABAP Editor
- Class Builder
- Function Builder
- Menu Painter
- Screen Painter
- Text Element Maintenance

58. What is a 'Spool Request'?

In the context of SAP systems, **spool requests** are an integral part of managing print jobs. They are created during dialog or background processing and contain details about the print job such as the printer information and formatting instructions. These requests are stored in the spool database, while the actual print data is held in 'Temporary Sequential' objects, commonly referred to as *TemSe*. This system ensures that large volumes of print jobs are handled efficiently and are correctly formatted for the specified output device.

59. What is 'CTS'?

The **Change and Transport System (CTS)** is an integral part of SAP's application development and customization, which ensures smooth transitions and consistent data across different environments. It streamlines the process of capturing development and configuration changes and migrating them through various stages, from development to testing and ultimately to production. This system is crucial for maintaining the integrity and continuity of the SAP system landscape, as it allows for controlled movement of changes, minimizing the risk of errors and ensuring that all systems are synchronized with the latest updates.

60. What is a 'Transport'?

In SAP, the **transport** system is a critical component for managing changes across different SAP systems and landscapes. It ensures that the necessary changes in configuration, development, or data are consistently and securely moved from one environment to another, typically from development to quality assurance and finally to production.

The **transport request** is the central element in this process, acting as a package that contains all the related objects and information required for the move. The export process collects all the objects listed in the transport request from the source system and packages them into a data file. This data file is then used by the import process to apply the changes to the target system's database, ensuring that the new or altered components are available in the new environment. The **transport log** records every step of this process, providing a detailed history of what was moved, when, and by whom. The **transport organizer** *(Figure 2.12)*, a tool within SAP, offers a comprehensive interface for administrators to manage and monitor these transports, making it an essential aspect of change management in SAP systems.

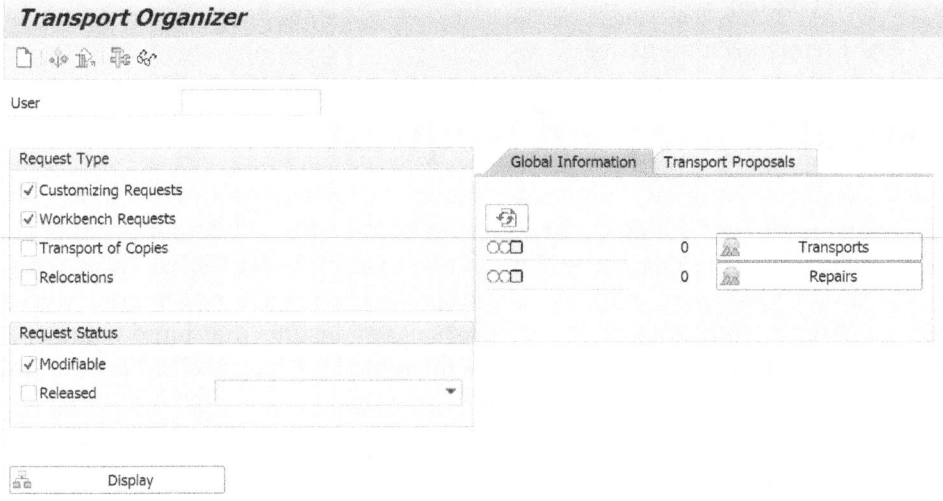

Figure 2.12: Transport organizer

Figure 2.13

61. How do you find out who has transported a transport request?

You can find out who has moved a transport request by looking at the Table *TPLOG* (use the Transaction Code **SE16** to access the table) and inputting the transport name in **CMDSTRING** field with '*': example, *SETCODE* (*Figure 2.14*):

Data Browser: Table TPLOG Select Entries   4

Table: TPLOG
Displayed Fields: 9 of   10 .   Fixed Columns: ⌐6⌐   List Width 0250

HOST	PID	USERNAME	SYDATE	SYTIME	COUNTER	CLIENT	CMDSTRING
s4h2022	11678	TMSADM	01.12.2022	18:24:12		000	SETCODEPAGE pf=/usr/sap/trans/b
s4h2022	20512	TMSADM	14.10.2022	08:25:50		000	SETCODEPAGE pf=/usr/sap/trans/b
s4h2022gen	6629	TMSADM	23.12.2022	17:37:46		000	SETCODEPAGE pf=/usr/sap/trans/b
s4hana2022	10499	TMSADM	13.12.2022	09:56:45		000	SETCODEPAGE pf=/usr/sap/trans/b

Figure 2.14: Table TPLOG with select entries

62. What is an 'Authorization' in SAP?

Authorization is a critical aspect of security and operational integrity in SAP systems. It involves defining and managing user privileges, ensuring that individuals have the appropriate level of access to perform their roles effectively. The SAP Basis Administrator plays a key role in this process, setting up roles and permissions that align with organizational policies and regulatory requirements. This ensures that sensitive data is protected and that the system's functionality is used responsibly and appropriately.

63. Explain the different types 'Client' in Customizing SAP.

In SAP, a **Client** represents the highest hierarchical level and holds master records essential for the company's operation. These settings and data are crucial to ensure consistency and control across all Company Codes within the organization. It is a fundamental requirement for a Client to have at least one Company Code, which is the primary organizational unit for which individual financial statements can be created (more about Company Code in a later chapter). This structure is pivotal in maintaining an organized and efficient business environment.

During SAP project implementation, you will create different *'types'* of Clients like:

- Development Client
- Test Client
- Production Client

In any implementation, it is necessary that you have at least three types of Client, as aforementioned. There may be instances in which you may need to define more than three Clients, like:

- Development Client
- Test Client
- Quality Assurance Client
- Training Client
- Production Client

The **Development Client**, often called the 'Sandbox' Client, serves as a crucial testing ground for new configurations and program development. It is a space where developers can experiment and 'play' with various scenarios (hence sometimes known as 'Play Client'), ensuring that all Customizations are thoroughly vetted before being finalized and moved to a more stable environment. This sandbox approach is fundamental to maintaining the integrity of live systems while fostering innovation and continuous improvement.

Once a new program or configuration is approved, it is transported to a *'Test Client'* for thorough testing, including both modular and integration tests. Training for end-users is conducted using a separate Client designed for that purpose (*'Training Client'*). Sometimes, the test and training environments may coexist within a single instance. Finally, a *'Quality Assurance Client'* is utilized to conduct essential quality checks before the configuration or program is deployed to the *'Production Client'* (also called 'Golden Client') via CTS functionality, ensuring reliability and performance in the live environment. With very limited access to the Production Client, not everyone can access the Client. That way, the Customizing settings, and the business transactions are safeguarded. That is why the Production Client is also called the *'Live System.'*

Do not confuse this term with the 'client,' which denotes a customer or supplier in normal business parlance.

64. How can you find the field/data underlying an 'SAP Transaction'?

Understanding the technical data in SAP transactions is crucial for effective troubleshooting and system analysis. The 'F1' key and 'Technical Data' buttons provide a gateway to this information, but their utility is limited when dealing with structures rather than transparent tables. Structures, often a composite of various sources, including the 'Includes' and calculated fields, require a more focused approach. The logical database structure can provide a lot of information, revealing the underlying tables that drive specific business areas and how they interconnect.

To go deeper, techniques such as 'debugging,' 'SQL Trace,' and 'Runtime Analysis' become invaluable:

- **Debugging** allows you to set watchpoints and observe the code execution in real-time, pinpointing where and how fields are populated.

- **SQL Trace** offers a behind-the-scenes look at the database operations, detailing table interactions during a transaction. Although not all tables will be visible, especially those that are buffered, it provides a comprehensive overview of the database activity.

- **Runtime Analysis** expands the scene by showing all tables accessed, giving a complete picture of the transaction's footprint on the system (*Figure 2.15* and *Figure 2.16*).

These methods, whether used individually or in combination, enable you to systematically uncover the field information you seek. The process requires patience and persistence, but the resulting understanding of the technical data is invaluable for maintaining and optimizing the SAP environment.

Figure 2.15: Runtime Analysis (via Transaction SAT)

ABAP Runtime Analysis: Initial Screen

Tips & Tricks

Measurement

Reliability of Time Values

Short Descriptn

In Dialog		In Parallel Session
Transaction		Switch On/Off
Program		
Function module		Schedule
Execute		For User/Service

Measurement Restrictions

| Variant | DEFAULT | From user |

Performance Data File

Other File...

Figure 2.16: ABAP Runtime Analysis (via Transaction SE30)

Transaction Code **SE30**
SAT

Figure 2.17

Join our book's Discord space

Join the book's Discord Workspace for Latest updates, Offers, Tech happenings around the world, New Release and Sessions with the Authors:

https://discord.bpbonline.com

CHAPTER 3
SAP HANA

Introduction

The chapter provides you with a brief introduction to SAP HANA. Here, you will learn how SAP HANA is different from other databases, its evolution, its benefits, and its architecture. You will also learn how to migrate to SAP HANA from traditional databases.

65. How 'SAP HANA' is different from other databases?

As discussed earlier (in *Chapter 1, SAP Basics*) **SAP High-performance Analytic Appliance (HANA)** is a column-oriented in-memory database that stores data in its memory instead of the conventional way of storing it on a disk. This in-memory storage enables the processing of a high volume of data (transactions) as well as analytics in a single system with lightning-fast performance: it is 3600 seconds faster than a conventional database, and you can get your database query returned with a result in less than a second. It also takes care of application development.

SAP HANA stores data in column-based tables in the main memory. By combining **online transactional processing (OLTP)** and **online analytical processing (OLAP)**, the system's performance increases manifold: The SAP HANA database is capable of 3.5 billion scans per second and about 15 million aggregations per second per core (*Figure 3.1*).

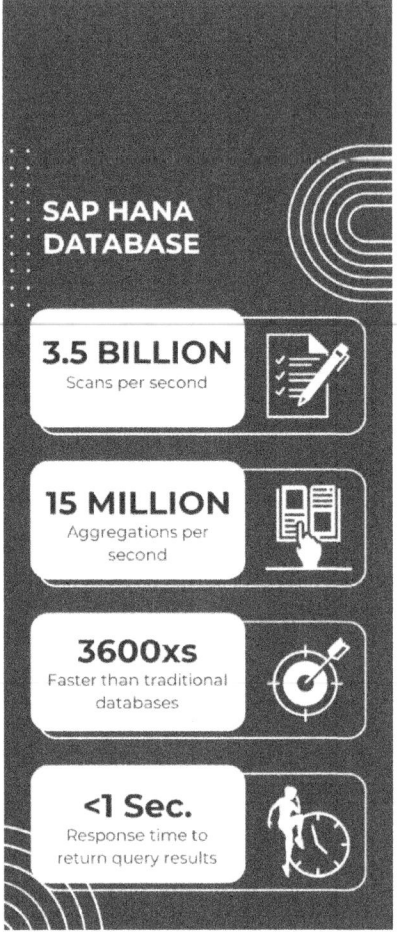

Figure 3.1*: SAP HANA – highlights*

66. Explain the 'In-Memory Database.'

In an **in-memory database (IMDB)** database, the data is stored in the computer's main memory (RAM) instead of the conventional or traditional way of storing on disk drives (floppy disks and hard drives) or **solid-state drives (SSD)**. Even with increased in-memory capabilities, in recent times, the traditional databases are still disk-based.

Unlike traditional databases, SAP HANA was built from scratch to work with data in memory. You can add secondary storage mechanisms as and when required to balance performance and cost. Since data retrieval from main memory is several times faster than from a disk / SSD, this leads to lightning-fast response times.

You will normally go in for *in-memory* databases for applications requiring top speed besides handling large volumes of data traffic, such as banking systems. This database is most suited for applications that call for real-time analytics, predictive modeling, etc.

67. Outline the 'Benefits of SAP HANA'.

SAP HANA, on top of being a database and the one point of truth for all data and data functions, offers a host of benefits, regardless of where you deploy it: on-premises or in the cloud. These benefits include the following:

- **Completeness**: It is not just a database. It has database services, application development, OLAP, OLTP, and data integration.
- **Efficiency**: It comes with a relatively smaller data footprint with zero duplication of data and with advanced compression that reduces the number of data silos that would otherwise be required.
- **Flexibility**: It can be deployed in multiple options: on-premise, in-the-cloud, or as a hybrid.
- **Intelligence**: It has built-in **machine language** (**ML**) to complement transaction and analytical processing.
- **Power**: With its unmatched **multiple parallel processing** (**MPP**), it queries large datasets quickly.
- **Quickness**: It is quicker to return database query results in less than a second, even from a large production application with voluminous data.
- **Scalability**: Its modularity enables easy scalability to meet changing data volumes and user numbers. It can support several terabytes of data in a single server.
- **Security**: It provides for a secured setup besides offering unparalleled and comprehensive data and application security that is comprehensive.
- **Simplicity**: It comes with advanced data virtualization and a single data gateway.
- **Versatility**: It supports hybrid processing of transactional and analytical data and several data types.

68. Explain the 'History of SAP HANA'.

The co-founder of SAP, *Hasso Plattner*, wanted a database that could process analytical and transactional data at record speed in real-time. Accordingly, he demonstrated the prototype of a new database known as **Hasso's New Architecture**, which was further improved, later renamed **SAP HANA**, and launched in 2010.

As you can see from *Figure 3.2*, SAP HANA (aka SAP HANA 1.0) was released in 2010. Only ten new customers went live with that. In 2012, SAP HANA was released as a product for cloud computing and was termed 'SAP HANA Cloud PaaS' ('Platform-as-a-Service'). 2013 saw the launch of 'SAP **HANA Enterprise Cloud**' (**HEC**), an '**Infrastructure-as-a-Service**' (**IaaS**) tool that offered a managed cloud to its 3,000+ customers. In 2015, SAP released SAP HANA 2.0 and SAP S/4HANA ERP, which were written specifically for SAP

HANA. By 2016, SAP launched SAP BW/4HANA, the data warehouse solution for the SAP HANA platform. 'SAP HANA Cloud' was released in 2019 as SAP's next generation **'Data Platform as a Service' (DPaaS)**. SAP HANA 2.0 SPS 06 was released in Dec. 2021. More than 33,000 customers now run their business on SAP HANA.

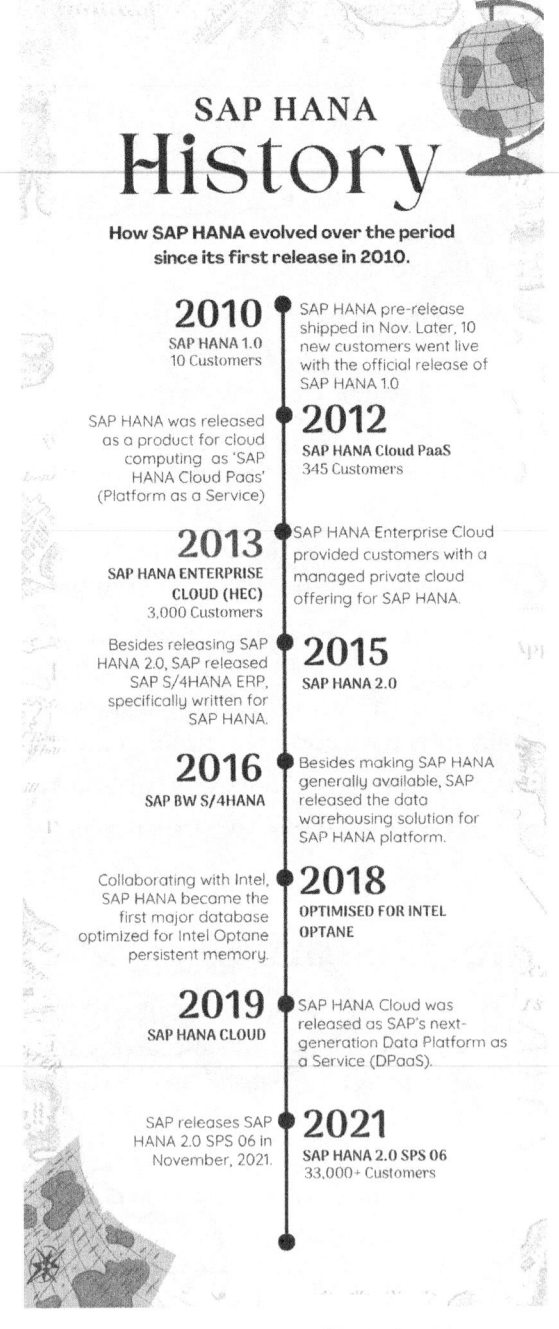

Figure 3.2: *History of SAP HANA*

69. Explain SAP 'HANA Architecture'.

The SAP HANA system, in its simplest format, is made up of three major components, as shown in *Figure 3.3*:

- An index server
- A name server
- A preprocessor server

The main component of the SAP HANA database is the **'index server.'** It contains the actual data and the data engines required for data processing. It uses SQL/MDX processor to process incoming SQL/MDX statements. This server also has a *persistence layer* that takes care of the integrity and durability of the transactions. It is responsible for restoring the HANA system to its last saved state when there is a system restart, because of which the transactions are either fully *done* or fully *undone*. The index server also contains a **session and transaction manager** (**STM**) to keep track of transactions, both running and completed.

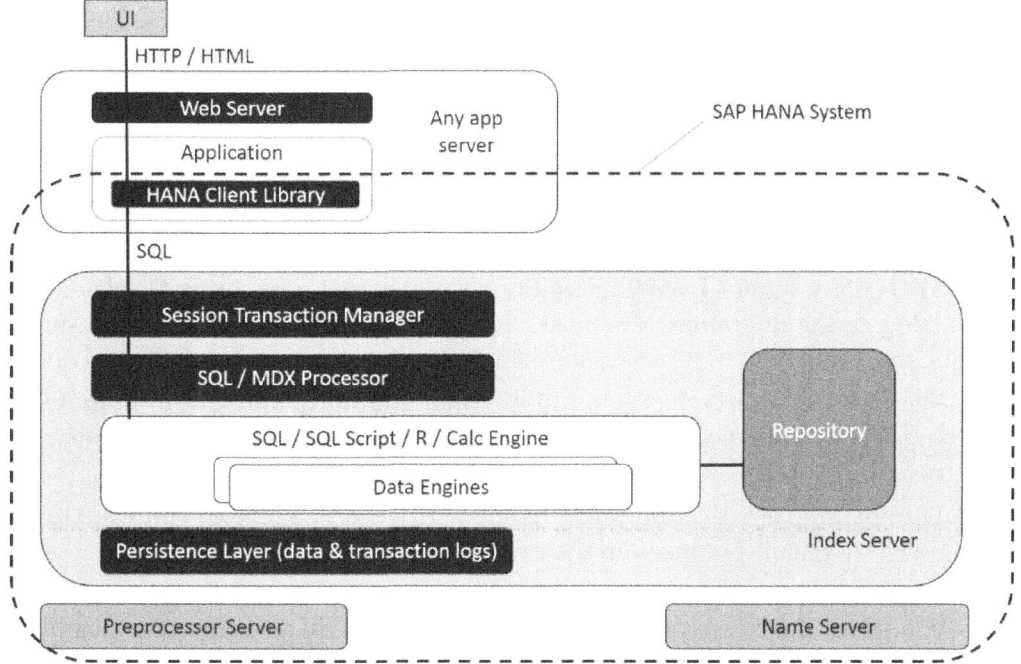

Figure 3.3: *SAP HANA architecture (classical)*

The **'preprocessor server'** in SAP HNA is used by the index server to analyze and process text data, thereby providing the user with the results of a text search.

The information on SAP HANA's system landscape (or topology) is stored in the **'name server'** (aka 'nameserver'). Hence, at any point in time, the name server has up-to-date information about which components are running and where they are running in a distributed landscape. It also knows what data is located on which server.

SAP HANA database uses SQLScript as its scripting language, which can embed data-intensive application logic vis-a-vis the classical ones that embed only a limited functionality into a database via SQL. The limited capability of classical applications leads to large data copying operations spread over several copying cycles with little scope for optimizing through parallel processing. But, with SQLScript, SAP HANA has the capability of simultaneous parallel processing using multiple processors. The SAP HANA database also supports functional libraries like SAP HANA **'Business Function Library'** (**BFL**) and SAP HANA **'Predictive Analytics Library'** (**PAL**). As these two libraries are fully integrated with the data engines (of the index server), SQLScript can directly call their functions for processing. Both SQL and SQLScript, in SAP HANA, share a common infrastructure accessing several meta definitions (say, row definition, column definition, index, etc.) that are stored in a single common catalog. In the case of programs written in the 'R' language, SAP HANA also supports them.

70. Is SAP HANA 'ACID' compliant?

Yes. SAP HANA is **Atomicity, Consistency, Isolation, and Durability (ACID)** compliant.

71. How to migrate from a traditional database to SAP HANA?

Since SAP HANA differs from the traditional databases, you need to plan carefully before taking up the migration. You need to complete the following steps for a successful migration that will result in much lesser data footprint compared to traditional ones:

1. The first step is to select what to migrate. You may not want to migrate all the legacy applications, data, and custom code. Accordingly, plan to migrate only the items you need in the new database.

2. The next step is to decide on the deployment strategy. How do you want to deploy SAP HANA: on-premises, in the cloud, or as a hybrid deployment?

3. Then comes sizing your SAP HANA database: how much of the main memory will you need? Take care to plan for both dynamic and static data, besides planning adequate disk size for persistent storage.

4. Take data cleansing seriously. This is an opportunity to remove bad, duplicate, and unwanted old data so that you have a reduced data footprint on the new system after the migration.

CHAPTER 4
SAP S/4HANA

Introduction

In this chapter, you will learn how SAP S/4HANA differs from SAP ERP. In the process, you will learn about the deployment options for SAP S/4HANA, the difference between SAP S/4HANA Cloud Public and SAP S/4HANA Cloud Private, the concepts of 'GROW with SAP' and 'RISE with SAP,' the release cycle of SAP S/4HANA, how to migrate to SAP S/4HANA together with the recommended tools and services for such migrations, and much more.

72. How is SAP S/4HANA different from SAP ERP?

SAP S/4HANA is the successor to SAP ERP (ECC). Unlike SAP ECC, which can work with any database, SAP S/4HANA works only with SAP HANA. Built specifically for SAP HANA, SAP S/4HANA is the latest enterprise applications business suite meant for the digital economy. Built to leverage the capabilities of in-memory computing, SAP S/4HANA is designed to use the most modern user experience via SAP Fiori. The core modules of SAP ERP have since been reorganized into several **Line of Business** (**LoBs**). You can deploy SAP S/4HANA in multiple ways: on-premises, in-the-cloud, or as a hybrid deployment.

73. What is a 'Cloud Software'?

Cloud Software is a **'Software-as-a-Service'** (**SaaS**) product in which you, as the consumer of a software application, are billed on a subscription basis. This model is highly flexible and agile, as you pay only for what you use. The other advantage is that you can scale up / down very quickly with no / minimum upfront investment. With the cloud platform and tools, you can develop your applications and deploy them on that cloud.

SAP's examples of SaaS solutions include SAP SuccessFactors, SAP Fieldglass, SAP Ariba, and SAP Concur, as well as the cloud editions of SAP S/4HANA.

74. In contrast to SaaS, what is 'PaaS'?

Platform-as-a-Service (**PaaS**) relates to an infrastructural arrangement in which a third-party cloud service provider hosts the software application and tools of your choice and makes them available to you over the Internet for a fee.

75. What is, then, 'Infrastructure-as-a-Service' (IaaS)?

In **Infrastructure-as-a-Service** (**IaaS**) computing, a third-party cloud service provider hosts the required servers, storage, and other computing infrastructure and makes them available to you as the consumer on a rental basis over the Internet. Essentially, you rent the required computing services on a pay-per-user basis without worrying about the maintenance and backup handled by the third-party providing the services.

76. What are the 'Deployment Options' available for SAP S/4HANA?

SAP offers different software deployment options for deploying SAP S/4HANA, as under:

- **Public cloud option**: The product is called SAP S/4HANA Cloud Public or simply SAP S/4HANA Cloud. It is also known as SAP S/4HANA Essential Edition.
- **Private cloud option**: The product is known as SAP S/4HANA Cloud Private.
- **On-premises option**: The product is known as SAP S/4HANA On-Premises.

Even with the cloud option, in addition to the private and public cloud options, you can also opt for a hybrid cloud deployment option to take advantage of a multi-cloud computing environment.

77. What is the 'SAP S/4HANA Cloud Public' edition?

SAP S/4HANA Cloud (aka *SAP S/4HANA Cloud Public*) is the ready-to-run cloud ERP solution from SAP. It delivers the latest industry best practices and continuous innovation. With this breakthrough cloud ERP solution, it is possible to implement and deliver the initial scope of SAP implementation within 30 days, with a 50% reduction in implementation cost, as well as a 40-60% quicker time-to-value. Accessed via the Internet, SAP S/4HANA Cloud is a SaaS product that is licensed on a subscription basis. The solution comes with the following:

- Proven industry-standard best practices
- Quicker time-to-value with guided implementation, faster technical setup, and intuitive **user interface (UI)**
- Automatic and continuous updates: all managed by SAP
- Continuous innovation resulting from updates on built-in **artificial intelligence (AI)**, **machine learning (ML)**, **robotic process automation (RPA)**, and analytics
- Best-in-class security, compliance, and scalability
- Open and extensibility enabling easy integration with business partners by leveraging ready-to-use APIs

78. Outline the 'Scope of SAP S/4HANA Cloud Public'.

The SAP S/4HANA Cloud Public comes with comprehensive ERP coverage with end-to-end business processes via pre-configured best practices and with select **industry solutions (IS)**. The scope is as outlined in *Figure 4.1.*

Figure 4.1: *Scope of SAP S/4HANA Cloud Public*

79. What is SAP S/4HANA Cloud Private?

SAP S/4HANA Cloud Private refers to the SAP enterprise application services hosted and maintained on a private cloud network protected by a firewall. You can build a private cloud within SAP's data center. Alternatively, you can use one of the commercially available *IaaS* like AWS, Azure, Alibaba Cloud, etc. As against the SAP S/4HANA Cloud Public, the private cloud option offers tight security and control. So, SAP S/4HANA Cloud Private is a single-tenant dedicated environment where the cloud/infrastructure provider runs SAP S/4HANA services.

80. Explain the 'Scope of SAP S/4HANA Cloud Private'.

The scope of SAP S/4HANA Cloud Private and SAP S/4HANA On-Premises is one and the same. It covers extended business processes of various LoBs with 25 IS. The scope is as outlined in *Figure 4.2*:

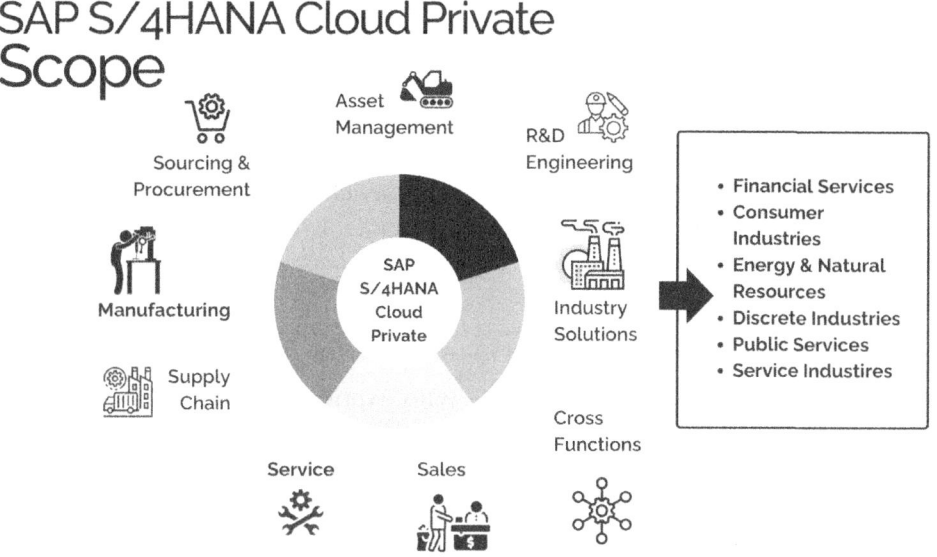

Figure 4.2: *Scope of SAP S/4HANA Cloud Private*

81. How does 'SAP S/4HANA Cloud Private' differ from 'SAP S/4HANA Cloud (Public)'?

The major difference between 'SAP S/4HANA Cloud Private' and 'SAP S/4HANA Public Cloud' is how the services are deployed and maintained.

With *SAP S/4HANA Public*, the customers are provided with services hosted and maintained over a public cloud and network. This means that if you are a customer of SAP S/4HANA Public, you would share such services together with several other customers, and this kind of deployment is known as 'multi-tenant.' Since it is a shared arrangement, this is very affordable besides being efficient as the services are maintained by SAP themselves (SAP is the default service provider for this SaaS solution).

In contrast, *SAP S/4HANA Private* services are kind of exclusive (not shared with any other customer) and maintained over a private network behind a firewall. Hence, this is often termed a 'single tenant' environment, as the services are run from a dedicated setup.

The other major differences are as follows:

* When you opt for SAP S/4HANA Cloud Private, you can go in for a 'greenfield' or 'brownfield' or selective data transition implementation (aka 'partial conversion'), unlike SAP S/4HANA Cloud Public in which you can only do a 'greenfield' implementation.

- With SAP S/4HANA Cloud Private, you can customize (including structural changes) and/or modify the SAP source code. You cannot do such a modification in SAP S/4HANA Cloud Public.

- With SAP S/4HANA Cloud Private, you have full access to the system's backend through SAP GUI, which is not available in SAP S/4HANA Cloud Public.

- With SAP S/4HANA Cloud Private, you have full access to SAP IMG. You can also opt for expert configuration. This is not available in SAP S/4HANA Cloud Public.

- SAP S/4HANA Cloud Public is a SaaS product, but SAP S/4HANA Cloud Private is an IaaS product.

- SAP S/4HANA Cloud Private is more suited for the following:

  o Existing SAP ERP customers who want to move to the cloud without redesigning their processes and retain their existing ERP investments.

  New customers who require a full, extensive ERP functionality, including partner add-ons, and with the ability to extend/enhance as and when required. In contrast, SAP S/4HANA Cloud Public is for the customers (existing or new) wanting to move to the cloud and start afresh with a clean system, open for process redesign, and are 'ok' to give up any existing ERP investment.

- While SAP S/4HANA Cloud Private is available for all industries, SAP S/4HANA Cloud Public is available only for selected industries with selected LoBs.

- While the best practices and periodic enhancements are automatically pushed to all the subscribed customers in SAP S/4HANA Cloud Public, you, as a customer, can decide when you want to install the best practices (and enhancements) if you are on SAP S/4HANA Cloud Private. This is true, provided you stay with the mainstream maintenance (7 years).

- Since it will be a single tenant dedicated environment, the **total cost of operation** (**TCO**) is higher in the case of SAP S/4HANA Cloud Private as against SAP S/4HANA Cloud Public, wherein the TCO is the lowest with higher **return on investment** (**ROI**).

82. What are all the 'LoBs in SAP S/4HANA Cloud'?

As already mentioned, the erstwhile modules of SAP ERP have since been reorganized to LoBs to cover the various business scenarios with the launch of SAP S/4HANA. These LoBs, together with additional SAP Cloud solutions, like SAP Business Technology Platform, SAP SuccessFactors (Employee Central), SAP Cloud for Customer, SAP Fieldglass, Ariba Network, Concur, SAP Jam social collaboration platform, etc., enable SAP S/4HANA solutions to tackle end-to-end business processes required by various enterprise customers.

These LoBs (*Figure 4.3*) are:

- **Finance**: This LoB encompasses everything related to money, including financial accounting and close, financial operations, cost managemnt, treasury and risk management, subscription billing, and revenue management.

- **Sourcing and procurement**: Takes care of business activities from sourcing and fulfilling raw materials. Includes sourcing and contract management, operational procurement and invoice management, central procurement, and procurement analytics.

- **Manufacturing**: This LoB is all about production planning, production operations, manufacturing insights, and quality management.

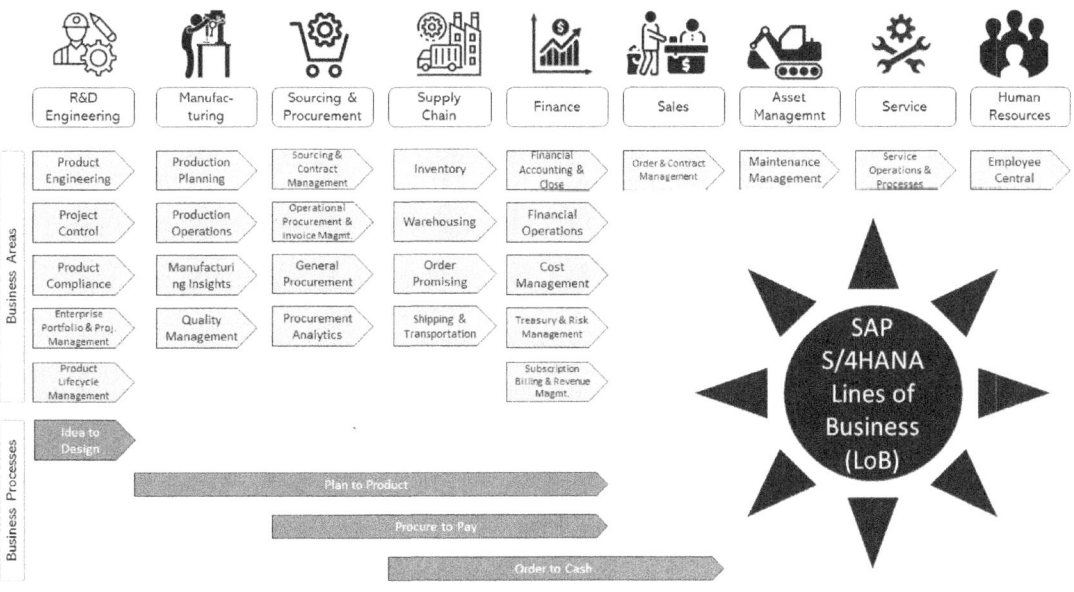

Figure 4.3: *LoB in SAP S/4HANA Cloud*

- **Supply chain**: This is all about inventory, warehousing (including EWM), order promising, and shipping and transportation.

- **Sales**: This LoB covers business processes and scenarios related to sales orders, billing, sales order fulfillment and monitoring, returns management, pricing management, contract settlement, foreign trade, credit management, and revenue accounting.

- **R&D engineering:** Focusing on a product's lifecycle, this LoB covers product engineering, project control, product compliance, enterprise portfolio and project management, and product lifecycle management.

- **Asset management**: This LoB manages an enterprise's fixed assets, as well as plant maintenance and **environment, health, and safety (EHS)** monitoring.

- **Service**: This takes care of business processes and scenarios in service operations, including professional services.
- **Core HR**

83. Which SAP S/4HANA Cloud edition is suitable for which Company? How to decide?

Companies' ERP needs are different: one size does not fit all. Each company would have different requirements. Keeping that in mind, SAP has developed two different cloud ERP journeys for deploying SAP S/4HANA Cloud Private and SAP S/4HANA Cloud Public editions: "GROW with SAP" and "RISE with SAP."

'GROW with SAP' and 'RISE with SAP' supports customers in different but unique ways irrespective of the starting point. Whatever the journey route you take, at the center is the cloud ERP core, which can be either SAP ERP S/4HANA Public or Private Edition. See *Figure 4.4* for more details:

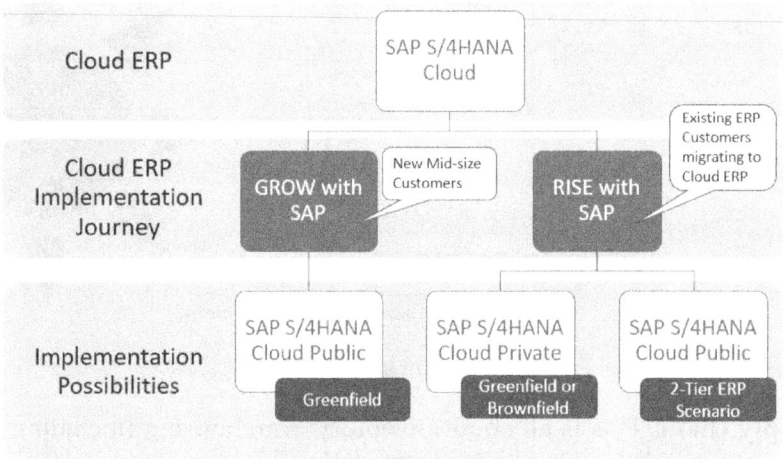

Figure 4.4: *SAP S/4HANA Cloud ERP implementation journey*

SAP recommends *SAP S/4HANA Cloud Public* to companies that require ready-to-run standardized business processes with little or no lead time and for those who expect that their cloud ERP solution will always be updated with the latest releases and changes. For this section of customers, SAP recommends the 'GROW with SAP' journey, which brings together the required adoption services, accelerators, access to the SAP community, and learning, in addition to the cloud ERP solution that is SAP S/4HANA Cloud Public edition.

However, SAP recommends *SAP S/4HANA Cloud Private* to those customers who require higher customization and more control over the cloud solution. This approach allows such customers to take their own time to innovate on the solution, and this kind of tailored fit enables such customers to leverage their existing ERP investments. SAP recommends going ahead with 'RISE with SAP' for this group of customers, offering the prospective customers a choice between 'brownfield' system conversion and 'greenfield' new deployment of SAP S/4HANA Cloud Private. As with 'GROW with SAP,' the 'RISE with SAP' journey also brings in many tools, accelerators, and services that support the journey.

84. Explain 'GROW with SAP.'

The '**Grow with SAP**' offering is tailored to help mid-size companies take advantage of SAP's cloud ERP solution. It provides the required solution (SAP S/4HANA Cloud Public), best practices, select industry solutions, and ready-to-run services that will enable your business to be up and running on the cloud ERP in the quickest possible time. This is meant for 'greenfield' implementations for new customers who want to start on a clean slate.

The offerings are listed in *Table 4.1*:

Feature	Details
Solution	• SAP S/4HANA Cloud Public • SAP Business Technology Platform • Industry best practices for select industries
Adoption and accelerators	• SAP Activate • SAP Cloud ALM • SAP Baseline Packaged Activation Service (Optional)
Community and learning	• SAP Community • SAP Learning

Table 4.1: *The offerings under GROW with SAP*

85. What is 'RISE with SAP'?

'**RISE with SAP**' enables enterprises to migrate their existing ERP solutions to SAP S/4HANA Cloud (Private) at their own pace with a personalized migration journey. Since it follows a guided approach based on the SAP Activate methodology, one can confidently migrate. 'RISE with SAP' combines cloud solutions, infrastructure, and services to create a clear migration path.

86. What is the 'Release Cycle for SAP S/4HANA Cloud Private'?

SAP S/4HANA Cloud Private follows a two-year release like the SAP S/4HANA On-Premises edition. To remain in mainstream maintenance, you need to install at least one upgrade every five years as a customer of SAP S/4HANA Cloud Private.

After the annual base release, SAP releases the non-disruptive **Future Pack Stack (FPS)** every six months till the next base release. After a new base release, the previous annual release version will receive a quarterly **Service Pack Stack (SPS)** from SAP. SPS releases will contain only the corrections and not any new functionality.

87. What is the 'Release Cycle for SAP S/4HANA Cloud Public'?

SAP S/4HANA Cloud Public's major releases are twice a year and enhance the existing functionality. SAP installs such enhancements to customers' existing scope. Besides the major releases, SAP provides **Continuous Feature Delivery (CFD)** updates monthly that offer customers new features. Note that these new features are just pre-delivered via CFD but not automatically installed; this gives the customers the flexibility to decide if they want to switch to the new features. However, if you, as a customer of SAP S/4HANA Public, do not switch to the newly offered features, SAP will install them automatically during the next major release.

The releases are referenced by combining the last two digits of the year of release together with the two-digit month reference. For example, the Feb 2023 major release will be denoted as 2302. Then, a CFD update is mentioned as a suffix to the release reference: for example, 2302.1, 2302.2, and so on.

88. How to 'Migrate to SAP S/4HANA Cloud Public'?

You can migrate your legacy data to S/4HANA Cloud Public via 'Migration Cockpit' by the following methods:

- Transferring data using template files delivered by SAP (Local SAP S/4HANA Database Schema connection)
- Data can be transferred using a separate HANA staging database (Remote SAP HANA Database Schema connection).

Either way, you would push the legacy data into the staging tables before they get migrated to the cloud system (*Figure 4.5*).

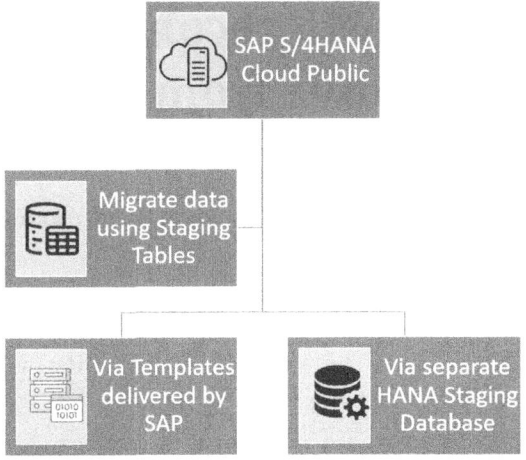

Figure 4.5: *Migration to SAP S/4HANA Cloud Public*

89. How to 'Migrate to SAP S/4HANA Cloud Private'?

There are a couple of ways (*Figure 4.6*) with which you can migrate your legacy enterprise data to SAP S/4HANA Cloud Private:

- As outlined in the previous question, migrate data using staging tables (in two ways) as you would to SAP S/4HANA Cloud Public.
- Migrate legacy data directly from the SAP source system (via an RFC connection) to the target SAP S/4HANA Cloud Private system.

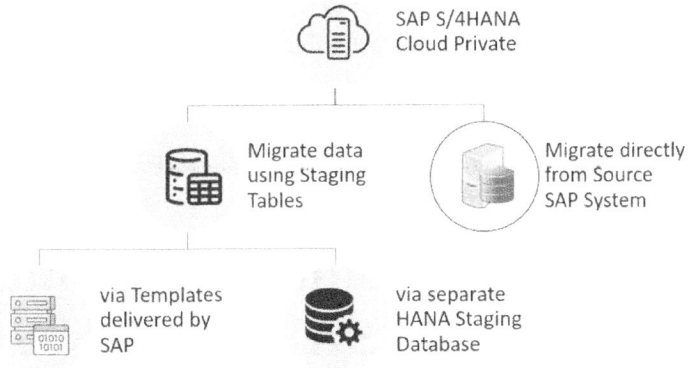

Figure 4.6: *Migration to SAP S/4HANA Cloud Private*

Note: The above migration paths are applicable to the SAP S/3HANA On-Premises edition as well.

90. What are the SAP recommended 'Tools and Services to move from SAP ECC to SAP S/4HANA Cloud'?

SAP recommends several tools and services that support moving from SAP ECC to SAP S/4HANA Cloud. They are as follows:

- **SAP S/4HANA readiness check**: Use this tool to assess the readiness (both technical and functional) of your current SAP ECC system for the proposed move to SAP S/4HANA Cloud. The tool will flag potential issues, if any, and provide recommendations for preparing the system and adopting the custom code.

- **SAP transformation navigator**: Using this, you can get guidance on the most suitable path for moving to SAP S/4HANA Cloud. Based on the current landscape and business needs, this tool will provide the scope, effort, and timeline for the proposed migration.

- **SAP customer evolution kit**: It enables you to start your digital transformation to SAP S/4HANA Cloud, provides you with one-to-one expert guidance, and is free from SAP. With this, you can tailor the transformation plan based on your business needs.

- **SAP advanced data migration by Syniti**: The software with data profiling, data quality management, and data migration automation features will help you to set up a framework for managing large-scale data migration from the current SAP systems to SAP S/4HANA Cloud. Syniti works well with 'GROW with SAP' and 'RISE with SAP.'

- **SAP S/4HANA migration cockpit**: With a guided step-by-step approach, this will make it easier to migrate data from SAP ECC to SAP S/4HANA Cloud. The pre-configured templates and workflows in the tool will take care of both data migration and data quality.

- **SAP landscape transformation**: Supporting both homogenous and heterogeneous system landscapes, it enables real-time data replication and transformation from SAP ECC to SAP S/4HANA Cloud.

91. What technical requirements must be met before migrating to SAP S/4HANA Cloud?

You need to meet the following technical requirements so that you can migrate from SAP ECC to SAP S/4HANA Cloud:

- Adapting your legacy/custom code to work with the simplified data model of SAP S/4HANA Cloud.

- Converting the system to Unicode. You may use the Software Provisioning Manager tool.
- Ensuring that the current system meets the system requirements for SAP S/4HANA Cloud.
- Migrating your existing database to SAP HANA. You can use the 'SAP Database Migration Testing' cloud service.

92. List the 'Tools and Services for SAP Data Migration.'

For migrating your data from SAP ECC to SAP S/4HANA Cloud solutions, you can make use of the following data migration tools and services:

- **SAP data services:** Using 'SAP Data Services', you can extract, transform, and load data from any source into SAP S/4HANA. Loaded with comprehensive data validation and data quality checks and features, this tool supports both real-time and batch processing.
- **SAP legacy system migration workbench**: Providing step-by-step guidance, this workbench helps data migration from legacy systems to SAP systems. It offers data mapping, data validation, and field conversion.
- **SAP information steward**: A data governance software that offers data profiling, data lineage, and data quality scorecards, ensuring quality and compliance when you migrate data into SAP systems.
- **Rapid data migration to SAP S/4HANA**: This is another tool for migrating data from legacy systems into the SAP system. Offering a simplified approach, this comes with pre-configured templates, workflows, and best practices to accelerate data migration.
- **SAP advanced data migration and management by Syniti**: Refer to *Question 90* for details.

93. Outline the 'Highlights of SAP S/4HANA Cloud Private 2023 Release'.

With the 2023 release of SAP S/4HANA (on-premises) and SAP S/4HANA Cloud Private editions, SAP has delivered about 1,500 new and updated apps, functionality APIs, and innovations, including the following:

- **Artificial Intelligence:** SAP has made **Artificial Intelligence (AI)** an essential and integral asset for any business, both current and future. The ever-advancing use of AI enables your business to streamline processes for enhanced customer experience with reduced errors, leading to better growth and profitability. For example, in **Finance**, an all-new machine-learning enabled 'predictive scenario late payment risk' helps business users predict the risk of late payment of outstanding invoices. This intelligent scenario has also been updated for Public Sector (FI-CA). Further, in **Finance**, during the financial closing process, you can now define/execute balance validation rules to ensure the completeness and correctness of P&L and B/S accounts.

- **Data insights:** The latest innovations in **Sourcing and Procurement** assist sourcing managers in managing multiple projects via streamlined sourcing processes and valuable inputs. In **Master Data Management (MDM)**, the latest innovations bring federated visualization of **Master Data Governance (MDG)** processes. In the **Application Development and Integration**, with the 2023 innovations, you can now monitor the life cycle situations via the 'Monitor Situations – Extended' app. In **Sales**, with the innovations, you can now suspend product valuation in the customer return process when processing a refund. Now, you also have role-based access to price elements of documents at the header or item level. In **Product Compliance**, you can now avoid ambiguity or confusion as there will be continuous provisioning of listed substances via a regulatory content service.

- **Connectivity:** In **Inventory Management and Physical Inventory**, with the 2023 innovations to SAP S/4HANA Cloud Private, you can now scan bar codes with internal and external scanning devices in several of the SAP Fiori apps, such as 'Stock—Single Material,' 'Post Goods Receipt for Process Order,' 'Transfer Stock—In Plant,' etc. SAP has introduced a simplified Kanban in **Extended Warehouse Management (EWM)** without centralized deliveries for decentralized EWM.

- **Digital-age user experience**: The new 2023 release includes several new SAP Fiori apps, such as 'Manage Charges for Freight Orders' and 'Manage Credit Memo Requests—Version 2'.

Join our book's Discord space

Join the book's Discord Workspace for Latest updates, Offers, Tech happenings around the world, New Release and Sessions with the Authors:

https://discord.bpbonline.com

CHAPTER 5
SAP Fiori

Introduction

This chapter introduces you to SAP Fiori: the concept, evolution, different dimensions, different types of SAP Fiori apps, deployment options, etc. You will also learn about SAP Fiori Launchpad, SAP Fiori Mobile Start, SAP Fiori Apps Reference Library, and SAP Companion.

94. What is SAP Fiori?

Based on **SAP User Experience (SAP UX)**, **SAP Fiori** is the design system with which you can create top-class business apps for ERP applications, turning even a casual user into an SAP expert. The resulting SAP Fiori apps will work seamlessly on desktops, tablets, and smartphones. With consistent tools, technology, and templates, SAP Fiori helps build, test, and deploy apps that come with a unified user experience that is role-based, adaptive, intuitive, coherent, simple, and delightful. In simple terms, SAP Fiori is a **user experience (UX)** for SAP applications.

95. Describe the evolution of SAP Fiori.

Unlike SAP R/3, which provided the **Graphical User Interface (GUI)** for the presentation layer to interface the SAP system with the users, the introduction of SAP S/4HANA brought in the need for a new, better, and improved UI that powered the business apps, enabling the users to access the SAP system on the go via smartphones and tablets, besides the conventional access on desktops or laptops.

First introduced in 2013, SAP Fiori was initially meant to be accessed on mobile devices. At that time, there were only about 25 SAP Fiori apps (currently, there are more than 3100 SAP Fiori apps for the SAP S/4HANA product suite alone). By 2016, SAP brought out SAP Fiori 2.0 (based on SAPUI5 technology), which provided the app design concepts for SAP ERP and SAP S/4HANA. The year 2017 saw the release of SAP Fiori 3.0 with better design elements, customization, and machine learning capabilities. This version came with the famous 'Quartz' theme (the earlier theme being 'Belize'), offering light and dark options. Initially, SAP Fiori 3.0 was made available only to SAP S/4HANA customers (via 1908 release). However, with the 1909 release of SAP S/4HANA, it was made available to on-premises customers as well (*Figure 5.1*).

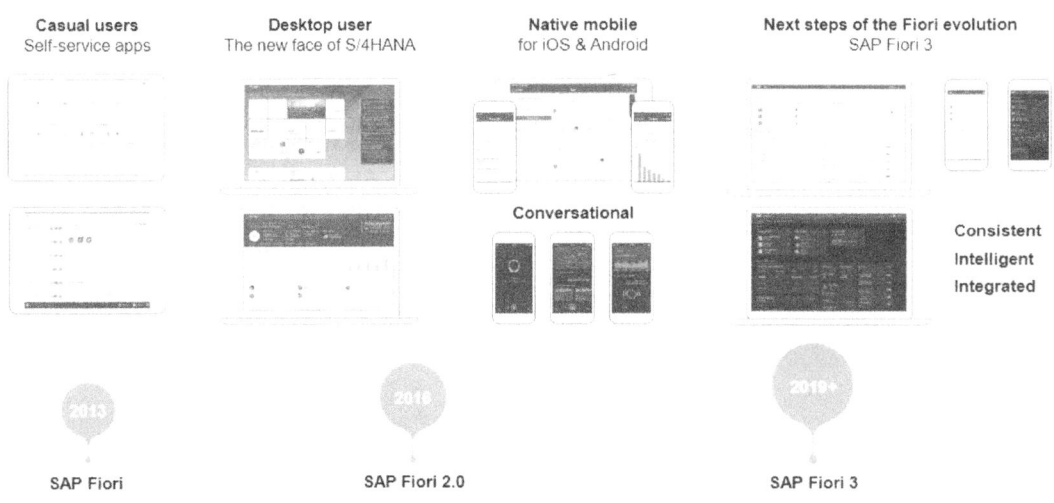

Figure 5.1[1]: Evolution of SAP Fiori

You can now use SAP Fiori across various solutions, such as SAP S/4HANA, SAP SuccessFactors Employee Central solution, SAP Ariba mobile solutions, and SAP Hybris Cloud for Customer solution.

96. What is SAPUI5?

SAPUI5 provides the UI technology you need to build enterprise-ready web apps. You can use SAPUI5 on all main SAP platforms and outside them, as most are open-sourced from OpenUI5.

---

1   (Image courtesy: SAP)

Technically speaking, SAPUI5 is a Client UI technology based on JavaScript, CSS, and HTML. You can run apps developed with SAPUI5 in a browser on any device: mobile, tablet, desktop computer, or laptop PC.

97. What are the three dimensions of SAP Fiori?

SAP Fiori has the following three dimensions:

- **SAP Fiori concept**: A simplification of SAP UX relying on modern design principles that are role-based, adaptive, simple, coherent, and delightful.
- **SAP Fiori design**: This dimension is all about the visual design, information architecture, colors, and interaction patterns that you will come across in the SAP Fiori design guidelines.
- **SAP Fiori technology**: This encompasses the system architecture, technology, infrastructure, and programming elements that you may require to build, test, and deploy SAP Fiori apps, as well as the SAP Fiori launchpad.

98. What is 'SAP Fiori Launchpad'?

SAP Fiori Launchpad is the single entry point for launching and navigating between SAP Fiori apps on mobile devices and desktop PCs. Centered on your specific needs, it provides you an overview of those apps that you normally need with the relevant information thereon (as shown in *Figure 5.2*):

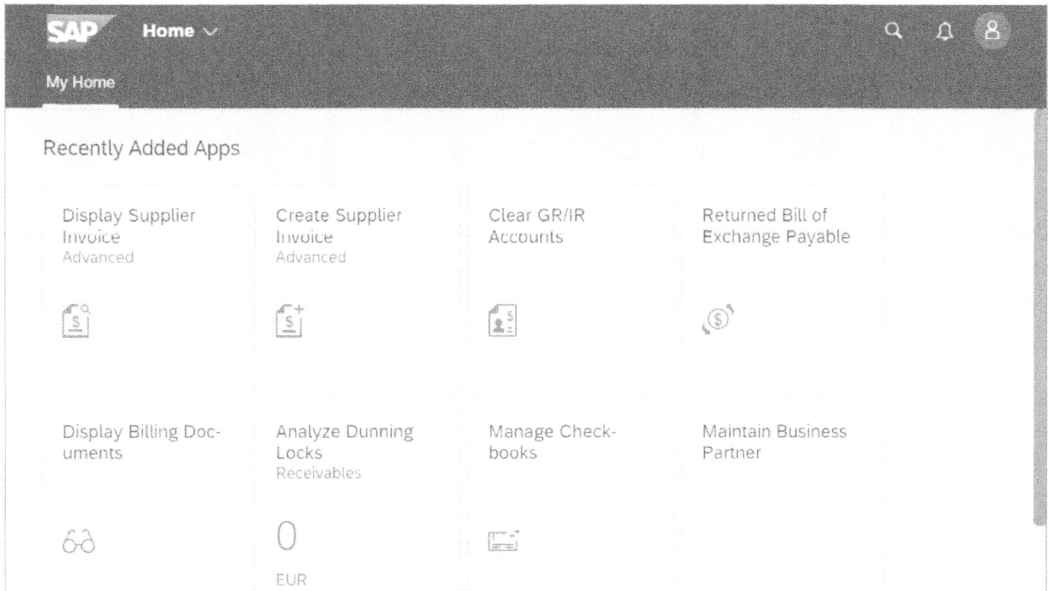

Figure 5.2: *SAP Fiori Launchpad*

SAP Fiori Launchpad is a role-based, real-time personalized environment that runs all your SAP Fiori apps. You can also include non-SAP Fiori apps like Dynpro or even the classic SAP GUI in the launchpad.

99. What is 'SAP Mobile Start' in the context of SAP Fiori?

With the release of SAP S/4HANA 2021 and the SAP Fiori front-end server 2021 for SAP S/4HANA, SAP has improved the SAP Fiori launchpad experience for the web. It has provided an all-new native mobile single-entry point known as "**SAP Mobile Start**" (also known as '**SAP Start**').

The SAP Start includes several evolutionary improvements in the UX for SAP S/4HANA applications, besides bringing in the much-required AI support to the UX. With this, SAP has enabled the launching of a new native mobile application for all SAP users that addresses all those needs that are tailored to an individual's tasks and workstyle (as shown in *Figure 5.3*):

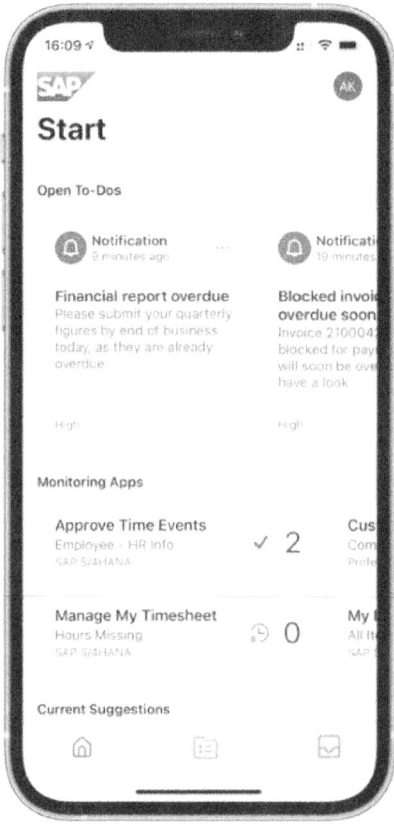

Figure 5.3: *SAP Mobile Start (aka SAP Start)*

100. What are the available 'Options to Deploy SAP Fiori'?

You can deploy SAP Fiori in the following two ways:

- **As a stand-alone deployment for single back-end systems**: Here, you will deploy a dedicated AS ABAP front-end server with SAP Fiori front-end server in a standalone system in front of the back-end system, either behind or in front of the firewall. In such a stand-alone deployment, you will install and configure the front-end components and the SAP Fiori launchpad separately from the back-end system. Hence, when you customize/ (adjust the default configuration) on the back-end system, note to perform the equivalent customization/(adjustment) on the front-end as well. This is to preserve the consistency of both systems.

- **As embedded deployment**: Here, you deploy the SAP Fiori front-end server into the AS ABAP of a back-end system.

101. What do you mean by 'SAP Fiori Apps Reference Library'?

The **SAP Fiori Apps Reference Library** is a comprehensive library consisting of all relevant SAP content for the SAP Fiori launchpad. With this library, you can explore, plan, and implement SAP Fiori apps. Currently, there are more than 16,200 apps (including non-SAP Fiori ones) from which you can select the required apps according to your needs (as shown in *Figure 5.4*):

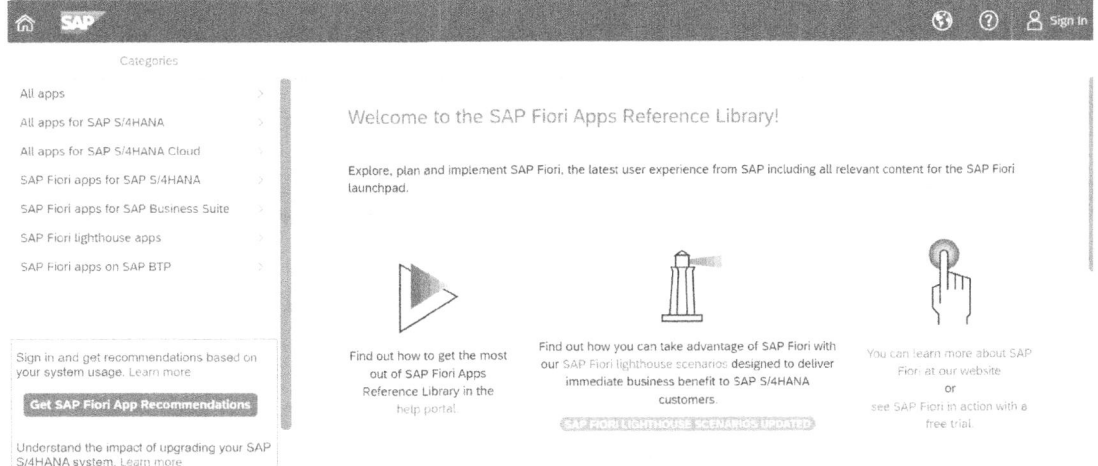

Figure 5.4: SAP Fiori apps reference library

With the SAP Fiori apps reference library, you can perform the following actions:

- Directly navigate to the app's related resources, like its documentation, maintenance planner, etc.
- Display the installation and configuration information aggregated for selected apps.
- Have an overview of all SAP Fiori apps available on that day.
- Look at app-specific key information and the technical data you may need to install/configure that app.
- View the data relating to the previous versions of an app.
- View the recommended SAP Fiori apps that may suit your specific needs.

102. What is the 'SAP Fiori Apps Recommendations Report'?

The **SAP Fiori Apps Recommendations Report (FAR)** inspects your current SAP usage information and identifies and recommends the most valuable and relevant SAP Fiori Apps for your enterprise. To achieve this, FAR automatically investigates the history of your SAP GUI transactions. Then, it identifies the relevant SAP Fiori apps depending on how many other transactions you use in the same area. Essentially, FAR comes up with recommendations for closely related SAP Fiori apps. FAR report works for both SAP S/4HANA and SAP Business Suite environments.

103. What are 'SAP Fiori Lighthouse Scenarios'?

The **SAP Fiori Lighthouse Scenarios** is a collection of SAP Fiori apps that offer immediate business benefits to the users of SAP S/4HANA Cloud and SAP S/4HANA compared to SAP Business Suite. The list gets updated as and when new apps are made available. You can easily locate the Lighthouse apps marked in the Fiori apps reference library.

104. What are the different 'Types of SAP Fiori Apps'?

There are three different types of SAP Fiori apps, divided based on their focus and infrastructural requirements (*Figure 5.5*):

Figure 5.5: *Types of SAP Fiori apps*

105. Explain 'Transactional Apps' in SAP Fiori.

The **Transactional Apps** in SAP Fiori let you perform transactional tasks, such as creating, changing, or approving purchase requests or purchase orders, creating or approving a leave request, etc. They represent simplified views and interaction with existing business processes and solutions. Though these apps run better on an SAP HANA database, you can also port to other databases with decent performance.

For these transactional apps, the UI layer is stored on the ABAP front-end server with the necessary product-specific UI add-ons for the respective products, such as on-premises SAP ERP, SAP S/4HANA, CRM, etc. The infrastructure components comprise the central UI SAPUI5, SAP Fiori Launchpad, and SAP NetWeaver Gateway with OData enablement.

Some examples of SAP Fiori Transactional Apps are as follows:

- Clear Outgoing Payments
- Edit Supplier Invoice Settings
- Manage Automatic Payments
- Post Outgoing Payments
- Supplier Invoice (S/4HANA)

106. Describe 'SAP Fiori Fact Sheets'.

The **SAP Fiori Fact Sheets** (aka **'Object Page'**) display contextual information about the central objects of your business operations. They are intuitive and harmonized. From a fact sheet area (aka 'tile'), you can drill down to the underlying details. You can easily navigate from one fact sheet to another but related fact sheets (say, navigating from a document to the related business partner or the master data). From a fact sheet, you can also access related SAP transactions. You can call up the fact sheets from:

- The search results displayed in the launchpad
- Other fact sheets
- Transactional or analytical apps

Note that SAP Fiori Fact Sheets run only on an SAP HANA database with an ABAP stack. You cannot port them to any other database.

Some examples of SAP Fiori Fact Sheets apps include:

- Billing Document
- Credit Memo Request
- Customer Returns
- G/L Account
- Sales Order

107. Describe 'SAP Fiori Analytical Apps'.

The **SAP Fiori Analytical Apps** provide real-time, role-based insight into your business's operations by collecting and displaying KPIs directly on a browser. They can be SAP Smart Business applications or any other analytical, predictive, and planning applications.

These apps combine the data and analytical power of SAP HANA with the integration and interface components of SAP Business Suite. They provide real-time information on a large volume of data in a simplified front end for effective management control. To achieve this, you can use the pre-delivered KPIs and 'insight-to-action' scenarios. Alternatively, you can define your own based on the KPI modeler tool. These apps run only on an SAP HANA database.

A few examples of SAP Fiori Analytical Apps include the following:

- Analyze Dunning Locks
- Cash Flow Analyzer
- Data Migration Status
- Outstanding Billing Overview
- Overdue Materials - Stock in Transit

108. What is 'SAP Companion' that you can use with SAP Fiori Launchpad?

You can use the '**SAP Companion**' for the SAP Fiori launchpad to display the current online help for the applications directly on a web browser. For you (as an SAP end-user) to be able to display this web help, the corresponding catalog and group information for SAP Fiori must have been assigned properly. Note that for SAP Companion to work properly, you must set up the Web Dispatcher correctly.

Join our book's Discord space

Join the book's Discord Workspace for Latest updates, Offers, Tech happenings around the world, New Release and Sessions with the Authors:

https://discord.bpbonline.com

CHAPTER 6

Project Implementation

Introduction

In this chapter, you will learn about the different project methodologies in SAP: past and current. In the process, you will learn about SAP Solution Manager and its versions. There is also a brief overview of how to Customize the SAP solution, with an introduction to SAP IMG.

109. What is 'SAP Activate'?

SAP Activate is a framework that enables SAP project managers and consultants to deliver SAP projects more quickly, with ease, and with clarity. It is not just a project management methodology but a framework that is much more than that. With the shift in implementation from the traditional 'design to blueprint' way (as in SAP R/3 via 'ASAP' methodology marked by the consultative, waterfall project management approach that consumed a lot of time and effort) to the current transformative 'fit-to-standard' approach, SAP Activate offers agile, modular, scalable implementation with rapid delivery steps for fitting to the standard but best business processes. With this game-changing methodology, you can now deploy a fully configured SAP ERP system iteratively in a few weeks (*Figure 6.1*):

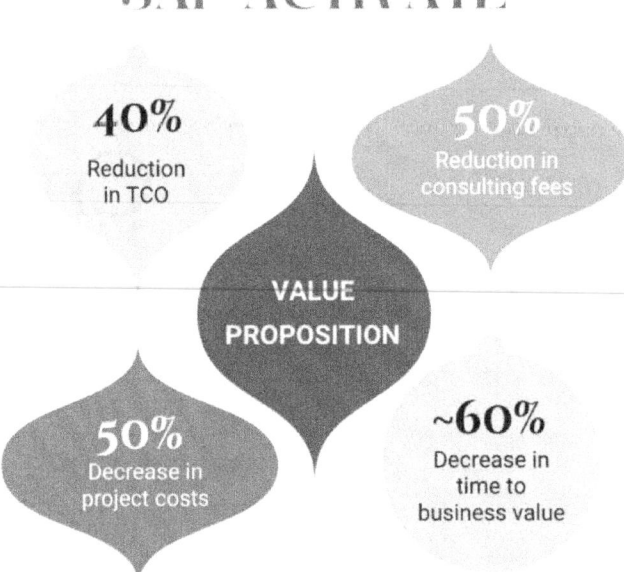

Figure 6.1: *SAP Activate: the value proposition*

110. What are the 'Key Elements of SAP Activate'?

The three key elements (or pillars) of SAP Activate are as follows:

- **SAP best practices**: SAP Activate comes with ready-to-run best business practices (with the required process documentation) that can dovetail customer's processes. The 'SAP Best Practice Explorer' comprises business process flows across LoBs, roles and responsibilities, and standard test scripts. You can also use this documentation as a user manual.

- **SAP Activate Methodology**: SAP Activate Methodology is the latest project implementation methodology for implementing and delivering SAP solutions for the digital economy. Based on the Agile methodology, it is iterative and continuously improves and delivers business value for increased project quality and confirmed project success. You can view the different general and solution-specific SAP Activate methodologies in the SAP Roadmap Viewer.

- **Guided configuration**: Powered by SAP Cloud ALM, SAP Activate comes with guided configurations powered by integrated configuration tools for deployment and running. This makes the life of project managers and consultants easy in project implementation, as they can now work with industry-specific standard configurations together with user-specific self-service guided configurations.

111. How is 'SAP Activate' different from the erstwhile 'ASAP' and 'SAP Launch'?

Accelerated SAP (ASAP) was a project management methodology used in SAP for faster and cost-effective implementation of SAP R/3 projects. It comprised three components: ASAP Roadmap, Tools (Questionnaires, templates, etc.), and R/3 services and training (Hotline, Early Watch, Remote Upgrade, Archiving, etc.). Aimed at providing a step-by-step direction and guidance throughout the project implementation, the ASAP roadmap meandered through the following four milestones or phases in the project implementation life cycle:

- Project preparation
- Business blueprint
- Realization
- Final preparation

A successor to ASAP, SAP Launch methodology, released in 2014, was meant for SAP SaaS implementation, tailored specifically to meet the implementation requirements of SAP's Cloud ERP portfolio. It consisted of four main phases with the corresponding quality gates, as shown in the following *Table 5.1*:

Detail	1	2	3	4
Phase name	Prepare	Realize	Verify	Launch
Quality gate	Project verification	Solution acceptance	Readiness acceptance	Go-live

Table 6.1: *Phases and Quality Gates in SAP Launch methodology*

Figure 6.2 summarizes how SAP Activate is different from that of its predecessors, ASAP and SAP Launch:

Type	Earlier	Now	Supports implementation of	Improvements in SAP Activate
New implementation	ASAP	SAP Activate (for On-premise editions)	-> SAP S/4HANA On-Premise -> SAP Business Suit (SRM, CRM etc.,)	* Agile methodology
	SAP Launch	SAP Activate (for Cloud editions)	-> SAP S/4HANA Cloud editions -> SAP Success Factors, SAP Ariba, SAP Concur, SAP Analytics Cloud, SAP Concur & SAP Fieldglass, SAP Sales Cloud, Datasphere etc.,	* Iterative * Leverages SAP Best Practices * Less than 10 deliverables per phase
System Conversion	NA	SAP Activate (for System Conversion)	-> SAP S/4HANA On-Premise, SAP BW/4HANA, SAP S/4HANA Central Finance	* Guided Configuration * Solution fit/gap workshops replace earlier Blueprint
Landscape Transformation	NA	SAP Activate (for Landscape Transofrmation)	-> SAP S/4HANA On-Premise -> SAP S/4HANA Cloud editions	

Figure 6.2: *SAP Activate: the value proposition*

112. What is known as 'SAP Roadmap Viewer'?

The **SAP Roadmap Viewer** is a tool that provides access to the different SAP Activate methodologies (aka 'roadmaps'). With a visual representation of the implementation process, these roadmaps are user-friendly, providing a comprehensive view of the progress of the implementation and making it easier for SAP project managers / consultants to view and track the project's activities, tasks, and deliverables. Through hyperlinks, you can also access the appropriate accelerators relating to a specific task. From the viewer, you can explore all the roadmaps or see the details for your favorites that are pinned to the home screen (*Figure 6.3*):

Figure 6.3: *SAP Activate Roadmap Viewer*

113. Outline the various SAP Activate Roadmaps that are available for a business.

You will see that the different SAP Activate roadmaps have been organized into four logical categories with which you can track all your project deliverables of all your SAP implementation, migration, or upgrade projects:

- **Cloud-specific methodology**:
  - SAP Activate for SAP S/4HANA Cloud Public Edition (3-system landscape)
  - SAP Activate for SAP S/4HANA Cloud Public Edition (2-system landscape)
  - SAP Activate Methodology for RISE with SAP S/4HANA Cloud Private Edition

- o   Baseline Activation Service for SAP S/4HANA Cloud (3-system landscape)
- o   SAP Activate Methodology for SAP Cloud for Sustainable Enterprises
- o   SAP Activate for SAP Integrated Business Planning for Supply Chain
- o   SAP Activate Methodology for SAP Concur
- o   SAP Activate Methodology for SAP SuccessFactors
- o   SAP Activate Methodology for SAP Service Cloud Roadmap
- o   SAP Activate Methodology for SAP Datasphere
- o   SAP Activate Methodology for SAP Ariba and SAP Fieldglass
- o   SAP Activate Methodology for SAP Analytics Cloud
- o   SAP Activate Methodology for the Intelligent Enterprise
- o   SAP Activate Methodology for SAP Sales Cloud Roadmap
- o   SAP Activate for SAP S/4HANA Cloud, public edition (3-system landscape)- Early Adopters
- **On-premises specific methodologies:**
  - o   SAP Activate Methodology for Transition to SAP S/4HANA
  - o   SAP Activate Methodology for Transition to SAP BW/4HANA
  - o   SAP Activate methodology for S/4HANA Central Finance
- **Upgrade methodologies:**
  - o   SAP Activate for Upgrade of SAP S/4HANA Cloud Public Edition (3-system landscape)
  - o   SAP Activate Methodology for SAP S/4HANA Upgrades
- **Generic methodologies**:
  - o   SAP Activate Methodology for New Cloud Implementations (Public Cloud-General)
  - o   SAP Activate Methodology for Business Suite and On-Premise- Agile and Waterfall

In each of these methodologies, you get to know the following, as shown in *Figure 6.4*:

- Overview (phase-wise)
- Content (phases, workstreams, product, tags, and roles)
- Accelerators

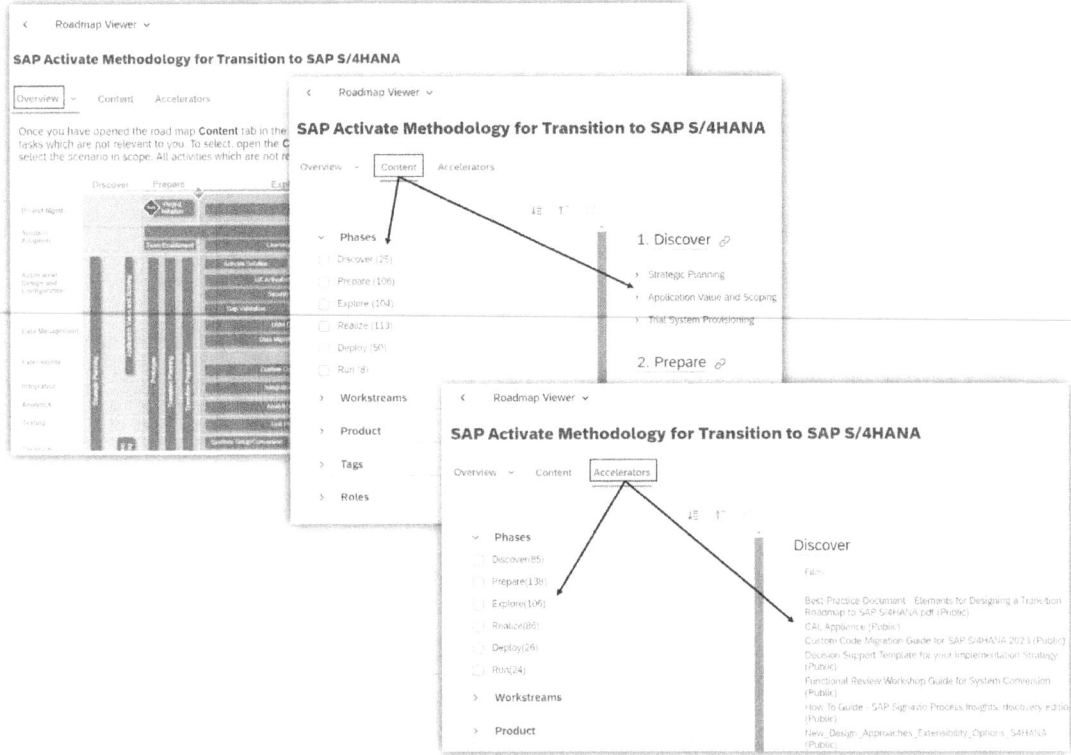

Figure 6.4: SAP Activate methodology: overview, content and accelerators

114. What are the different 'Phases in SAP Activate'? Explain.

There are six implementation phases in a typical SAP Activate methodology:

1. **Discover**: As a customer, you will understand the features, scope, and extent of the proposed solution (say, RISE with SAP S/4HANA Cloud Private Edition). You will understand what it can bring as value to your existing business. At the end of this first phase, you will agree on the implementation scope, target solution model, and project timeline with the sales team. The key activities include the following:

   a. Stakeholder identification.

   b. Value Discovery using a trial system.

2. **Prepare**: In this phase, you will undertake the initial preparation for the project. This marks the start of the project, the finalization of the project plan, and the assignment of the project team. This phase signifies that the project is underway. The quality gate to exit this phase is 'Prepare to Explore.' The key activities are as follows:

a. Project initiation, project plan/schedule preparation, and assignment of roles.

b. Project team onboarding.

c. Project kick-off.

d. Provisioned product verification.

e. Starting of preparation of 'fit-to-standard' workshops (by answering the *Business Driven Configuration* questionnaire).

f. Readying the initial system for 'fit-to-standard' workshops.

g. Initiating the 'Integration and Interface' list.

h. High-level technical architecture plan preparation.

i. Preparing for the next phase ('Explore').

3. **Explore**: Here, you will develop detailed plans for all the workstreams to be executed in the next phase (Realize). You need to ensure the entire gamut of the implementation project (scoping, testing, end-user enablement, operations, and solution configuration) is covered. The quality gate to the next phase will be Explore to Realize.' The activities are as follows:

a. Carrying out a 'fit-to-standard' workshop.

b. Confirming to-be business processes with process models.

c. Identifying master data and organizational requirements.

d. Obtaining business sign-off on delta requirements and design documents.

e. Collecting end-user information and learning needs and developing a learning strategy.

f. Establishing project management: tracking, monitoring, and reporting.

g. Signing off plans and validating exceptions to the Golden Rules.

4. **Realize**: In this phase, you will complete executing all the plans you made and signed off on in the previous 'Explore' phase. You will notice that the implementation team iteratively configures the system besides extending, integrating, testing, confirming, and documenting the end-to-end solution. The team will also carry out conversion programs for legacy data migration. By all this, you will ensure that the solution's configuration is according to the backlog collected and approved previously. Prepare your users for the switch, and prepare & complete end-user training. Prepare and keep the production system ready for a cutover. The quality gate to be crossed is 'Realize-to-Deploy.' The following will be the key activities of this phase:

a. Implementing the solution in the DEV system, in iterations using incremental build.

b. Conducting end-to-end testing of the full solution in the QA system.

    c. Configuring, extending, and integrating the PRD system ('production' environment).

    d. Preparing for data migration and data archiving.

    e. Carrying out project team/key-user training.

    f. Finalizing training materials and documentation for the end-user.

    g. Tracking and reporting on value delivery.

5. **Deploy**: With the readiness confirmation from the organization, business, and operations, you will cut over to the production environment. This marks the end of the implementation phase. You will now prepare for the 'Run' phase, which will hand over all the project deliverables to the customer for ongoing maintenance. The tasks are as follows:

    a. Resolving all open issues, particularly the crucial ones.

    b. Executing transition and cutover plans (including organizational change management plans)

    c. Completing end-user training.

    d. Identifying and documenting all issues you encountered while transitioning to the new solution.

    e. Monitoring business process results and production environment.

    f. Tracking and reporting on value delivery.

6. **Run**: In this phase, you, as the customer, will aim towards the smooth running of the solutions for value generation. This is the phase for continuous learning. The tasks are as follows:

    a. Establishing governance model.

    b. Monitoring system and running the solution.

    c. Realizing the business benefits.

    d. Continuous learning to improve and identify innovation opportunities.

    e. Managing end-to-end service delivery.

115. What is SAP 'Solution Manager'?

SAP Solution Manager is used in the **'application lifecycle management'** (**ALM**) of SAP solutions. It helps customers to manage their SAP and non-SAP applications more effectively. By centralizing, enhancing, automating, and improving the management of the entire system landscape, the SAP Solution Manager helps reduce the **total cost of ownership** (**TCO**). It also supports adapting the SAP landscape to new requirements, like implementing new business processes. SAP Solution Manager is no longer a single-stack system. It now consists of an ABAP system and a Java system.

In any project implementation, the recommended sequence for the implementation of an SAP Solution Manager system includes the following steps:

1. Plan the overall implementation with respect to scope, hardware, and software requirements.
2. Plan the appropriate system landscape that will meet your use cases.
3. Install SAP Solution Manager system components.
4. Configure the system
5. Set up the required connection to the managed system.

116. What is the latest version of SAP 'Solution Manager'?

SAP Solution Manager 7.2 is the latest version. It covers the complete application lifecycle (ALM) of your IT solution running on-premises, hybrid, or in the cloud. With this highly integrated solution, you can implement, maintain, run, and adopt all enterprise solutions, including non-SAP applications. It supports business innovation, business continuity, and efficient operations.

With SAP Solution Manager 7.2, you can take care of the following:

- Application Operations
- Business Process Operations
- Change Control Management
- Cross Topics
- Custom Code Management
- Data Volume Management
- Focused Build and Focused Insights
- IT Service Management
- Landscape Management
- Process Management
- Project Management
- Test Suite

If you are not using the SAP HANA database but still want to upgrade to SAP Solution Manager 7.2, install **Text Retrieval and Information Extraction (TREX)**. TREX is a powerful engine for intelligent search, automatic document classification, and retrieval of information from both structured and unstructured text.

117. How many SAP Solution Manager systems do you need to install?

To have a tight functional integration, it is sufficient and recommended to have only one SAP Solution Manager system installed so that you run all the processes in the same system. This is because it makes sense and logical to have all solution information (systems and business processes) and messages (incidents, issues, and change requests) accessible to the entire support organization from a single system for efficient production solutions. However, there may be situations in which you may want to work with more than one SAP Solution Manager system when there is a complete segregation of business units. However, this may lead to restrictions in collaboration among the business units. It is perfectly alright to have SAP Solution Manager as a separate instance on the same hardware in which you are running the SAP application software.

118. What do you mean by 'Focused Build' for SAP Solution Manager 7.2?

The '**Focused Build**' for SAP Solution Manager is a seamless, tool-based, out-of-the-box methodology for managing requirements-to-deploy processes. It provides pre-configured standard SAP Solution Manager features and processes as well as additional build functions. Note that the usage rights of SAP Solution Manager already include SAP Focused Build; you do not need to pay anything additional to use this, and there is no restriction on the number of users.

119. What is 'Focused Insights' for SAP Solution Manager 7.2?

The '**Focused Insights**' for SAP Solution Manager contains the best practices (800+ best practice KPIs) and experiences from past projects, offering you a set of pre-packaged dashboards tailored to your business needs. Using this, you can build your custom dashboards via state-of-the-art user experience in minutes. As with SAP Focused Build, you do not need to pay anything additional to make use of SAP Focused Insights, and this comes with no restriction on the number of users.

120. What is 'Customizing' in SAP? Is this different from 'Configuration'?

Broadly speaking, **Customizing** is the process of modifying a standard SAP system to meet the specific needs of a customer, which sometimes requires code changes. This may involve adding fields, tables, etc. However, **Configuration** is adapting the standard system to meet the business requirements. This may not involve changing the standard coding of the SAP system. In the practical world, you will come across SAP users, consultants, and others using these two terms interchangeably.

121. What is 'SAP Customizing Implementation Guide?

SAP Customizing Implementation Guide or the **SAP Implementation Guide** (IMG) provides the various configuration/Customizing steps in a tree-like structure for easy access, with the nodes representing the Customizing objects. This is the central repository for Customizing, providing step-by-step guidance for various Customizing tasks. Besides the steps/activities, the IMG (let us continue to call this IMG for simplification) also contains the detailed notes of that task, including the order in which you need to make the settings. When you execute an activity from the IMG, you are indirectly changing the values (parameters) in the underlying table(s) in the SAP system.

The IMG structure is a logical group of IMG activities (*Figure 6.5*), which, when executed, will take you to the relevant tables/structures in the system wherein you can configure the parameters to meet the specific requirements of the business. At the group level (say, 'Financial Accounting'), you will have the documentation detailing what elements or objects are in that group. When you expand such a group, you will see the list of IMG activities (say, 'Define company,' 'Define Profit Center,' etc.) that you will double-click or execute by pressing the 'Execute' icon to reach the configuration screen. In the IMG, you chose to display 'Additional Information' that can display the 'Maintenance Object,' the last four characters (in most cases) of which is the 'Transaction Code' for that IMG activity (say, **OX15** for the IMG activity 'Define Company').

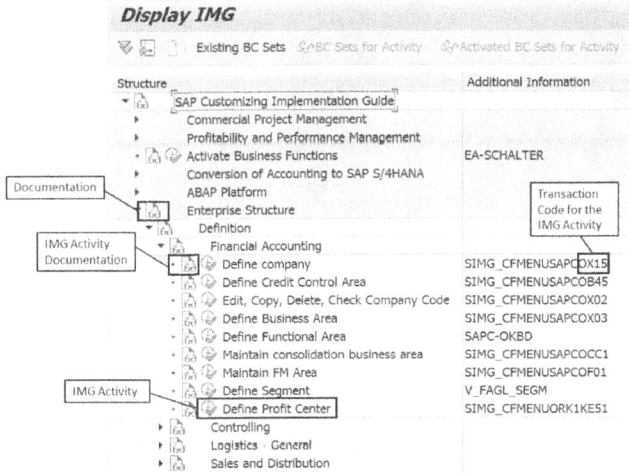

Figure 6.5: SAP Customizing Implementation Guide

Figure 6.6

122. Explain various 'Types of IMG'.

There are three types of **IMG** (*Figure 6.7*):

- **SAP Reference IMG** provides all the Customizing steps for all the functional areas. This, as the name suggests, is the 'reference IMG' from which you may create your IMG to meet the exact requirements of the enterprise and the project.

- The **Enterprise IMG** is usually an exact copy of the 'SAP Reference IMG' but is limited to the countries where the implementation is carried out. From the Enterprise IMG, you may create your Project IMG, which will contain the application components/business processes required in the current project.

- It is also possible that you create the **Project IMG** by directly generating from the SAP Reference IMG. In this case, the country selection is done when the Project IMGs are created. You may have more than one project IMG if you run different projects concurrently.

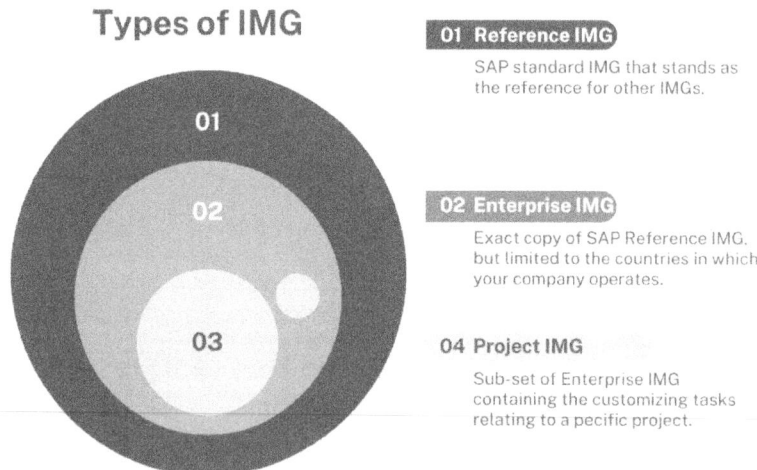

Figure 6.7: *Types of IMG (Reference, Enterprise and Project)*

123. What are the various ways of 'Customizing'?

You can customize SAP using the following:

- **IMG**: Follow the IMG tree step-by-step. No technical knowledge (about Tables, Views, etc.) is required. You can access SAP IMG via Transaction Code **SPRO (or SIMG)**.

  For example: Configure 'Company'. Follow the IMG Menu Path "*SAP Customizing Implementation Guide | Enterprise Structure | Definition | Financial Accounting | Define Company.*"

- **Transaction Codes**: Need to know how to customize Transaction Codes.

  For example: Configure 'Company Code.' Use Transaction Code: **OX15**. Enter the details on the resulting screen.

124. Why is the 'IMG' route of customization recommended?

IMG is a logical way to access data from multiple physical tables without even knowing where the data are flowing from. This is because many transactions affect more than one table. There is no need to know about the names of the associated Transaction Codes. IMG gives you a step-by-step way of progressing from one activity to the other. Also, you could classify the activities into various views like 'mandatory/critical/optional,' 'Client-dependent/client-independent, ' etc., so that you can proceed according to your requirements and time. Since IMG provides you with the functional view, it becomes easier to 'configure' and test the same immediately as with most standard configurations like account group, chart of accounts, etc.

125. What is a 'User Parameter'?

SAP provides a way of lessening your day-to-day data entry operations by facilitating default entries for fields and bringing out the most suitable *display variant* for document display, document entry, open/line-item processing, etc. The **user parameter**, also known as '*Accounting Editing Options*', is a boon as it saves time and results in more accuracy as data entry errors are eliminated with the default values. You can make the settings for document entry, document display, open and line items, cash journal etc.

Figure 6.8: User parameter settings

You can, for example, set the following parameters (*Figure 6.8*):

- System to default the 'exchange rate' from the first line item
- The user does not process any 'special G/L transactions' or 'foreign currency transactions.'
- The document needs to be complete before it is 'parked.'
- The system always calculates the tax component on the 'net' invoice and not on the 'gross.'
- Your document currency defaults to the 'local currency', the one used in the last document, or the functional currency, for example.
- The system needs to convert currency if documents are to be fetched from 'archives.'
- Documents need to be displayed using 'reference number.'
- 'Payment reference' is used as a selection item in open item processing.
- Activate branch/head office 'dialog' while processing line items.

Transaction Code **FB00**

Figure 6.9

CHAPTER 7

SAP S/4HANA Finance

Introduction

This chapter on SAP S/4HANA Finance will help you understand why SAP launched SAP S/4HANA Finance, replacing the erstwhile SAP ERP. Besides, you will learn about the different solution areas within SAP S/4HANA Finance, as well as its advantages and capabilities.

126. Why did SAP launch 'SAP S/4HANA Finance'?

SAP's erstwhile financial accounting applications or ERP solutions were not agile enough to meet the demands of today's digital economy. Most of those applications were marked by disconnected data processing, which called for a lot of manual intervention for reconciliation as the data was not flowing in real-time. This prompted SAP to launch a solution that would be seamlessly integrated, prevent data duplication, enable timely financial or accounting closing, and provide appropriate reports on the fly.

Accordingly, SAP launched **SAP S/4HANA Finance** (earlier known as '*SAP Simple Finance*') in 2015 to suit the digital market economy. It is a business suite that combines ERP, CRM, SRM, and others into a single ERP running on the in-memory SAP HANA database. This revamped solution, available for on-premises and cloud deployments, supports general & management accounting, financial planning, financial operations accounting & financial close, accounts payable & accounts receivable, treasury & cash management, risk management, and much more.

127. Explain the advantages of implementing SAP S/4HANA Finance.

The following are some of the advantages of going in for SAP S/4HANA Finance implementation:

- SAP S/4HANA Finance is a comprehensive financial solution for the modern digital enterprise with advanced digital data architecture as the core of the enterprise solution. Besides being a single source of truth for both transactions and analytics, it enables future innovations with its modular architecture. The 'digital core' of SAP S/4HANA Finance integrates several application extensions such as SAP Ariba, SAP Concur, SAP SuccessFactors, and SAP Fieldglass solutions.

- SAP S/4HANA Finance solution, powered by SAP Fiori, offers a simple and intuitive **user experience (UX)**. It offers a common, real-time view of financial and accounting information, enterprise-wide consistency, and a reduction in the need for manual reconciliation and errors.

- SAP S/4HANA Finance can predict, simulate, and analyze financial alternatives to optimize business processes.

- SAP S/4HANA Finance can deliver end-to-end business benefits across the five capability areas (aka 'solution areas') spread across the **lines of business (LoB)**.

- SAP S/4HANA Finance is available for on-premises, in-cloud, and hybrid deployments. It is suitable for both new 'greenfield' implementations and 'brownfield' conversions of existing SAP ECC implementations.

128. Outline the Primary Capabilities of SAP S/4HANA Finance.

A comprehensive financial solution for the modern digital enterprise, **SAP S/4HANA Finance,** comes with several primary capabilities, as outlined in *Figure 7.1*. As you can see from the figure, SAP S/4HANA Finance takes care of all financial requirements across all roles, providing the required granular solutions. With this comprehensive solution, you will now be able to track &monitor financial accounting information in an integrated framework that supports multiple countries, multiple currencies, multiple languages, and several charts of accounts.

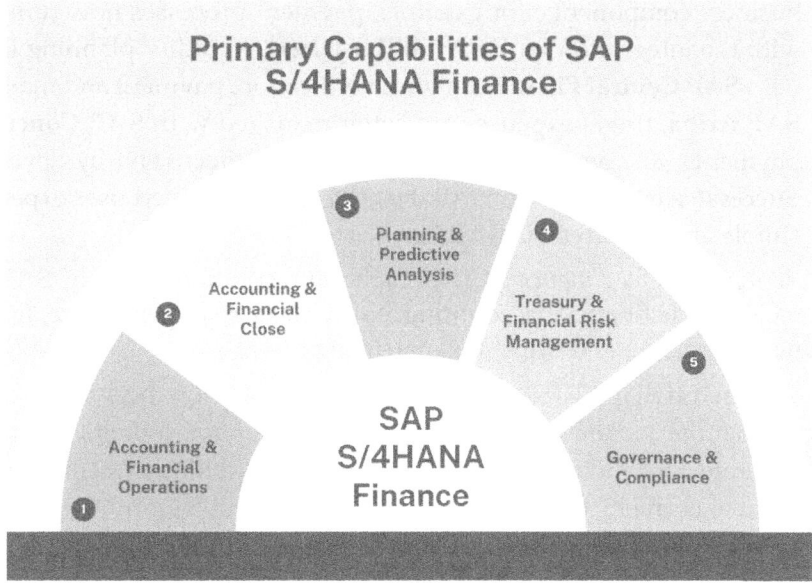

Figure 7.1: Primary Capabilities of SAP S/4HANA Finance

129. Describe the solution areas within each primary capability of SAP S/4HANA Finance.

In each of the primary capabilities, **SAP S/4HANA Finance** provides the required solution to manage the business processes thereon (*Figure 7.2*):

- There are several solution areas within the primary capability of '*Accounting & Financial Operations*' in SAP S/4HANA Finance, such as record to report, order to cash, procure to pay, real estate management, travel expenditure management, financial process governance, and indirect tax management:

  o Historically, in SAP R/3 and other ERP solutions of that era, the various business processes like invoice payment, vendor or customer management, credit administration, real-estate management, travel expenses management, depreciation of fixed assets, etc., across different FI components and sub-ledgers, were all spread across multiple solutions or systems involving manual integration and reconciliation. At times, it would nearly be impossible to collate, analyze, and forecast expenses & revenues because not much data was flowing in real-time.

  o With SAP S/4HANA Finance, several of these pain points have since been removed by streamlined end-to-end business processes cutting across multiple business components; for example, payment processes now run like a breeze with the integration with **SAP Biller Direct**, liquidity planning is centralized with **SAP Central Finance**, invoice verification, payment and management via **SAP Ariba**, travel expenses are better managed with **SAP Concur**, employee payments & compensations are handled effectively by leveraging **SAP SuccessFactors**, and so on. All these have an improved user experience that is simple and intuitive via **SAP Fiori.**

- In '*Accounting and Financial Close*' capability, solution areas of SAP S/4HANA Finance include financial accounting, entity close, enterprise close, financial close, financial reporting and direct tax management:

  o The traditional ERPs, before SAP S/4HANA Finance, were characterized by manual reconciliations because of several sub-ledgers, delay in closing, separate consolidation activities as the consolidation systems were disparate, manual currency conversion, no real-time inventory, and the like.

  o SAP S/4HANA Finance overcomes all these pain points. For example, with a single '*universal journal*' for data entry across application areas like G/L accounting, controlling, asset accounting, etc., it obviates the need for separate revenue recognition, reconciliation, and consolidation of the data flows in real-time. Also, by removing redundancies and aggregates, SAP S/4HANA Finance enables faster accounting & financial closing. It also adds more value with its live reports supporting the legal and statutory requirements.

SAP S/4HANA
SOLUTION AREAS

ACCOUNTING & FINANCIAL OPERATIONS
- Record to Report
- Order to Cash
- Procure to Pay
- Real Estate Management
- Travel Management
- Tax Management (indirect)
- Financial Process Governance

GOVERNANCE & COMPLIANCE
- Enterprise Risk Mgmt.
- Controls & Compliance Management
- Policy Lifecycle Mgmt.
- Automated Monitoring & Screening
- Audit Management
- International Trade Management

ACCOUNTING & FINANCIAL CLOSE
- Financial Accounting
- Entity Close
- Corporate Close
- Financial Reporting
- Financial Close Governance
- Tax Management (direct)

TREASURY & FIN. RISK MANAGEMENT
- Payments & Bank Communications
- Cash & Liquidity Mgmt.
- Debt & Investment Mgmt.
- Fin. Risk Management
- Risk Mgmt. for Commodities
- Treasury Governace

FIN. PLANNING & PREDICTIVE ANALYSIS
- Planning, Budgeting & Forecasting
- Profitability & Cost Management
- Management Reporting

Figure 7.2: *Solutions areas within SAP S/4HANA Finance*

- Under the capability *'Financial Planning & Predictive Analysis,'* SAP S/4HANA Finance covers the solutions areas like planning, budgeting, & forecasting, profitability & cost management, and management reporting:

  o Before the advent of SAP S/4HANA Finance, financial planning was a headache for most enterprises. There were separate, disconnected systems, tools, and processes for planning; budget allocations were static and manual, and difficulties in simulating business innovation, etc.

  o All these have changed now. SAP S/4HANA Finance integrates all the financial planning processes. It functions into a single transactional system, enabling a consolidated view of planning & forecasting via the *'SAP Business Objects Planning and Consolidation'* application that, besides enabling planning at any level, also facilitates simulation and 'what-if' analysis in real-time, helping the business to visualize the impacts of changes (to profitability) before committing to plans. The solution, with its real-time financial data, can drill down even to the line-item level.

- Payments & bank communications, cash & liquidity management, debt & investment management, financial risk management, treasury governance, and risk management for commodities are some of the solution areas within *'Treasury and Financial Risk Management'* capability of SAP S/4HANA Finance:

  o The pre-SAP S/4HANA Finance ERPs were plagued by multiple and separate treasury systems with many bank communication interfaces that resulted in minimal integration of treasury data with financial accounting. The cash forecasting was often manual and was riddled with inaccuracies and delays. All these, with the fluctuating commodity prices, led to a situation in which it became next to impossible to manage currency exposures centrally, which impacted timely forex risk mitigation.

  o Enter SAP S/4HANA Finance. With its integrated liquidity management via **SAP Cash Management**, it enables liquidity planning and analysis using automated processes. Relying on the built-in 'one exposure' functionality, it supports centralized forex risk management and takes care of 'hedging.' The **SAP In-House Cash** and **SAP Bank Communication** add-ons provide the required integration.

- There are several solution areas, including enterprise risk management, controls & compliance management, policy lifecycle management, audit management, integrated trade management, and automated monitoring and screening within the *'Governance & Compliance'* capability of SAP S/4HANA Finance:

  o Earlier, you needed to extract financial data manually from multiple systems to examine the financial audit trail while trying to identify accounting or financial fraud. Such a fragmented process did not aid in transparency and lacked accountability. Often, the business strategy was not in sync with the **governance, risk, and compliance (GR)** activities. Hence, the audit function was not very scalable with the expansion of the business.

o SAP S/4HANA Finance changed all these with its cloud and LoB extension enhancements. For example, the **SAP Fraud Management** application, with its full lifecycle of fraud management capability, enables the detection, investigation, quantification, & remediation of fraud. With this, you can now monitor and optimize the investigation process as well. SAP S/4HANA Finance uses **SAP Process Control** and **SAP Risk Management** applications, together with **SAP Audit Management**, to streamline automated controls, thereby building an effective defense framework.

Note: In the next few chapters, we shall discuss the various application areas within financial accounting (FI) in SAP S/4HANA Finance for easy understanding. To give a better grasp of the content, we have modeled the questions in a way that almost reflects the SAP Customizing Implementation Guide (IMG) so that it is easy for you to relate and follow up.

Join our book's Discord space

Join the book's Discord Workspace for Latest updates, Offers, Tech happenings around the world, New Release and Sessions with the Authors:

https://discord.bpbonline.com

CHAPTER 8
FI: General

Introduction

This chapter explains SAP FI briefly and provides the necessary information on each of the functional areas within financial accounting.

130. Explain 'Financial Accounting (FI)' in SAP.

SAP FI (**Financial Accounting**) is the backbone that records, collects, or processes financial transactions or information in real-time to provide the necessary inputs for external (statutory) reporting. SAP FI is integrated with other functional areas (such as Material Management-MM, Sales and Distribution-SD, Logistics, Supply Chain Management, Production, Quality Management, Transportation Management, Human Resources-HR, Production Planning-PP, Controlling-CO, etc.).

131. What are all the 'Functional Areas of SAP FI'?

SAP FI is made up of several functional areas, including G/L accounting, **accounts receivable & payable (A/R & A/P)**, bank accounting, revenue accounting, asset accounting, and much more (*Figure 8.1*):

Figure 8.1: *SAP IMG showing Sub-functional areas within FI*

As you can see from *Figure 8.1*, the financial accounting application area in SAP is made up of the following:

- **FI-G/L, General Ledger Accounting**:
  - o This is integrated with all other application areas within FI and outside FI.

- **FI-A/R & FI A/P, Accounts Receivable &Accounts Payable**:
  - o Integrated with FI-G/L, FI-AA, MM, SD, and **Plant Maintenance (PM)**, this application area manages customer & receivables, vendor & payables. It is well-known for credit management functionalities (from the FI side), 'dunning,' and 'payment' programs.

- **FI-CA, Contract Accounts Receivable and Payable**:
  - o A sub-ledger to SAP FI, this is an alternate application for SAP FI-AR/AP and is mainly used in businesses like media, telecom, utilities, etc., where there are many business partners and a massive volume of documents.

- **FI-BL, Bank Accounting**:
  - o A sub-application within SAP FI that deals with bank account transactions and communications. Unlike SAP ECC, now in SAP S/4HAA Finance, bank accounts are treated as master data.

- **FI-RAR, Revenue Accounting & Reporting**:
  - ○ This solution enables users to comply with the requirements & regulations of IFRS 15 by providing a comprehensive solution for revenue recognition & reporting.
- **FI-RTC, Real-Time Consolidation**:
  - ○ A consolidation solution with the integration of SAP S/4HANA and 'SAP Business Planning and Consolidation' (SAP BPC), SAP FI-RTC (Real-Time Consolidation), which considers both data quality and flexibility, and leverages the consolidation capabilities of SAP BPC.
- **FI-AA, Asset Accounting**:
  - ○ A mandatory sub-ledger, this works with the G/L accounting in SAP S/4HANA Finance. This application takes care of end-to-end life cycle management of fixed assets of an enterprise, from acquisition to retirement of an asset.
- **FI-SL, Special Purpose Ledger**:
  - ○ This provides summary information from multiple applications at a level of detail the user defines. It is generally used for reporting purposes in SAP S/4HANA Finance. You may keep this as a G/L or subsidiary ledger with the appropriate account assignment objects.
- **FI-CF, Central Finance:**
  - ○ An optional parallel operational application linked to the source ERP. With its real-time integration of financial data, it enables quick consolidation of businesses.
- **FI-CIT, Corporate Income Tax Framework**:
  - ○ This solution helps classify, settle, and report corporate income tax, besides other types of taxes.

Join our book's Discord space

Join the book's Discord Workspace for Latest updates, Offers, Tech happenings around the world, New Release and Sessions with the Authors:

https://discord.bpbonline.com

CHAPTER 9

FI: Enterprise Structure

Introduction

This chapter introduces the enterprise structure in SAP FI. You will learn about the various organizational units, including Company, Company Code, business area, functional area, etc., that make up the FI enterprise structure. You will also learn about the important global parameters for a Company Code.

Before answering the questions, let us examine the FI organization structure depicted below (*Figure 9.1*) to understand how the enterprise structure is within SAP FI. As we progress through the questions, if you need clarification on the arrangement of the various organizational elements, visit this section again.

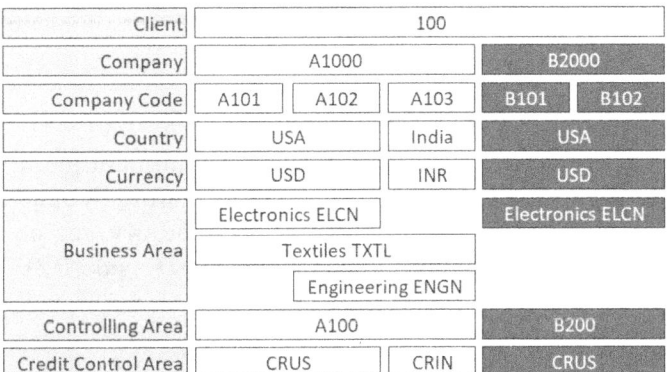

Figure 9.1*: FI Organization Structure*

The starting point of any SAP implementation is to define the 'enterprise structure' that is made up of various 'organizational units' used in different applications like SAP FI, SAP SD, SAP MM, etc. Since the scope of this book is related to financial accounting in SAP S/4HANA, Finance, we shall restrict ourselves to the concept and definition of these units under SAP FI.

132. What do you mean by 'Organizational Units' in SAP?

The '**Organizational Units**' in SAP are the elements or structures representing the business functions and are used in reporting. For example, Client (across the various modules), Company Code (FI), Controlling Area (CO), Plant (logistics), Sales Organization (SD), Purchasing Organization (MM), Employee Group (HR), etc.

133. What are the important 'Organizational Units' in FI, in SAP?

You use the organizational units in SAP FI to structure the business functions to aid in external reporting. The various logical elements of the SAP FI system include the following:

- Client (mandatory)
- Company (optional)
- Company Code (mandatory)
- Business Area (optional)
- Credit Control Area (mandatory)
- Functional Area (optional)
- Functional Management Area (optional)
- Profit Center (optional)
- Segment (optional)

134. What is a 'Company'?

A **Company** in SAP is represented by a 6-character alphanumeric code and usually represents the enterprise or the Group Company. The definition of a Company enables it to meet the statutory and/or legal requirements of the country/region where it is located. A Company can include one or more Company Codes (*Figure 9.2*). The Company sits below the Client in the SAP enterprise structure.

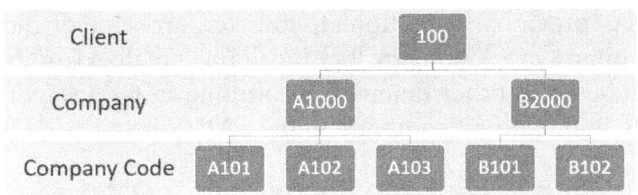

Figure 9.2: *Company code and Company code structure*

Figure 9.3

The creation of a Company in SAP is optional. Use Transaction Code OX15 to create a Company (*Figure 9.4*).

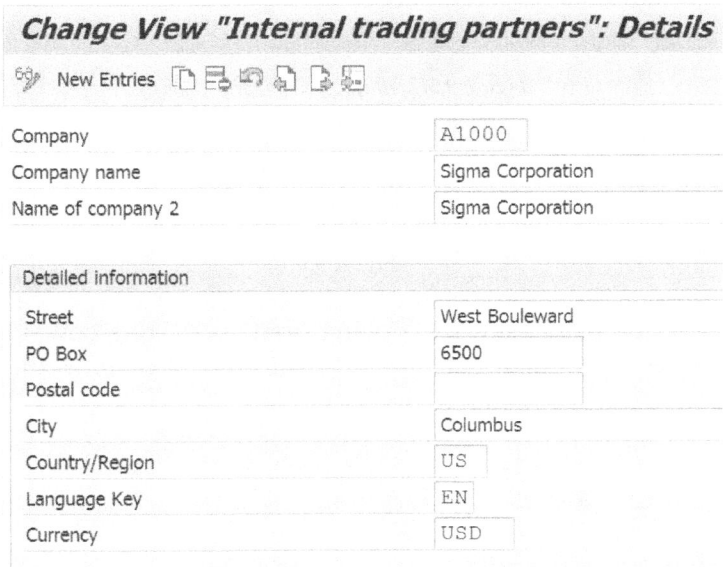

Figure 9.4: *Defining a Company*

135. What is a 'Company Code,' and how is this different from a 'Company'?

A **Company Code** in SAP is the smallest organizational unit where you can draw individual Financial Statements (Balance Sheet and Profit & Loss Account) for your external legal or statutory reporting. It is denoted by a 4-character alphanumeric code. Creating a Company Code is mandatory; you must have at least one Company Code defined in the system for implementing FI. As previously mentioned, you can have one or more Company Codes under a single Company in SAP (*Figure 9.2*). You must create a Company Code according to tax/commercial law and other financial accounting criteria (*Figure 9.5*). Remember, it represents a legally independent company in the SAP system.

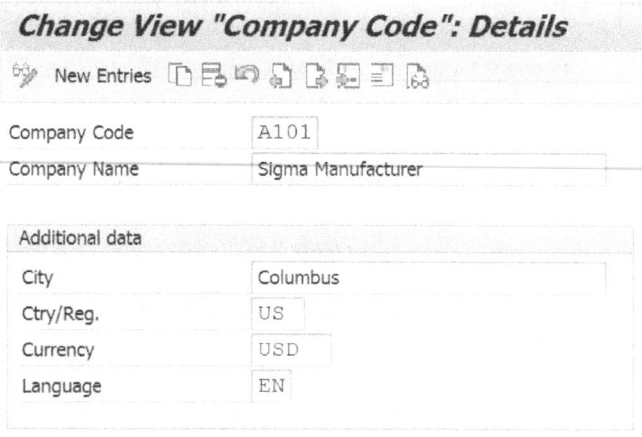

Figure 9.5: *Defining a Company Code*

Figure 9.6

You may define a Company Code by copying from an existing one ('*Copy, Delete, Check Company Code*' option as shown in *Figure 9.7*). You may also define the Company Code anew (the second option in *Figure 9.7*) from scratch.

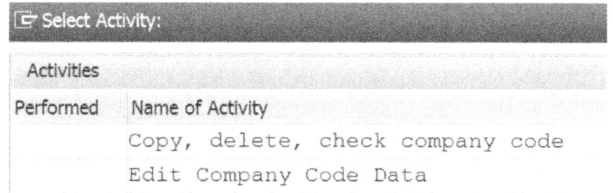

Figure 9.7: *Options to define a Company Code*

136. What are the important 'Global Settings (Parameters)' for a Company Code?

The global settings or global parameters for a Company Code are divided into two broad categories: accounting organization data and processing parameters, as shown in *Figure 9.8*:

Change View "Company Code Global Data": Details

≡ Additional Data ◀ ▶ 🖨

Company Code	A101	Sigma Manufacturer	Columbus
Country/Reg.	US	Currency	USD	Language Key	EN

Accounting organization

Chart of Accts	CANA	Alternative COA	
Company	A1000	FM Area	
Credit Control Area	CRUS	Fiscal Year Variant	K4
External CoCode	☐	Global CoCde	
Company Code Is Productive	☐	VAT Registration No.	
Hide Company Code in F4	☐		

Processing parameters

Document Entry Screen Variant	2	✓ Business Area Fin. Statements
Field status variant	0001	✓ Propose Fiscal Year
Pstng period variant		✓ Define default value date
Max. exchange rate deviation	10 %	☐ No Exch. Rate Diff. When Clearing in LC
Sample Acct Rules Var.		☐ Tax base is net value
Workflow Variant		✓ Discount base is net value
Inflation Method		✓ Financial Assets Mgmt active
Tax Crcy Translation		☐ Purchase Acct Proc.
CoCd -> CO Area		☐ JV Accounting Active
Cost of Sales Accounting Actv.	2	☐ Hedge request active
☐ Negative Postings Permitted		☐ Enable Amount Split
		☐ Tax Reporting Date Active
☐ Manage Postg Period		

Figure 9.8: *Company Code Global Parameters*

Accounting organization data

This comprises several parameters such as the chart of accounts, alternative chart of accounts, Company, **financial management area (FM area)**, credit control area, fiscal year variant, global Company Code, external Company Code, VAT registration number, etc. This is where you will mark your Company Code as *productive* ('*Company Code Is Productive*') after it goes live.

Processing parameters

The processing parameters for a Company Code provide the required parameters for processing and controlling the accounting data in the system. The parameters include document entry screen variant, field status variant, posting period variant, maximum exchange rate deviation, sample account rules variant, inflation method, tax currency translation, Company Code – Controlling Area assignment indicator, whether the cost of sales accounting is active, if negative posting is permitted, do you need to generate business area financial statements, is the system to propose the fiscal year during transaction posting, define default value date, if the tax base should be of net value, no exchange rate difference when clearing in local currency, if the discount base is to be net, whether financial asset management is active, if joint venture accounting is active, is the system to enable amount split during invoice posting and the like.

Figure 9.9

137. Can you assign more than one 'Company Code' to a 'Company'?

Yes, you can assign more than one Company Code to a single Company. All the Company codes within a Company should use the same *Chart of Accounts* and the same *Financial Year*, though they all can have different *Local Currencies*.

138. What is a 'Business Area'?

Business Areas correspond to specific business segments of a Company and may cut across different Company codes (for example, product lines). They can also represent different responsibility areas (for example, branch units). The definition of business area is optional in SAP. The business area is represented by a 4-character alphanumeric identifier. Some examples are provided in the following figure (*Figure 9.10*):

Business Area	Description	
ELCN	Electornics	
TXTL	Textiles	
ENGN	Engineering	

Figure 9.10: Business Area

Use Transaction Code **OX03** to define the required business areas.

Figure 9.11

The financial statements drawn per business area are for internal reporting purposes. You need to put a 'tick' mark in the *'Business Area FS'* checkbox in the configuration against the Company Code(s) for which you want to enable business area financial statements (*Figure 9.12*). You can do this for all the Company Codes using the Transaction Code **OB65** or do that individually for each of the Company Codes when configuring the Company Code global parameters (Transaction Code **OBY6**). When transactions are posted in FI, you have the option of assigning the same to a business area so that the values are properly captured business-area-wise for internal financial statements.

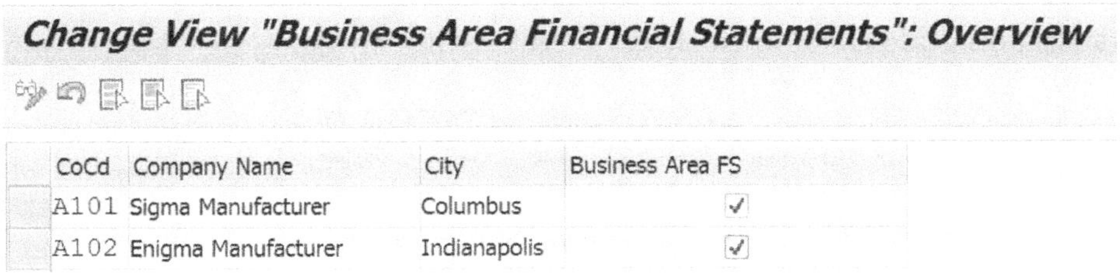

Figure 9.12: Enable Business Area Financial Statements

139. Can you attach a 'Business Area' to the transaction without assigning it in a posting?

Yes. The business area can also be derived from other account assignments, such as cost centers. However, to do this, you need to define the business area in the master record of that cost center.

140. How to post 'Cross-Company Code Business Area' postings?

By using a 'cross Company Code transaction,' you will be able to post to different business areas cutting across various Company Codes. Any number of 'Business Area–Company Code' combinations are possible.

141. What is a 'Credit Control Area'?

The **Credit Control Area**, a mandatory organization unit in SAP, helps administer the credit management functions related to the customers. This organizational unit is used in FSCM, SD, and FI-A/R applications (*Figure 9.13*):

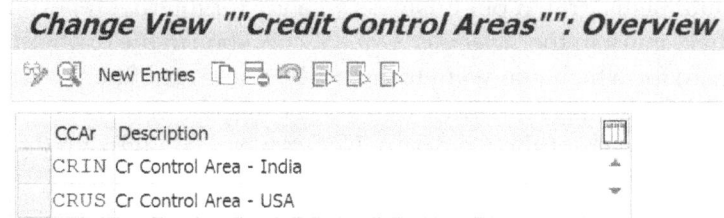

Figure 9.13: Credit Control Area

Use Transaction Code **OB45** to create the credit control area(s).

Figure 9.14

By definition, you can have more than one credit control area in a Client, and each Company Code is assigned exactly to one credit control area. However, you can indeed attach many Company Codes to the same credit control area (*Figure 9.15*):

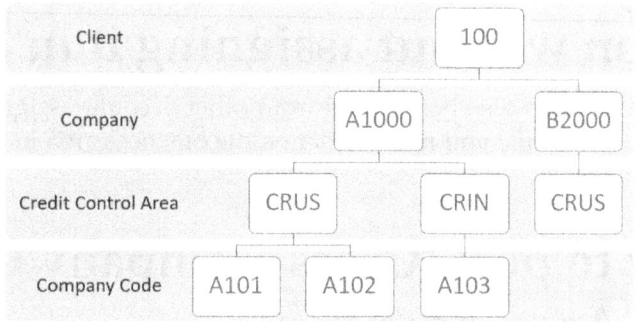

Figure 9.15: Credit Control Area – Company Code Assignment

With SAP S/4HANA Finance, credit risk management is handled via **Financial Supply Chain Management (FSCM)**. The credit management component of FSCM (FIN-FSCM-CR) determines the loss of receivables from business partners (customers) via a BAdI that is integrated with SAP SD. You will define the required credit evaluation/management checks in FSCM. Since this is essentially handled in FSCM, we will not discuss more about credit control area and credit management in this book.

142. What is a 'Functional Area' in SAP?

A '**functional area**' is an SAP FI organizational unit used in 'cost of sales' accounting. Also used in **SAP Funds Management**, they help to classify your company's expenses according to the various functions performed by your staff, such as production, sales, marketing, accounting, etc. The standard SAP system comes delivered with several functional areas, all starting with "Y" (*Figure 9.16*); you may use them as such or create your own.

Functional Area	Name
YB10	Sales Revenue
YB15	Sales discounts and allow
YB18	Cost of Goods Sold
YB20	Production
YB25	Consulting/Services
YB30	Sales and Distribution
YB35	Marketing
YB40	Administration
YB50	Research & Development
YB70	Other gains
YB75	Other expenses

Figure 9.16: *Default Functional Area*

To create a new functional area, you may use the Transaction Code **FM_FUNCTION**, as the earlier Transaction Code **OKBD** is now obsolete.

Figure 9.17

143. What is an 'FM Area' in SAP?

Used in 'SAP Funds Management' and 'SAP Cash Management', an **FM area** aka 'Financial Management Area') structures your business for cash and funds management. You can assign more than one Company Code to a single FM area. The FM area is, then, derived from the assigned Company Code. You can do such an assignment even if the Company Code currency of such Company Codes differs from that of the currency of the FM area. However, remember that you will not be able to change the currency of the FM area if you have already posted to that in FI or other application areas. Also, note that you must maintain the characteristics of FM areas separately for SAP Cash Management and SAP Funds Management while defining those areas in SAP IMG.

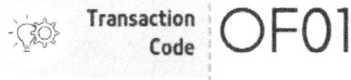

Figure 9.18

144. What is a 'Segment'?

Denoting a geographical area or line of business, you use **segments** to generate reports that meet the requirements of '**International Accounting Standards**' (**IAS**), '**International Financial Reporting**' (**IFRS**), or '**Generally Accepted Accounting Principles**' (**US GAAP**), or any other similar standards.

When you model a segment based on **lines of business (LOB)**, then it is known as a **business segment** that represents a single product/service or a group of products/services. On the other hand, a **geographical segment** represents, for example, assets or customers of a specific location or one that provides services/products in a specific economic zone or area.

When you define a profit center, you can then enter the appropriate segment over there. However, for this to happen, you need to define the segments beforehand, well before defining the profit centers. The system derives the segment from the assigned profit center. Of course, you can also derive segments using other criteria; for that, you must use BAdI.

Join our book's Discord space

Join the book's Discord Workspace for Latest updates, Offers, Tech happenings around the world, New Release and Sessions with the Authors:

https://discord.bpbonline.com

CHAPTER 10

FI Global Settings: Ledgers

Introduction

In this first chapter on FI global settings, you will learn all about ledgers and the associated settings. You will start with the standard and custom fields before discussing the field status, field status variant, and field status groups. Besides learning about the accounting principles and parallel accounting in SAP, you will learn about the different types of ledgers, ledger groups, universal journals, etc., and how SAP posts to the various ledgers. You will learn about the usage of currencies in SAP S/4HANA Finance, fiscal year, fiscal year variant, posting period & special period, posting period variant, and finally, the retained earnings account.

There are several global settings that you need to complete in Customizing before making the settings for individual application areas like G/L Accounting, Accounts Receivable and Accounts Payable, Bank Accounting, Asset Accounting, etc. The important ones include the settings related to the following:

- Ledgers
- Documents
- Tax on sales/purchases
- Withholding tax
- Inflation accounting

145. What do you mean by 'Standard Fields' in SAP?

The **standard fields** (aka 'dimensions') are pre-delivered in an SAP system, supported natively by the 'Data Model.' Used across the system, all such fields come with default settings, and you do not need to make any additional configuration to use them in the transactions and reports. The *business area, profit center,* and *segment* are some examples of the standard fields. It is possible that you may not be using all the standard fields. In such a situation, you may want to use them for a different purpose. However, SAP recommends refraining from using them for alternative purposes because, later, you may not be able to use them again for the originally intended purpose. Instead, you may want to use the *customer fields* when you feel that standard fields are not meeting your exact business requirements in the system.

146. So, what exactly are 'Customer Fields'?

The **customer fields** (aka 'custom fields' or 'customer-specific fields') are the '**user-defined fields' (UDFs)** for use in SAP ERP and SAP HANA systems. You can use a custom field to store some structured information that you cannot otherwise store in a standard field. As you, as a customer, define such database table fields anew, they do not have any default settings; you need to configure them with the appropriate settings to use them in transactions or reports in SAP.

You may include such custom fields via the extensibility options in classic GUI (both HTML GUI and SAPGUI) screens beside the SAP Fiori apps. When defined, these fields are available across all SAP Clients, though you may not use them. You can use them either as such or combine them with other standard fields. Once you have defined these fields, and when they are in sync with the ERP system, you will not be able to change or delete them via standard means.

Name the custom fields (say, starting with 'ZZ' like ZZSPREG) in your customer namespace. This will avoid naming conflicts.

147. Why does SAP recommend caution when you want to add 'Customer Fields'?

When you want to add customer fields, you need to be mindful of the impact it will create in the system. Once defined, you need to enrich or fill them with content when you make journal entries via manual and automated postings and from the interfaces. So, the recommendation is not to define more custom fields than what is absolutely required.

148. What are the different uses of 'Custom Fields'?

You will normally use the **custom fields** to analyze values at the aggregate level. SAP outlines that you can make use of the custom fields in the following ways:

- **As product/activity related characteristics**: For example, as vehicle groups (like sedan, hatchback, SUV), as product group (like electrical consumables, lubricants), etc.

- **As managerial/organizational characteristics**: For example, geographies (like North America, Central America).

- **Industry/legal requirement characteristics**: For example, insurance contract types, banking contract types, etc.

149. Is there any functional restriction for the use of 'Custom Fields'?

When you plan to define **customer fields**, do not lose sight of the prerequisites for the usage of these fields, which are reporting requirements based on the information that is available in Financial Accounting, Financial Close, and Predictive Analysis & Planning in SAP S/4HANA Finance. You should not use custom fields for purposes that can be achieved otherwise via the standard fields; for example, you should not use custom fields to evaluate stock, payables, etc.; instead, use the B/S items for that purpose. The custom fields are also not required to replace the standard scenario but to provide specific information about your business.

Note that you cannot use customer fields in financial accounting for open item processing in SAP FI-AR/AP. However, you can assign customer fields (in the coding block) to G/L account items (accounts for financial statements).

150. What are the technical restrictions, if any, in making use of 'Custom Fields'?

Including **custom fields** does not trigger any process flow in SAP S/4HANA Finance. However, the value filling a custom field may trigger such a process. There is no fixed master data (like customers, bank accounts, G/L accounts, etc.) assigned to the characteristics of custom fields. Accordingly, no such value will flow during journal posting using custom fields. If you do not plan to fill the custom fields with data, then you need to fill them via BAdI with your own business rules.

Technically, the number of custom fields per se does not affect the data volume as there is no totals table in SAP S/4HANA Finance. However, that does not mean that you can add any number of custom fields because using custom fields, for example, as sender/receiver in allocations, can result in the increased processing time of allocations and the resulting number of journal entries.

151. How to create the 'Custom Fields'?

You can create your own **custom fields** in the 'coding block' of the system. Create the custom fields in your 'test' system and use a transport to move them to other Clients. Once created, you can use these newly created customer fields in SAP FI-G/L accounts and in SAP MM inventory accounting and purchasing. The system also updates them while creating line items in CO. All custom fields are updated during automatic postings. However, if you want to update them manually in a posting, then you need to add these fields to the entry variants of SAP Enjoy posting transactions.

Transaction Code OXK3

Figure 10.1

152. What precautions should you take when including 'Custom Fields'?

It is important that you do not make any postings in a 'live' system when you are creating a custom field. Also, you should not make any postings when you transport the custom fields to the production system.

153. What do you mean by 'Field Status' in SAP?

The 'field status' represents the behavior of a field on a data entry screen, whether it is for displaying the data or receiving the data as input. Every field on a data entry screen can have any one of the three statuses, namely, 'suppressed' (aka 'hidden'), 'required entry,' and 'optional entry.' By default, every field will have the stat-us of 'display,' and you need to decide which of the three statuses you are going to apply to a field to change its field status.

154. What is a 'Field Status Group'?

A **field status group** (**FSG**) is a collection of field statuses for a group of fields. Through an FSG, you will decide which fields in that group need to be made with the status of 'suppressed,' 'optional,' or 'required.' Once you complete the definition of FSG, you then need to associate that with the individual G/L account master records at the Company Code level. Note that you cannot enter FSG for customer/vendor accounts; you need to do that via the associated reconciliation (G/L) accounts. Then, based on the FSG in the reconciliation accounts, the system controls the field status of customer/vendor accounts during any transaction posting.

155. What is a 'Field Status Variant'?

You combine various field status groups into a **field status variant** (**FSV**) and then assign the FSV to one or more Company Codes. By doing this, it is possible that you can use the same FSV in multiple Company Codes without defining FSV for each of the Company Codes.

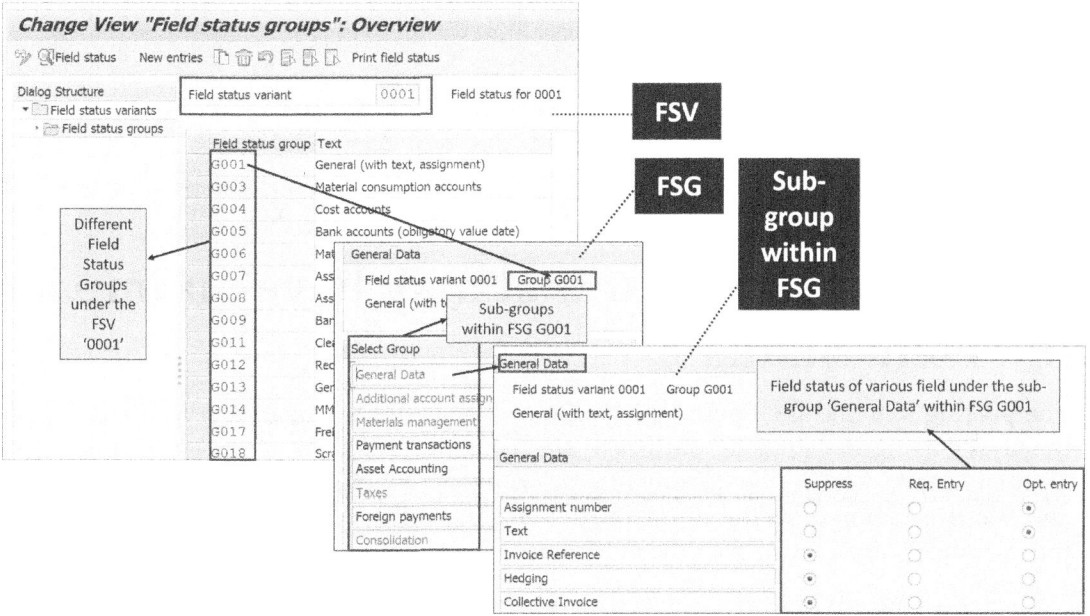

Figure 10.2: Field Status, Field Status Group, and Field Status Variant

The standard SAP comes with the FSV '0001' with various FSGs like G001, G003, G004, etc. If you look closely at the FSG (*Figure 10.2*), you will notice that each FSG comprises one or more sub-groups, namely general data, additional account assignments, materials management, payment transactions, and so on. Furthermore, you will also notice that some groups are shown in blue text while the rest are in black. The sub-groups in black text (say, payment transactions, for example) will have all the fields with their default status as 'suppressed,' and they may not be relevant to that FSG.

Transaction Code OBC4

Figure 10.3

You may assign FSV to a Company Code using the Transaction Code **OBC5**. You can also assign FSV to a Company Code while maintaining the Company Code global parameters vide the Transaction Code **OBY6** (*Figure 10.4*).

Figure 10.4: *Assign FSV to Company Code*

Transaction Code OBC5

Figure 10.5

156. Is there a factor that may have an impact on 'Field Status'?

The **posting key** and the **document type** may impact the status of a field. For example, the G/L posting key in a standard SAP system comes with the status of all fields as an 'optional' entry. And, in the document type, you may denote the fields '*Reference Number*' and '*Document Header*' as 'required entry' fields. In such cases, both the posting key and the document type may impact the field status, as well as the associated FSG.

In such a situation, you come across a conflicting situation; for example, you have a field with its status as 'suppressed' in FSG, but for the same field, you may have field status as 'required entry' in the posting key. In such a situation, SAP uses 'link rules' to resolve the conflict.

157. So, what are known as 'Link Rules'?

The '**link rules**' in SAP provide a resolution when there is a conflicting field status setting for a particular field. This may be because you maintained different statuses for a field in FSG and posting key, for example. The link rules, then, determine the final field status for that field. As you can see from *Figure 10.6*, for example, if the field status in the G/L account is 'suppressed' and if it is 'required entry' for the same field in posting keys, then the result will always be an 'error' because of conflicting statuses.

		Field Status in Posting Key			Final Field Status based on Link Rules
		Suppressed	Required Entry	Optional Entry	
Field Status in G/L Account	Suppressed	✓			Suppressed
			✗		Error (Conflict)
				✗	Error (Conflict)
	Required Entry	✗			Error (Conflict)
			✓		Required Entry
				✗	Error (Conflict)
	Optional Entry	✓			Suppressed
			✓		Required Entry
				✓	Optional Entry

Figure 10.6: Link Rules to overcome conflicting Field Status settings

158. What is an 'Accounting Principle'?

The '**accounting principle**' represents the rules and guidelines that your company should follow while reporting financial data and results. It governs accounting according to the general rules and concepts by forming the groundwork for the more complicated, detailed, and legalistic accounting rules. The accounting principles vary from government to government, and you will come across several accounting principles, including the 'going-concern principle,' the 'revenue-recognition principle,' the 'accrual principle,' and the 'matching principle.' Some of the popular accounting principles are as follows:

- International Accounting Standards (**IAS**)
- International Financial Reporting Standards (**IFRS**)
- US Generally Accepted Accounting Principles (**US GAAP**)
- Indian Accounting Standard (**Ind-AS**)

159. Can you combine more than one 'Accounting Principle' to post in a single transaction?

Yes. SAP allows you to combine more than one accounting principle when the posted data for each of the individual accounting principles are identical. For example, you can create a single accounting principle by combining both IAS and US GAAP.

160. What is 'Parallel Accounting' in SAP?

You will go for **'parallel accounting'** when you want to conduct valuations and closing operations in your company according to different accounting principles like group commercial accounting, local commercial accounting, local tax accounting, etc. When you use parallel accounting, you can denote the valuations and closing operations in additional parallel currencies besides the local currency. It is possible, in SAP, that you can use a total of 10 currencies for such purposes.

Consider, for example, that you have an Indian subsidiary of your American group Company. Now, for the Indian subsidiary, besides creating financial statements according to group commercial accounting principles (US GAPP), you also need to create financial statements meeting the local commercial accounting principles for India (Indian Accounting Standard – Ind AS). In this case, you will use USD as the group currency (type 30), representing the group accounting principle, and INR as the local currency (type 10), representing the local commercial principle, for valuation and closing operations.

161. What are the different approaches to 'Parallel Accounting'?

There are three approaches to portray parallel accounting:

- Account approach (using additional accounts)
- Ledger approach (using parallel ledgers)
- Company Code approach (using additional Company Codes)

Of the three, the last approach (using additional Company Codes) is almost obsolete and is not supported by all application components in SAP. In this approach, you will portray parallel accounting by defining an additional Company Code. SAP supports this approach only if you are upgrading to SAP S/4HANA Finance. In all other cases, SAP does not support this anymore. Even in the case of upgrades, you will not be able to make any new configuration settings.

162. Explain the 'Account Approach' to Parallel Accounting.

In the '**account approach**' to parallel accounting, you define additional G/L accounts to portray parallel accounting in the system. With this approach, you will have different account areas, as shown in *Figure 10.7*: one area with specific accounts for each of the accounting principles and one joint area that contains postings for both accounting principles. SAP recommends adopting the account approach if you are fine with having a relatively large number of accounts and the number of valuation differences arising out of different accounting principles is not large.

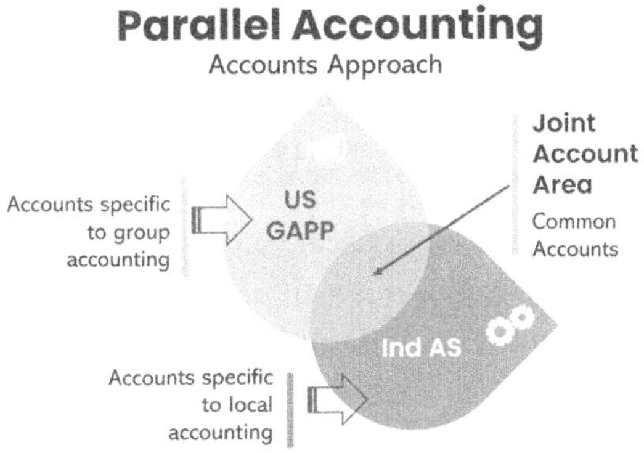

Figure 10.7: *Accounts approach to Parallel Accounting*

163. Describe the 'Ledger Approach' to Parallel Accounting.

Also known as the 'parallel ledgers approach,' in the ledger approach to parallel accounting, you will use multiple parallel general ledgers, according to different accounting principles, to portray parallel accounting in SAP. When posting, you can direct the system to post as follows:

- To all the ledgers
- To select the number of ledgers in a ledger group
- To a single ledger

Before defining the parallel ledgers, you should decide what accounting principle you want to represent in the leading ledger (usually, this will be the group accounting principle) and what are the other accounting principles (for example, local commercial accounting, local tax accounting, etc.) that you want to be represented in the non-leading ledgers. We shall discuss leading and non-leading ledgers in a while.

164. When will you go for Parallel Accounting using 'Parallel Ledgers'?

You will resort to a ledger approach to parallel accounting when you feel that using additional accounts to portray parallel accounting will be unmanageable.

165. What are all the advantages of using the 'Ledger Approach' to Parallel Accounting?

There are several obvious advantages of using **parallel ledgers for parallel accounting,** including the following:

- The number of G/L accounts becomes easily manageable.
- You can manage each accounting principle using a separate ledger in each Company Code.
- You will be able to use different **fiscal year variants** (**FYV**).
- You can use the standard reports (drill-down reports and reports generated using Report Writer and Report Painter) for both the leading and non-leading ledgers.

166. Is there a disadvantage to using the 'Ledger Approach' in Parallel Accounting?

While there are several advantages to using parallel ledgers for parallel accounting, this approach has disadvantages. One disadvantage is that the use of parallel ledgers will increase the data volume in the system.

167. What is SAP's recommendation for 'Parallel Accounting'?

SAP S/4HANA Finance provides both the 'account approach' and 'ledger approach' options for parallel accounting. However, SAP recommends the 'ledger approach' if it is a new implementation of SAP S/4HANA Finance.

168. What is a 'Ledger' in financial accounting?

Also known as *'book of final entry,'* a **ledger** in financial accounting classifies and records the information from 'journals' (aka *'book of first entry'*) as debits or credits and summarizes the same, showing the current balance. A ledger can be a **general ledger (G/L)** or a **subsidiary ledger (sub-ledger)**.

169. What is a General Ledger?

Segregated by various types like assets, liabilities, revenues, expenses, etc., the **G/L** records every financial transaction, according to a specific accounting principle, in a company during the company's lifetime. You will post such transactions to the various G/L accounts, which then flow into the G/L in a summarized format. Additionally, it is from this accounting information that you prepare different accounting/financial statements showing the financial health of the company.

SAP S/4HANA Finance supports multiple accounting principles via parallel accounting, for which you will define separate general ledgers representing different accounting principles. This may be required as different accounting principles may treat a particular transaction differently, such as accruals.

170. What are the different 'Types of Ledgers' in SAP S/4HANA Finance?

You will come across two types of ledgers in financial accounting in SAP S/4HANA Finance (*Figure 10.8*):

- Standard ledger
- Extension ledger

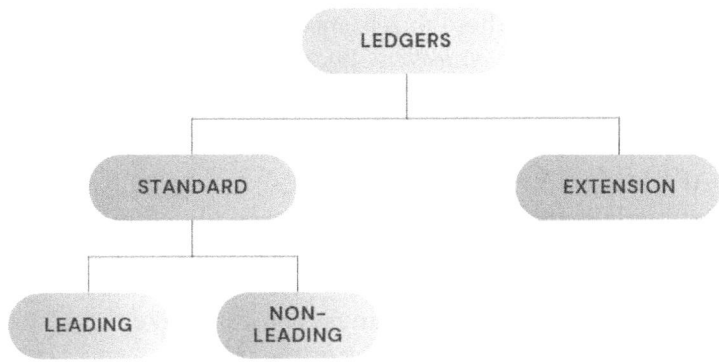

Figure 10.8: *Ledgers in SAP S/4HANA Finance*

171. What is a 'Standard Ledger'?

A ledger that is made up of all journal entries of all business transactions is termed the **'standard ledger.'** There can be several standard ledgers defined in the system. But you must designate a standard ledger either as a *'leading ledger'* or a *'non-leading ledger.'* SAP requires that you designate one of the standard ledgers as the 'leading ledger' (per Client) in G/L accounting. You can have any number of non-leading ledgers.

When you use the *'account approach'* in parallel accounting, you need only one ledger (the G/L), which will be the leading ledger by default. However, when you use the *'ledger approach'* for parallel accounting, you need more than one ledger: one leading ledger and one or more non-leading ledgers.

172. Explain the 'Leading Ledger.'

Represented by **0L** in the standard system, the **leading ledger** is mandatory and is linked to all the Company Codes in the system. By that, this ledger gets updated, by default, with all the transactions in all the Company Codes. The leading ledger is fully integrated with SAP CO and gets updated with all the actual data. The leading ledger's settings are the same as the underlying Company Code regarding currency, **fiscal year variant** (**FYV**), and **posting period variant** (**PPV**). The document numbers, once assigned to the leading ledger, apply to all the dependent ledgers as well.

173. What are 'Non-leading Ledgers'?

You will need **'non-leading ledgers'** when you use the ledger approach in **parallel accounting** for your company. The non-leading ledgers are also standard ledgers but are used to manage the different valuation approaches of your business in G/L Accounting. This may be required as the local accounting period or local tax year may differ from that of the global reporting period, for example. In this case, you may need to have a different FYV or currency to take care of these requirements, which may not be possible if you go in for defining additional *'extension ledgers'* because the extension ledgers, by definition, inherit the same settings and postings of the underlying standard ledger (more about extension ledgers later).

The standard SAP S/4HANA Finance system contains only the **leading ledger** (**0L**); there is no pre-defined non-leading ledger. Hence, you need to define/activate all the required non-leading ledgers for the required Company Codes in the system according to your requirements. Besides defining these ledgers, you will also need to make appropriate customizing settings to manage their postings: you can make the system post to all the non-leading ledgers or select ledger(s) via the *ledger groups*.

Unlike the leading ledger with the same FYV and PPV of the assigned Company Code, you can configure the non-leading ledgers to have a different FYV and PPV than that of the Company Code. Also, it is optional to define a second and third currency for non-leading ledgers. However, if you plan to assign a non-leading ledger with a second and third currency case, you must define those currencies in the respective Company

Codes. Only then will you be able to use those currencies in the non-leading ledgers. You cannot assign a currency to these ledgers if the same has not been defined for that Company Code.

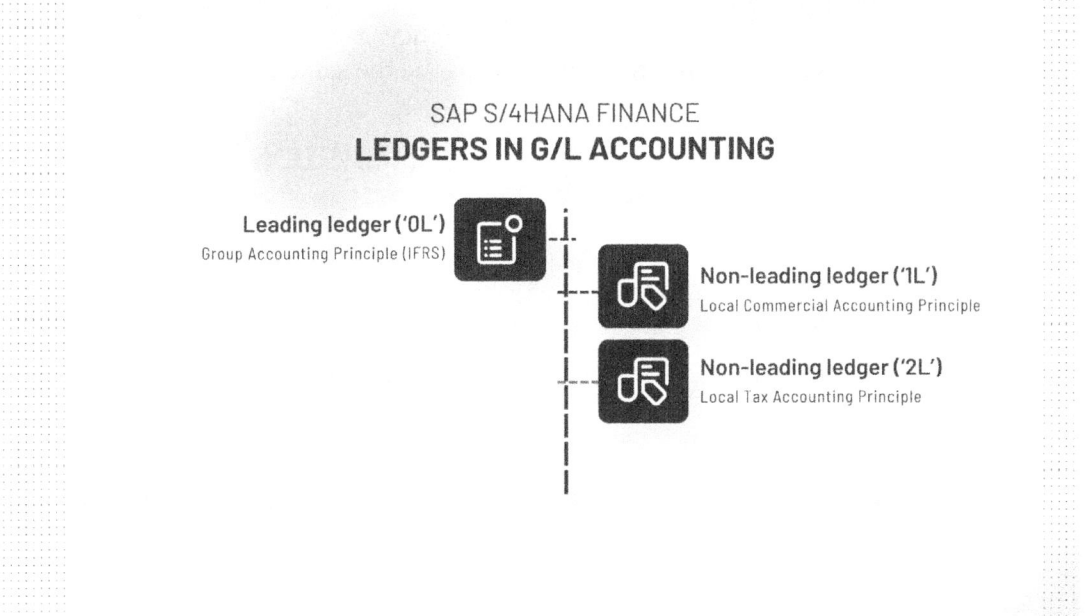

Figure 10.9: *Leading and non-leading ledgers*

Take the case of a company that, besides the group valuation (IFRS), needs financial statements to meet the local commercial accounting principle (where the Company Codes operate) and the local tax accounting principle. So, in a case like this, you will manage group valuation by using the leading ledger and two non-leading ledgers that represent the local and tax accounting principles (*Figure 10.9*).

174. What is an 'Extension Ledger'?

You define an '**extension ledger**' based on an underlying standard ledger. The underlying standard ledger may be a leading ledger or a non-leading ledger. While defining an extension ledger, you also need to specify the *'extension ledger type'* that identifies the type of journal entries that you can post to the extension ledger (we shall discuss more about 'extension ledger type' later).

The extension ledger inherits all the settings of the underlying standard ledger on top of inheriting the postings. However, it is possible that you can explicitly make some postings only to the extension ledgers; such delta postings will not get updated in the underlying standard ledger. This means that only such delta postings are stored in the database per extension ledger, thereby avoiding duplication in the underlying standard ledger.

It is possible to create more than one extension ledger based on a single underlying standard ledger. It is also possible that you create an extension ledger based on another extension ledger (*Figure 10.10*). Because of these, you may assign a different PPV accounting principle, or Company Code to the extension ledgers than that of the underlying standard ledger. But you will not be able to change the currency or FYV of the extension ledgers from that of the underlying standard ledger: it must be the same.

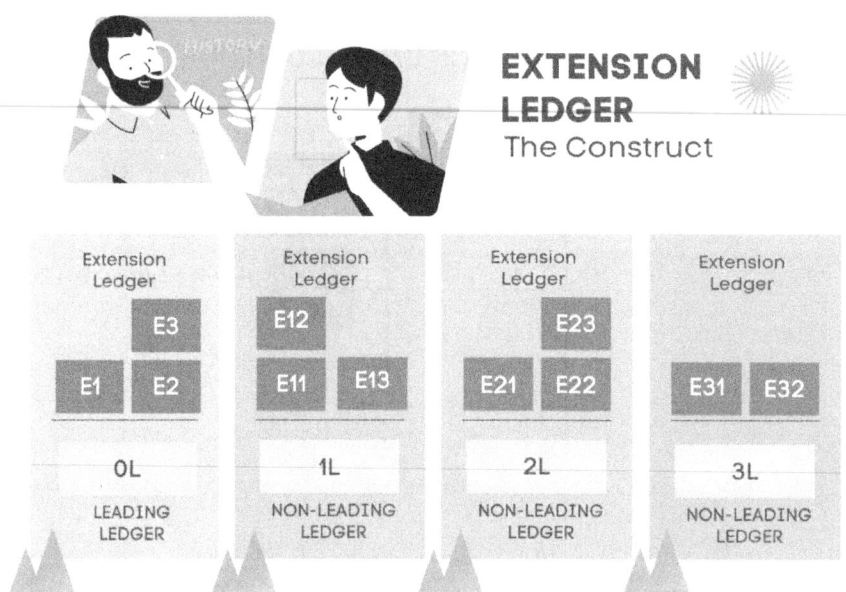

Figure 10.10: *Extension Ledger: the construct*

When you generate a report based on an extension ledger, the system brings up not only the extension-ledger-only postings but also all the inherited postings from the underlying standard ledger. This is a very useful and flexible way of providing additional views within G/L Accounting in SAP S/4HANA Finance, besides the regular legal views of the standard ledgers. So, the extension ledgers will come in handy for storing predictive/simulation data, manual adjustment postings that you may make for management accounting, etc.

175. Differentiate 'Extension Ledger' from 'Standard Ledger.'

Using *Table 10.1*, let us understand how an extension ledger differs from a standard ledger in terms of activation, postings, etc.

Standard ledger	Extension ledger
Independent ledger. May be a leading or non-leading ledger.	Always based on an underlying standard ledger that can be a leading or non-leading ledge
You can define various ledgers to meet different legal and reporting requirements. While doing so, you must designate one ledger as the leading ledger, and the rest as non-leading.	You can add one or more extension ledgers on top an underlying standard ledger. Also, you can have one extension ledger on top of another.
You can make postings specific to or to all ledgers. By default, the leading ledger receives all postings in all the Company Codes.	You can make postings that are updated only in the extension ledgers. However, an extension ledger inherits all the settings and postings of the underlying standard ledger.
The total balance equals the ledger balance.	The total balance is the sum of balance of the underlying standard ledger and the balance of the specific extension ledger.
When migrating from classic G/L in SAP ECC to SAP S/4HANA Finance, you cannot activate standard ledgers on day1. However, you can activate the same later.	You can activate the extension ledgers on day1, when you are migrating from classic G/L in SAP ECC to SAP S/4HANA Finance.

Table 10.1: *Standard Ledger vs. Extension Ledger*

176. What kind of postings are received by the 'Extension Ledger'?

Postings, including manual postings, posted without a ledger group to the leading ledger will all be received in the extension ledger as well. Similarly, all postings, including manual postings, posted **with a ledger** group assigned to a non-leading ledger are also received in a leading ledger.

177. How are 'Non-Leading Ledger' and 'Extension Ledger' different?

We have already seen that there could be instances wherein your business requirements may not be met by defining non-leading ledgers alone, and in such a situation, you may need to go for extension ledgers. So, compared to the leading ledger, both the non-leading and extension ledgers differ in some characteristics that you need to be aware of to make an informed decision. The differences are summarized in *Figure 10.11*:

Ledger	Compared to 'Leading Ledger'				
	Can a different currency be defined?	Can a different FSV be used?	Can a different PPV be used?	Can a different 'company code' be assigned?	Can a different 'accounting principle' be used?
Non-leading Ledger	✓	✓	✓	✓	✓
Extension Ledger	🚫	🚫	✓	✓	✓

Figure 10.11: Non-leading and extension ledgers: How different from a leading ledger?

178. What is an 'Extension Ledger Type'?

While defining an extension ledger, besides denoting the underlying standard ledger, you need to specify the appropriate '**extension ledger type**' to indicate what kind of journal entries will get posted into that extension ledger. SAP provides four ledger types, as shown in *Figure 10.12*. The journal entries are listed, from top to bottom, according to how extensive they will be. The topmost one, *standard journal entries*, comes with the most extensive one, and the bottommost one, *journal entries for valuation differences*, comes with the least extensive data. The entries are as follows:

- The *'standard journal entries'* are like the regular journal entries posted to the underlying standard ledger. When posted, such entries are stored in the extension ledger with the document numbers. Once posted, as in any other document entry in SAP, you will only be able to reverse but will not be able to delete. You will normally use this extension ledger when you need to manually adjust the journal entries according to a new accounting principle or for some management adjustment postings that need not affect the underlying standard ledger. As mentioned already, this kind of journal entry comes with the most extensive data of all the four types.

- In the case *'P, Line items with technical numbers/no deletion possible'* type of extension ledger, the system stores the journal entries only with technical numbers without the regular document numbers. Here, you can only reverse the entries that have already been posted and cannot delete them. SAP recommends that you use such a type of extension ledger for predictive accounting or recording commitments.

- When you create an extension ledger of type *'S, Line items with technical numbers/ deletion possible'*, as in the case of type 'P', here also, the system saves the journal entries only with technical numbers (and not document numbers). The only difference from type 'P' is that, here, you can delete the journal entries if required. You can use this type of extension ledger for simulation purposes, which is often called a 'simulation ledger' in SAP S/4HANA Finance.

- As the name suggests, you will use the extension ledger of type *'journal entries for valuation differences'* to post journal entries that account for valuation differences of accounting principles.

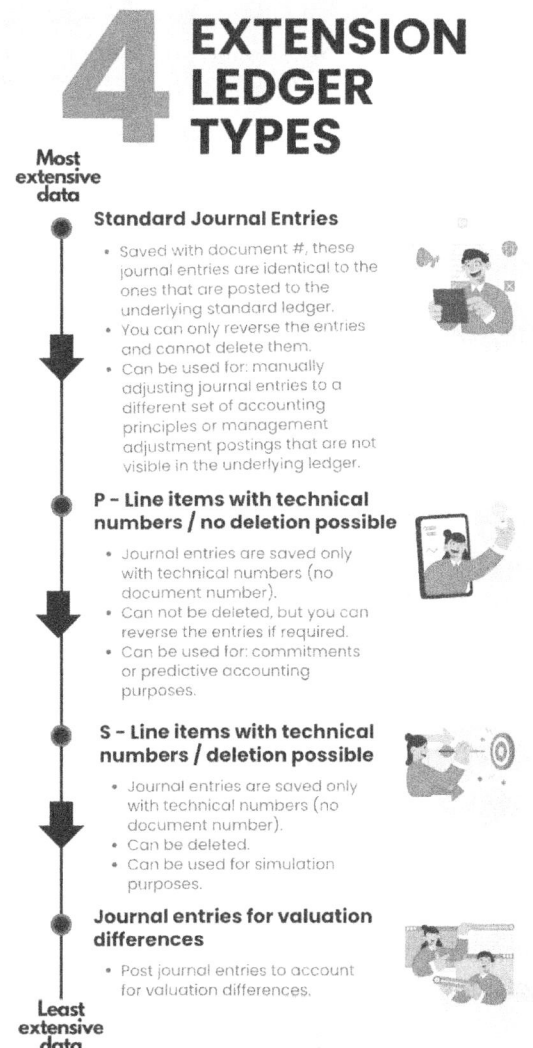

Figure 10.12: Extension ledger types

179. Any restriction in creating one 'Extension Ledger' on top of another?

Creating multiple extension ledgers on top of another extension ledger is restricted by the 'extension ledger type.' The logic is as shown in *Figure 10.13*:

- 1: You can create any type of extension ledger on top of another extension ledger of type *standard journal entries*.

- 2: You can create extension ledger types 'P' and 'S' on top of another extension ledger of type 'P'.

- 3: You can create only the 'S' type of extension ledger on top of another extension ledger of type 'S'.

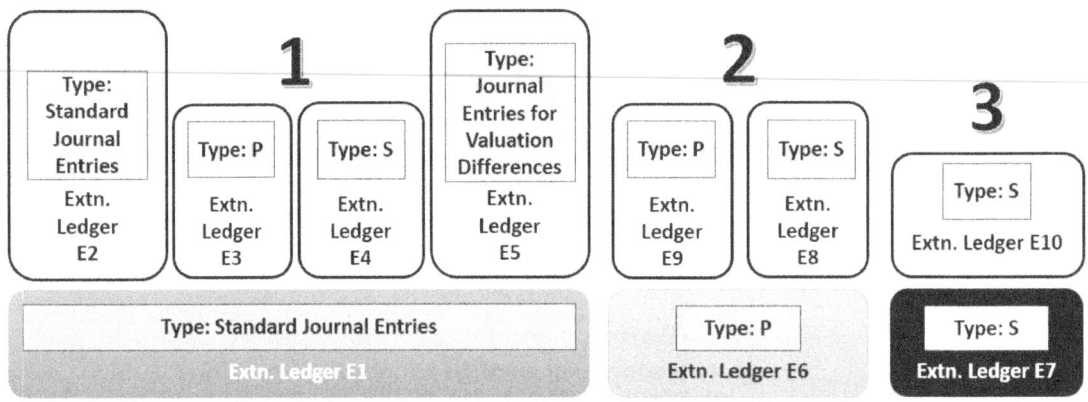

Figure 10.13: *Logic for creating an extension ledger on top of another extension ledger*

180. What is a 'Ledger Group'?

The **ledger group** is a combination of standard ledgers to which you can apply the functions and processes of G/L Accounting as a whole. Once defined, you can use the groups to apply the same, for example, journal postings, to a number of ledgers via the ledger group in one go instead of doing it individually to each of the ledgers.

When you define a standard ledger in SAP S/4HANA Finance, the system creates a ledger group, by default, with the same name as the ledger. So, when there is only one ledger, then the name of the ledger, as well as the ledger group, is the same. You only need to create and name ledger groups explicitly when you want to combine more than one ledger.

While defining the ledger group, you need to designate a ledger of the group as the 'representative ledger,' which is used to determine the posting period and check if that posting period is open or not for posting. Then, the system uses the relevant FYV of the assigned individual ledgers and posts to them. When the posting period of the representative ledger is open, irrespective of whether that posting period is open for the rest of the assigned ledgers, the system posts to all the ledgers in the group.

181. Explain the rules governing the specification of a 'Representative Ledger' of a 'Ledger Group.'

The following rules (denoted by A, B, C, and D in *Figure 10.14*) apply while specifying the representative ledger of a ledger group in G/L Accounting in SAP S/4HANA Finance:

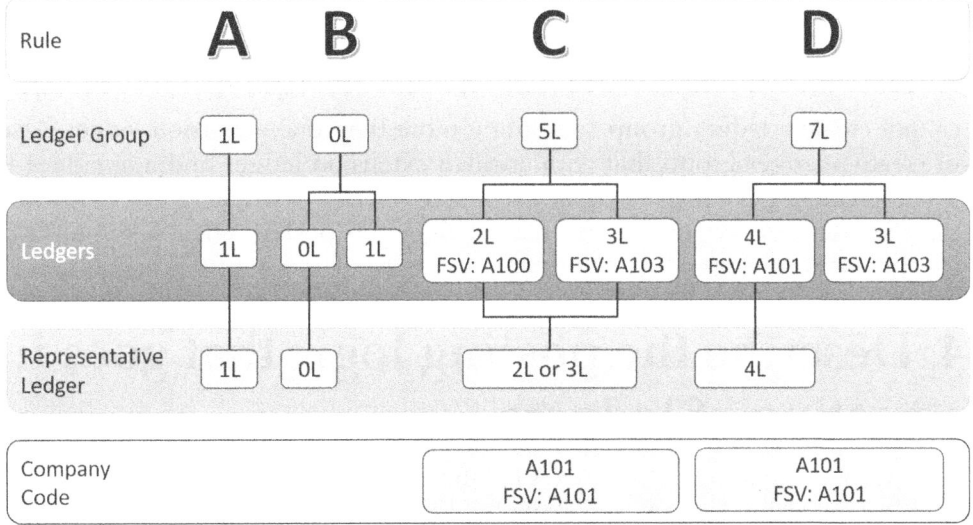

Figure 10.14: *Representative Ledger in Ledger Groups*

- **Ledger group has only one ledger (A)**: When the ledger group contains only one ledger, then that ledger will be the representative ledger.

- **Ledger group contains a leading ledger (B)**: When the ledger group contains a leading ledger, then that leading ledger must be specified as the representative ledger.

- **Ledger group without a leading ledger (C)**: (All ledgers having an FYV different than the FYV of the Company Code) When the ledger group is without a leading ledger, and when the FYV of the assigned ledgers is different from that of the Company Code, then, any of the assigned ledgers in the group can be specified as the representative ledger.

- **Ledger group without a leading ledger (D)**: (With one ledger having the same FYV as that of the Company Code) When the ledger group is without a leading ledger and when the FYV of one of the assigned ledgers is the same as that of the Company Code, then that ledger, having the same FYV as that of the Company Code, has to be specified as the representative ledger.

182. What if you cannot use the same 'Ledger Group' for several Company Codes?

In a situation where you cannot use the same ledger group for all the Company Codes, you first create several ledger groups, and in each group, specify a different representative ledger before using the ledger groups in the Company Codes.

183. What about creating 'Ledger Groups' for Extension Ledgers?

You cannot create a ledger group combining more than one extension ledger. Also, you cannot create a ledger group that combines an extension ledger and a standard ledger. When you create an extension ledger, the system creates a ledger group with the same name as the extension ledger. The extension ledger gets posted whenever you post to the underlying standard ledger.

184. Describe the posting logic that goes into the posting of ledgers.

The G/L Accounting in SAP S/4HANA Finance uses different logic while posting to the standard and extension ledgers, as detailed in *Figure 10.15*:

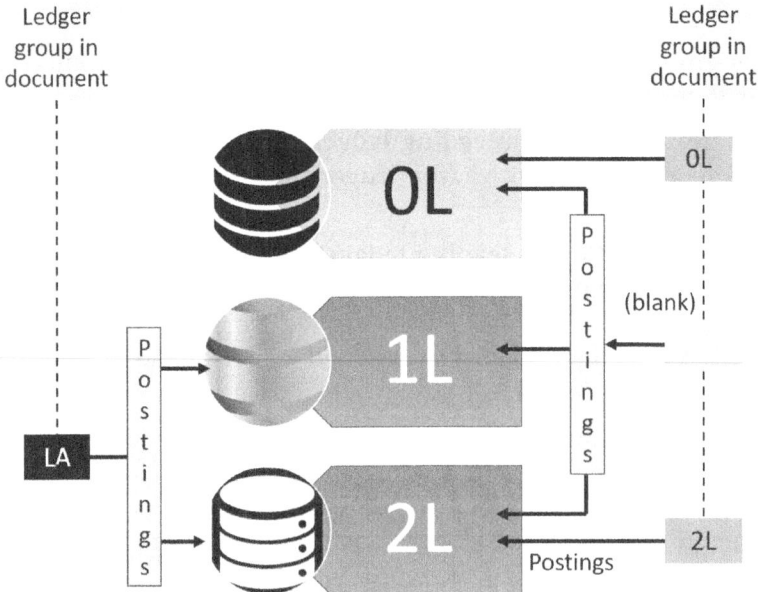

Figure 10.15: *Ledger Posting Logic*

- If you do not specify the ledger group in the document, the system posts it in all the ledgers.

- If you specify a ledger group in the document, then the system posts the document only to the ledgers that are assigned to that ledger group.

185. What are all the shortcomings of using 'Ledger Group' for posting?

Though ledger groups offer a convenient way of posting to multiple ledgers simultaneously, it is not without disadvantages that include:

- You will not be able to make tax-relevant postings, postings directly to tax accounts, and postings to accounts that you manage on an 'open-item' basis.

- You will be able to make postings only in the currencies that are assigned to the ledger group or assigned ledgers. You cannot post in any other currency.

- The system uses the representative ledger to check if the posting period is open via the FYV and the Company Code of the representative ledger. When the system finds that the posting period is open, it posts all the assigned ledgers even if the posting period of other ledgers is not open.

186. What is a 'Daily Special Ledger'?

Also known as the 'day ledger,' a **daily special ledger** is a totals table with an FYV having 366 posting periods. This ledger will contain all the original postings for the G/L. When defining such a ledger, ensure that it is neither a leading ledger nor the representative ledger of a ledger group, and you do not define the fiscal year and the posting periods differently than those of the representative ledger of the ledger group.

187. When will you go for a 'Daily Special Ledger'?

You may define a **daily ledger** when you want to have reports that display the average daily balances. You can enable drill-down reporting for the daily special ledger by activating that functionality.

188. How do you 'Deactivate a Ledger' in SAP S/4HANA Finance?

You can deactivate a G/L for future fiscal years for a given Company Code. However, you should understand the following before proceeding with ledger deactivation:

- You cannot deactivate a leading ledger.
- If you have a ledger that has been denoted as a representative ledger and used in FI-AA, you should not deactivate such a ledger because you will not be able to post in FI-AA after the deactivation.

189. Which table gets updated when you post to the ledgers?

When you post to the ledgers, leading, non-leading, or extension ledger, the system updates the table ACDOCA.

190. Explain ACDOCA.

Historically, the earlier versions of SAP ERP used totals and index tables for data storage and retrieval. With the introduction of SAP HANA architecture, which aids in in-memory processing, SAP removed these tables, thereby overcoming data duplication and redundancy. In SAP S/4HANA Finance, with the introduction of the ACDOCA table (*Figure 10.16*), data from all SAP applications, including asset accounting, material ledger, profitability analysis, and controlling, can now flow into this table. This table receives the data from the **Universal Journal.**

With ACDOCA, the following is possible:

- You can now configure currency using a central currency configuration in SAP S/4HANA. The ACDOCA's currency amount field can now accommodate 23 digits, including two decimal places (this was 9 to 22 earlier).
- There is no limitation to the number of line items in the document for posting; earlier, this was restricted to 999 per document.
- You can add custom fields.
- With most of the tables removed in various applications of SAP FI / CO, and most of them now part of ACDOCA, there is no need for extensive reconciliation at the period end. For example, there is no need to reconcile asset accounting with financial accounting, as that remains always reconciled.
- Though all the transactions from FI-AA, FI-A/R, and FI-AP are dovetailed into ACDOCA together with the SAP G/L Accounting, you will still see the presence of the table BSEG (a cluster table earlier, which has now been converted into a transparent table).
- The universal journal now records all the actual costs, both primary and secondary.
- The profit center accounting is activated by default.

- There are up to sixty characteristics, including the fixed ones (both standard and additional) for the operating concern, that help in margin analysis and segment reporting.

- The erstwhile **Material Ledger (ML)** fields are now made available in the universal journal, making it compulsory to use the ML functionality with SAP S/4HANA Finance.

- Despite the reduction of the number of database tables in FI-CA, the original document of the accrual postings is now available in the universal journal as the SAP S/4HANA Accrual Engine is tightly integrated with SAP G/L Accounting.

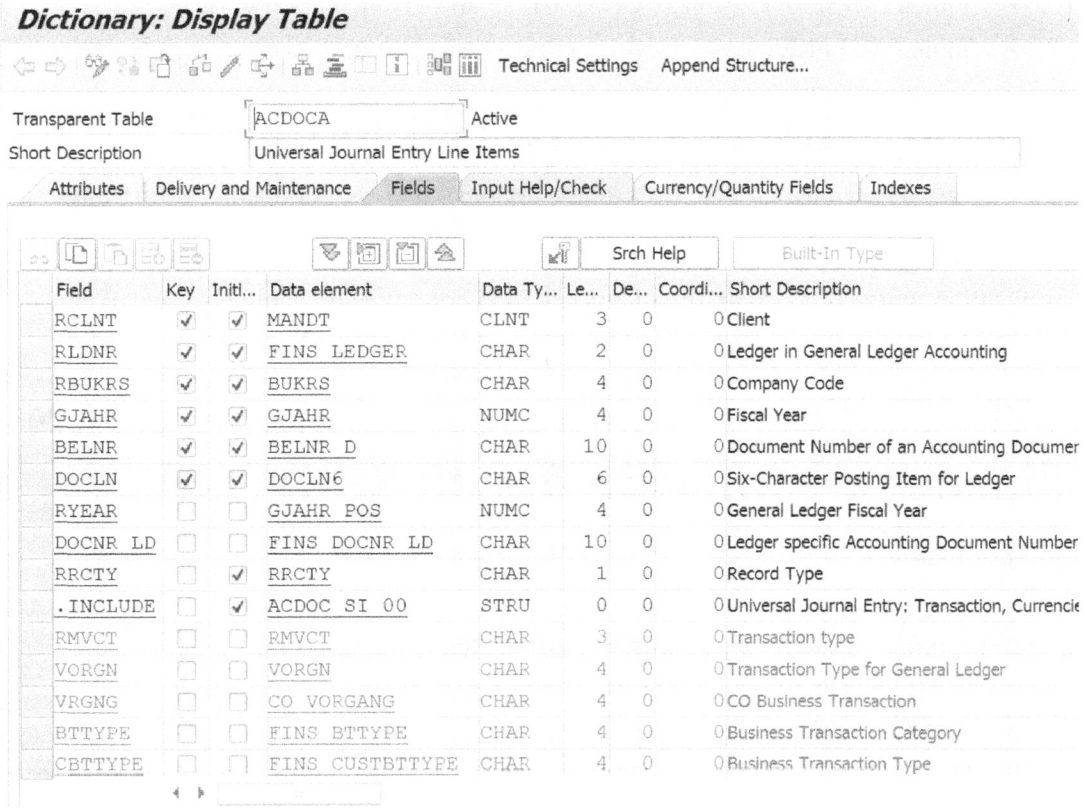

Figure 10.16: *Table ACDOCA*

191. Which of the earlier tables in SAP has since been removed in ACDOCA?

ACDOCA's aim is to remove data duplication and data redundancy. Also, SAP HANA's in-memory processing platform obviates the need for extensive indexing of the tables unless the data records are millions and millions. Accordingly, the following tables have now become defunct/obsolete in SAP S/4HANA Finance:

- Tables BSIS (index for G/L accounts) and BSAS (index for G/L cleared items. This information is available in BSEG.
- Tables BSIS / BSAS holding the secondary index.
- Tables BSID (index for customers) and BSIL (index for vendors). These are available in BSEG.
- Table GLT0 (G/L totals). The table held the same data as that of BSEG.
- Tables KNC1 (customer transaction figures) and LFC1 (vendor transaction figures).
- Tables BSID, BSAD, BSIK, BSAK, BSIM, FAGLBSIS and FAGLBSAS.
- Tables GLT3, KNC3, LFC3, COSS, COSP and FAGLFLEXT.
- Table FAGLFLEXA.

192. So, what is a 'Universal Journal'?

The **universal journal** in SAP records all the financial (FI) and controlling (CO) transactions as journal entries and stores the same in the ACDOCA table. The journal represents an integrated book of entries consisting of line items in one place, irrespective of the application where it is originating. Hence, this is known as the 'single source of truth' for both financial and management accounting.

193. What application areas of SAP S/4HANA Finance are integrated with 'Universal Journal'?

The following application areas of finance (FI) and controlling (CO) within SAP S/4HANA Finance have been integrated with the universal journal:

- **FI-GL**: SAP General Ledger Accounting
- **FI-AA**: SAP Asset Accounting
- **CO**: SAP Controlling
- **CO-PA**: SAP Profitability Analysis
- **CO-PA-ACT**: Material Ledger

Regarding CO-PA, note that only margin analysis is fully integrated with the universal journal. All the business transactions in the above application areas flow into the universal journal, and they are all updated in ACDOCA.

194. What happened to CO 'Cost Elements' with the introduction of Universal Journal?

With the advent of table **ACDOCA**, you no longer define the cost elements as separate master data in SAP CO. They are now a part of SAP G/L Accounting, and you shall create them as a special type of G/L accounts when you define the G/L account master records.

195. How many 'Currencies' can you use with Universal Journal?

As previously mentioned, while discussing parallel accounting, you can use a total of 10 currencies in the universal journal: two pre-configured and eight user-definable. The two pre-configured currencies (that you cannot change) include the 'Company Code currency' (or local currency) and the 'CO area currency' (when you use the SAP CO application component).

196. How do you maintain 'Currency' in SAP?

A **currency** (the legal means of payment in a country) in SAP is denoted by a three-character *Currency Code* maintained as per the ISO standards. For example, **US Dollars (USD)**, **Indian Rupee (INR)**, **Great Britain Pound (GBP)**, etc. Each currency code in the system will have a validity defined. You may not need to define a new currency, as SAP has defined all that is required. However, you can use the Transaction Code **OY03** to define or view the currencies in a standard SAP system. This is where the validity is also maintained.

Figure 10.17

197. How are 'Exchange Rates' maintained in SAP?

An '**exchange rate**' is defined for each pair of currencies, and each 'exchange rate type' is defined in the system. The exchange rate is defined at the document header level.

198. What is an 'Exchange Rate Type'? List some of them.

The **exchange rate type** is defined according to various purposes like valuation, translation, planning, conversion, etc. The commonly used exchange rate types include the following:

- Average rate (M)
- Bank buying rate (G)
- Bank selling rate (B)
- Historical exchange rate
- Key date exchange rate

The system generally uses the exchange rate type M (average rate) while posting/clearing documents.

Figure 10.18

199. What is known as the 'Translation Factor'?

The relation between a pair of currencies per 'exchange rate type' is known as the '**translation factor**.' For example, the translation factor is one when you define the exchange rate for the currencies USD and INR, as follows:

$$\frac{USD \quad 1}{INR \quad 1}$$

200. What is known as 'Exchange Rate Spread'?

The difference between the 'bank-buying rate' and the 'bank selling rate' is known as the **exchange rate spread**, which remains almost constant. When you maintain the exchange rate spread, it is sufficient if you maintain the '*average rate*' for that currency in question in the system, as you will be able to deduce the buying/selling rate by adding/subtracting the spread to/from the average rate.

201. Explain the usage of 'Direct' or 'Indirect Quotation.'

It is possible to maintain the exchange rates in SAP using either of these two methods: direct and indirect. What decides the usage of a particular type of quotation is the business transaction or the market standard (of that country).

SAP adopts two prefixes to differentiate the direct and indirect quotes during entering/ displaying a transaction:

- ' '– Blank, no prefix. Used in Direct Quotation
- '/' – Used in Indirect Quotation

When no prefix is entered (blank), the system construes the quotation as the 'direct quote'.

The possible scenarios are as follows:

- The company in question mainly uses *'Direct Quotation'*.

  Use ''(blank) as the prefix for default notation for direct quotation. Use '*' as the prefix for the rarely used direct quotation. If someone tries entering a transaction using direct quotation but without the '*' in the exchange rate input field, the system will issue a warning.

- The company in question mainly uses *'Indirect Quotation'*.

  You do not need to make any specific settings as the default is the ''(blank) prefix for the direct quotation and '/' for the indirect quotation. So, unless you make a transaction entry with the '/' prefix, the system takes all the entries as direct quotations.

- There could be instances of requirements wherein you are required to configure in such a way that a prefix is mandatory irrespective of the type of quotation. In this case, define the direct quotation prefix as '*' and the indirect one with the system default '/' prefix. This necessitates prefixing each of the entries either by '*' or '/'. Else, the user will get a warning to correct the entry.

202. What is a 'Currency Type' in SAP?

The **'currency type'** in SAP signifies the purpose for which it is used, such as document currency, Company Code currency, controlling area currency, and so on.

203. List the important 'Currency Types' that you will come across in SAP S/4HANA Finance.

There are several **currency types** that are pre-defined in the system to meet various purposes. Each currency type comes with a two-digit numeric identifier. Though there are several, we are listing only the important ones here:

- **00**: Document currency
- **10**: Company Code currency
- **20**: Controlling area currency
- **30**: Group currency
- **40**: Hard currency
- **50**: Index-based currency
- **60**: Global Company currency
- **70**: Controlling object currency

204. What is a 'Document Currency'?

The **'document currency'** is the currency in which the system posts an accounting document. Denoted by 00, this currency can be different from the Company Code currency, controlling area currency, group currency, etc. You can either enter this manually or the system can automatically enter it in the document header.

Within document currency, you will come across two more types:

- Document currency in group valuation
- Document currency in profit center valuation

205. What is a 'Company Code Currency'?

When you define a Company Code, you also need to mention in which currency you will be maintaining the accounts/ledgers in financial accounting. This is the **Company Code currency and** is also known as the 'local currency'. Though not common, some people also refer to this as the 'functional currency'. You will normally use this currency to bring out the financial statements of the Company Code. It is denoted as '10' in the system.

You will also come across two more Company Code currencies that are used for specific purposes:

- **11**: Company Code currency (group valuation)
- **12**: Company Code currency (profit center valuation)

206. What is a 'Controlling Area Currency'?

You will use **'controlling area currency'** (aka 'CO area currency') for cost accounting purposes in SAP S/4HANA Finance. It is the default currency for the various CO objects. As in the case of Company Code currency, you will assign the controlling area currency while defining the controlling area using the assignment indicator, as shown in *Table 10.2*:

Assignment indicator	CO area currency type
Controlling area same as Company Code	10 (Company Code currency). You will not be able to change this.
Cross-Company Code-cost accounting	The currency type can be anything: 10, 20, 30, 40, 50 and 60.

Table 10.2: *CO area currency type and the assignment indicator*

207. How many currencies can you assign in the Company Code settings for Ledgers?

Besides the local currency (Company Code currency) and the group currency, you can assign eight more freely definable currencies in SAP S/4HANA Finance while you maintain the Company Code settings for the ledgers (*Figure 10.19*):

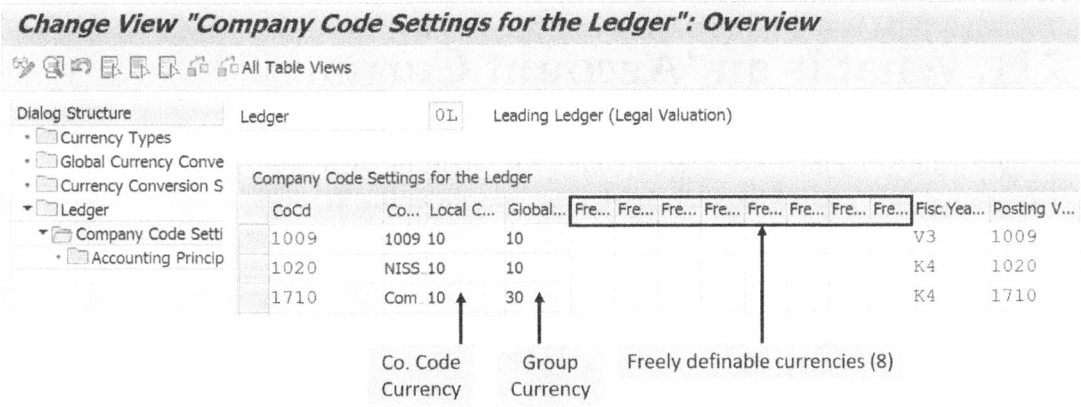

Figure 10.19: *Currency Assignment for Company Code – Ledger combination*

208. What is a 'Group Currency'?

This is the currency defined at the Client level. This is denoted as '30'. When you combine the valuation view with the **'group currency'**, the second digit of the group currency identifier will represent the valuation view. For example:

- **31**: Group currency / group valuation (the digit '1' in the currency type '31' signifies group valuation)
- **32**: Group currency / profit center valuation

209. What do you mean by 'Hard Currency'?

Denoted as '40', you will use **'hard currency'** for external reporting if your Company Code operates in a country with high inflation. You will normally input this currency type when you maintain the country settings.

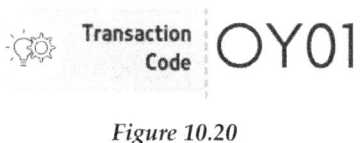

Transaction Code **OY01**

Figure 10.20

210. What is the 'Global Company Code Currency'?

The currency defined for the Company (or the consolidated Company) is called as the **'global Company Code Currency'**. It is denoted as '50' and you will maintain this currency against the Company while defining the Company.

211. What is an 'Account Currency'?

When defining the G/L accounts in the system, you must define a currency in which an account will be maintained. This is called the **'account currency'**. This is defined in the 'Company Code' area of the G/L master record (under the 'Control Data' tab) and is used for postings and account balance display (*Figure 10.21*):

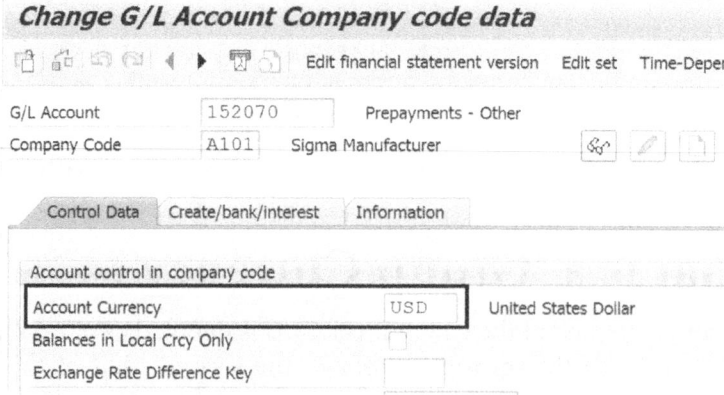

Figure 10.21: *G/L Account Currency*

For defining the account currency of a G/L account master record, you have two options:

- Maintain the account currency the same as that of the Company Code currency. With this, you will be able to post transactions in any currency. However, the system converts all foreign currency postings into local currency for balance display and reporting.

- Maintain the account currency that is different from that of the Company Code currency. Here, you can post only in that foreign currency, and the G/L account will be denoted as a 'foreign currency B/S account'. However, the system maintains the transaction figures and the account balance in both local and foreign currencies.

212. What are all the 'pre-requisites' for posting in a 'Foreign Currency'?

The following are the **pre-requisites**, you need to take care of before posting in a foreign currency:

- Local currency already defined for the Company Code (in the global parameters)
- Foreign currency defined in the currency code Table
- The exchange rate as defined for the foreign currency and the local currency
- Translation Ratio maintained for the local and foreign currency

213. What is a 'Fiscal Year'?

A **fiscal year** is an accounting period that, in general, is made up of 12 months. You will draw your company's financial statements every fiscal year.

214. What is a 'Posting Period'?

A month in a fiscal year is known as the **'posting period.'** When you post a transaction in SAP FI, the system assigns a posting period based on the month and year of that transaction. Normally, you will have 12 posting periods. However, it is possible that you can have more: for example, you can have 366 posting periods when you define a 'daily special ledger' (we have discussed the daily special ledger in *Questions 186* and *Question 187*).

215. What is a 'Special Period' in SAP?

Apart from the concept of the posting period, SAP also uses another one known as the special period, which is used to carry out activities relating to the period-end (or year-end) closing of accounting. Usually, the last posting period in a fiscal year is divided into one or more special periods (*Figure 10.22*). However, the special periods that you create this way by subdividing the last posting period does not create new posting periods. If you do not use all the 12 regular posting periods in a fiscal year, you can designate the unused ones as special periods. The special period in a fiscal year helps you to create more than one supplementary financial statement, all within the same fiscal year. This comes in handy during the year-end closing operations. The special periods cannot be determined automatically by the system based on the posting date of the document: the special period needs to be manually entered into the 'posting period' field in the document header.

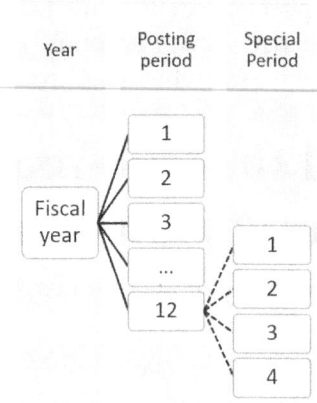

Figure 10.22: *Posting periods and special periods*

216. What are the three 'Types of Fiscal Year'?

In SAP, you will come across the following three types of fiscal years (*Figure 10.23*):

- Calendar fiscal year
- Non-calendar fiscal year
- Shortened fiscal year

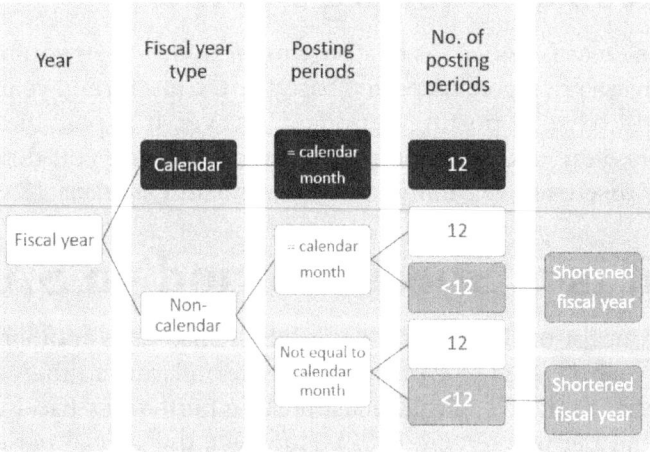

Figure 10.23: *Types of fiscal year*

217. Explain 'Calendar Fiscal Year'.

A '**calendar fiscal year**' is an accounting year that corresponds to the calendar year. Here, the posting periods correspond exactly to the calendar months, with the start and end of posting periods being the same as those of the calendar months. In a calendar fiscal year, you do not need to explicitly define the posting periods: the first posting period always corresponds to the first calendar month, and so on.

218. Explain 'Non-Calendar Fiscal Year.'

When a fiscal year does not correspond to a calendar year, then you call that a '**non-calendar fiscal year.**' The posting periods may or may not correspond to the calendar months. When defining a non-calendar fiscal year, specify the number of posting periods. If a non-calendar fiscal year comprises less than 12 posting periods, it is known as the 'shortened fiscal year'.

For example, 1-Apr-2022 to 31-Mar-2023 is a non-calendar fiscal year but with calendar months as the posting periods. 16-Jul-2022 to 15-Jul-2023 is also a non-calendar fiscal year but with non-calendar months as the posting periods.

Besides specifying the calendar month for the posting period, you also need to specify the 'day limit' (the start and end for each period) and the 'year shift' (aka 'year displacement factor') while defining the non-calendar year. This year-shift (0, +1, or -1) enables the system to adjust the non-calendar fiscal year to reflect the correct fiscal year.

219. How does the system post correctly in non-calendar FY with calendar PP?

As you can see from *Table 10.3*, the transaction dated 15 March 2023 falls under calendar month three but relates to posting period 12. The system uses the year shift (-1, in this case) to identify the correct fiscal year as 2022 (=2023-1) and posts to the correct posting period of 12.

Calendar year	Calendar month	Fiscal year	Posting period	Start date	End date	Year shift
2022	4	2022	1	01-Apr	30-Apr	0
2022	5	2022	2	01-May	31-May	0
2022	6	2022	3	01-Jun	30-Jun	0
2022	7	2022	4	01-Jul	31-Jul	0
2022	8	2022	5	01-Aug	31-Aug	0
2022	9	2022	6	01-Sep	30-Sep	0

Calendar year	Calendar month	Fiscal year	Posting period	Start date	End date	Year shift
2022	10	2022	7	01-Oct	31-Oct	0
2022	11	2022	8	01-Nov	30-Nov	0
2022	12	2022	9	01-Dec	31-Dec	0
2023	1	2022	10	01-Jan	31-Jan	−1
2023	2	2022	11	01-Feb	29-Feb	−1
2023	3	2022	12	01-Mar	31-Mar	−1

Table 10.3: Non-Calendar Fiscal Year (with Posting Periods = Calendar Months)

220. How does the system post correctly in non-calendar FY with non-calendar PP?

When a non-calendar fiscal year is made up of non-calendar months as the posting periods, with the start date/end date of posting periods not corresponding to the start/end of calendar months, you need to maintain the 'period-end' information to enable the system to identify the correct posting period.

Calendar year	Calendar month	Fiscal year	Posting period	Period-end	Year shift
2022	8	2022	1	15-Aug	0
2022	9	2022	2	15-Sep	0
2022	10	2022	3	15-Oct	0
2022	11	2022	4	15-Nov	0
2022	12	2022	5	15-Dec	0
2022	12	2022	6	31-Dec	0
2023	1	2022	6	15-Jan	−1
2023	2	2022	7	15-Feb	−1
2023	4	2022	8	15-Mar	−1
2023	4	2022	9	15-Apr	−1
2023	5	2022	10	15-May	−1
2023	6	2022	11	15-Jun	−1
2023	7	2022	12	15-Jul	−1

Table 10.4: Non-Calendar Fiscal Year (with Posting Periods not equaling Calendar Months)

As you can see in *Table 10.4*, in this case, there will be two periods for the sixth posting period: one ending with 31-Dec-2022 (for the calendar month 12), and the other ending with 15-Jan-2023 (for the calendar month 1). If you do not maintain the data like this, the system will not be able to identify the correct posting period for the transactions posted between 1-Jan-2023 and 15-Jan-2023. Now, in our case, both the transactions dated 22-Dec-2022 and 13-Jan-2023 will be correctly identified by the system as the ones belonging to the posting period 6; for the first transaction, the year 2022 is arrived at using the year-shift of 0 (=2022-0), and for the second transaction, the system uses the year-shift of -1 to correct the fiscal year (=2023-1).

221. What is a 'Shortened Fiscal Year'?

A fiscal year is normally made up of 12 posting periods. However, there may be instances wherein the fiscal year may have less than 12 periods. In such a case, the fiscal year that is made up of less than 12 posting periods is known as a **'shortened fiscal year.'** The shortened fiscal year is usually a non-calendar fiscal year. You will normally use a shortened fiscal year, for example, when you switch over from a calendar fiscal year to a non-calendar fiscal year (or vice versa), when you first start your business operations in the middle of a fiscal year or when you combine your current company with another to form a new enterprise and so on.

222. What is a 'Fiscal Year Variant'?

The fiscal year, in SAP, is defined using a **'Fiscal Year Variant'** (**FYV**) as shown in *Figure 10.24*:

- All **calendar year fiscal year variants** in standard SAP are usually denoted as 'K1', 'K2' etc. The FYV 'K1', for example, comprises 12 posting periods plus one special period, 'K2' comes with 12 posting periods plus two special periods, and so on.

- SAP denotes the **non-calendar fiscal year variants** using the FYV 'V3', 'V6,' and 'V9'.

- The standard SAP system comes with two FYV for **shortened fiscal years**: 'R1' and 'AM.' It is recommended that you use 'R1' in SAP FI and 'AM' in FI-AA.

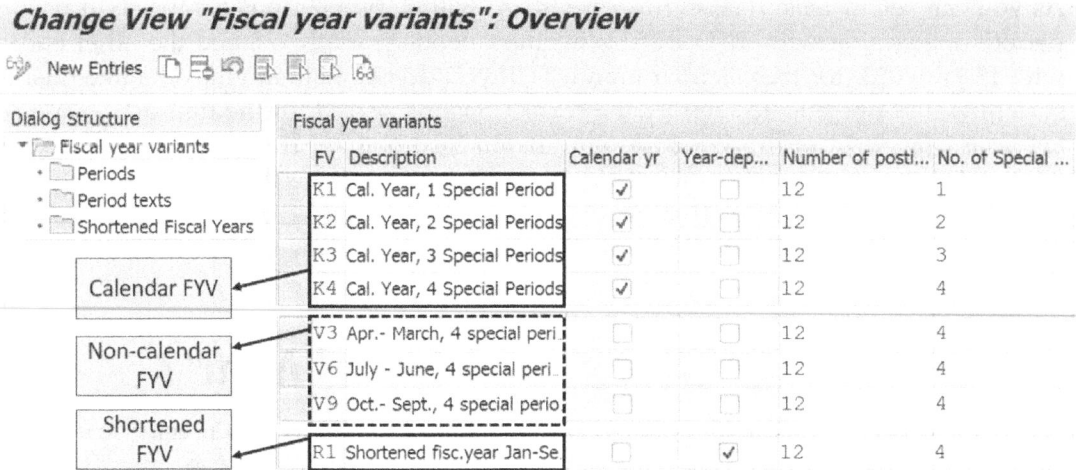

Figure 10.24: *SAP's standard fiscal year variants*

When you define your own FYV, you will define an FYV using a two-character alphanumeric FYV identifier, and you need to specify the number of postings and special periods. If you define a calendar fiscal year, then there is no need to maintain the posting periods explicitly; you just need to select the *'Calendar yr'* checkbox. However, when you define a non-calendar FYV, you need to specify the posting periods, the day limit, and the year shift, as we discussed earlier. You may also specify the names for the posting periods: short name (three characters) or long name (up to 20 characters). Through the assignment with a Company Code, the FYV enables the system to identify the correct posting period during transaction postings.

Transaction Code OB29

Figure 10.25

223. How do you assign a 'Fiscal Year Variant' to the Company Code?

You can assign an FYV to one or more Company Codes (*Figure 10.26*). However, you cannot assign more than one FYV to a single Company Code. In a standard SAP system, a Company Code is assigned, by default, to the FYV 'K4' (calendar year with four special periods). However, you can assign a different one if you have not made any postings yet to that Company Code.

Change View "Assign Comp.Code -> Fiscal Year Variant".

CoCd	Company Name	Fiscal Year Variant	Description
A101	Sigma Manufacturer	K4	Cal. Year, 4 Special Periods
A102	Enigma Manufacturer	K4	Cal. Year, 4 Special Periods

Figure 10.26: *Assign Fiscal Year Variant to a Company Code*

Transaction Code **OB37**

Figure 10.27

224. How does the system identify a 'Posting Period'?

Based on the posting date entered in the system while posting a document, the system automatically determines the period by looking at the document date and the year. However, for this to occur, you should have properly defined the fiscal year variant.

225. What happens when you try posting to a previous year?

First, to post a document relating to a previous year, say, 2022, when you are in 2023, the relevant posting period should be 'open' in the system. When such a posting is done, the system makes some adjustments to the background:

- **One**: The carry-forward balances of the current year, already done, are updated in case the posting is affecting B/S items.

- **Two**: If the posting is going to affect the P & L accounts, then the system adjusts the carried forward profit or loss balances to the **retained earnings** (**RE**) account(s).

226. What do you mean by 'opening' of Posting Periods?

Postings in SAP are controlled by the 'opening' of posting periods via the **posting period variant** (**PPV**). Normally, the current posting period is open for document posting, and all other periods are closed. At the end of the period (month), this posting period is closed, and the new one opened for postings. This way it provides better control. It is, however, possible to keep all the periods or select periods open.

Transaction Code OB52

Figure 10.28

227. What is a 'Posting Period Variant'?

A **'Posting Period Variant'** (PPV) is useful in 'opening' the posting in one or more Company Codes. First, you will define a PPV and assign it to the Company Code(s).

If you need better control of the opening of posting periods at the Company Code level, define a PPV for each Company Code. For easy administration, the best practice is to denote the PPV with the same identifier as the Company Code (*Figure 10.29*). This is the standard setting in SAP.

However, instead of doing it individually for different Company Codes, if you want to open posting periods simultaneously across several Company Codes, you just need to define only one PPV and assign it to all the Company Codes. Since the PPV is a cross-Company Code, you just need to open that PPV: it will then impact all the assigned Company Codes in one go.

Change View "Assign Comp.Code -> Posting Period Variants

CoCd	Company Name	City	Variant
A101	Sigma Manufacturer	Columbus	A101
A102	Enigma Manufacturer	Indianapolis	A102

Figure 10.29: Assign PPV to a Company Code

Use the Transaction Code **OBBO** to define PPV and **OBBP** to assign a PPV to a Company Code.

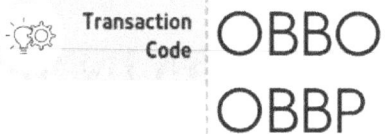

Transaction Code OBBO
OBBP

Figure 10.30

228. Can you selectively 'Open' and 'Close' accounts for posting?

Yes, it is possible to selectively control the opening of posting periods for various types of accounts (*Figure 10.31*). Usually, a '+' is mentioned in the topmost entry, indicating that all the account types are allowed for posting. Now, against the G/L accounts (S), customer accounts (D), vendor/supplier accounts (K), material accounts (M), and contract accounts (V), specify the period that needs to be opened. This ensures that all the account types are open for the current period, indicated by '+', and other types of accounts are open for the previous period as well. Not only can select account types be opened or closed for a specific period, but select accounts within an account type can also be opened or closed.

Change View "Posting Periods: Specify Time Intervals": Overview

New Entries

Posting Periods: Specify Time Intervals

Var.	A	From Acc...	To Account	From Per.1	Year	To Per. 1	Year	AuGr	From Per.2	Year	To Per. 2	Year
A101	+		3		2023	3	2023					
A101	A		ZZZZZZZ_1		2023	12	2023	13		2023	16	2023
A101	D		ZZZZZZZ_1		2023	12	2023	13		2023	16	2023
A101	K		ZZZZZZZ_1		2023	12	2023	13		2023	16	2023
A101	M		ZZZZZZZ_1		2023	12	2023	13		2023	16	2023
A101	S		ZZZZZZZ_1		2023	12	2023	13		2023	16	2023
A101	V		1		2023	12	2023	13		2023	16	2023

Figure 10.31: Opening (and closing) of posting periods via PPV

229. Why cannot you post to a customer a/c in a previously closed 'Posting Period'?

When you want to selectively 'close' or 'open' the posting period of some accounts (account range), there will be no problem with that if you are doing it for G/L accounts. However, if it is a sub-ledger account (like the customer), the same has to be achieved via opening or closing the account interval of the '*reconciliation account*' of that account type.

230. Can you open a 'Posting Period' only for a particular user?

Yes. SAP allows you to open or close the posting period only for specific users. This can be achieved by maintaining an **authorization group (AuGr)** at the document header level.

231. What can be the maximum number of 'Posting Periods' in SAP?

Under G/L accounting, you can have a maximum of 16 posting periods (12 regular + 4 Special Periods). However, you can have up to a maximum of 366 posting periods in the case of a '*special purpose ledger*'.

232. What is a 'Special Purpose Ledger'?

Special Purpose Ledgers (FI-SL) are used in reporting. These are all basically user-defined ledgers, which can be maintained either as G/L or subsidiary ones with various account assignment objects (with SAP dimensions like a cost center, business area, profit center, etc. or customer-defined dimensions like region, area, etc.). Once defined, this functionality helps you to report at various levels. Ideally, you collect the information, combine it, and create the totals. This is something like an additional reporting feature, and usage of this feature will have no effect on the regular functionalities of SAP.

233. What is a 'Year-dependent' FYV?

A calendar year fiscal variant, when defined as 'year-dependent', is relevant and valid only for that year.

234. What precautions must you take while defining 'Shortened Fiscal Year'?

Note that the **shortened fiscal year** is always year-dependent. This must be followed or preceded by a full fiscal year (12 months). Both the shortened and the full fiscal year, in this case, have to be defined using a single fiscal year variant.

235. What do you understand by 'Edit Fiscal Year Calendar' in SAP?

The '**edit fiscal year calendar**' task is maintaining a fiscal calendar based on the FYV configuration. You must execute this only when setting up your new system or if you are already 'live' but want to introduce a new FYV in between.

In an already 'live' SAP system, the 'balance carryforward' functionality automatically determines the fiscal calendar data, and there is no need for this specific task. When you execute this task for a specific FYV, the system determines the fiscal calendar data (such as the fiscal year, periods, and quarters with start and end dates) that you can use in analytical applications, such as the Trial Balance Fiori app, or in other Fiori apps.

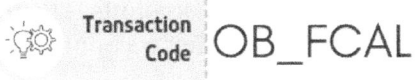

Figure 10.32

236. How do you open a new 'Fiscal Year' in the system?

You do not need to 'open' the new fiscal year as a separate activity: once you post into the new fiscal year, the new fiscal year is automatically opened, or the new fiscal year is automatically opened when you run the *'balance carry forward'* program.

However, you need to have the relevant posting period already opened in the new fiscal year, complete the document number range assignment if you are following a year-dependent number range assignment, and define a new fiscal year variant if you follow a year-dependent fiscal year variant.

237. How do you 'Carry-Forward' the account balances?

If you have already posted into the new fiscal year, you do not need to 'carry-forward' the balances manually; it is done by the system automatically. Else, use the various 'carry-forward' programs supplied by SAP for this task.

238. Can you explain how 'Carry-Forward' happens in SAP?

For all the B/S items, the balances of these accounts are just carried forward to the new fiscal year, along with account assignments, if any. This is also true for customer and vendor accounts. In the case of P & L accounts, the system carries forward the profit or loss (in the local currency) to the *retained earnings* account, and the balances of these accounts are set to '0'. No additional account assignments are transferred.

239. Is there a pre-requisite for 'Carry-Forward' activity?

Yes, for Profit & Loss accounts, you should have defined the 'Retained Earnings' account in the system. Additionally, you should have specified the *'Profit & Loss Account Type'*, in the master record of each for Profit & Loss accounts. There are no such requirements for G/L accounts, customer, and vendor/supplier accounts.

240. How many 'Retained Earnings' accounts do you normally need?

You can define as many **retained earnings accounts** as you need. But normally, companies use only one retained earnings account. Remember, to define more than one retained earnings account, you should use the *'Profit & Loss Account Type.'*

241. Can you have multiple 'Retained Earnings' accounts?

Normally, it is sufficient to use one **'retained earnings' account**. However, if you are configuring for a multinational company where the legal requirements require treating some of the tax provisions differently from that of other countries, then you may require more than one retained earnings account to take care of such a situation.

Join our book's Discord space

Join the book's Discord Workspace for Latest updates, Offers, Tech happenings around the world, New Release and Sessions with the Authors:

https://discord.bpbonline.com

CHAPTER 11

FI Global Settings: Document

Introduction

This is the second chapter on FI global settings. In this chapter, you will learn all about documents, tolerance and tolerance groups, clearing, partial and residual payments in payment processing, and the like. You will also learn about configuring some default values, including default value date, fiscal year default, etc. Towards the end of the chapter, you will learn about archiving in SAP S/4HANA Finance: document and account archiving.

242. What is a 'Document' in SAP?

SAP is based on the '*document principle*,' which means that a document is created for every business transaction in the system. The **'document'** is the result of a posting in SAP accounting and is the connecting link between various business operations. There are two types of documents:

- **Original documents**: These documents relate to the origin of business transactions. For example, invoices, receipts, statements of accounts from banks, etc.

- **Processing documents**: These include '*accounting documents*' generated out of postings in the system and '*reference documents*' that include account assignment models, sample documents, and recurring entry documents. These reference documents are also known as 'special documents' and aid in simplifying document entry in the system.

Every document is made up of the following (*Figure 11.1*):

- A *Document Header*
- Two or more *Line Items*

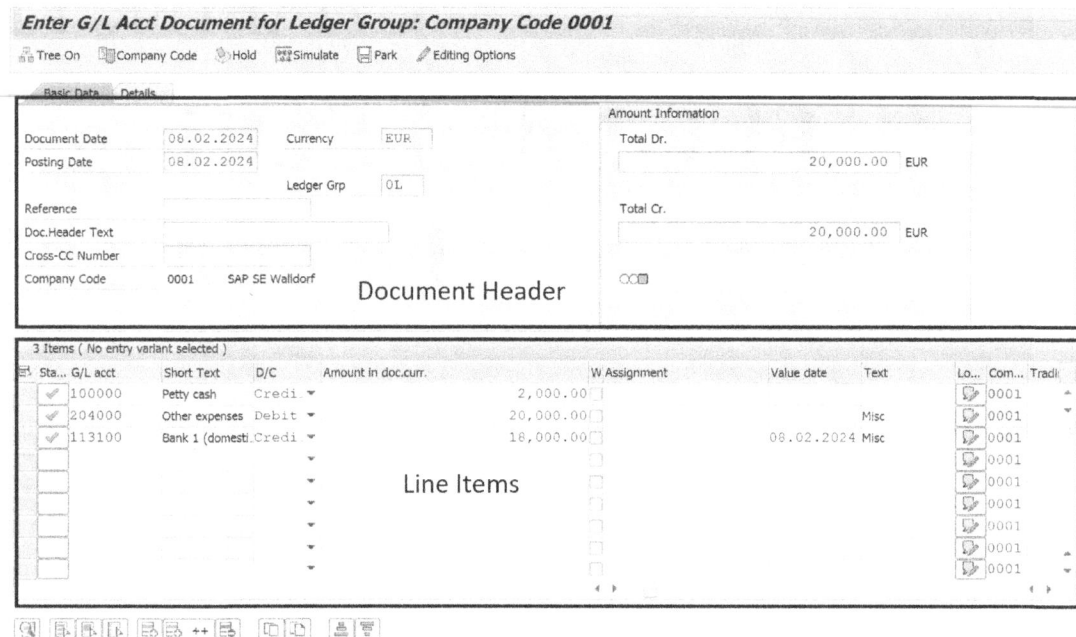

Figure 11.1: Document in SAP

Before attempting to enter a document, note to call up the relevant *document entry function*. The system provides a variety of readymade document entry templates suited to different transactions, such as regular G/L entry, customer invoice posting, etc. The details entered in a document can be *simulated* and displayed before it is posted in the system. You may also choose to '*park*' the document and post it later.

243. What is a 'Document Header'?

The '**document header**' contains information that is valid for the **whole document,** such as:

- Document date
- Posting date
- Currency
- Ledger group

- Reference
- Document header text
- Cross-CC number
- Company code

The document header (*Figure 11.1*) also contains information such as trading partner BA, translation date, exchange rate, etc. The fields on the document header are divided into two tabs: 'basic data' and 'details'.

Apart from these, you also have the amount information (total debit and total credit) on the right-hand side of the header, along with three 'traffic lights' showing the document's readiness for posting. A 'green' light indicates that you can go ahead and post the document.

244. What is a 'Line Item' in a Document?

You will see the **line items** just below the header in a document (*Figure 11.1*). A line item contains details like a G/L account number, a short text, a debit/credit indicator, an amount, a value date, an assignment, a long text, a Company Code, a business area, a cost center, an order, etc. A document must contain at least two line items: one for the debit and the other for the credit. A document can have any line items in SAP S/4HANA Finance (this was limited to a maximum of 999 in the earlier versions of SAP ERP).

While entering the line items, there may be situations in which the system adds certain line items to the document before posting. These are known as 'system generated line items,' and they depend upon the type of posting that you are trying to complete.

245. What is the system-generated 'Line Item'? Give some examples.

After you have made the entries in a document, just before posting, the system may automatically add some line items to make the document complete, depending upon the type of document that you are about to post. You can add more information, like text, additional account assignments, etc., even to the system-generated line items.

The system-generated line items may include the following:

- Bank charges or residual items during open item clearing or customer/vendor payment postings.
- Cash discounts received/paid in payment postings.
- Inter-company payable/receivable items in cross-Company Code transactions.
- Profit (gain) or loss from exchange rate differences between invoice and payment.
- Tax amounts on sales/purchases during invoice (customer/vendor) posting.

246. When is a Document said to be 'Complete'?

A document is said to be 'complete' when the total debits equal the total credits. That is, the total of all the debit items should equal the total of all the credit items of the document, resulting in zero balance. Unless this is achieved, you will not be able to post the document as it is considered an 'incomplete' document. It is, however, possible that you can 'hold' such a document, come back later, make the required changes (say, changing the line items or adding more line items, etc.), and then post when the document becomes 'complete.' Just by looking at the traffic lights in the header, you can say whether the document is complete or not. A complete document will have the 'green' light, but an incomplete one will have the 'red' light glowing.

247. What is a 'Document Type'?

SAP comes delivered with several standard **document types**, which are used in various postings. The document type, besides classifying an accounting transaction within the system, helps in orderly document storage. It controls the account types a particular document type can post to. For example, document type 'AB' allows you to post to all the accounts, whereas document type 'DZ' allows you to post only customer payments. Every document type is assigned to a number range.

Valid across all Clients, SAP comes delivered with a number of standard document types (more than 40, in fact) that you can use across various applications. Some of the commonly used documents are listed in *Table 11.1*.

Type	Description	Type	Description
AA	Asset Posting	KP	Account Maintenance
AB	Journal Entry	KR	Vendor Invoice
AD	Accruals/Deferrals	KZ	Vendor payment
AF	Depreciation Pstngs	ML	ML Settlement
AN	Net Asset Posting	PR	Price Change
AP	Periodic asset post	RA	Sub.Cred.Memo Stlmt
AR	Asset Reorg Posting	RE	Invoice - Gross
BC	Foreign Currency Rev	RK	Invoice Reduction
CC	Sec. Cost CrossComp.	RN	Invoice - Net
CH	Contract Settlement	RP	Spl Invoice Price Change
CJ	Petty Cash	RT	Retentions

Type	Description	Type	Description
CL	CL/OP FY Postings	RV	Billing doc.transfer
CO	Secondary Cost	SA	G/L Account Document
DA	Customer document	SB	G/L Account Posting
DG	Customer credit memo	SC	Transfer P&L to B/S
DR	Customer invoice	SE	Inventory Postings
DV	Customer interests	SJ	Cash Journal Document
DZ	Customer Payment	SK	Cash Document
ER	Manual Expense Travel	SU	Intercomp./Clearing
EU	Euro Rounding Diff.	UE	Data Transfer
EX	External Number	WA	Goods Issue
KA	Vendor Document	WE	Goods Receipt
KG	Vendor Credit Memo	WI	Inventory Document
KN	Net vendors	WL	Goods Issue/Delivery
KP	Account maintenance	WN	Net Goods Receipt

Table 11.1: *SAP's Standard Document Types (Example)*

Figure 11.2

248. How is the 'Account Type' connected to the 'Document Type'?

The '**document type**' is characterized by two-character codes like AA, DG, etc., whereas an 'account type' is denoted by a one-character code like A, D, etc., specifying as to which are all the accounts a particular document can be posted to.

The common account types are as follows:

- **A**: Assets
- **D**: Customer (Debtor)
- **K**: Vendor (Creditor)
- **M**: Materials
- **S**: G/L

When you consider, for example, the document type 'DZ' (*Figure 11.3*), the letter 'D' represents the account type ('customer,' in this case), and 'Z' represents the type of posting ('payment' in this case). Likewise, the document type 'KR' denotes the invoice (R) posting to the vendor (K) accounts.

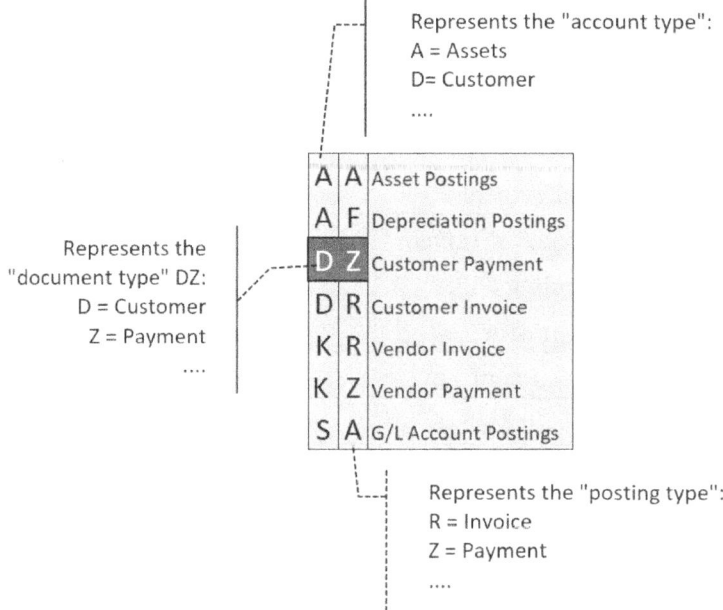

Figure 11.3: Document Account types

249. Describe 'Number Range' in Documents.

A '**number range**' refers to a number interval defined in the system so that when documents are posted, the system assigns a number from this range. You will define different number ranges for different document types. Each document in SAP is uniquely identified by the combination of document number, Company Code, and fiscal year.

The number range for a document type can be defined as follows:

- Per fiscal year
- Until a fiscal year in the future

If defined to last only one fiscal year, then this needs to be defined every year. When number ranges are defined every fiscal year, at the start of the year, the system starts from the first number in the range for that particular year, and this will help in not reaching the upper limit fast. In this case, you do not need to define a very large range interval; a small interval will do fine. Even when a number is repeated in another fiscal year, the system will not have difficulty bringing up the right document as it also looks at the fiscal year besides the document number.

Edit Intervals: Accounting document, Object RF_BELEG, Subobject A101

Number Range No.	Year	From No.	To Number	NR Status	External
14	9999	1400000000	1499999999	0	☐
15	9999	1500000000	1599999999	0	☐
16	9999	1600000000	1699999999	0	☐
17	9999	1700000000	1799999999	0	☐
18	9999	1800000000	1899999999	0	☐
19	9999	1900000000	1999999999	0	☐
20	9999	2000000000	2099999999	0	☐
47	9999	A470000000	A479999999	0	☑
48	9999	4800000000	4899999999	0	☐
49	9999	4900000000	4999999999	0	☐
50	9999	5000000000	5099999999	0	☐
51	9999	5100000000	5199999999	0	☐
52	9999	AAAAAAAAAA	ZZZZZZZZZZ	0	☑
X1	9999	9100000000	9199999999	9100000000	☐
X2	9999	9200000000	9299999999	9200000000	☐

Figure 11.4: Document Number Range for Company Code A101

If you specify the fiscal year as '9999' (*Figure 11.4*), then the document number range is valid forever, and you do not have to do this exercise of maintaining number ranges every fiscal year. Every year, the system starts with the last number used in the previous year. When defining the number ranges that are valid forever, note that you must define a fairly large number range per document type so that you do not run out of numbers in the immediate future.

250. How do you determine the optimum 'Number Range Interval' documents?

It is important that you define an adequate interval for a number range that is used by different document types so that you do not run out of numbers in between. This is more important when you define number ranges that are valid forever (999 years). SAP recommends using the process flow shown in *Figure 11.5* to arrive at the optimum number interval for the documents:

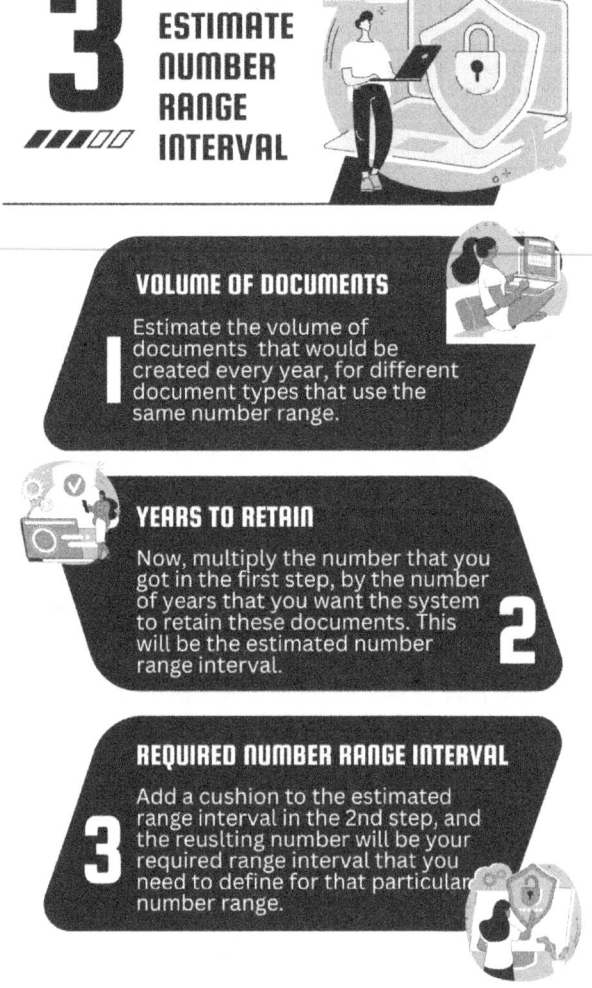

VOLUME OF DOCUMENTS

Estimate the volume of documents that would be created every year, for different document types that use the same number range.

YEARS TO RETAIN

Now, multiply the number that you got in the first step, by the number of years that you want the system to retain these documents. This will be the estimated number range interval.

REQUIRED NUMBER RANGE INTERVAL

Add a cushion to the estimated range interval in the 2nd step, and the reuslting number will be your required range interval that you need to define for that particular number range.

Figure 11.5: Determining the Optimum Number Range Interval

251. How does 'Document Type' control the Document Number assignment?

For every document type, you will assign a number range. Then, you define a number interval for this number range. Finally, while defining the number interval, you must denote whether the number range is for internal or external number assignment (*Figure 11.6*).

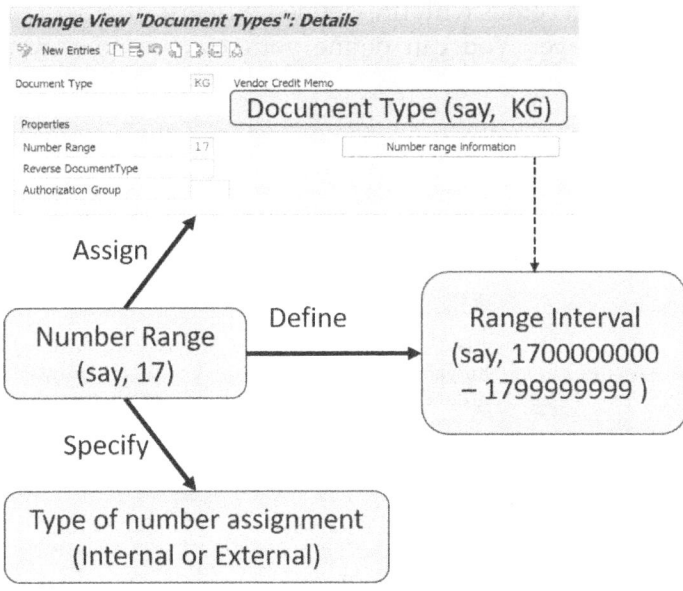

Figure 11.6: *Number Range Assignment process*

252. What are the two kinds of document number range assignments?

With regards to the assignment of numbers to the documents, there are two kinds of number assignment, as shown in *Figure 11.7*:

- *Internally* assigned by the system
- *Externally* input when the same is created

The number ranges can be defined so that the system generates the number automatically when a document is created. This is known as *'internal number assignment.'* Under this, the system stores the 'last number' used for a document in the *'Current Number'* field and will bring up the next number when another document is created.

If *'external numbering'* is used, the user must input a document number every time a new document is created in the system. Since the user supplies the number every time, the subsequent numbering may not be sequential. Unlike internal numbering, the system does not store the 'last number' in the *'Current Number'* field. When using external numbering, care should be taken on how you define these numbers: for example, you can define a number that is 'numeric' like 0000000001 to 9999999999 or 'non-numeric' like AAAAAAAAAA to ZZZZZZZZZZ or A470000000 to A479999999, but not like 0000000001 to ZZZZZZZZZZ or AAAAAAAAAA to 9999999999. The length of the number cannot exceed ten digits (or characters).

The standard SAP system comes with pre-defined numeric number ranges that are 'fiscal year- dependent'. However, you can define your own number range intervals with appropriate validity if required.

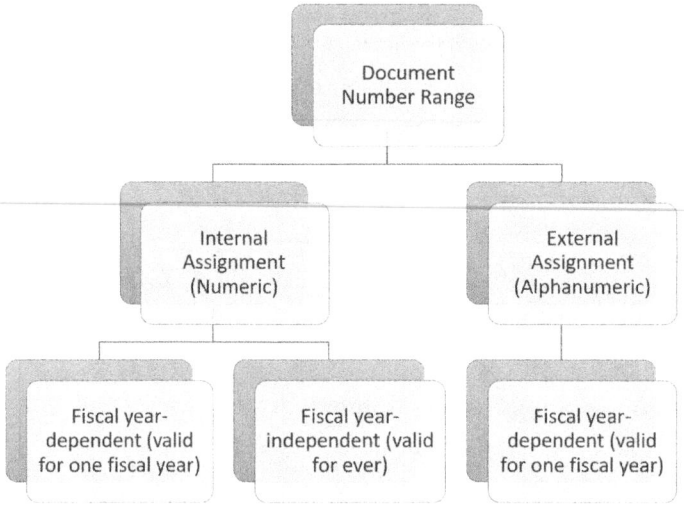

Figure 11.7: Document Number Range – the Classification

253. Explain the types of number ranges that you can use for document numbering.

The numbers in a number range can either be *numeric* or *alphanumeric*.

When the numbers are **numeric**, the system will prefix the number with the required zeros to make the number length uniform at ten digits. In numeric numbers, you can go in for 'fiscal year-specific' number ranges or 'fiscal year-independent' number ranges: the fiscal year-specific number ranges are valid for a particular, fiscal year, and you need to maintain the number ranges every fiscal year. However, if you are following 'fiscal year-specific' numbering, it is better not to mix numeric and alphanumeric numbering for a particular document type in various fiscal years.

If you use **alphanumeric numbering**, the number is padded with zeros from the right to maintain the length if it is less than ten characters. For obvious reasons, SAP recommends using fiscal year-specific numbering if you plan to use alphanumeric number ranges.

254. List the activities for configuring the number ranges in SAP.

The following are the activities that you need to complete to configure the number ranges properly in the system:

- Defining the number ranges (Transaction Code **FBN1**).
- Copying the number ranges to Company Code (Transaction Code **OBH1**).
- Copying the number ranges to fiscal year (Transaction Code **OBH2**).

255. Can you use the same 'Number Range' across Company Codes?

Yes. Since the number ranges are defined per Company Code, you may use the same number ranges across different Company Codes.

256. Can you use the same 'Number Range' for both the master records and documents?

Yes, SAP allows you to use the same number range intervals for both master records and documents. Of course, you can also use different ranges.

257. Can you use the same 'Number Range' for the same document type but in a different Company Code?

Yes, you can use the same number range interval for the same document type but in a different Company Code. This is because you define the number range intervals per Company Code. It is also possible that you use the same number range for a different document type in a different Company Code.

258. What is the recommended 'Number Range' for 'Sample and Recurring Entry Documents'?

SAP recommends using the following number range objects for the special documents, viz., sample and recurring entry documents:

- X1: Recurring entry documents
- X2: Sample documents

259. What 'Number Range' is used for 'Reversal Documents'?

By default, the system will use the same number range of the main document for reversal unless you have defined a separate number range that needs to be used for the reversed documents. For example, the system uses the number range '17' for the document type 'KG.' Since the number range for *'Reverse Document Type'* is left blank, the system, by default, uses the same number range '17' for the reversal as well. However, if you specify a different number in the *'Reverse DocumentType'* field (*Figure 11.8*), then the system will use that number range for all the reversals associated with the main document type.

You need to exercise caution while using a different number range for reversals: this number range should be 'numeric' even if the number assignment is 'external' for the main document. Otherwise, the reversal will not happen, and the system will throw an error.

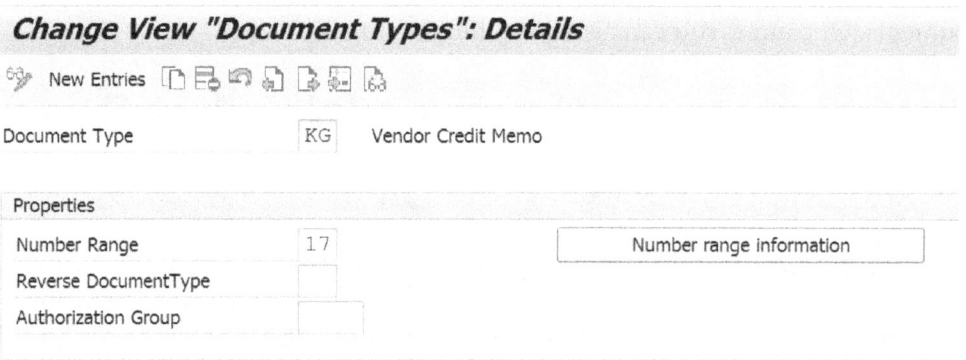

Figure 11.8: Document number range for reversal document

260. Is there any special attention to be paid in SAP S/4HANA Finance while defining document number ranges?

Yes. You need to ensure that the document numbers assigned to the 'leading ledger' (0L) do not have any gaps. So, it is recommended that you define a specific document type with its own number range that will be used for the valuations in the leading ledger. You can use this document type for the 'non-leading ledgers' as well.

261. Can you change a 'Number Range' later, after the initial definition and assignment?

Once you have defined and assigned a number range to a Company Code and document type, you may get into a situation where the originally defined number range interval or validity is insufficient. In such a case, you can change both the lower and upper limits of the range provided that the number range's lower limit has not yet been used in the system and the proposed upper limit of the range is not less than the current document number. Even if you try to define a new range, ignoring these guidelines, you will not be able to proceed further as the system will not allow you to 'save' the changes.

As far as validity is concerned, you can change it for a future fiscal year at any time in the system.

262. Explain how you can 'Delete' a document number range.

The best practice is not to delete any number range once defined and assigned to a Company Code. However, you can delete an already defined internal number range if it is not used at the time of deletion. Even if the system has used a single number from that range, you will not be able to delete that entire range. In the case of an external number range, you can delete it at any point in time; even if the range is in use, you can delete the range, overriding the warning message issued by the system.

263. What is the best practice for 'filing' original documents?

The system creates at least one document when a transaction is created/completed. SAP recommends 'filing' of original documents (under the number of the processing document generated in SAP). The best practice is to enter the (external) number of the 'original document' in the *'Reference'* field of the processing document created in the SAP system. For easy cross-reference and verification, note down this SAP document number created on the 'original document.'

264. What do you mean by 'Net' Postings?

Usually, when a transaction is posted, say vendor invoice (document type: KR), the system posts the 'gross' amount with the 'tax' and 'discount' included. However, SAP provides you with the option of posting these items as 'net'. In this case, the posting excludes 'tax' or 'discount.' Remember to use the special document type 'KN'. Similarly, you will use the document type 'DN' for 'customer invoice – Net' against the normal invoice postings for the customer using the document type 'DR'. For using this 'net method' of posting, you should have activated the required settings while entering the Company Code global parameters, using Transaction OBY6, and selecting the two checkboxes (under 'processing parameters'): *'Tax base is net value'* and *'Discount base is net value'* (*Figure 11.9*):

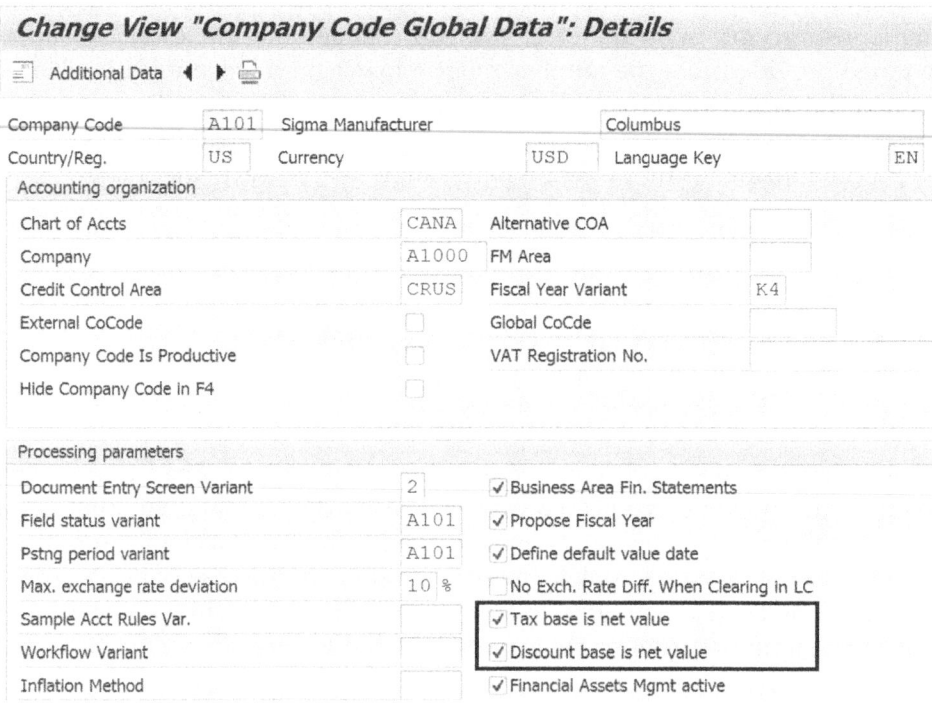

Figure 11.9: *Net Postings setting in Company Code global parameters*

265. Explain the various 'Reference Methods' in the document entry.

SAP recommends **'reference methods'** as a *'document entry tool'* to facilitate faster and easier document entry into the system when it is required to enter the same data repeatedly. Besides making the document entry process less time-consuming, this also helps ensure error-free document entry.

The various reference methods used in SAP are as follows:

- Reference documents
- Account assignment models
- Sample documents (reference document type 'M')
- Recurring entry documents (reference document type 'D')

266. Explain posting with 'Reference Documents'.

When you want to post a new document with 'reference' to an existing document in the system, you can do that by selecting the 'Document Entry' from the application like FI-G/L, FI-A/P, or FI-A/R and then selecting the option *'Post with Reference'* under *'Document'* on the menu bar when using certain Transactions like **F-02**, **F-05** (for G/L documents), **F-22** (for customer documents) etc., for example. However, when you use Transactions like **FB50** or **FB50L**, the *'Post with Reference'* option is available under *'Goto'* on the menu bar.

To use this option, you need to enter the document number, Company Code, and fiscal year (optional), then select the appropriate processing options like *'Enter G/L account items,'* *'Do not propose amounts', 'Display line items,' 'Copy text'* etc., to proceed further. The system copies the line items from the reference document if you have selected the option *'Display line items.'* When you press *'Enter,'* you will be taken to the overview screen, where you can check and correct the accounts, amounts, etc., and then post the document.

267. What is an 'Account Assignment Model'? When can you use it?

The **account assignment model** is a reference method used in document entry when the same distribution of amounts to several Company Codes, cost centers, accounts, etc., is frequently used. Instead of manually distributing the amount among accounts or Company Codes, you may use equivalence numbers for distributing both the credit and debit amounts (*Figure 11.11*). A cross-Company Code account assignment model can also be created. The account assignment model may contain any number of G/L accounts. The G/L account items need not be completed. The model can be used across several Company Codes and can even include Company Codes from non-SAP systems.

The use of the account assignment model is limited to G/L accounts only. Also, unlike a sample document, an account assignment model may be incomplete, which can be completed during document entry by adding, deleting, or changing the data already saved in the model.

Transaction Code FKMT

Figure 11.10

Account Assignment Model: Change Line Items

🗑 Delete selected area 🖨 🖹 🖫 ↩ 📄 📋

Acct assgnmt modelA101-MD

Currency	USD

Account Assignment Model Items

PK	CoCd	G/L	Tx	Jurisdictn Code	BusA	Cost Ctr	Equiv
40	A101	215120			ELCN		30
40	A101	215120			TXTL		20
40	A101	215120			ENGN		50
50	A101	111000					100

Figure 11.11: Account assignment model

268. What is a 'Sample Document'?

A '**sample document**' is like a template (*Figure 11.12*), created and stored so that the information contained therein can be easily copied into new documents and posted in the system. The sample documents, when posted, are stored in the system but, unlike accounting documents, will not update the transaction figures. You will normally use sample documents when you want to copy the contents to another document: for example, you create a sample document with an assignment to multiple cost centers and use this document as the reference document to create a new document with the same cost center assignment. It is possible that you can create a new sample document via the '*Posting with Reference*' option.

Display Sample Document: Data Entry View

🔧 📄 ▣ 🖨 ⓘ Taxes ⇅ Display Currency

Data Entry View

Document Number	9200000000	Company Code	A101	Fiscal Year	2024
Document Date	09.02.2024	Posting Date	09.02.2024	Period	2
Reference		Cross-Comp.No.			
Currency	USD	Texts Exist	☐	Ledger Group	

🔲 📄 📑 🔍 📊 ▽ Σ 📊 🖨 📄 📊 📋 ⓘ

CoCd	Item	Key	SG	Account	Description	Amount	Currency	Tx	Profit Center	Assignment
A101	1	40		650010	Purchased Services	500.0	USD	E0		
	2	50		630020	Water	500.0-	USD	E0		

Figure 11.12: Sample document

After you have created a sample document, you can make the system propose the values from this document that you can adopt without any change or change the data by omitting/ supplementing it into the new document. You can reuse a sample document any number of times. The sample documents have separate number ranges (X2).

In general, the sample documents are user-specific: that is, they are available only to the user who has created the same. The user can change, display, or delete, but not the others. If you want your sample documents to be accessed and used by others, then you need to provide them with the necessary access. Then, these documents will be denoted as 'all-user' sample documents.

You can 'hold' a sample document, and you can also retrieve, edit, and save an already 'held' document as a sample document.

Use Transaction Code **F-01** to create a sample document, **F-57** to delete, **FBM2** to change, **FBM3** to display, and **FBM4** to display changes.

269. What is a 'Recurring Entry Document'?

You can use the **'recurring entry document'** as a 'reference document' for enabling quicker posting of periodically recurring postings such as loan repayments, insurance premium payments, rent, etc. Since this document is not an accounting document, the account balances are unaffected. In a recurring entry original document (*Figure 11.13*), you will not be able to change the posting key, account, and amount. They are defined with a special number range ('X1'). Unlike an account assignment model, the recurring entry document **cannot** be used for cross-Company Code postings.

The *recurring entry document* **per se** does not update transaction figures but acts only as a reference and as the basis for creating accounting documents. The system creates the accounting documents from the recurring entry original document. There are two ways of setting the exact date when this document should be posted:

- **Posting frequency**: Enter the day of the month and the period (in months) between two postings.
- **Scheduled run**: Configure the 'run schedule' specifying the calendar days the program should post these documents.

You need to use Transaction **FBD1** to create a recurring entry original document. To execute the same use Transaction Code **F.14** (G/L account periodic processing).

Enter Recurring Entry: Header Data

Company Code	A101

Recurring entry run

First Run On	16.02.2024
Last Run On	16.02.2025
Interval in Months	1
Run Date	16
Run Schedule	

✓ Transfer amounts in local currency
✓ Transfer tax amounts in local currency
✓ Copy Texts

Document header information

Document Type	SA	Currency/Rate	USD
Reference		Translatn Date	
Document Header Text			
Trading Part.BA			

Enter Recurring Entry Display Overview

🗐 ↕ Display Currency   Account Model   📄G/L item fast entry   ⓘ Taxes

Document Date	09.02.2024	Type	SA	Company Code	A101
Posting Date	09.02.2024	Period	2	Currency	USD
Document Number	INTERNAL	Fiscal Year	2024	Translatn Date	09.02.2024
Reference				Cross-CL Number	
Doc.Header Text				Trading Part.BA	

Items in document currency

	PK	BusA	Acct		USD	Amount	Tax amnt	
001	40		ELCN	0000650010 Purchased Services		5,000.0		E0
002	50		ELCN	0000630020 Water		5,000.0-		E0

Figure 11.13: Recurring Entry Document

Transaction Code **FBD1**

Figure 11.14

270. What is a 'Document Change Rule'?

The functionality '**document change rules**,' when configured in the system, maintain the information relating to 'what fields can be changed?' and 'under what circumstances?'. As you know, SAP's *document principle* does not allow changing the 'relevant' fields once a document is posted; any changes can only be achieved through *'document reversal'* or additional postings. The fields like Company Code, business area, account number, posting key, amount, currency, etc., can never be changed once the document is posted. However, SAP allows changing some fields in the line items like payment method, payment block, house bank, dunning level, and dunning block, etc. These can be changed document by document or using '*mass change*' for several documents in a single step.

You may also change the contents of the field '*Doc. Header Text*', '*Reference*', etc., of a document (*Figure 11.16*). Again, you need to configure in the system 'what fields can be changed' and 'under what circumstances'. In any case, as already pointed out, SAP does not allow you to change the contents of fields that are central to document principle (say, account, amount, posting date, etc.) and the accounting objects (like business area, cost center, etc.) that have already been posted to.

Figure 11.15

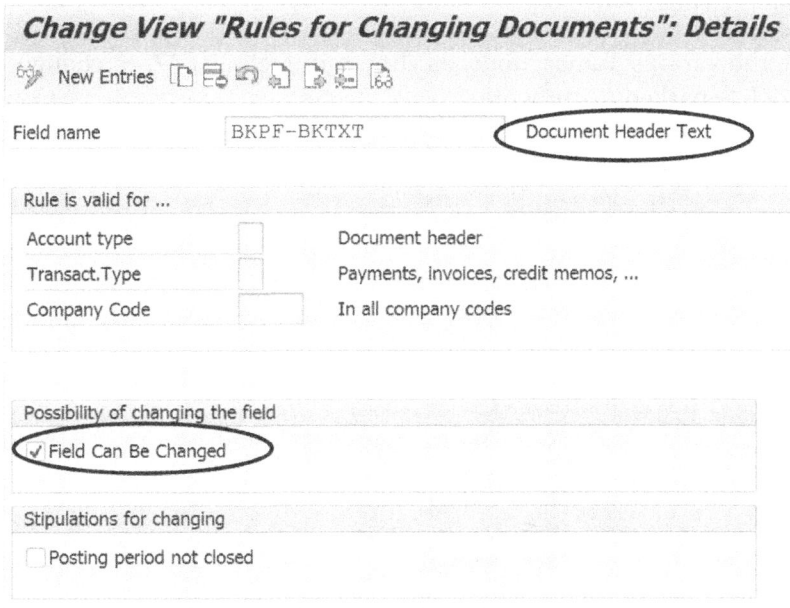

Figure 11.16: *Configuring Document Change Rule (Header)*

271. What is 'Parking of Document' in SAP?

'Parking of document,' in SAP, is one of the two preliminary postings (the other being 'Holding' of documents) in the system referring to storing incomplete documents in the system. These documents can later be called upon for completion and posting. While 'parking' is a document, the system does not carry out the mandatory 'validity checking'. The system does not also carry out any automatic postings (like creating tax line items) or 'balance checks.' As a result, the transaction figures (account balances) are not updated. This is true in all financial transactions except in TR-CM (Cash Management), where 'parked' documents will update the transactions.

You can use the parking of documents functionality to 'park' data relating to customers, vendors, or assets (acquisition only). When a cross-Company Code document is 'parked,' only one document is created in the initial Company Code; when this 'parked' document is posted, all other documents relevant to all other Company Codes will be created. However, it is to be noted that *substitution* functionality cannot be used with document 'parking,' as substitution is activated only upon transaction processing.

The added advantage of parking a document is that a document 'parked' by an accounting clerk can be called upon for completion by someone else. The 'parked' documents can be displayed individually or as a list from where the required document can be selected for completion and posting. The number of the 'parked' document is transferred to the posted document. The original 'parked' document, if necessary, can be displayed even after the same has been posted.

You can use the various Transactions, as shown in *Figure 11.17*, to change, display, post, process, or delete parked documents.

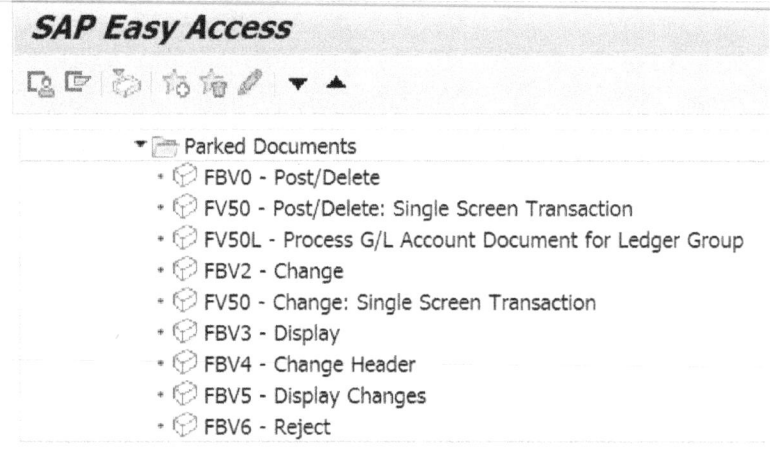

Figure 11.17: Parked Document: Transactions for various functions

272. How to change the Posting Date of 'Parked Documents'?

With respect to every Company Code, you can define if the posting date of parked documents is to remain unchanged or can be overwritten with the system date. SAP provides three options to configure the settings: < blank> option will keep the posting data unchanged, 'option 1' will result in a change of the posting date to the system date, and 'option 2' is the same as that of 'option 1' when the posting period is closed. With the settings, if the change of posting date of a parked document leads to a new fiscal year, then the system does not change the posting date to the system date but keeps to the original date.

Also, this functionality of changing the posting date of a parked document is available only for classic FI document parking transactions (**FBV0**) and not for 'SAP Enjoy' single-screen transactions. With the 'SAP Enjoy' transactions, you can change the system date at any point before posting.

273. What is a 'Hold Document' in SAP?

During a transaction, when the user finds that they do not have a piece of information required to be entered, they can '**hold document**' and complete the same later. As in the case of 'parked' documents, here also the document does not update the transaction figures. Though user-specific and available only for the user who has created the documents, the 'held document' can also be accessed by other users if the user-creator has given the necessary authorizations to access the held document.

In most accounting transactions, you will be able to 'park' or 'hold' a document (*Figure 11.18*).

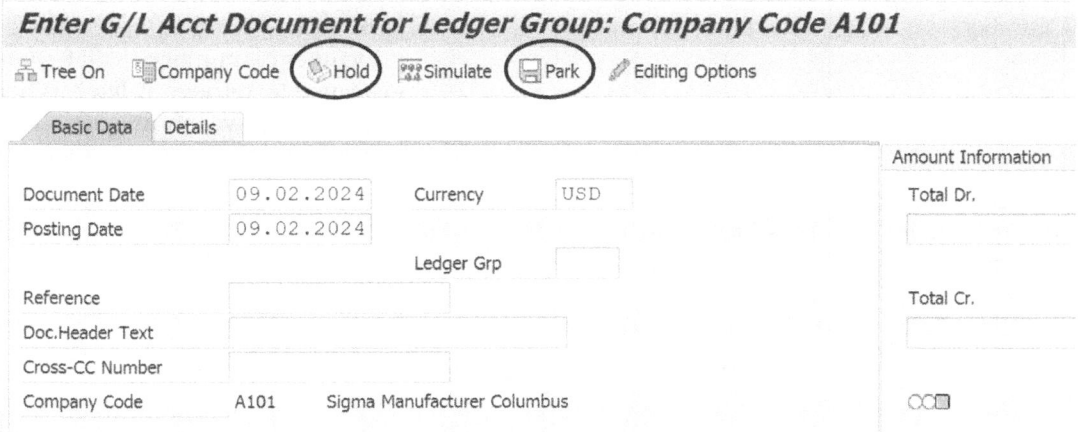

Figure 11.18: *Park / Hold document*

274. What are the essential differences between 'Parking' and 'Holding'?

The essential differences between 'parking a document' and 'holding a document' can be summarized as shown in *Table 11.2*:

Attribute	'Park' document	'Hold' document
When to use?	During document entry you find that, for example, the required account assignments are missing. In such a case, you may want to 'park' the document and come back later to complete the same when you have the required inputs. Unlike in 'holding' a document, this may take a while.	You will 'hold' a document when you are interrupted while entering it. The idea is to store the data temporarily.

Attribute	'Park' document	'Hold' document
View the document in 'Account Display'?	Yes.	No.
Changes to the document?	Any user can access, view and/change the document.	None other than the creator, will be able to access, view and/change the document, unless the creator provides access rights to other users.
Document number?	When 'parked', the system assigns a document number.	When you 'hold' a document, you need to enter a 'temporary document number' that you can use to retrieve it later. When posted, the system assigns a new document number as in any other case.
Use of data in the document for evaluation purposes?	Possible, even though the system does not update the account balance.	Not possible.

Table 11.2: *Parking / Holding a Document: the differences*

275. What is an 'Automatic Posting'?

When you post documents in SAP, the system sometimes adds additional line items (like input/output tax, cash discount gain/loss, foreign exchange rate differences, etc.) to the ones you have entered in the document. This helps to reduce your work as the system calculates them automatically.

However, you need to define the appropriate G/L accounts that you want the system to post to for the automatically added additional line items, this will bring in a control whereby no manual posting is allowed to any of these accounts. Also, you need to configure the rules according to which the system will post to these accounts automatically. For example, you can configure the system to post to different tax G/L accounts based on different tax codes.

It is also possible that you can manually supplement, for example, an account assignment (say, cost center) to the automatically generated line items. To achieve this, go and select '*Supplement Auto. Postings*' checkbox in the G/L account master record that you have defined for automatic postings (*Figure 11.19*):

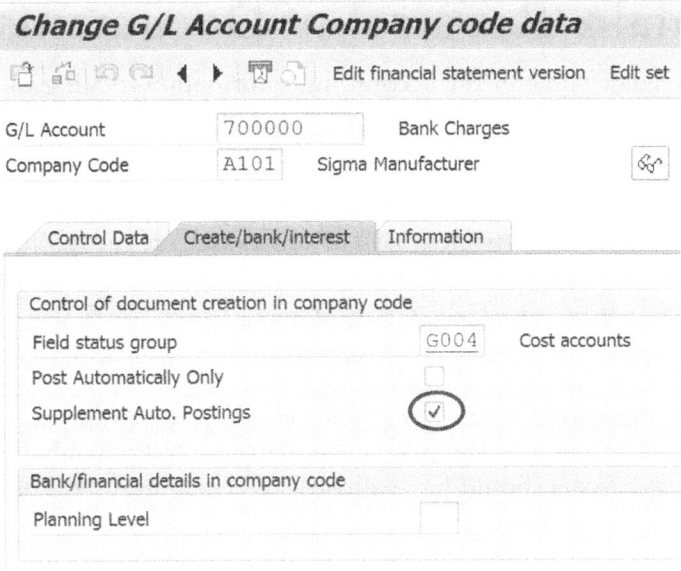

Figure 11.19: *Supplementing automatic postings*

276. What is 'Clearing'?

A **clearing** in SAP refers to the squaring-off of open debit entries with that of open credit entries. The clearing is allowed in G/L accounts maintained on an 'open item' basis and in all customer/vendor accounts. The clearing can either be manual or automatic. In case of *manual clearing*, you will view the open items and select the matching items for clearing. In the case of *automatic clearing*, a program determines what items need to be cleared based upon certain pre-determined open item selection criteria and proposes assignments before clearing these assigned items. Whatever the type of clearing, the system creates *a clearing document* with the details and enters the 'clearing number' against each of the cleared open items. The *clearing number* is derived from the document number of the clearing document.

You will also be able to do a *'partial clearing'* when you cannot match open items exactly; in this case, the balance amount not cleared is posted as a new open item. You need to configure *clearing tolerance* and define rules for tackling the situation (like writing off, posting the difference to a separate 'clearing difference' account, etc.) if the net amount after clearing is not zero.

In the case of customers who are also vendors/suppliers, you will be able to distinguish between them provided the same is duly configured in the relevant master data (by entering the customer number in the vendor master record, and *vice versa*).

277. Explain 'Reversal of Documents' in SAP.

If you need to change some of the accounting information relating to an already posted document, you can only achieve the same by **reversing** the original document and posting a new one with the correct information. However, reversal is possible only when:

- The document's origin is in FI (not through SD, MM, etc.)
- The information like business area or cost center, etc., are still valid (that you have not deleted these business objects)
- The original document has no cleared items
- The document relates only to the line items of customer/vendor / G/L

While reversing, the system automatically selects the appropriate document type for the reversal, besides defaulting to the relevant posting keys. Remember that the document type for *reversal documents* should have already been configured (refer to *Question 259* for more details) when document types were defined in the system. As already discussed, the system uses the same number range as that of the original document for the reversed documents unless you have specified a different number range. Also, note that if you do not specify the posting date for the reversal document, the system defaults to the posting date of the original document.

278. Explain 'True Reversal'. How it is different from regular 'Reversal'.

As you know, any document reversal results in postings that are opposite the credit/debit sides of the original posting, leading to an increase in the account balances, and the 'trial balance' is automatically inflated on both sides. This is against the legal requirement in some countries like France, wherein it is required that even after reversal, it should not result in increased account balances. As a result, SAP came out with '**true reversal**' which overcomes this problem by *'negative postings'* to the same line item(s) during reversal. The account balance that was originally increased was restored to the actual balance during the reversal (see *Table 11.3* for more details):

Type of Reversal	Type of posting	Account 100000		Account 200000	
		Debit	Credit	Debit	Credit
Traditional Reversal	Original Posting	$ 2500			$ 2500
	Reversal		$ 2500	$ 2500	
	A/c Balance	$ 2500	$ 2500	$ 2500	$ 2500

Type of Reversal	Type of posting	Account 100000		Account 200000	
		Debit	Credit	Debit	Credit
'True' Reversal	Original Posting	$ 2500			$ 2500
	Reversal	-$ 2500			-$ 2500
	A/c Balance	0			0

Table 11.3: *Example of True Reversal*

279. What is 'Fast Entry'?

Instead of the regular document entry screens, SAP provides '**Fast Entry**' screens, facilitating a quick way of entering repetitive line items in a transaction. To achieve this, you need to define a *Fast Entry Screen Layout*, which will specify what fields you will require for data entry and in which order. You may configure these fast entry screen layouts for G/L account line items, credit memos, and customer/vendor invoices. Each of these fast entry screen layouts will be denoted by a 5-character screen variant in the system. Fast-entry screens are used in *complex (general) postings*.

SAP's *Enjoy Postings* are also meant for similar data entry screen; but the difference is that while in case of 'fast entry' you will start from scratch in identifying the fields, positioning them in the line item etc., whereas in Enjoy Postings, the system comes with all the fields activated and you will deselect the fields that you do not want to be made available on the data entry screen.

280. What is a 'Posting Key' in SAP?

A **'posting key'** in SAP is a two-digit alphanumeric key, which, together with the 'account number,' controls the entry of line items in a document. The posting key determines the following, as shown in *Figure 11.20*:

- What *account* (D, K, S, M, A) can be posted to
- Which side of the account (*debit or credit*) to be posted to
- What is the document entry screen layout that needs to be used for that particular transaction
- Whether any other *special requirements* are to be taken care of (for example, you can indicate if the sales figures are to be updated)

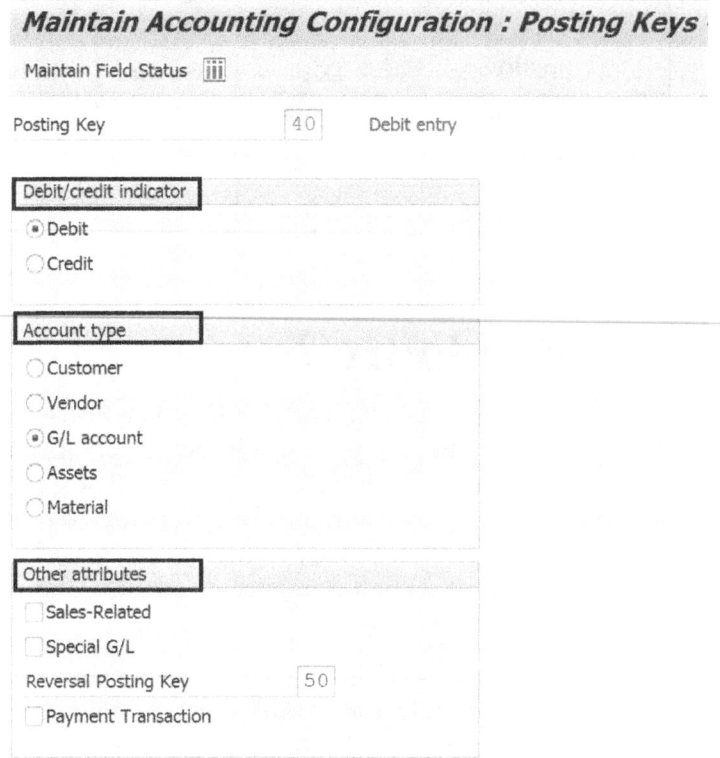

Figure 11.20: Posting key configuration

SAP comes with several posting keys for meeting the different business transaction requirements: '40' (G/L debit), '50' (G/L credit), '01' (customer invoice), '11' (customer credit memo), '21' (vendor credit memo), '31' (vendor payment), etc.

Figure 11.21

It is recommended that you do not change any of the default posting keys in the system, as additional or new posting keys are very rarely required. However, you can create your own posting keys if you really need them.

281. What do you mean by 'Tolerance' in SAP transaction processing?

You need to define **'tolerances'** in the system to facilitate dealing with the payment differences (always in the 'local currency') arising out of accounting transactions and to instruct the system on how to proceed further. Normally, you define tolerances (either in 'absolute terms' or in 'percentage') beyond which the system will not allow you to post a document should there be a difference. In exact terms, you instruct the system as to how to proceed further when there is a payment difference: when the payment difference is within the defined tolerance limits, the system proceeds to complete the transaction either by adjusting the cash discount or by making postings to separate expense/revenue account.

282. What are all the types of 'Tolerances' that you will come across in SAP?

In SAP, tolerances are defined per Company Code, and there are three types:

- Employee tolerance
- Customer or vendor/supplier tolerance
- G/L account clearing tolerance

283. What is a 'Tolerance Group'?

You will manage the tolerances via '**tolerance groups**' in the system. You will define the tolerance groups, per Company Code, that specify the upper amount limit for posting a transaction and the permitted payment differences. It is a best practice to define at least two tolerance groups: one, the 'null tolerance group' will be the one with stringent tolerance rules, and the second specific tolerance group, which you attach to a group of employees or group of customers/suppliers, which is kind of 'relaxed' compared to the null group. However, it is mandatory to have at least one tolerance group per Company Code.

284. Explain the Employee Tolerance Groups.

Since the tolerance rules usually apply to a group of employees, you define '*employee tolerance groups*' in the system and assign the employees to these groups. Again, you may define several employee tolerance groups with one null tolerance group that applies to all employees not assigned to a specific not-null tolerance group.

While defining this employee tolerance group, you will specify the following (*Figure 11.22*):

- Upper limits for various posting procedures:
  - o Amount per document
  - o Amount per open account item
  - o Cash discount, in percentage
- Permitted payment differences:

How much over or underpayment an employee is allowed to process? This is defined both in absolute value and in percentage, and the system will take into account the lower of the two during transaction processing.

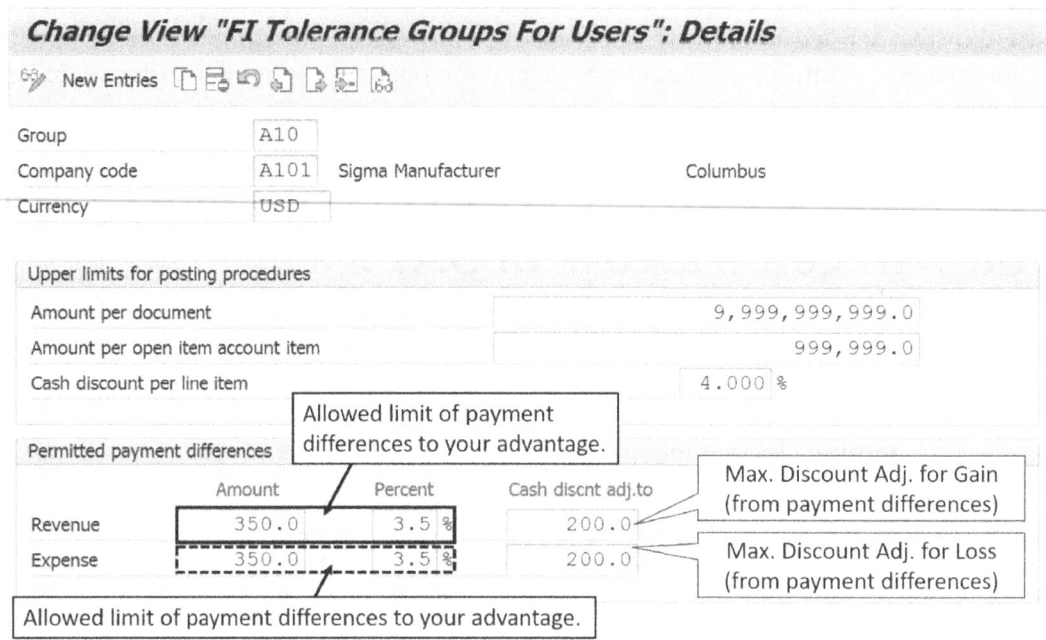

Figure 11.22: FI Tolerance Group for Users (employees)

Example: You want to define tolerance group A10 for your Company Code A101 besides a 'null' tolerance group. Once defined, you will allocate specific employees to tolerance group A10, and the 'null' group will be for all.

You stipulate that the tolerance group A10 will have the following rules (*Figure 11.22*):

Posting of accounting documents allowed up to a maximum value of USD 9,999,999,999 per document, with a limit of USD 999,999 per open item.

Maximum cash discount per line item at 4%.

Under 'permitted payment differences,' the system allows a maximum payment difference of 3.5%, the absolute amount being USD 350. The payment differences can be adjusted with a cash discount of up to USD 200.

285. Explain the 'Customer/Supplier Tolerance Groups.'

Like that of employee tolerance groups, you will also be defining **customer/vendor (supplier) tolerance groups**, in SAP, which you will enter in the respective master records.

By such a tolerance group, you specify, for example, how large the payment difference (of a customer or vendor/supplier) the system can still accept to process the payment transaction. Besides the payment difference settings, you can also define the grace days for cash discounts and how you want the system to manage the residual items.

286. What is 'G/L Account Clearing Tolerance'?

For **G/L account clearing tolerance**, you need to define the limits to which the system will accept the differences and post them automatically to pre-defined G/L accounts. Once defined in IMG Customizing, you must attach the appropriate tolerance group to the G/L account master record. As in the case of the employee tolerance group, you may define the upper limit for clearing both in absolute amount and in percentage, both for debit (clearing differences to your advantage) and credit (clearing differences to your disadvantage) postings.

287. List the Transaction Codes to maintain tolerance groups in SAP.

The following are the Transaction Codes in SAP that you will use in configuring the tolerance groups in the system:

- Define Employee Tolerance Group: **OBA4**
- Define Customer / Supplier Tolerance Group: **OBA3**
- Define G/L Account Tolerance Group: **OBA0**

288. With different tolerances defined, what tolerance will the system apply?

So, when tolerance limits are defined for employees (employee tolerance groups), customers/suppliers (customer and vendor/supplier tolerance groups), and G/L accounts (G/L account clearing tolerance groups), the system considers the lowest of all three while processing the transaction.

289. Explain, with examples, how the system applies 'Tolerance' settings while posting.

Example: You have an A/R from one of your customers for USD 1,000, net due immediately. You have configured the employee tolerances as indicated in *Table 11.14*:

Details	Amount (USD)	Percent	Cash discount adj. to (USD)
Permitted payment differences			
Revenue	25	0.5	5
Expense	25	0.5	5

Table 11.4: Employee Tolerance Settings (Example)

Now, let us consider the following scenarios (*Figure 11.23*):

Scenario	1	2	3	4	5	6
A/R outstanding (USD)	1,000	1,000	1,000	1,000	1,000	1,000
Amount received from customer (USD)	990	970	997	1,020	1,050	1,003
Underpayment to the tune of (USD)	10	30	3			
Overpayment to the tune of (USD)				20	50	3

Figure 11.23: Different scenarios in A/R payment processing

Scenario one

The customer sends in a payment of USD 990 against the receivable amount of USD 1,000. As this is an underpayment, the system will use the tolerance rules for the 'Expense' row. First, the system will try to adjust the cash discount for the shortfall: here, the payment difference is USD 10, which is more than the discount amount that can be adjusted to (USD 5). As the discount cannot be adjusted, the system will ignore this rule and move on to check the upper limit set for the payment differences. The permitted payment difference is USD 25, lower than 'Amount' USD 25 and 'Percent' 0.05*1000 = 50. Since the payment difference (USD 10) is within the permitted payment difference of USD 25, the system clears the transaction by posting a loss of USD 10 to an expense account.

Scenario two

The customer sends in a payment of USD 970 against the receivable of USD 1,000. This is an underpayment, and the shortfall is USD 30. As in *Scenario one*, the system will look up the 'Expense' row to clear this transaction. It tries to determine whether the cash discount amount can be adjusted towards the payment difference and finds that it cannot do so because the actual shortfall is USD 30, more than the cash discount adjustment amount (USD 5) allowed in the system. Now, the system looks up the 'Amount' and 'Percent' configurations under permitted payment differences: it understands that it can tolerate a maximum of only USD 25 (amount allowed in absolute terms = USD 25, amount allowed as percentage = 0.05*1000 = 50). As the payment difference of USD 30 exceeds the permitted payment difference of USD 25, the system does not clear the transaction. Here, you may need to clear the same manually.

Scenario three

The customer sent in a payment of USD 997 against the total receivable amount of USD 1,000. That is an underpayment to the tune of USD 3. As with the two previous scenarios, the system will also look at the rules configured for the 'Expense' row since this is also an underpayment. The system adjusts the cash discount amount allowed against the payment difference (USD 3). As the tolerance settings permit adjusting the cash discount to a maximum of USD 5 towards any payment difference, this transaction is cleared, and the cash discount account is posted accordingly.

Scenario four

The customer sends in a payment of USD 1,020 against the receivable amount of USD 1,000, an overpayment of USD 20. Since this is an overpayment, the system will now consider the settings maintained for the 'Revenue' row. First, it checks whether it can adjust the cash discount amount: this is not possible since the allowed cash discount adjustment amount is only USD 5 (against the payment difference of USD 20). Now, the system checks whether this could be cleared using the 'Amount' and 'Percent' settings. Since the payment difference (overpayment) is well within the permitted payment difference upper limit of USD 25 (lower of 'Amount' 25 and 'Percent' 0.05*1000 = 50), the system proceeds to book the overpayment of USD 20 as profit and credits the same to a revenue G/L account, and clears the transaction.

Scenario five

This is also regarding an overpayment. From the customer, you receive a payment of USD 1,050 against the receivable of USD 1,000. As in the case of *Scenario four*, since this is also an overpayment, the system will consider the tolerance rules configured for the 'Revenue' row. As against the allowed cash discount adjust amount of USD 5, the payment difference (overpayment) in this case is 50, and hence, the system does not adjust the cash discount amount towards this payment difference. Now, looking at the upper limit of USD 25 as the permitted payment difference (lower of 'Amount' and 'Percent' settings), the system stops processing the transaction any further as the payment difference (USD 50) is much more than the allowed limit of USD 25. Again, manual intervention is required to process the posting.

Scenario six

Consider that the customer sends in a payment of USD 1,003. This is against the A/R outstanding of USD 1,000 by an overpayment of USD 3. The system considers the settings under the 'Revenue' row as this is a case of overpayment. Since the payment difference is well within the allowed cash discount adjustment amount of USD 5, the system completes the transaction and posts it to the relevant accounts.

290. How do we process the payment difference that exceeds the tolerance?

When the payment difference exceeds the tolerance limits set for the automatic clearing of transactions, you can process the transactions via *partial payments* or *residual items* in SAP S/4HANA Finance. Though both methods will have the same effect on your customer's account balance, they differ from one another because of their differing impacts on A/R line items.

291. Explain 'Partial Payments'.

A **'partial payment'** situation arises when, for example, a customer does not pay the full invoice amount but pays only a portion of that. In this case, the system does not clear the original invoice: the initial invoice and the payment remain open items until the balance amount is received. This is the opposite of what happens in a 'residual item' processing. When posting a partial payment, you may use the pre-defined reason codes, or you may create your own reason codes if required. Whatever the reason code you use, ensure you do not set the *'Charge Off Diff'* indicator.

Example: Assume that you have an A/R outstanding of USD 1,000 against a customer. Supposing that the customer sends in a payment of only USD 700. In this case, you resort to partial payment processing. When you post USD 700 as the incoming payment, a new open line item is created for this amount (USD 700), and the customer's liability is reduced to USD 300. This way, the partial payment, and the initial invoice remain open until the customer pays the remaining amount of USD 300. In SAP S/4HANA Finance, if you are using the Fiori app "Edit Options for Journal Entries," you can select the field 'Use Invoice Ref' so that the system links this partial payment to the original open item.

Instead of processing via the partial payment route, you may charge off the payment difference (when it is small) by posting it to an expense G/L account. Here, you may also use a reason code configured with the *'Charge Off Diff'* indicator set.

292. Explain 'Residual Payments'.

Creating a **'residual item'** happens when, for example, you receive a payment from a customer (against an A/R outstanding) that leads to a payment difference that cannot be processed automatically using the tolerances configured in the system. When you manually post the incoming payment, you clear the original invoice amount to the tune of the current payment and post the (payment) difference to the customer's account as a residual item. In the process, the system clears the original invoice with the payment. Still, it creates a new open item (for the payment difference) linked to the initial invoice (via the *'Invoice Reference'* field). You may need to provide a 'reason code' while posting the residual item in the system. As in the case of posting a partial payment, you may also use the pre-defined reason codes here, or you may create your own reason codes if required. Whatever the reason code that is used, make sure that you do not set the '*Charge Off Diff*' indicator.

Example: Consider that you have an A/R outstanding against a customer for USD 1,000. Instead of receiving full payment, you receive only USD 900 from the customer, which the system does not clear automatically as the payment difference is much more than the tolerance limits. While processing the incoming payment, you want to post a residual item. In this case, the system posts the incoming payment of USD 900 and clears the original invoice of USD 1,000 but creates a new open item (the residual one) for USD 100, with reference to the original invoice. This new line item will be open and outstanding until you get that payment from the customer.

Instead of posting a residual item, you may want to post the payment difference to an expense account, as we discussed earlier in case of underpayment scenarios. In this case, while using a pre-defined reason code, you will select the '*Charge Off Diff*' checkbox to indicate that the payment difference is being charged off using a separate expense G/L account.

293. How does 'Partial Payment' differ from 'Residual Payment'?

A **partial payment** results in posting a credit to the customer's 'open item' but leaving the original item intact. As a result, no open item is cleared. During partial payment, the system updates the '*invoice reference*' and '*allocation*' fields.

As against the partial payment, the **residual payment** clears the particular 'open item' against which the payment is applied. However, since there is not enough to clear the entire open item, the system creates a new open item, which is the difference between the original invoice item and the payment applied. Note that the new invoice/open item created by the system will have the new document date and new baseline date, though you can change these dates.

294. What are 'Reason Codes' in SAP S/4HANA Finance?

SAP S/4HANA Finance offers '**reason codes**' that help document the reason while processing payment differences. You may use such reason codes, per Company Code, to manage payment differences in partial payments and residual items and post them on an account. SAP comes delivered with several reason codes that you may use, or you may create your own codes if required. For every reason code (identified by a 3-character identifier), you enter the required explanation (*Figure 11.24*), correspondence type (SAP50, SAP51, etc.), select or deselect the '*Charge Off Diff*' indicator, etc.:

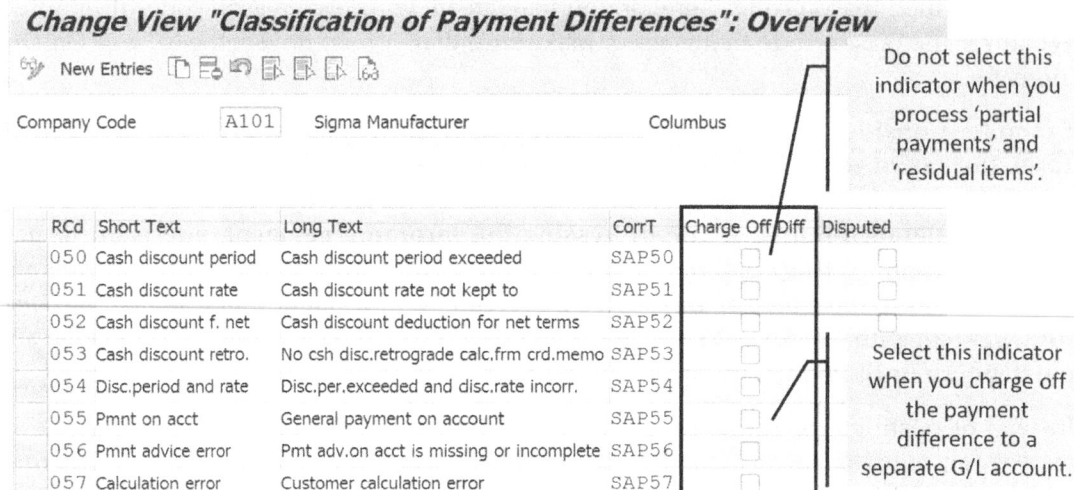

Figure 11.24: Pre-defined Reason Codes in SAP

Figure 11.25

As discussed previously, when using the reason codes for partial payments, residual items, etc., you need to ensure that the '*Charge Off Diff*' indicator checkbox is unselected. However, when you charge off the payment difference to an expense G/L account, you may use a reason code with the '*Charge Off Diff*' indicator checkbox selected.

295. What are 'Text IDs' in SAP S/4HANA Finance that you can use in documents?

During document entry in SAP, you will enter a header text in the '*Doc. Header Text*' field (that relates to some explanation or notes for the whole document) and some text for each line item (the 'item text' in the '*Text*' field). However, at times, you may find that the space available for entering such explanatory header text or item text is not sufficient to put in all the information that you want to document. In such cases, you may want to use the '**text ID**' option available in SAP. Here, you define a text ID, and for each text ID, you store detailed information either for the header or for a line item. So, how does this work?

Define the required Text IDs if the standard ones do not meet your requirements. To define your own text IDs, use the following Transaction codes:

Details	Transaction code
Define Text ID for Documents (Header)	**OBT8**
Define Text Identifications for Line Items	**OBT10**

Table 11.5: Transaction Codes for Text ID Definition

Now that you have the required text IDs created in the system let us understand how to input the additional information when entering a document: while entering a document, to maintain a detailed '*Doc. Header Text*', you call up a pop-up screen from '*Extras | Document texts*' on the menu bar, and from there, you can enter any additional text by clicking on the '*Detailed text*' button at the bottom of the 'Texts in Accounting Document' pop-up screen. This will open a text editor that you can use to enter the information (*Figure 11.26*):

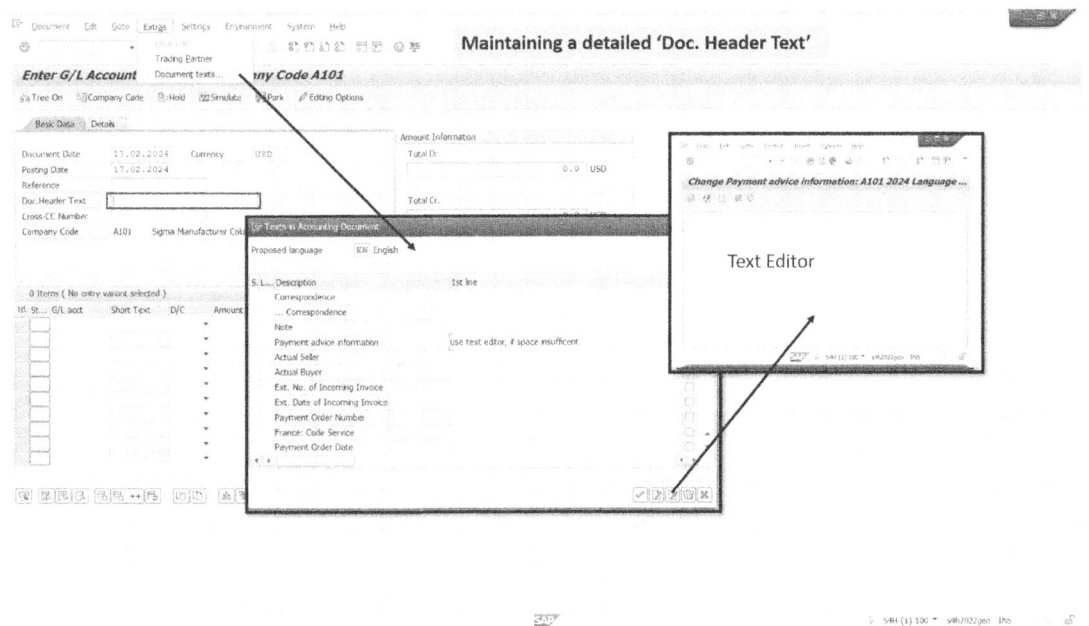

Figure 11.26: Entering detailed Document Header Text

To enter *line-item text*, you will normally use the '*Text*' field. However, this field may not be sufficient to include all the details, as the length is only 50 characters. In such a situation, you may click on the '*Long Text*' icon adjacent to the '*Text*' field, which will open a 'Long Text for Document Line Item' pop-up screen. From that pop-up, open a text editor by clicking on the '*Editor*' icon, then enter the text you want to document for the line item (*Figure 11.27*):

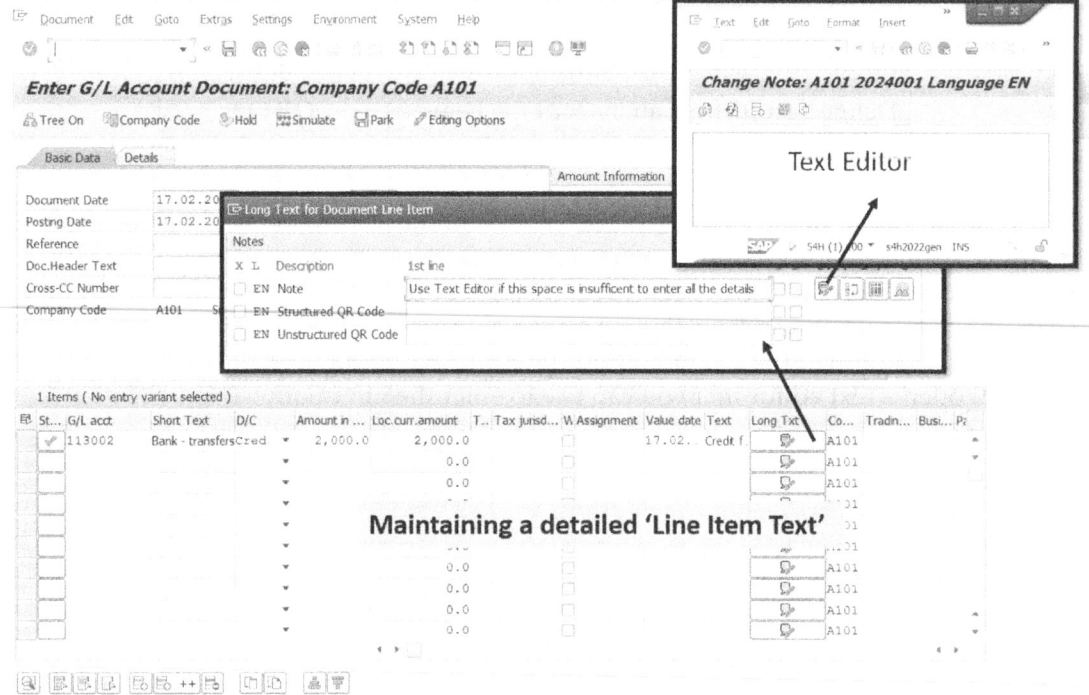

Figure 11.27: Entering detailed Line Item Text

296. Define 'Line Item Text'. How is it different from 'Text ID'?

Instead of entering an explanation for a line item, every time, you may want to use some shortcuts that enable you to automatically input some pre-determined text in the *'Text'* field. In this case, you will configure 'text keys' using a 4-character identifier (say, A101, for example). Then, for each key, you enter the text (not more than 50 characters) that you want to get transferred to the line-item text. While entering such text, you may also use variables like document date, posting date, baseline date for payment, etc. To use such a variable, you must use the 3-character variable identifier (say, BLD for document date, BUD for posting date, XBL for reference document number, etc.) prefixed with the '$' sign. Once defined, when you enter a line item in the *'Text'* field, you just need to enter the text key with the '=' sign prefixed (like =A101), and the system will populate the text field automatically with the relevant text. You can edit/adapt this pre-filled text if you have selected the *'Control Display'* checkbox while creating the text keys (*Figure 11.28*):

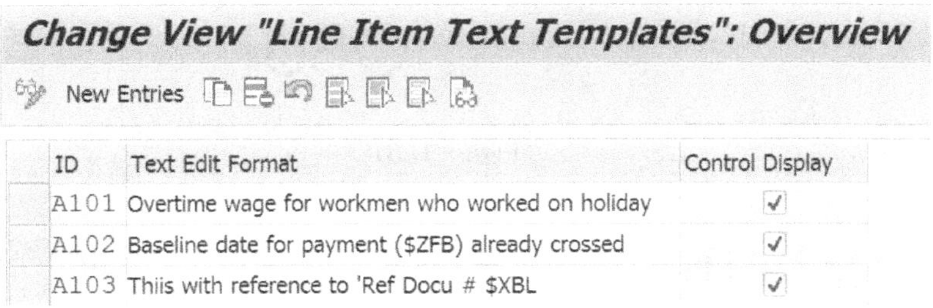

Figure 11.28: *Configuring pre-defined texts for line item text*

Transaction Code OB56

Figure 11.29

297. Explain the settings 'Define Default Values for Document Types and Posting Keys.'

For a given Transaction, you can store the default document type and the posting key in the system so that when you are starting that Transaction (say, **F-27** 'Enter Customer Credit Memo'), the system proposes the document type 'DG' and the posting key '11' as default values, instead of you entering them every time. This is called 'define default values.' SAP comes delivered with several such defaults for most of the Transactions (*Figure 11.30*) that you can use as such (recommended) or modify if required. Note that these settings are cross-Client; any change will affect all the Clients.

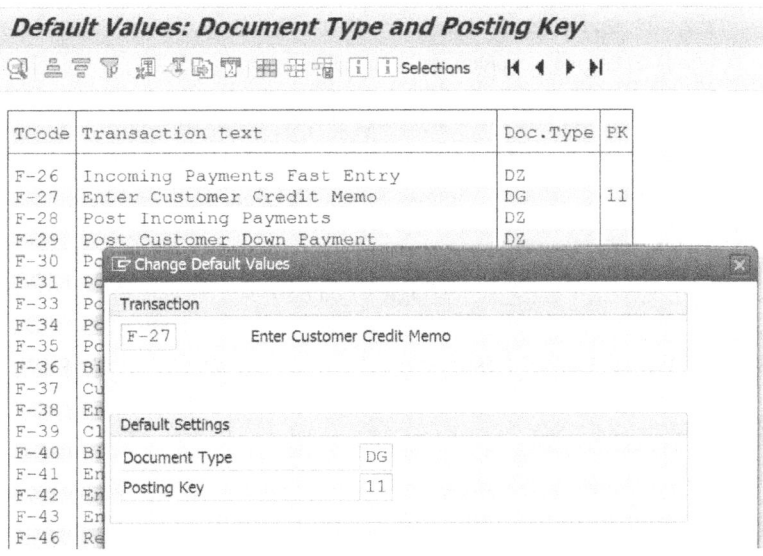

Figure 11.30: *Defining Default Values (Document Type and Posting Key)*

Figure 11.31

298. Explain the 'Enable Fiscal Year' Customizing activity.

You use the **'Enable Fiscal Year'** Customizing activity to decide if you want the system to propose the fiscal year during document change/display functions. When enabled, the system brings up the fiscal year that you used in your last work session. You will normally enable this option if your Company Code works with 'year-dependent' document number ranges. In such a situation, besides bringing up the last document number, the system also displays the appropriate fiscal year during document display/change functions. You do not need to enable this option (leaving the *'Propose Fiscal Year'* indicator blank, as shown in *Figure 11.32*) if your Company Code works with 'year-independent' document number ranges. In this case, for your document change/display functions, the system brings up only the last document number processed.

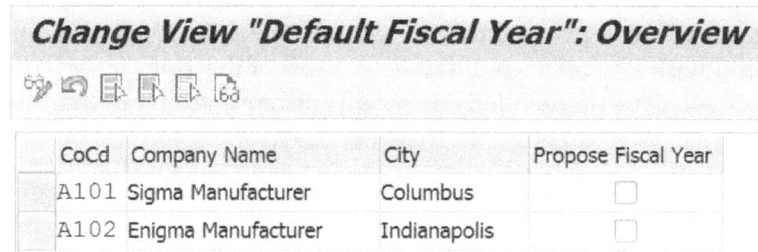

Figure 11.32: Enabling 'Propose Fiscal Year'

Figure 11.33

Instead of configuring 'propose fiscal year' this way, you can also achieve the same via Transaction **OBY6** when you maintain the Company Code global parameters (refer to *Question 136*).

299. Explain Configuring 'Default Value Date.'

While entering the line items in a document, you may want to input the value date. Instead of entering the value date, you can configure the system to propose the same by selecting the *'Propose Value Date'* checkbox (*Figure 11.34*). In this case, the system will propose the CPU date as the **default value date,** which you can change if required. You need to make these settings per the Company Code.

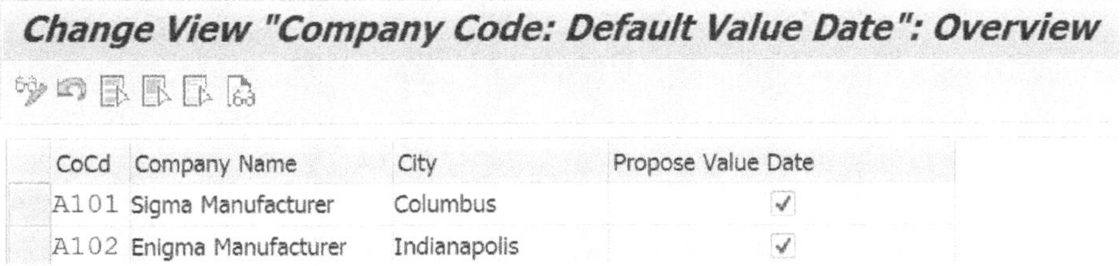

Change View "Company Code: Default Value Date": Overview

CoCd	Company Name	City	Propose Value Date
A101	Sigma Manufacturer	Columbus	✓
A102	Enigma Manufacturer	Indianapolis	✓

Figure 11.34: Configuring Default Value Date

Transaction Code **OB68**

Figure 11.35

As in the case of the Customizing activity 'propose fiscal year,' you may also use the Transaction **OBY6** (Company Code global parameters) for making the desired settings for 'default value date': in this case, you will select/deselect the checkbox *'Define Default Value Date'* (refer to *Question 136*).

300. Is it possible to Configure the way the 'System Messages' are displayed?

Yes, you can control how the system displays the various system messages (**Error**, **Warning,** and **Information**). Through this Customizing activity, you can decide if a message is to be displayed in a dialog box or as a footer if you want to change 'E' messages to 'W,' and if you want the system to switch the messages altogether (not showing any message).

While configuring, first, you will select the *'Work Area'* (say, 1E – BCA: Account, AA – Messages for Asset Accounting, BE – General Document Entry, etc.) for which you want to configure the message display. Then, using the **'New Entries'** option, you can configure the system behavior for each of the message numbers (*'MsgNo'*). While doing so, you can configure this for select users (*'User Name'*) or the entire Client. Also, you need to configure the settings for both online (dialog) transactions and batch input transactions (*Figure 11.36*):

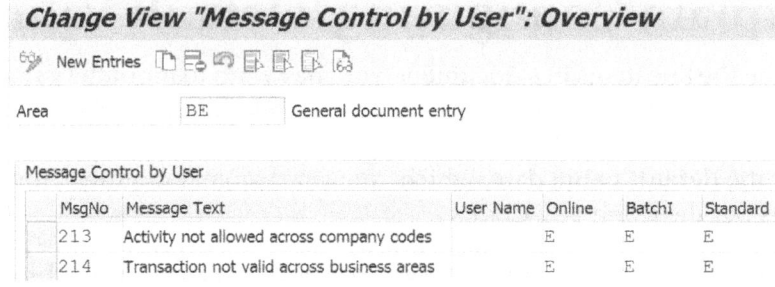

Figure 11.36: Configuring Message Control

Figure 11.37

301. What is a 'Business Transaction Type' in SAP S/4HANA Finance?

A '**business transaction type**' is a business transaction category that leads to a journal entry in SAP. It is a type of business event that signifies value/quantity change for a Company Code that needs to be accounted for in SAP FI (Financial Accounting). Simply put, they are the 'value flows'. The business transaction types help you to classify the various transactions in a more detailed way (*Figure 11.38*):

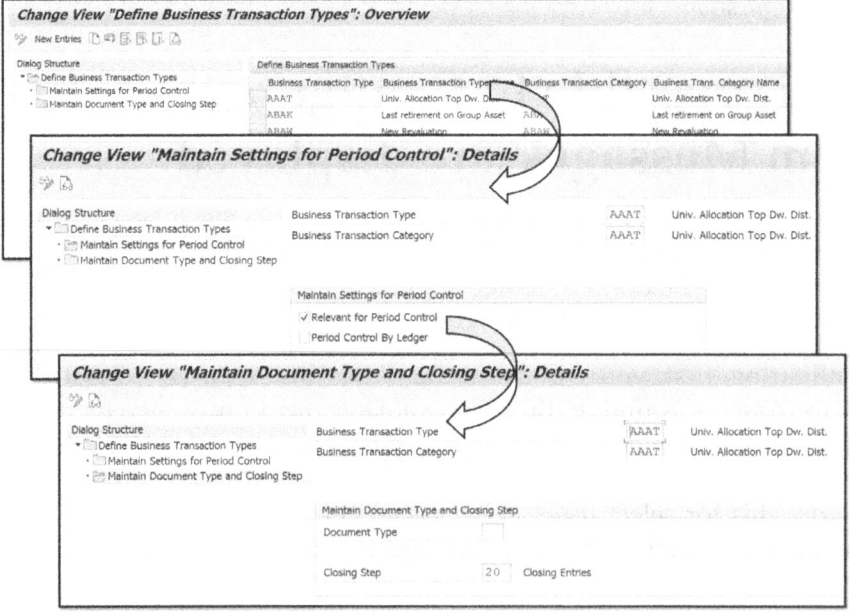

Figure 11.38: Business Transaction Types

SAP comes with several business transaction categories and types that will be sufficient to meet all your business transaction requirements. If you need any additional categories or types, you can still define them using the customer namespace 'Y*.'

302. What is an 'Archiving Object' in SAP S/4HANA Finance?

A central component in 'SAP Data Archiving,' an **archiving object** is a logical object of business data. It specifies which data is archived in what manner. Describing which database objects need to be handled together (as a single business object), it is read from the database table by a 'write' program and deleted by a 'delete' program after the system has successfully archived the data.

It is also possible that some of the archiving objects may need some 'pre-processing' that just *marks* and *prepares* the data for archiving without deleting the same. The 'write' program reads the data and writes them to archive files without deleting them from the database. If you have configured the system to start the 'delete' program, once the 'write' program completes its job, the system will begin the deleting process. Otherwise, it must be triggered manually. Either way, the 'delete' program deletes the data (in the archive files) from the database. You can specify if the 'delete' program is to write the deleted data to an external storage device. You can also use an optional 'post-processing' program that will start after the 'delete' program has completed its task: the idea is to delete any undeleted data from the database by the 'delete' program. However, this post-processing may not be available for all the archiving objects.

303. What are the common 'Archiving Objects' in SAP S/4HANA Finance?

You can use the Transaction **AOBJ** to view the archiving objects and their details, including the 'write' and 'delete' programs (*Figure 11.39*):

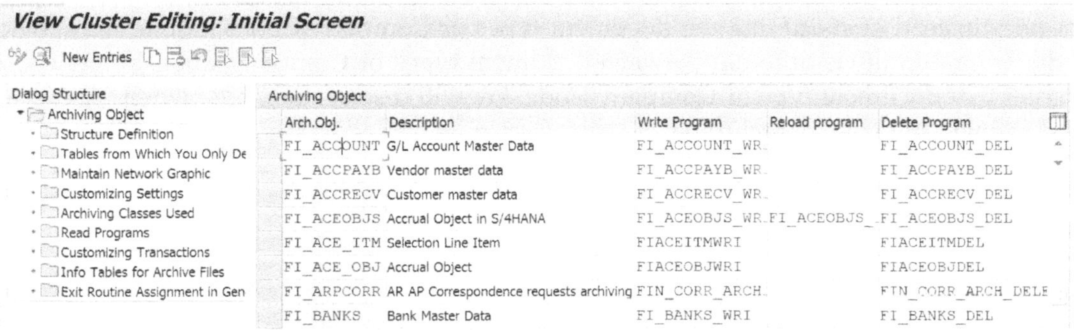

Figure 11.39: SAP Archiving Objects

The following are some of the common archiving objects across various functional components in SAP (*Table 11.6*):

Functional component	Archiving Object	Details
Financial Accounting (FI)	FI_DOCUMENT	Financial Accounting Documents
	FI_ACCOUNT	G/L Account Master Data
	FI_ACCPAYB	Vendor Master Data
	FI_ACCRECV	Customer Master Data
	FI_BANKS	Bank Master Data
	FI_ELBANK	Electronic Bank Details
	FINCS_DOC	Group Journal Entries
Cost Center Accounting	CO_COSTCTR	Cost center data
	CO_ITEM	CO Line items

Table 11.6: Common Archiving Objects in SAP FI

304. Explain 'Account Document Archiving' in SAP.

SAP provides you with the archiving functionality to help you delete and **archive the accounting documents** that you no longer require to be made available online. To proceed with the archiving, you will set the minimum number of days that a document and its secondary index should be alive in the system; only after that time frame will the 'write' program select such documents for archiving. While making the settings for document archiving, you need to configure that for every 'document type' and 'account type'. The system considers the posting date of the document and the key date you mention for archiving to arrive at the reference date for selecting the documents that are to be archived. While proceeding with the parameters for starting the archiving program, you can enter an '*' if the minimum life is the same for several document types or several Company Codes instead of specifying the document types or Company Codes individually. When the minimum life is different between document types or Company Codes, you need to enter that document type or Company Code. We will discuss this more when we explain 'document type life' in archiving.

305. How is 'Account Document Archiving' different from 'Account Master Data Archiving'?

Unlike 'account document archiving,' in the case of 'archiving account master data', first, you need to set the *'Mark for Deletion'* flag for all those master records that you want to delete. Then, SAP uses a special program that archives all such marked master records, subject to the condition that no other dependent data remains in the system. You will be able to use this archiving program only to delete the test data before going 'live'.

306. What is the use of the function 'Data Aging' in SAP FI?

The '**data aging**' function frees up large space from the database to get more working memory. The process moves the data (via the aging object 'FI_DOCUMENT,' the journal entry) from the current area to a historical ('cold') area based on the 'data temperature' (the minimum life of a document mentioned in terms of days or years) that you define in Customizing.

You can define different settings for each of the 'journal (document) type' and 'account type'. You can use the following SAP IMG menu path to Customize the settings relating to journal document/account data aging: *SAP Customizing Implementation Guide | Financial Accounting | Financial Accounting Global Settings | Tools | Data Aging | Data Aging for Accounting Documents*:

- *Define Life for Account Types*
- *Define Life for Document Types*

You can access the data aging function either via the SAP Easy Access Menu: *Accounting | Financial Accounting | General Ledger | Periodic Processing | Data Aging | Posting Documents* or the Transaction *DAGRUN*. When you run the functionality, the system moves the corresponding database tables to the historical area of the database. The system moves the documents that are no longer required for day-to-day operations only after ensuring that the pre-spelt conditions are met.

307. What 'Checks and Conditions' are to be met to apply 'Data Aging'?

Only after the system ensures that the required conditions are met for data aging in SAP FI, it moves the documents to the 'cold area' of the database. Some of the conditions that are to be met are shown in *Table 11.7*:

#	Explanation
	Checks at the 'Header' level
101	No recurring, sample and parking documents are included.
102	The document has been in the system for the minimum number of days specified.
103	The retention time for the document type has exceeded.
	Besides the above, the system also runs some basic checks like 'entry date not initial' (090), 'clearing document with line items' (092) etc.
	Checks for the line items
201	Documents with withholding tax should meet the country-specific retention requirements.
202 (105)	Document should not have any open items.
203	Account type retention time has expired.
204	No payment block set.
	Other basic settings include that the AP/AR items are managed on open-item basis.

Table 11.7: Data Aging- Checks and Conditions

The above list is not exhaustive. The are some more checks and conditions relating to various business objects in FI-G/L, FI-A/P, F-A/R, FI-AA, FI-ML, and CO.

308. What is 'Account Type Life' in Archiving?

By '**account type life**' in archiving, we mean the minimum life (days) of accounts in the system before an archiving program can select those accounts for archiving. While defining the account type life, you will be specifying the 'Company Code,' 'account type,' 'from account,' and 'to account' details along with the 'minimum life' (Life) and 'secondary index life' specifications in days. In the case of vendor/supplier and customer accounts, while specifying the range numbers, you specify the 'from' and 'to' of the associated G/L accounts.

You can enter the details per Company Code if the minimum life specifications are different across Company Codes, or you can just use an '*' in the Company Code field indicating that the minimum life is the same across several Company Codes. This is the same for the account types. However, you need to be aware that the system always uses the most exact specifications for an account. Any specification with an '*' is not termed as 'exact,' and the specification decreases with the length of the G/L account interval.

Consider a situation like the one in the following *Table 11.8*, wherein neither of the specifications is termed 'exact.' In such a situation, the system considers the entry with the maximum number of days (120, in the example shown below) under 'minimum life' for proceeding with archiving. However, the system also considers the shortest relevant G/L account interval for the 'Company Code – account type' combination. If no specification exists in the system, a minimum life of 9,999 days is considered by default.

Company Code	Account Type	Minimum Life
*	D	120
A101	*	100

Table 11.8: Document Type Life - Minimum Life Specifications: An Illustration

Figure 11.40

Besides the account life, you may also define the (secondary) index life (which will be discussed later).

309. Explain 'Document Type Life' in Archiving in SAP.

As in the case of account type life, you need to specify the '**document type life**,' which is the minimum period; in days, the documents should be available online in the system before they can be deleted and archived using the document archival programs. Here also, you will make the specifications for a combination of 'Company Code' and 'document type': you can enter an '*' if you want to have the same document type life across multiple Company Codes or several document types, or you can also specify the entries with the specific Company Code or document type (*Table 11.9*). Similar to account type life, the system looks for the most specific entry; an entry with an '*' is not considered specific enough. If the system does not come across a specific entry, then it goes with the specification containing the maximum document type life for the combination of 'Company Code – document type.' If the system does not find any entry or combination, then the default document type life of 9,999 days will be considered.

Company Code	Document Type	Minimum Life
*	SA	120
A101	*	90

Table 11.9: Document Type Life - Minimum Life Specifications: An Illustration

Figure 11.41

Besides the Company Code, document type, and minimum life specifications, you also need to maintain the settings for the indicator '*FBRA Check.*' When you select this checkbox (*Figure 11.42*), the system examines, during the execution of Transactions FBRA and FCH8, if the document is included in the current archiving run: if this is not true, then the system allows resetting of cleared items. Otherwise, when the checkbox is not selected and when the document archiving life has already been reached, the system does not allow resetting the already cleared items.

Change View "Document Archiving: Document Life": Overview

New Entries | Variable list | Archive test

Document Archiving: Document Life

Company Code	Doc. Type	Document Life	FBRA Check	
*	SA	120	✓	
A101	*	90	☐	

Figure 11.42: *Document Type Life in Archiving*

310. What do you mean by 'Secondary Index Life' in Archiving in SAP?

Besides specifying the 'account type life' and 'document type life,' you may also specify the **'secondary index life'** while maintaining the settings for archiving in SAP S/4HANA Finance. The system makes use of the secondary index (containing the information on G/L, vendor, and customer accounts) to display the line items besides double-entry invoice verification.

The system considers the secondary index life to decide for how long such an index for documents that have been selected for archiving, based on the document posting date and secondary index removal key date, should remain in the system after the documents have been archived. If the secondary index life is more than the 'account type life' / 'document type life', then the system deletes the account/document from the database but keeps the secondary index alive in the system.

311. What is an 'Archive Index' in SAP S/4HANA Finance?

When you archive the accounting documents, the system creates an '**archive index**' (like a "library catalog"), enabling you to search and locate the archived documents quickly. It is like a map that contains details like archive objects, their location, etc. SAP provides you with a generic tool called **Archiving Information System** (**AS**) that is used in indexing data archives. 'AS' is fully integrated with the 'SAP Data Archiving' environment. The archiving indexes that are created using 'AS' are known as *'Archive Information Structures'* and are used to retrieve archived documents for display.

312. Explain 'Document Archiving' in SAP with an example.

Let us look at the following example to understand how account document archiving works in SAP (*Table 11.10*):

Parameters	Value	Remarks
Company Code	A101	
Document Type	DR	
Account Type	D	
Account Type Life (days)	90	
Document Type Life (days)	60	
Secondary Index Life (days)	300	
Invoice date	10-APR-23	
Clearing Date	30-APR-23	
Archiving key date1	20-JUL-23	Archiving not successful
Archiving key date1	20-AUG-23	Archiving successful

Table 11.10: Document Archiving Parameters (Example)

Consider that you have the above details for document/account archiving in your SAP S/4HANA system. Assuming that there was a document with an invoice date of 10/Apr/2023, which was cleared on 30/Apr/2023, the system will take the clearing date in association with the archiving key date (20/Jul/2023) to determine if the 'document type life' or 'account type life' has exceeded the number days set for them. Considering the archiving key date of 20/Jul/2023, the system would not archive this document because the account type life of 90 days had not exceeded the clearing date of 30/Apr/2023. However, instead of 20/Jul/2023, had the archiving key date been 20/Aug/2023, then the system would have archived the document as the account type life of 90 days had already been exceeded. Even after archiving, the system would keep some sections of the document in the secondary index until 300 days from the clearing date (30/Apr/2023).

313. How can you 'Display an Archived Document'?

You can **display archived accounting documents** individually, either via 'AS' or the general 'display document' or 'display line items' functions from different application areas like G/L, A/R, A/P, etc. You can display an archived accounting document only when you have the appropriate archive index for the same. For example, the system makes use of 'AS' to index FI_DOCUMNT archives in the following ways:

- To display archived documents via 'AS' (Transaction Code **FB03**), you need to have the 'archive information structures' (archive indexes) created in the system with any one of the standard SAP field catalogs, such as FI document by header (SAP_FI_DOC_001) or FI document by account (SAP_FI_DOC_002).

- To display an archived accounting document using the Transaction **FB03L** (G/L view), you would need the archiving index created with the standard field catalog SAP_FI_DOC_003.

- If you want to display the line items from archived accounts, make sure that the 'secondary index life' is set to more than the 'account type life'. The system allows you to view the line items from the database even when the associated accounting documents have been archived and the corresponding secondary indexes deleted from the system.

314. Explain 'AS' in SAP S/4HANA Finance.

The **AS** is a generic tool with which you can create indexes on archived objects like accounting documents. As already mentioned, you can use 'AS' to display archived data. The components in 'AS' include the **Archive Retrieval Configurator** (**ARC**) and *Archive Explorer*.

Figure 11.43

Via **ARC,** you will be able to generate the 'archive information structures' (archive indexes) using the field catalogs. Once generated, the archive information structures will be the basis for reporting archived information. While generating the archive information structures, you can decide if you want to store the archive indexes on SAP's standard database system or on Sybase IQ (secondary database). If you store the archived indexes on a secondary database system, retrieving archived data will be much faster as it takes some stress off SAP's standard database.

The **Archive Explorer** helps provide quick access to archived data. Through the archive information structures stored in transparent tables by ARC, the archive explorer enables faster searching of archived data and allows access to individual data objects in archives for display in technical/application-specific views.

CHAPTER 12

FI Global Settings: Tax on Sales/Purchase

Introduction

This chapter on FI global settings discusses the concept and configuration of tax on sales/ purchases. You will learn about different taxes supported in SAP S/4HANA Finance and how taxes are calculated in SAP, including calculation via an external tax calculation system.

315. What are all the taxes supported in SAP S/4HANA Finance?

SAP S/4HANA Finance supports several taxes, calculations, and reporting, including the following:

- Tax on Sales/Purchases
- Withholding Tax (Extended Withholding Tax)

316. What is Tax on Sales/Purchases?

The '**tax on sales & purchases**' (*sales & use tax*) is levied on goods and services based on VAT (*Value Added Tax*) principles. The tax on sales & purchases includes input tax, output tax, additional tax, and acquisition tax. The calculation and reporting of this tax are supported by SAP's FI-G/L, FI-A/P, and FI-A/R application components.

317. What is 'Sales Tax'? Differentiate that from 'Use Tax.'

Levied on the sale of goods and services, you as the customer (or buyer of goods/services) bear the **'sales tax.'** The seller (vendor) of goods or the service provider collects the sales tax at the time of sales and remits the same to the tax authorities.

Unlike sales tax, the **'use tax'** is imposed on the purchaser. That is, the customer or the purchaser is liable to pay the tax and not the vendor or service provider. The buyer of the goods and services pays this tax to the local tax authority wherein the goods/services are consumed.

In general, a transaction is subject to either of the taxes: sales tax or use tax, not both.

318. Explain how 'Input Tax' differs from 'Output Tax'.

Charged by the vendor, the **'input tax'** is calculated on the invoice amount (net of discounts). In contrast, the **'output tax'** is charged to the customer and is calculated on the net price of the products/services. You can always offset input and output taxes and pay only the balance to your tax authorities.

319. What is 'Additional Tax'?

The 'additional tax' is calculated over and above the tax on sales and purchases in a particular country. It may be in the form of clearing tax, investment tax, luxury taxes, environmental taxes, etc., or it may even represent the tax postings under the postponed accounting system (BENELUX countries).

320. What is 'Acquisition Tax'?

A type of VAT, the **'acquisition tax,'** is levied on moving goods and services across the border within the European Union. The receiving party applies it at the local VAT rate. However, this can also be posted as input tax. Though it varies across the EU, it corresponds to the standard domestic VAT rate of a particular country.

321. What is 'Withholding Tax'?

You, as a receiver of services, withhold a portion of the invoice amount from the vendor (service provider or employee) and remit that withheld tax collected to the tax authorities. The balance tax will be paid directly by the vendor to the tax authority. In the employer-employee relationship, this is often termed as (income) **'tax deducted at source'** (**TDS**). SAP, with the introduction of **Extended Withholding Tax** (**EWT**), has moved from the erstwhile classic withholding tax and offers a migration path to EWT.

322. At what levels can you handle taxation in SAP?

SAP's versatile tax-handling capabilities reflect the complexity of global taxation systems. With SAP, you can handle taxation at various levels as indicated as under:

- At the national (or federal) level, SAP can manage broad tax regulations that apply to entire countries, such as VAT in Europe or GST in Australia.
- For countries like the USA, SAP can handle taxes at the regional or jurisdiction level, accommodating state-specific tax laws.
- In nations where national and regional taxes apply, such as India, Canada, and Brazil, SAP manages the intricate interplay between different tax layers, ensuring compliance and accuracy in tax reporting.

323. What are the three major Customizing settings for Tax on Sales/Purchases?

SAP has grouped all the Customizing settings relating to tax on sales/purchases into:

- Basic settings
- Calculation
- Posting

324. List out the major 'Customizing Tasks in Basic Settings.'

The global settings you make in the system for tax on sales/purchases are grouped under **'basic settings.'** The important ones are as follows:

- Check Calculation Procedure (**OBYZ**)
- Assign Country/Region to Calculation Procedure (**OBBG**)
- Check and Change Settings for Tax Processing (**OBCN**)
- Specify Structure for Tax Jurisdiction Code (**OBCO**)
- Define Tax Jurisdictions (**OBCP**)
- Change Message Control for Taxes (**OBA5**)

- Change Field Control for Tax Base Amount
- Switch Off Tax Translation between Local and Document Currency
- Define and Check the Tax Reporting Date
- External Tax Calculation

(Transaction Code is shown in brackets for each of the Customizing tasks)

325. What is 'External Tax Calculation'?

Besides using SAP's country-specific tax calculation procedures to calculate/post the tax on sales & purchases, SAP also provides you with the option of using some external systems (Vertex, Taxware, OneSource, etc.) for tax calculation. So, by using the external tax calculation system, you can determine the tax jurisdiction code from the customer/vendor/Cost Center/Plant master records, calculate tax for FI – G/L, A/R, and A/P: document entry, orders & invoicing in SAP SD & SAP MM, and update external tax calculation system.

326. List the Customizing tasks for 'External Tax Calculation.'

There are various Customizing activities that you need to complete before interfacing with an external system for tax calculation, like:

- Define Number Ranges for External Tax Returns (**OBETX**)
- Define Physical Destination (**SM59**)
- Define Logical Destination
- Activate External Tax Calculation
- Activate External Updating
- Develop Enhancements for External Tax Calculation (**CMOD**
- Transfer Tax for Cross-Company Code Transactions)
- Define Connection with External Tax System

(Transaction Code is shown in brackets for each of the Customizing tasks)

327. What are the important Customizing tasks under 'Calculation' in SAP IMG?

The following are the major Customizing tasks that you need to complete for tax calculation on sales & purchases in SAP S/4HANA Finance:

- Define Tax Codes for Sales and Purchases (**FTXP**)
- Assign Company Code to Document Date for Tax Determination (**OBCK**)
- Specify Base Amount (**OB69**)
- Change Foreign Currency Translation (**OBC8**)
- Determine Exchange Rate for Tax Items
- Tax Codes for Tax-Exempt Sales

(Transaction Code is shown in brackets for each of the Customizing tasks)

328. What are SAP IMG settings for 'Posting' Tax on Sales/Purchases?

You will make the following Customizing settings for the successful posting of tax calculated in the system:

- Define Tax Accounts (**OB40**)
- Assign Country/Region and Tax Code to G/L Accounts
- Define Account for Exchange Rate Difference Posting (**OBYY**)
- Assign Tax Codes for Non-Taxable Transactions (**OBCL**)
- Transfer Tax for Cross-Company Code Transactions

(Transaction Code is shown in brackets for each of the Customizing tasks)

329. Outline how Tax on Sales & Purchases is handled in SAP.

SAP uses *condition methods* via a *tax calculation procedure* together with *tax codes* and *jurisdictions* to calculate the tax on sales & purchases. The tax procedure is also called the 'tax calculation procedure' or simply the 'calculation procedure'. You will get to know that these terms are used interchangeably. The whole process involves:

- Definition of tax rate per tax code. Each tax code is associated with a tax type (output or input tax) in the tax procedure.

- Definition of country-specific tax procedures. The system uses such a tax procedure to calculate the tax via the tax codes. The tax procedure iterates the condition records and the access sequences for the tax calculation. You can also assign a tax calculation procedure to a country using the Transaction Code **OY01**.

- Assignment of tax procedure in the appropriate G/L accounts helps post the tax to the relevant G/L accounts.

- Once calculated, the system posts the tax to the respective G/L accounts. The exchange rate differences, if any, due to tax adjustments will also be handled.

330. How the Tax is calculated in SAP?

In SAP, the 'Condition Method' (*Figure 12.1*) is utilized for all tax calculations (except for withholding tax calculation), applying 'Tax (Calculation) Procedures' predefined within the system. These procedures are designed to work with Tax Codes, ensuring accurate tax amounts are determined for transactions.

Change View "Conditions: Condition Types": Details

New Entries

Condition Type	MWVI Input Tax Round.up	Access Sequence	MWST Tax Classification
			Records for Access

Control Data 1

Condition Class	D Taxes	Plus/Minus	positive and negative
Calculation Type	A Percentage		
Condition Category	D Tax		
Rounding Rule	A Round up		
Structure Condition	None		

Group Condition

Group Condition		Group Cond. Routine	
RoundDiffComp			

Changes which can be made

Manual Entries	No limitations	Amount/Percent	
Header Condition		Quantity Relation	
Item Condition	✓	Value	
Delete			

Master Data

Proposed Valid From	Today's date	Pricing Procedure	
Proposed Valid To	31.12.9999	Delete from DB	Do not delete (set the deletion flag only)
Ref. Condition Type		Condition Index	
Ref. Application			

Scales

Scale Base Type		Scale Routine	
Check Scale	None	Scale Unit	
Scale Type	can be maintained in condition record		

Control Data 2

Currency Conversion		Exclusion	
		Pricing Date	Standard (KOMK-PRSDT; tax and rebate KOM
Accruals			
Used for Var.Config.		Rel. for Acct Assigt	Relevant for account assignment
Invoice List Cond.			
Quantity Conversion			
Intercomp.Billing			

Text Determination

TextDetermProcedure		Text ID	

Figure 12.1: *Condition type (tax processing)*

The **tax codes** are the starting point for tax calculations in SAP. Being country-specific, they are tailored to each country's unique tax laws, ensuring compliance in financial transactions. The tax code determines not only the type of tax and the amount but also the correct G/L account for posting. Additionally, it calculates any supplementary tax amounts that may be applicable.

Each tax code corresponds to a specific Tax Rate, which is then linked to various 'tax types' within the tax procedures. This system allows for a single tax code to potentially have multiple rates, depending on the tax type it is associated with. These tax codes are assigned to a tax procedure associated with a G/L account master record, triggering the correct tax calculation whenever a transaction involving that G/L account occurs.

A **Tax (Calculation) Procedure** (*Figure 12.2*) includes the steps that define the 'sequence of operations', 'condition types' that specify the tax calculation model (such as fixed amounts or percentages and whether these can be automated), and 'reference steps' to determine the source of values used in calculations (like the base amount).

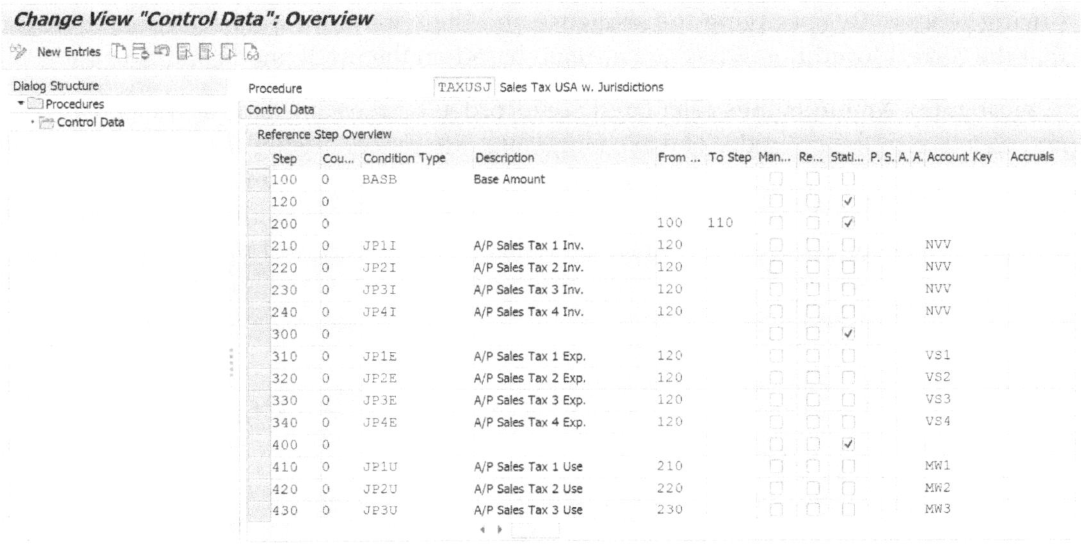
Change View "Control Data": Overview

New Entries

Dialog Structure
- Procedures
  - Control Data

Procedure TAXUSJ Sales Tax USA w. Jurisdictions

Control Data

Reference Step Overview

Step	Cou...	Condition Type	Description	From ...	To Step	Man...	Re...	Statl...	P.	S.	A.	A.	Account Key	Accruals
100	0	BASB	Base Amount			☐	☐	☐						
120	0					☐	☐	☑						
200	0			100	110	☐	☐	☑						
210	0	JP1I	A/P Sales Tax 1 Inv.	120		☐	☐	☐					NVV	
220	0	JP2I	A/P Sales Tax 2 Inv.	120		☐	☐	☐					NVV	
230	0	JP3I	A/P Sales Tax 3 Inv.	120		☐	☐	☐					NVV	
240	0	JP4I	A/P Sales Tax 4 Inv.	120		☐	☐	☐					NVV	
300	0					☐	☐	☑						
310	0	JP1E	A/P Sales Tax 1 Exp.	120		☐	☐	☐					VS1	
320	0	JP2E	A/P Sales Tax 2 Exp.	120		☐	☐	☐					VS2	
330	0	JP3E	A/P Sales Tax 3 Exp.	120		☐	☐	☐					VS3	
340	0	JP4E	A/P Sales Tax 4 Exp.	120		☐	☐	☐					VS4	
400	0					☐	☐	☑						
410	0	JP1U	A/P Sales Tax 1 Use	210		☐	☐	☐					MW1	
420	0	JP2U	A/P Sales Tax 2 Use	220		☐	☐	☐					MW2	
430	0	JP3U	A/P Sales Tax 3 Use	230		☐	☐	☐					MW3	

***Figure 12.2**: Tax procedure: Control data*

The **Account/Process Keys** (*Figure 12.3*) are crucial in linking tax procedures with G/L accounts for seamless tax data posting. This integration is vital for automating tax account assignments. To ensure these keys are equipped for automatic assignments, it's essential to define the default 'posting keys' for debit and credit (typically 40 and 50, respectively), establish 'rules for account determination' based on specific fields such as tax code or country key, and designate the appropriate 'tax accounts' for postings. Since the standard SAP system comes with various pre-defined account/process keys, it is recommended that they be used without making any modifications.

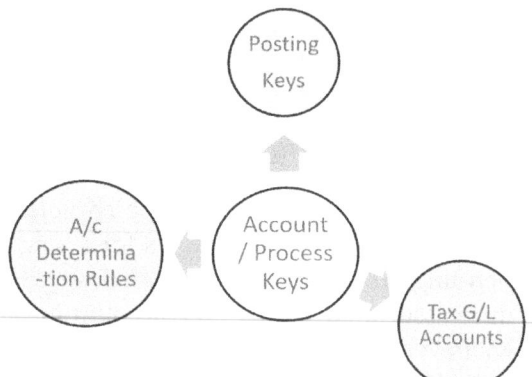

Figure 12.3: *Account / Process key for tax processing*

The **Access Sequence** is a critical component in determining the correct order in which 'Condition Tables' (nothing but a group of 'condition types') are accessed during the pricing process. By specifying the sequence and the criteria for data selection, it ensures that the correct 'condition types' are applied based on the predefined conditions.

Typically, **Tax Amounts** thus calculated are recorded on the same side as the G/L account associated with the tax code. The exchange rate differences arising from tax adjustments in foreign currencies are posted to specially designated accounts for exchange rate differences. However, you have the flexibility to define, at the Company Code level, how exchange rates for tax-related items are handled, whether entered manually or based on the posting or document date, with any resulting differences being allocated to a specific account designed for this purpose.

331. Explain the Configurations required for Taxes in SAP.

You need to define the following in the Customizing for calculating taxes in SAP:

- **Base Amount:** For each Company Code, define whether the *Base Amount* for tax calculation includes the cash discount. If the tax calculation base amount includes the cash discount, then the tax base is termed 'Gross'; otherwise, it is '*Net*.' You may also want to define a similar base amount for arriving at the 'cash discount.' Here, you will also define the settings per Company Code.

- **Tax Codes:** You use the 2-digit *Tax Code* to specify the percentage of tax to be applied to the base amount for tax calculation. During the definition of a tax code, you also need to maintain the '*Tax Type*' associated with the tax code to classify that either as '*Input Tax*' or '*Output Tax*.' Being country-specific, the tax types help determine how a tax is calculated and posted.

- **Tax Rate:** *Tax Rate* is the percentage of tax applied on a base amount to arrive at the tax amount. You can define tax rates for one or more types in a single tax code.

- **Check Indicators:** When configured, the *Check Indicators* enable the system to issue Error/Warning Messages if the manually entered tax amount differs from the tax amount calculated automatically by the system using a tax code.

332. What is a (Tax) 'Jurisdiction Code'?

In the United States, a **tax jurisdiction code** is a unique identifier that combines various codes representing different levels of tax authorities, from the state down to the city or district. This system allows for the precise allocation of tax revenues to the appropriate governing bodies. For instance, a typical tax jurisdiction code might include four levels representing the state, county, city, and district (sub-city), ensuring that each transaction's taxes are distributed correctly.

A systematic setup is essential to utilize jurisdiction codes effectively for tax calculations. First and foremost, you need to set up an 'Access Sequence,' which includes the country, tax code, and jurisdiction fields. This sequence is a roadmap for the system to determine the correct tax rates based on the criteria. Then you need to establish the 'Condition Types' which reference the 'Access Sequence' and dictate the tax calculation logic. Finally, you need to define the 'Jurisdiction Codes' themselves in the system, which, with their unique identifiers, the system can apply the correct tax rates to transactions based on geographical boundaries.

You define the tax rates in the tax code per jurisdiction. However, the system may process the tax calculation per jurisdiction code or tax level. If the calculation procedure contains an entry for jurisdiction code, then the system automatically uses the tax jurisdiction code method of processing the tax via the calculation procedure. In this case, you can specify if taxes should be calculated at the line item level or cumulated at the 'tax code/ tax jurisdiction code' level.

333. What if the 'Jurisdiction Code Structure' is not 2/3/4/1 in External Tax Calculation?

Supposing that you are using 'Vertex' as your external tax calculation system, you find that the jurisdiction code structure defined in the system (*Figure 12.4*) does not conform to '2/3/4/1'. In this case, you need to change the jurisdiction structure configuration.

Change View "Jurisdiction Code Structure": Overview

New Entries 🗋 🖶 ↩ 🖺 🖺 🖟 🖟

Schema	Name	Lg	Lg	Lg	Lg	Tx In
OTXUSX	External US Tax Jurisdiction Code	2	3	4	1	✓
TAXBRA	Brazil: External Tax (CBT)	3	7			✓
TAXBRJ	Brazil: External tax calculation	3	7			✓
TAXCAJ	Canadian Sales Tax, with Jurisdiction	2	2			☐
TAXUSJ	Standard US Tax Jurisdiction Code	2	2	5	1	✓
TAXUSX	VERTEX Standard Jurisdiction Code	2	3	4	1	☐

Figure 12.4: *Jurisdiction Code Structure*

Use Transaction Code **OBCO** or **V_TTXD**. However, before performing the configuration changes, you must first verify the tax jurisdiction code structure with your external system provider (say, 'Vertex'). Then, proceed to make the required changes. You also need to bear in mind that you cannot make any changes to this configuration if you are using an internal tax calculation solution for the US and you have any US tax postings in your 'P' system because any changes you make in your 'Q' system are automatically transported to 'P' because the system will trigger a veto block for such a transport.

> **Note: For the external tax calculation solution 'Taxware', the tax jurisdiction structure needs to be set to '2/5/2/0'. And, for ONESOURCE ('Sabarix') this will be '2/2/5/5'**

334. How does the system calculate tax on sales/purchases in External Tax Calculation?

We have already seen that you can use external tax calculation solutions like Vertex, Taxware, etc., to automatically calculate your company's tax. In this case, the external tax solution, via its interfaces with the SAP S/4HANA Finance system, determines the tax jurisdiction codes, applies the relevant tax rates, calculates the tax, and returns the tax information to the SAP system for appropriate posting to the relevant G/L accounts. To make use of the automatic calculation using an external tax solution, you need to complete the Customizing tasks that we have discussed previously. You must use the standard tax calculation procedure (external) '0TXUSX' and the standard SD pricing procedure 'RVAXUS.'

During the tax calculation process in **SAP FI and SAP MM**, the system computes the sales or purchase tax for each line item of the PO (purchase order) or invoice. Since the system needs to know where (=geographic location) the tax is to be charged, you must specify a 'ship-to' location as the tax jurisdiction code. Now, the system calculates the tax as outlined under:

1. The SAP system looks at retrieving the 'ship-to' tax jurisdiction code from the master record of the plant, cost center, asset, internal order, or project (WBS):

   a. If no such jurisdiction code exists (on the asset, order, or project), the system defaults the jurisdiction code associated with the cost center of the asset, order, or project into the purchase order or invoice verification document at the time of document creation and treats that jurisdiction code as the 'ship-to' destination.

   b. Since you can influence taxation by 'ship-from' destination, in addition to the 'ship-to' destination, the system may also use the jurisdiction code that you have maintained in the vendor master as the 'ship-from' tax destination.

2. The SAP system automatically retrieves the jurisdiction codes from the external tax solution (say, 'Vertex') whenever you create or change the address information in the master records associated with the plant, cost center, or supplier/vendor. It is possible that you can list all the valid jurisdiction codes from the external system just by placing the cursor on the jurisdiction code field of an asset, project, or internal order and hitting the function key *F4*.

3. The MM and FI modules of SAP utilize 'country' and 'tax code' data to access tax condition records effectively. The tax calculation procedure '0TXUSX' is integral to this process, incorporating condition formulas such as 300 - 306 and 311 - 316, which trigger the interface with the tax calculation system.

4. When the SAP system invokes the tax interface, it populates the communication structure with the necessary data required by your external tax solution to calculate taxes.

5. The SAP system's integration with the external tax solution results in transferring the communication data structures via **Remote Function Call** (**RFC**) to the tax solution's API. This external tax package processes the data through its tax calculation engine and returns the calculated tax details to the SAP system through the API.

6. The external tax package's (say, 'Vertex') API then passes this tax information, thus calculated, back to SAP's MM and FI application components.

In **SAP SD**, the tax calculation (amount of tax on each line item within a sales document) considers various parameters to determine the correct tax amounts and rates for sales orders and invoices. The system takes into account parameters like 'delivery Country' (origin) that signifies the tax authority and regulations that apply to the transaction in terms of tax laws and rates specific to that country, 'tax class of the "ship-to" partner' as a tax class could differentiate between exempt or taxable partners, 'tax class of the material' being shipped as certain materials might be exempt from specific taxes, 'date of tax calculation', the 'jurisdiction code' from 'ship-to-party' (Customer) and 'ship-from address' (Plant) as the tax rates can vary by jurisdiction and the 'point-of-order acceptance' and 'point-of-order origin' which define the location where the order is accepted and originated from. During the tax calculation, the steps are as follows:

1. As in the case of tax calculation in SAP FI and SAP MM, here in SAP SD, the system also retrieves the jurisdiction codes from the external tax solution during the creation/change of address information in the master records (of plant or customer). The system considers the 'ship-from' jurisdiction (of the plant) as the "point-of-order acceptance" and the 'ship-to' jurisdiction (of the customer) as the "point-of-order origin" as defaults.

2. The system then utilizes the 'country,' 'customer tax indicator, and 'material tax indicator' to accurately read the tax condition records. When a sales order is processed, during pricing execution, if the system encounters the specific condition type 1 ('UTXJ'), it exits the standard (=normal) pricing procedure. It then retrieves the relevant tax condition records using the 'country' and 'tax code' from the pricing condition record, ensuring that the correct tax amount is applied.

3. The tax procedure '0TXUSX' together with the SD pricing procedure 'RVAXUS' (with condition formulas such as 300-306 and 500, 510, 301-306) triggers the tax interface with an external tax system (say, Vertex).

4. As stated earlier, as soon as the tax interface system is invoked, the system fills a communication structure with header and item data required by the external tax package solution (say, 'Vertex') to calculate taxes. The system passes this communication structure to the external tax solution's API via an RFC.

5. Now, the external tax solution's API passes this data on to its tax calculation engine, which calculates the appropriate tax and returns it to the external solution's (say, 'Vertex') API for onward transmission to SAP's tax interface system.

6. The SAP system then applies these tax amounts and rates to the SD document for item pricing at the jurisdiction level via the condition types (XR1 - XR6).

335. Tell me about the 'Tax Reports' in SAP.

Incorporating SAP's default **tax reports** can streamline compliance with country-specific tax regulations. While third-party software is an option for tax reporting, completing closing operations within SAP before generating tax reports is crucial. This step is vital as it allows the system to make necessary adjustments (such as reconciling payables and receivables and accounting for exchange rate variations), which contributes to the accuracy of the reported tax amounts.

FI Global Settings: Withholding Tax

Introduction

In this chapter, we discuss the FI global settings relating to withholding tax. From the discussions, you will learn all about withholding tax, including the framework, the country-specific requirements, the difference between classic and **extended withholding tax** (**EWT**), the configuration settings required for using EWT, and the procedure that you need to follow if you want to change from classic withholding tax to EWT.

336. Explain the framework of 'Withholding Tax' in SAP.

Levied in countries like the UK, USA, India, Argentina, Brazil, etc., **withholding tax** is a type of tax that is deducted at source by the customer, from the vendor/supplier, for the goods and services provided by the vendor/supplier to the customer (*Figure 13.1*). The vendor/supplier is the one who is liable to pay the tax. However, the local tax authorities in these countries stipulate that the customer withholds (deducts) the tax on behalf of the vendor/supplier and remits the same to the tax authorities. It is also possible that the customer is expected to deduct or withhold only a portion of the tax, with the remaining paid by the vendor/supplier himself. For example, if the total tax payable by the vendor/supplier is USD 1,000, the customer may be asked to withhold only 20% (USD 200) as withholding tax. The vendor/supplier then pays the rest of the tax as in the normal course of business. If there is an overpayment of tax, including the total amount paid by the customer as withholding tax, then the vendor/supplier gets that as a 'refund' from the tax administrators.

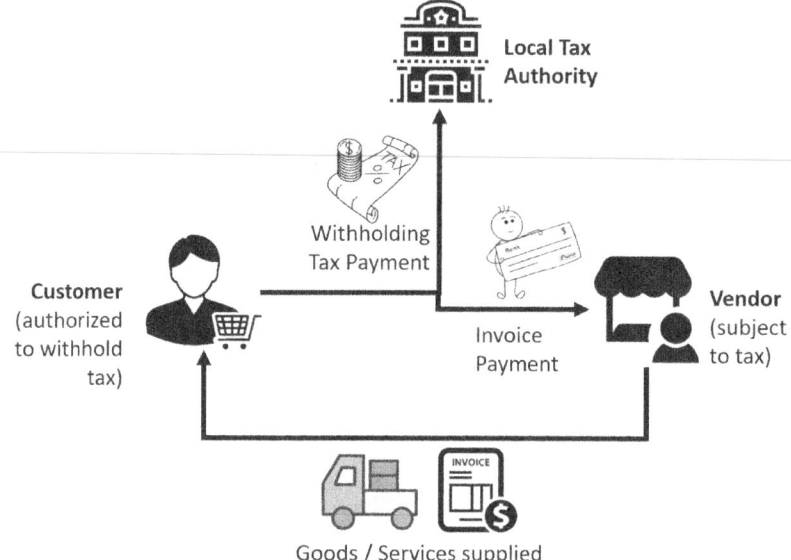

Figure 13.1: *Withholding tax framework*

However, there is another form of this tax known as **'self-withholding tax'**: here, the vendor/supplier himself deducts the tax and pays the same to the tax authorities.

The withholding tax is called differently in different countries: while it is called as such in countries like the USA, it is termed as 'income tax' in India, and the portion of the tax that is withheld by the customer is known as **tax deducted at source (TDS)**. In the USA, the invoice recipients (Company Code as a customer) are required to collect withholding tax on behalf of vendors like self-employed persons or foreign nationals who are non-residents working in the US. The withholding tax so collected is remitted periodically to the **Inland Revenue Service (IRS)**, and the relevant statements are sent to the respective vendors and IRS once a year, using the pre-printed forms including 1099-G, 1099-MISC, 1099-K, 1099-INT, and 1042-S.

In India, the self-withholding tax is known as the 'self-assessment tax.' In Columbia, withholding tax includes income tax, industry and commerce tax (levied by municipal governments), and VAT. Here, normally, a portion of VAT is withheld as withholding tax; however, if payment is made to non-resident individuals or companies, the Columbian tax authorities authorize deducting the entire VAT as withholding tax.

337. What are the two withholding tax options that are provided in SAP?

SAP provides you with two options under withholding tax type depending upon the ERP solution that you have deployed for your Company:

- Withholding tax (also known as '*classic withholding tax*')
- **Extended withholding tax (EWT)**

Released before the SAP R/3 4.0 version, the '**classic withholding tax,**' or simply the 'withholding tax,' was limited in functionality. It was mainly used to withhold tax per line item of vendor's invoice and support tax payment during calculation. It only supported the A/P viewpoint of withholding tax calculation as a solution.

For each Company Code, you may decide if you want to use classic or extended withholding tax. As EWT comes with more extended functionalities than the classic version, it is always recommended that you go to EWT. For example, if you are in the US and are required to report withholding tax both at the state and federal levels, then you have to only use EWT.

338. Explain 'Extended Withholding Tax.'

Unlike classic withholding tax that can process withholding tax only from vendor (A/P) view, in '**extended withholding tax**' (**EWT**), you can process withholding tax both from customer and vendor views:

- In the **A/P view**, your vendor is subject to withholding tax, and you, as the company, are liable to withhold tax and pay the same to the tax authorities.
- In **A/R**'s **view**, your company is subject to withholding tax as a vendor, and your customers have the mandate to withhold tax while making payments to you on the invoices that you raise on them. Then, your customers pay the tax withheld from you (=vendor) to the tax authorities. So, whether it is an A/P or A/R view, your business partners have the authorization to withhold tax on your behalf.

EWT allows to withhold tax both at the time of payment (including partial payments) and at invoicing:

- Normally, withholding tax is calculated when you post a payment in the system; by this, your outgoing payment in A/P or incoming payment in A/R is suitably reduced from the invoice, and the balance is paid to the vendor and customer, respectively.
- In countries like Brazil, Spain, and the Philippines, the withholding tax is stipulated to be posted during invoice posting. This means you effectively reduce the payable (A/P) or receivable (A/R) to the extent of the withholding tax calculated in the system.

- In general, you withhold the tax and reduce that tax amount from the invoice amount before making payment to the vendor. However, in countries like Italy and Argentina, the law requires that you do not reduce the invoice amount by withholding tax but post the calculated withholding tax as an offsetting expense amount.

Also, EWT allows for multiple withholding types to be levied on a single transaction, besides allowing for the accumulation of the withholding tax. So, when resetting cleared items, the system automatically reverses the clearing document if it contains any withholding tax; because of this, for all withholding tax types with accumulation, the system then adjusts the accumulated amount when the payment is reversed.

339. Is there a country-specific requirement that you use only EWT?

Yes, several countries legally require only EWT: the USA, Argentina, Brazil, Colombia, Mexico, Peru, Venezuela, EU countries, Africa, the UK, Slovakia, Turkey, India, Philippines, South Korea, and Thailand.

340. Compare 'Withholding Tax' with 'Extended Withholding Tax'.

The following table summarizes the functions covered under both the classic **withholding tax (WT)** and EWT:

Function		EWT	WT
Withholding tax on outgoing payment		✔	✔
Withholding tax on incoming payment		✔	
Withholding tax posting at time of payment		✔	✔
Withholding tax posting at time of invoice		✔	
Withholding tax posting at time of partial payment		✔	
No. of withholding tax type for each line item of document		>1	1
Withholding tax base	Net amount	✔	✔
	Modified net amount	✔	
	Gross amount	✔	✔
	Tax amount	✔	
	Modified tax amount	✔	

Function	EWT	WT
Rounding rule	✔	
Cash discount considered	✔	
Accumulation	✔	
Min. / Max. amounts and exemption limits	✔	
Certificate numbering	✔	
Calculation formulas	✔	✔

Table 13.1: *Extended withholding tax vs withholding tax: Salient functions*

341. List out the major configuration groups for setting up EWT.

The following are major configuration groups that you need to complete for setting up EWT implementation for each of your Company Codes:

- Basic settings
- Calculation
- Company Code
- Posting
- Reports

342. Enumerate the most important Customizing activities for EWT.

The most important IMG settings across the five groups of Customizing activities include:

- **Checking withholding tax countries/regions**: Carry out this task if you need to define or change the withholding tax country / region ID in the system. Even if you do not need to define your IDs, check this out to ensure that the IDs in the standard system correspond to the legal requirements for the country / region.

- **Defining withholding tax keys**: Here, you define withholding tax keys for classifying withholding tax items. You can use SAP-delivered country-specific withholding tax keys as such or modify or create your keys to meet the reporting requirements of a country / region.

- **Defining withholding tax types for payment posting/invoice posting**: Complete these settings if you want the system to calculate and post withholding tax while posting payments or invoices. The settings you define here control the various calculation options for EWT.

- **Defining exchange rate type for withholding tax type**: Set up the required currency exchange in the system so that the system can use this rate (of payment) for translating withholding tax from foreign currency to local currency,

- **Defining withholding tax codes**: Maintain the tax rate (in percentage), including withholding tax exemptions, to meet the country's legal withholding tax requirements.

- **Defining formulas for calculating withholding tax**: Configure the withholding tax base amount, withholding tax rate, and the related parameters, per formula header, that the system requires to calculate withholding tax. Once defined, a formula consists of the currency key, the withholding tax type, the withholding tax code, the country/region key for withholding tax, and the validity date.

- **Defining min/max amounts for withholding tax types**: Maintain the minimum/maximum amount for withholding tax and withholding tax base, per withholding tax type or withholding tax code, to calculate withholding tax.

- **Assigning withholding tax types to company codes**: Once you have defined the required withholding tax types, use this Customizing step to assign withholding tax types with each of the Company Codes.

- **Activating extended withholding tax**: Make the settings for activating EWT in your system after migrating master and transaction data from classic withholding tax. Once you have activated EWT, you cannot revert to classic withholding tax.

- **Determining accounts for withholding tax**: Maintain the tax G/L accounts that you want the system to post the withholding tax transactions.

- **Certificate numbering for withholding tax**: Set the appropriate settings for numbering withholding tax certificates. SAP offers four 'certificate numbering concept options'.

343. Explain, in detail, the process flow of EWT (A/P view).

Let us understand how the system, in A/P view, processes EWT for the taxable transactions:

- During invoice entry, you enter withholding tax data for each line item in the document. If withholding tax is to be posted during invoice entry, the system calculates the withholding tax for each 'withholding tax type' with a 'withholding tax code' already defined. The system posts the withholding tax, which is thus calculated. If the system encounters a situation where there is no withholding tax code available for a given withholding tax type, then the system skips calculating the tax for that line item.

- While entering the invoice, you can also manually maintain the withholding tax base and amount, provided you have made the relevant settings while defining the withholding tax type. Now, when the system comes across a manually entered tax base and tax amount, the system does not proceed to calculate withholding tax again. Otherwise, if these fields are blank, then the system proceeds to calculate the withholding tax as outlined in the previous point.

- If the system is to calculate the withholding tax only at payment, not at invoice posting, then the system stops at arriving at the withholding tax base amount; it does not proceed to calculate the tax. However, if the settings are such that the system calculates withholding tax during invoice posting, then, besides arriving at the withholding tax base, it also calculates the withholding tax amount.

- For all the withholding tax types that allow 'posting at the time of payment' (manual or automatic), the system calculates the withholding tax for the open items, reduces the invoice amount to the extent of tax thus calculated, and posts the payment.

- For all outgoing payments, including the system's automatic payment proposals, you can process the displayed details containing the withholding tax amount for each open item. While processing, if you change the open item selection or edit the automatically generated payment proposal, the system recalculates the withholding tax.

- When the system completes the calculation and posts the payments, you can display the withholding tax data for all the clearing line items of the payment document.

344. What is 'Withholding Tax Country/ Region ID'?

In setting up EWT, you must define the '**withholding tax country/region ID**,' which may differ from the normal (political) country ISO code like IN, US, etc. The system will use this country/region ID while printing the withholding tax form. The country/region ID in your standard system may differ from the one required by the specific country's tax authorities. Verify the standard settings in the system (*Figure 13.3*) and change the withholding tax country/region ID if required.

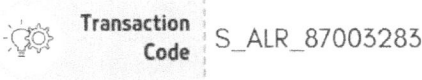

| Transaction Code | S_ALR_87003283 |

Figure 13.2

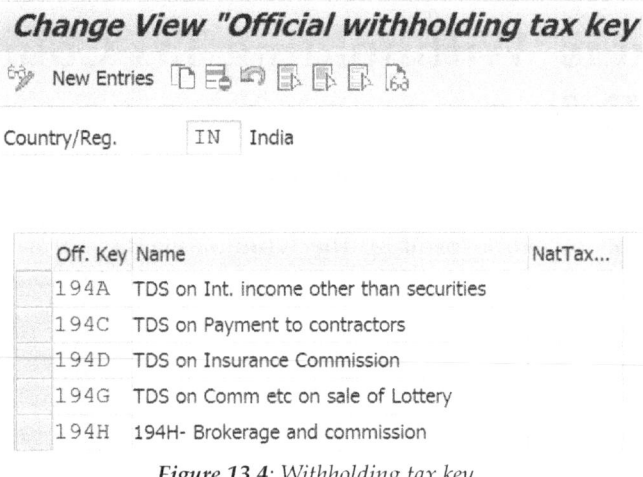

Change View "Countries/Regions for Withholding Tax

New Entries

C/R	WC/R	Description
US	SX	South Georgia Sandw.
US	SY	Syria
US	SZ	Switzerland
US	TB	St.Barthelemy
US	TC	United Arab Emirates
US	TD	Trinidad Tobago
US	TE	Tromelin Island
US	TH	Thailand

Figure 13.3: Withholding Tax Country ID

345. What is a 'Withholding Tax Key'?

Defined by a country's tax authorities, the '**withholding tax key**' is the official name of a withholding tax code. The tax authority of a country uses this key to identify the withholding tax type. This key helps prepare the withholding tax reports for submission to the tax authorities. You define withholding tax keys in the system and then assign the same to each of the withholding tax codes. SAP comes delivered with standard withholding tax keys that you can use as such. For example, for India, SAP provides you with withholding tax keys (*Figure 13.4*) that correspond to various sections of the Income Tax Act.

Change View "Official withholding tax key

New Entries

Country/Reg.   IN   India

Off. Key	Name	NatTax...
194A	TDS on Int. income other than securities	
194C	TDS on Payment to contractors	
194D	TDS on Insurance Commission	
194G	TDS on Comm etc on sale of Lottery	
194H	194H- Brokerage and commission	

Figure 13.4: Withholding tax key

Transaction Code	S_ALR_87003284

Figure 13.5

If you are using EWT in the USA, SAP S/4HANA Finance provides you with the following official withholding tax keys that you can use for reporting withholding tax (as shown in *Table 13.2*):

WT key	Description	WT key	Description
01	Interest pd by U.S. obligors - general.	27	Publicly traded partnership distribution (IRC 1446).
02	Interest paid on real property mortgages.	28	Gambling winnings.
03	Interest paid to controlling foreign corporation.	29	Deposit interest.
04	Interest paid by foreign corporation.	30	Original issue discount (OID).
05	Interest on tax-free covenant bonds.	31	Short-term OID.
06	Dividends paid by US corporation.	32	Notional principal contract income.
07	Dividend qual. for direct dividend rate	33	Substitute payment - interest.
08	Dividends paid by foreign corporation.	34	Substitute payment - dividends.
09	Capital gains.	35	Substitute payment - other.
10	Industrial royalties.	36	Capital gains distributions.
11	Motion picture or television copyright royalties.	37	Return on capital.
12	Other royalties.	38	Elig.defer.comp.items IRC 877A.
13	Royalties paid on public securities.	39	Distribution from nongrantor trust IRC 877A.
14	Real property income and natural resource royalty.	40	Other div. equiv. IRC 871.
15	Pensions, annuities, alimony, insurance premium.	41	Guarantee of indebtedness.
16	Scholarship or fellowship grants.	42	Earnings artist/athlete-no centr.w/h.
17	Compensation for independent personal services.	43	Earnings artist/athlete-central w/h.
18	Compensation for dependent personal services.	44	Spec. Federal procurement payments.
19	Compensation for teaching.	50	Inc. prev. rep. escrow procedure.
20	Compensation during studying/training.	51	Interest paid on actively traded securities.

WT key	Description	WT key	Description
22	Interest paid on deposit foreign branch.	52	Dividend paid on actively traded securities.
23	Gross income - Other	53	Subst. pmts from actively traded sec.
24	REIT distribution of capital gains.	54	Other income.
25	Trust distribution subject to IRC sec. 1445.	55	Taxable death benefits on life insurance.
26	Unsevered corporations and timber (IRC 1445).		

Table 13.2: Official withholding tax keys for the US

346. How do you Configure the 'Reason for Exemption' for EWT?

At times, you may want to exempt certain withholding tax types from withholding tax, say, for a specific period, after getting the appropriate permissions from the tax authorities. For such purposes, you need to define the '**reasons for exemption**' in the system using a 2-digit 'exemption reason' ID. SAP comes delivered with several such standard exemption reason IDs that are country-specific. For example, for the US, the exemption reason ID '03' is for 'income is not from U.S. source,''04-exempt from tax treaty', '12-payee subject to chapter 4 withholding tax', '20-dormant account', and so on.

	Transaction Code	S_ALR_87003287

Figure 13.6

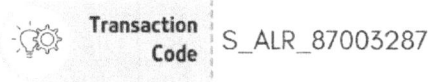

Figure 13.7: Withholding Tax Exemption Reason ID in Business Partner Master Record

Once defined, enter the 'exemption ID' against the required withholding tax type in the Business Partner (vendor/supplier) master in the Company Code area under the 'Vendor: Withholding Tax' tab (*Figure 13.7*). Before entering the exemption key as a line item, you need to enter the withholding tax type, withholding tax code, exemption certificate number, exemption percentage, and the exemption validity dates (from and to).

347. What is 'Recipient Type'?

The '**recipient type**' is used to group vendors based on certain characteristics ('occupation,' for example) who are subject to the same withholding tax type but may be charged at different rates. Used mainly in the US, it is for 1042-S reporting. Again, SAP comes with pre-defined standard recipient types per Company Code: for example, 01-US withholding agent – FI, 02-US withholding agent – Other, 05-US branch - not treated US person, 11-Withholding foreign trust, 15-Corporation, 16-Individual, 17-Estate, 18-Private foundation, 23-Pension, and the like. All these are defined for the withholding tax type '03' (1042-S).

348. Explain 'Withholding Tax Type'.

Representing various withholding tax types in a country, the 'withholding tax type' controls the calculation of extended withholding tax, unlike the withholding tax code, which controls only the percentage rate of the tax. You define the required withholding tax types and enter the same in the Business Partner's master data, in the Company Code data, under the 'Vendor: Withholding Tax' tab, for example.

You may need to define two categories of withholding tax types using the following Customizing tasks:

- Define Withholding Tax Type for Invoice Posting (Transaction Code: **S_ALR_87003264**)
- Define Withholding Tax Type for Payment Posting (Transaction Code: **S_ALR_87003266**)

Besides the above two tasks, you will also be completing the following Customizing activities while maintaining the withholding tax types:

- Define Exchange Rate Type for Withholding Tax Type
- Define Rounding Rule for Withholding Tax Type
- Assign Condition Type to Withholding Tax Type

For example, you will define the withholding tax types for different forms for the USA (*Figure 13.8*):

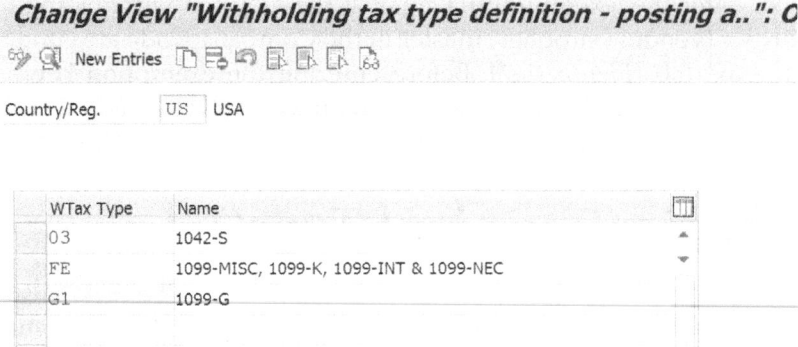

Figure 13.8: *Withholding tax types for the US for payment posting*

Then, for each of the withholding tax types, maintain the various Customizing settings, as shown in *Figure 13.9*:

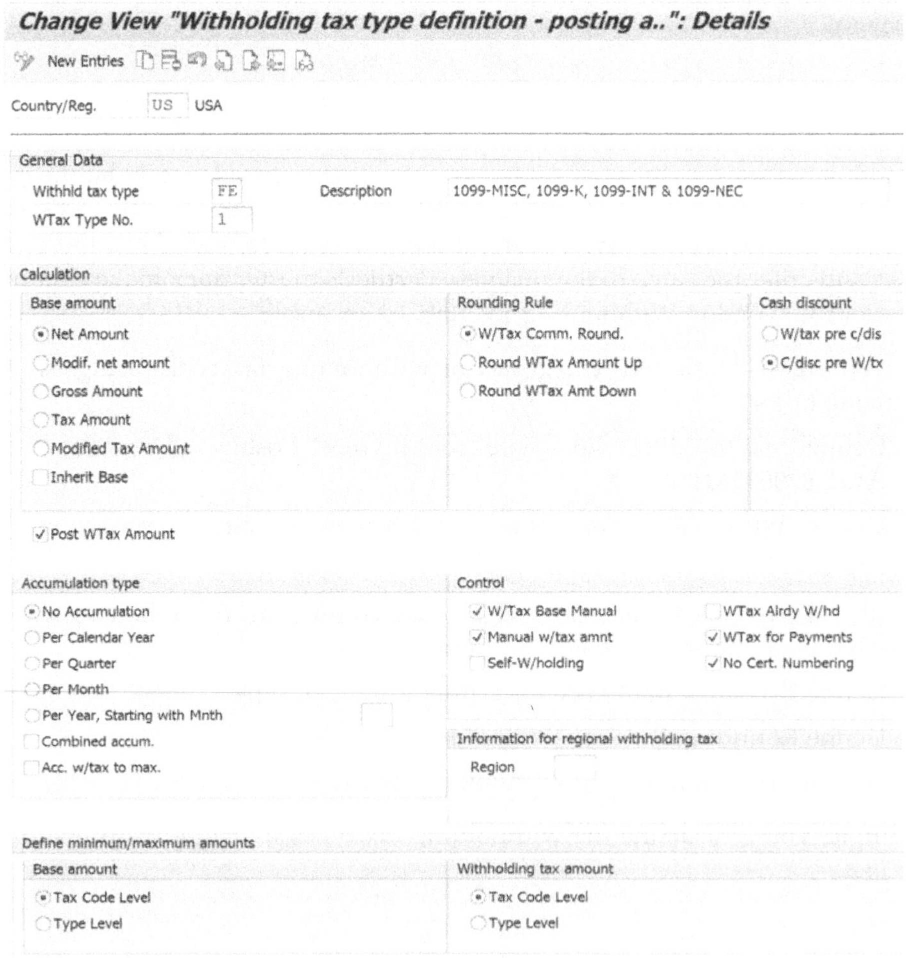

Figure 13.9: *Withholding tax types: Detailed settings*

The settings include the base amount, rounding rule, and cash discount under 'Calculation,' 'Accumulation type,' 'Control,' Defining minimum/maximum amounts' for the base amount and withholding tax amount, and the settings related to 'Central Invoice' and 'Minimum check.'

349. What is 'Central Invoicing'?

Used in Argentina, 'central invoicing' is a type of invoicing dealing with line items that are linked with other dependent documents, including credit/debit memos, down payment clearings, and partial amounts. You will establish the link when you post the dependent documents in the system by mentioning fields like invoice reference, document number, fiscal year, and line item. While calculating the withholding tax, the system takes note of all the line items that are linked together by the 'invoice reference.'

350. Explain 'Withholding Tax Code'.

By defining country-specific 'withholding tax codes,' you enable the system to assign a certain tax rate per line item, calculate the withholding tax automatically, and enable the system to automatically determine the appropriate tax G/L accounts to post the withholding tax amount thus calculated. Once you have defined a code that is in use in the system, do not try deleting or changing the settings for the code.

When defining a withholding tax code, you maintain several controlling parameters (like what the tax calculation base, what type of posting is required – standard entry or offsetting entry, the rate of tax, whether the withholding tax rate can be entered as a fraction, if the tax calculation should follow a special calculation procedure, what are all the reporting information – region, income type, etc.), as shown in *Figure 13.10*:

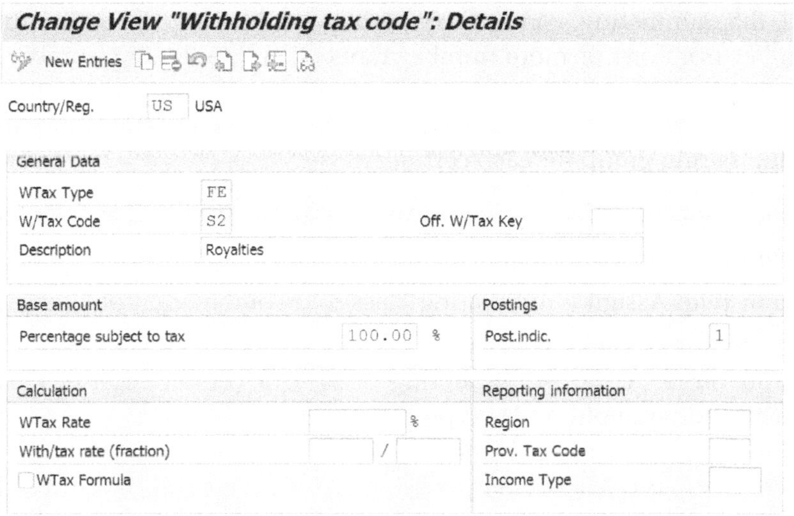

Figure 13.10: *Withholding Tax Code: Detailed Settings*

When you set up the Company Code for the USA using the Company Code template, for example, the system generates the required withholding tax codes for reporting and payment of withholding tax for 1099-MISC, 1099-G, 1099-K, and 1099-INT, and 1042-S vendors. If these system-generated tax codes are insufficient, you may create your own tax codes.

351. What are the three fields relevant in document entry, for Withholding Tax?

There are three important fields for withholding tax that you need to be cognizant of while entering a document:

- Withholding tax code
- Withholding tax base amount
- Amount exempted from withholding tax

You need to specify if a vendor's particular business transaction is subject to withholding tax. To make the relevant fields visible or suppressed, use the appropriate field status definition for the posting key and the relevant reconciliation G/L account. When a vendor is subject to withholding tax, you need to maintain the withholding tax code in the vendor master; the system defaults that withholding tax code during document entry. At the Company Code level, you need to assign the appropriate screen variant that allows you to enter the withholding tax-related data.

352. Explain 'Certificate Numbering' for EWT.

The **numbering of withholding tax certificates** needs to be as exact as possible. Towards this, define the numbering concept containing numbering class, numbering groups (the lot number from one or more number ranges), and assigning numbering groups to numbering classes. Then, you need to assign this numbering concept to the Company Code country and/or region. The system serially assigns a certificate number from the respective numbering group for each certificate.

SAP offers four concept options for certificate numbering in EWT, as follows:

- **Option one**: Assign a numbering class to the Company Code.
- **Option two**: Assign a numbering class to a combination of Company Code and withholding tax type.
- **Option three**: Assign a numbering class to a combination of Company Code, branch, and withholding tax type.

- **Option four**: Assign a numbering group to a combination of Company Code, account type, place of business, and withholding tax recipient type.

353. What is 'Withholding Tax Changeover'?

If you are in SAP, using a version before SAP R/3 4.0, and have been using classic withholding tax in your company, you can changeover to EWT if you have already migrated to version 4.0 in SAP R/3, or SAP ECC or SAP S/4HANA Finance. For this, it is not sufficient just to activate EWT; you need to complete the required Customizing settings for EWT, besides converting all the relevant master and transactional data. While doing so, you can make use of the SAP-supplied changeover tools but need to complete the tasks in the order that is recommended by SAP.

354. What are the 'Pre-requisites for Changing Over to EWT'?

Before starting the tasks for the actual changeover to EWT, complete the following pre-requisites:

- If you are in a software version less than SAP R/3 4.0, complete the release upgrade to the higher version.

- If you use invoice verification functionality, change to LIV (Logistics Invoice Verification), as EWT does not support traditional invoice verification.

- Carry out the data conversion in a test system; remember, once you have activated EWT, you cannot reverse the data conversion.

- Activate EWT only when the system prompts you to do so.

- You should not try posting any documents during the changeover, block the system access to the user, and, ideally, carry out the changeover during the weekend.

355. Outline the 'Process Flow' in changing over to EWT.

The automatic withholding tax changeover process consists of several procedures grouped into three categories ('Preparation', 'Data Conversion & Activation of Withholding Tax', and 'Postprocessing'). Remember to complete the procedures outlined in this section.

Preparations

The preparations are as follows:

- **Carrying out the financial accounting comparative analysis**
- **Archiving cleared items**: To reduce the processing time, the best practice is to archive all the cleared documents before you start the 'data conversion' step; otherwise, this step normally takes a very long time to complete.
- **Checking the system settings for EWT**: Here, in this step, you need to complete the various Customizing settings for EWT, including defining official withholding tax keys, defining withholding tax types and withholding tax codes, defining withholding tax formulas, and defining withholding tax minimum amounts. While making these settings, ensure that the new settings that you are making for EWT correspond exactly to the classic withholding tax settings that are already in the system. You do not need to make any new settings for the type of recipient for vendors, account determination, and assignment of withholding tax types to Company Codes, as the system takes care of these settings automatically during conversion. Do not activate EWT currently.
- **Setting up authorizations for the withholding tax changeover**: Create user authorization profiles (via the SAP-supplied authorization object 'F_WTMG') for the users who will all be involved in the withholding tax changeover activities. Once the changeover is completed, you need to remove these authorizations.
- **Blocking users:** During changeover conversion, you should not allow any user (other than those involved in the changeover) to access the system. Block system access so no one can post any document during the changeover.

Data conversion and activation of EWT

The points to be noted during data conversion and activation are as follows:

- **Creating and editing a conversion run**: With a 'conversion run' created in the system, you will be able to carry out and track the individual activities that are needed for the changeover. Complete the tasks in the same order as in the conversion run display screen (*Figure 13.11*). Once you have completed a particular conversion task, the traffic light will turn 'green' (or 'yellow,' if there are some warnings). Only then can you move on to the next activity. Once completed, you cannot go back to redo that completed activity.

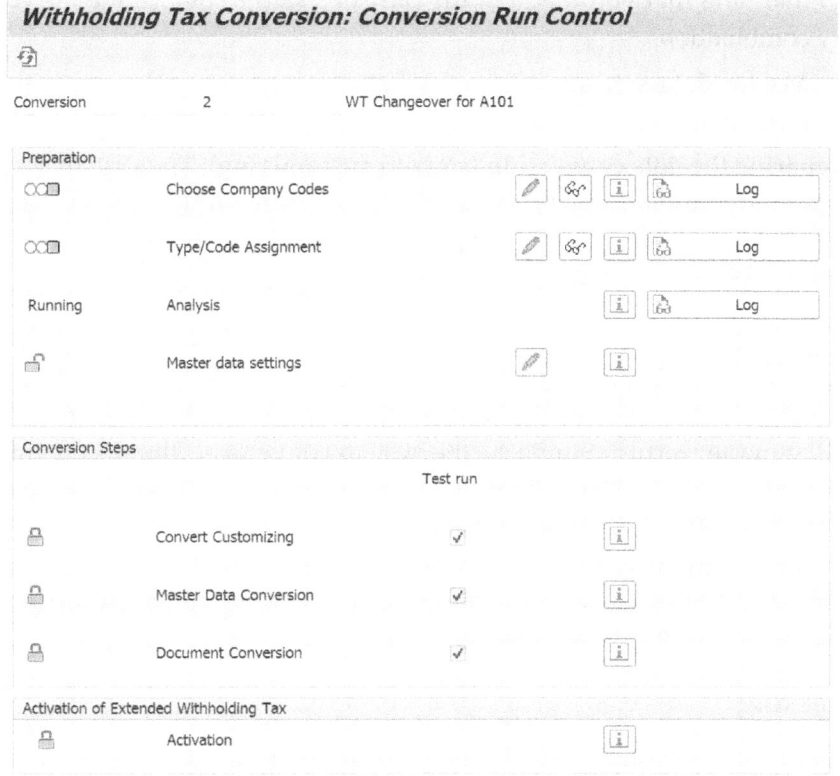

Figure 13.11: *Withholding Tax Changeover: Conversion Run Status*

Figure 13.12

- o **Choose Company Code**: Select all the Company Codes you want to convert the withholding tax data in the current run. The system will automatically add all the Company Codes that are involved in cross-Company Code clearing with that of the selected Company Code(s). Do not add any Company Codes that you have already included in a previous conversion run, or Company Codes in which EWT is already active.

- o **Type/code assignment**: Map the withholding tax codes of classic withholding tax to the withholding tax types/codes of EWT.

- o **Analysis**: The system will analyze the datasets per Company Code to determine the total number and the number of each withholding tax code of vendors, open items, cleared items, and parked items. It will also check the mapping that you made in the previous step to determine the correctness of combinations.

- o **Master data settings**: Choose whether you want only one withholding tax type or more than one per vendor.
- **Preparing the data conversion (convert customizing)**: The system assigns some of the classic withholding tax settings to the corresponding ones in EWT. Try the step with the 'Test run' checkbox selected. In that way, if you find any errors in the log, you can correct them and retry the step. When corrected, you can remove the test flag and complete the task.
- **Data conversion (master data & document)**: The system converts all the master data for all the Company Codes included in the current conversion run. While doing so, it converts only the masters that contain a withholding tax code assigned in the master record. Similarly, the system converts all the documents already in the system for which withholding tax is relevant. The system includes cleared and parked documents during this exercise.
- **Activating EWT:** Once you complete this task, EWT will be active for all the Company Codes you have included in the current conversion run. You cannot backtrack and make any changes.

Postprocessing

Carrying out postprocessing of withholding tax data conversion:

- The system does not automatically copy withholding tax exemption information in the classic withholding tax vendor master record to EWT vendor master records. You need to process each of the withholding tax types manually. Also, the reduced withholding tax rates defined at the tax code level in classic withholding tax (for exemptions) need to be defined at the vendor master now.
- Unlike classic withholding tax, reunification tax is not explicitly defined in EWT. You need to do that using a separate withholding tax type.
- The system does not convert certain documents, such as recurring entry documents, sample documents, and the noted items. You need to enter them again manually.
- Once everything is completed, you need to 'release' the system so that users can continue with their regular activities.

CHAPTER 14

FI Global Settings: Inflation Accounting

Introduction

This chapter discusses the last set of FI global settings. Here, you will learn about inflation accounting, how it is calculated using the inflation index, the two types of inflation index, and the other settings, including the inflation key and inflation method.

356. What is 'Inflation Accounting' in SAP?

Used in high-inflation countries, '**inflation accounting**' enables adjusting (= revaluating) your company's fixed assets regularly as a part of closing activities. With this, you will be adjusting the historical cost of the assets to the current costs using the *inflation index*. As in the normal case of recording the asset's **Acquisition & Production Costs (APC)** and depreciation in the regular depreciation areas, here in inflation accounting, you record the asset's revaluation amounts in '*revaluation areas*' that are nothing but a form of depreciation area.

SAP provides you with the '*Asset Revaluation (Inflation) Program*' that you need to use at the close of every month. This program calculates the revaluation amounts that you will store in the asset sub-ledger; when you execute the depreciation run, the system posts these amounts to G/L, together with the depreciation. When you bring in a new asset, you must enter the *revaluation key* into the new asset master record. Additionally, you must update the inflation indexes in SAP Customizing as and when they are made available.

357. What is an 'Inflation Index'?

The '**inflation index**' is a statistical measure that shows how much the prices of goods & services have increased over a period of time. It is arrived at on a basket of goods & services. You will then use this index to adjust your company's selected G/L accounts to account for inflation while preparing financial statements.

While maintaining the inflation index in SAP, you must define two indexes in the system: the general inflation index and the specific inflation index. The '*general inflation index*' signifies the general change in prices, and this is the index that you normally use to adjust most of the G/L accounts. In contrast, the '*specific inflation index*' represents the change in the price of specific goods & services (say, gold, silver, etc.). You will use a specific inflation index only when asked by the country's government where your Company Code operates.

Change View "Values": Overview

New Entries 🗅 🖶 🔁 🖺 🖺 🖺 🔂

Dialog Structure
- ▼ ☐ Header
  - ▼ ☐ Versions
    - • ☐ Values
  - • ☐ Composite Indexes

Inflation index   CL01   Inflation index (Chile)
Index version   1   Version 01

Index Date	Defi...	Accumulated	Percentage	Coefficient	Prov. (accum.)	Provisional (%)
30.04.1999	🗓	250	4.16667	1.041667	250	4.16667
31.05.1999	☐	260	4.00000	1.040000	260	4.00000
30.06.1999	☐	270	3.84615	1.038462	270	3.84615
31.07.1999	☐	280	3.70370	1.037037	280	3.70370
30.08.1999	☐	290	3.57143	1.035714	290	3.57143
30.09.1999	☐	300	3.44828	1.034483	300	3.44828
31.10.1999	☐	310	3.33333	1.033333	310	3.33333
30.11.1999	☐	320	3.22581	1.032258	320	3.22581

Figure 14.1: Sample Inflation index

SAP comes with sample inflation indexes (*Figure 14.1*) for several countries like Chile, Columbia, Mexico, Venezuela, and Turkey. You can use these sample indexes by updating them regularly, or you can copy them to create your version. While defining or updating the index values, you may also need to maintain '*composite inflation indexes*' in the system.

358. What is a 'Composite Inflation Index'? When will you use such an index?

A **'composite inflation index'** comprises more than one inflation index. This is useful when adjusting your G/L accounts using more than one inflation index. For example, assume that the government in Chile requires you to adjust all your real estate assets using a specific inflation index. In this case, you need to use both the specific inflation index and the general inflation index. Instead, you can achieve the same by using one composite inflation index that combines these two indexes.

359. What are all the 'Customizing Activities' in 'Inflation Accounting'?

There are several Customizing activities that you need to complete before using inflation accounting in SAP S/4HANA Finance, including:

- Maintain Inflation Indexes
- Maintain Time Base and Exposure to Inflation Variants
- Maintain Inflation Key
- Display Inflation Key Field in G/L Account (Per Activity)
- Display Inflation Key Field in G/L Account (Per Acct Group)
- Assign Inflation Keys to G/L Accounts
- Maintain Inflation Methods
- Assign Inflation Methods to Company Codes
- Assignment of Inflation Indexes to Line Items
- Maintain Inflation Adjustment Accounts
- Maintain G/L Accounts for Inflation Postings

360. What is 'Time Base and Exposure to Inflation Variant'?

A system object in SAP inflation accounting, the **Time Base & Exposure to Inflation Variant (TBE Variant)**, contains the settings (*Figure 14.2*) needed for the system to decide how often to adjust an item for inflation and how to adjust the items posted between time intervals.

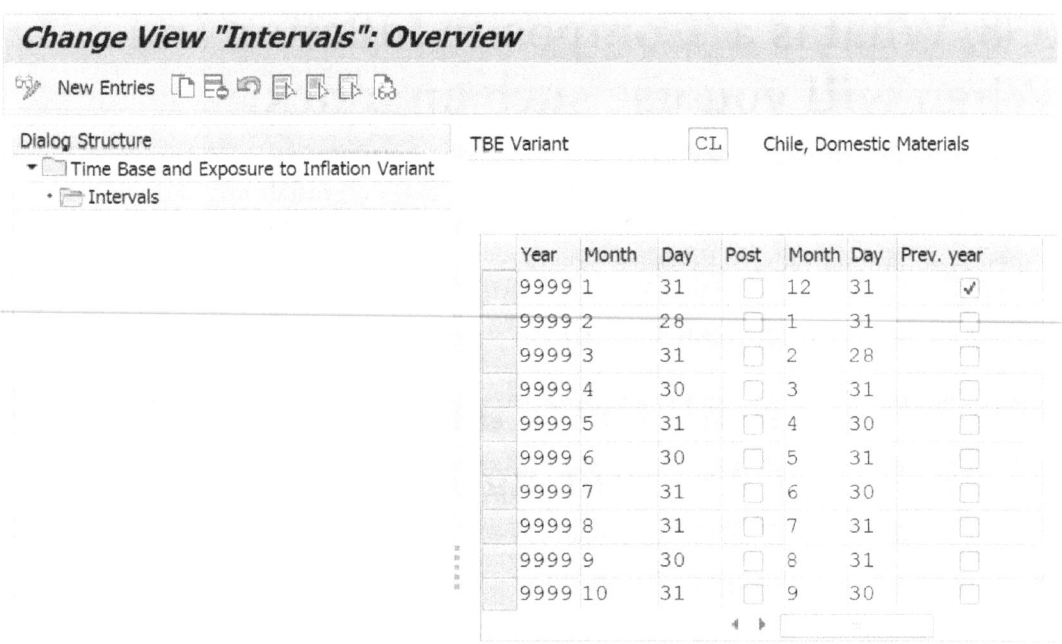

Figure 14.2: TBE Variant configuration

For example, consider that you need to adjust your fixed assets for inflation every quarter. To this effect, you will define the TBE variant. While maintaining the settings for the variant, you may also define that any asset acquisition in between a quarter will have to be adjusted for inflation only at the end of the month. Take the case that you acquire office equipment on 15 Mar 2023. Since the TBE variant adjusts all the assets at the last date of the month, 31 Mar 2023, the system considers this new asset as if purchased on 31 Mar 2023. However, for the month ending 30 Apr 2023, this new asset will be adjusted for inflation for the entire month.

361. What is an 'Inflation Key'?

The **'inflation key'** is a system object in SAP that controls how a G/L account is to be adjusted for inflation in terms of what inflation index is to be applied if the G/L account balance alone needs to be adjusted or if the G/L account line items are to be adjusted separately, and so on. Once you define the inflation keys, assign them to the appropriate G/L account master records (under 'Control Data'), as shown in *Figure 14.3*:

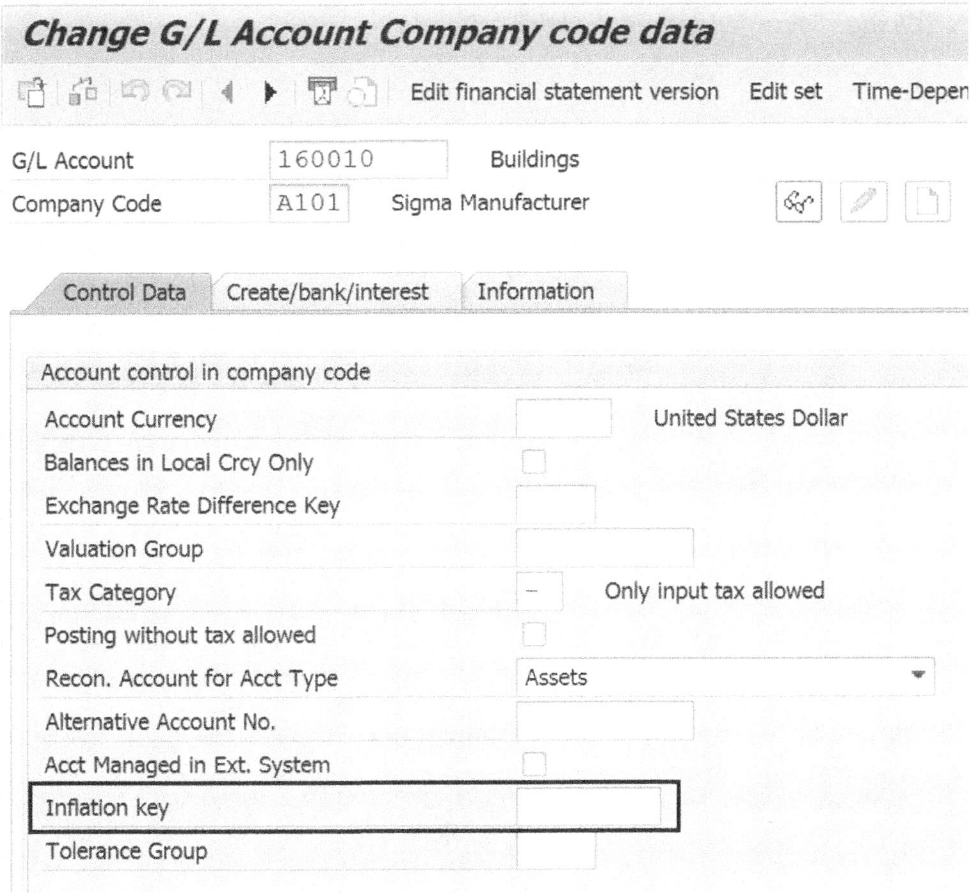

Figure 14.3: Inflation Key field in G/L Account Master record

362. What is an 'Inflation Method'?

A system object in SAP inflation accounting, the **'inflation method'** contains the settings for managing inflation accounting for a Company Code. It has all the information like the accounts (assets, material, etc.) that need to be adjusted for inflation, the general inflation index that is to be used, the TBE variant that is to be considered, and the specified document types for posting inflation adjustments. Each method comprises three sections: FI, FI-AA, and MM. If both FI-AA and MM components are active for the Company Code, then make the required settings for all three sections (*Figure 14.4*).

Change View "Inflation Methods": Details

New Entries 🗋 🖫 🖘 🕁 🗋 🖫 🖾

Country/Reg.	CL	
Method	CL01	Inflation Method Chile

General Settings

Ledger	AY

Inflation Accounting for Financial Accounting (FI)

☑ FI active

Basic Settings

General index	CL01		No Adjustment Split	☑
TBE Variant	M1		Exchange Rate Type	

Inflation Adjustment Documents

Doc. type (LC)	AB	Post. key (cr.)	50	Input tax code	C0
Doc. type (FC)	SA	Post. key (dr.)	40	Output tax code	D0

Inflation Accounting for Asset Accounting (FI-AA)

☑ FI-AA Active

Basic Settings		**Revaluation Transaction Types**	
Posting Variant	CL	CY Acq. (Dr.)	897
☐ Settle Revaluation Amts Propt'ly		CY Acq. (Cr.)	898
☐ Split Reval. of Depreciation			
		PY Acq. (Dr.)	891
Legacy Data Transfer		PY Acq. (Cr.)	893
Last rev. date			

Revaluation After Useful Life

Allow	No ▼

Inflation Accounting for Materials Management (MM)

☑ MM active

Basic Settings

☐ Post repl. cost		Valuation level	2
☑ Man. RC change		Exch. rate type	M
☐ Don't Post to MM			

Figure 14.4: Sample Inflation method

Once you define the inflation methods, you must assign a method to each Company Code that uses inflation accounting. SAP comes with standard inflation methods for each country's local version that you can use with some modifications, or you can define your methods.

CHAPTER 15

FI: General Ledger

Introduction

This chapter provides a comprehensive view of **SAP General Ledger** (**G/L**) Accounting in SAP S/4HANA Finance. The chapter discusses all the salient features of SAP G/L, besides outlining the important configuration settings required to be made in the system for making use of the G/L functionality. In the process, you will learn about the chart of accounts, G/L account master data, G/L account group, sample account, reference account, financial statement version, etc. You will also learn about document splitting, document clearing (both manual, automatic, and cross-Company Code), balance interest calculation, and the important SAP Fiori apps for G/L accounting.

363. What is the 'Purpose of SAP G/L Accounting'?

The main purpose of **SAP G/L Accounting** is to record all business transactions in a software application that is fully integrated with the various operational areas of an enterprise, like production, sales, marketing, purchasing, etc., to ensure that the recorded accounting information is complete and accurate. It helps meet the external legal and statutory requirements through financial statements like balance sheets and profit & loss statements. To meet the present-day financial accounting demands, SAP G/L Accounting in SAP S/4HANA Finance also handles parallel accounting, segment reporting, **cost of sales (CoS)** accounting, and even management accounting.

364. What SAP application components are integrated with SAP G/L Accounting?

SAP G/L Accounting is integrated with several application components for the smooth flow of accounting data that are posted into those components:

- Accounts Receivable and Accounts Payable
- Asset Accounting
- Controlling
- Human Capital Management
- Materials Management
- Public Sector Management - Funds Management Government
- Travel Management
- Treasury and Risk Management

365. Explain the salient features of SAP G/L Accounting.

With its centralized and up-to-date accounting information, **SAP G/L Accounting** is the single source of complete recording of all business transactions in SAP S/4HANA Finance. With its various functions for entering and evaluating accounting data, it allows you to select either the corporate group or the individual Company Code as the level of reporting. It enables automatic & simultaneous postings to sub-ledger accounts via reconciliation G/L accounts, updates the parallel ledgers and cost accounting areas simultaneously, and enables real-time evaluation & display of postings, account statements, and financial statements, with the drill-down option to get to the origin of an accounting transaction. This drill-down functionality helps you get real-time insight as you can display the original line items, documents, and total debits and credits.

366. How different is SAP G/L Accounting from the classic G/L Accounting of SAP ERP?

The *classic G/L accounting* in SAP R/3 required multiple ledgers and many application components, calling for time-consuming, extensive manual reconciliation to get a complete picture of a company's financial soundness. Also, it lacked the unified accounting interface to take care of segment reporting, parallel accounting, etc. You need to manually pass on the posting data from CO to FI periodically to have a view of management accounting. You also do not have integrated tools for planning and forecasting.

To overcome all these shortcomings, SAP came out with the *New G/L Accounting* as part of the later versions of SAP, called SAP ECC (SAP ERP). This brought in the required flexibility both in accounting and reporting. The New G/L Accounting was evolving with every release of SAP ERP, and with the introduction of SAP S/4HANA Finance, it became fully integrated with the other application areas, obviating the need for reconciliation. Simply called SAP G/L Accounting, it is versatile, flexible, and nimble, providing a single consolidated interface for both financial and management accounting. With its leading and non-leading ledgers, it effortlessly handles parallel, segment, and CoS accounting. It brings a big change in closing operations, resulting in no delay and real-time accounting information availability on the fly. It is the 'single source of truth' as far as the financial/accounting data is concerned.

367. Outline, in brief, the enhanced functionalities of SAP G/L Accounting.

SAP G/L Accounting, with its new and enhanced framework, addresses the varying legal, statutory, and reporting requirements of local and international accounting principles and introduces various functional enhancements for simplified data entry, analysis, and reporting. *Figure 15.1* depicts the multi-various capabilities or functionalities of SAP G/L Accounting.

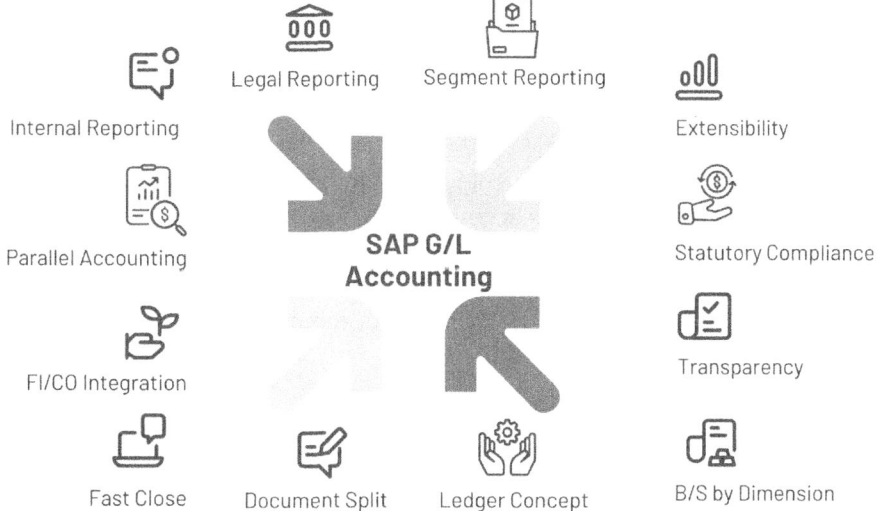

Figure 15.1: *SAP G/L Accounting: Enhanced functionalities*

368. What Customizing tasks are required to work with SAP G/L Accounting?

There are several general Customizing settings that you need to complete before you can start using the functionalities of SAP G/L Accounting. They are as follows:

- You should have defined the required Company Code(s) and CO area in the system.
- You should have completed the global settings for the fiscal year, posting periods, and currencies.
- You should have defined the required ledgers, both leading and non-leading.
- You should have made the required definition and settings for parallel accounting, if applicable.
- You should have configured FI integration with CO.

369. What are the three types of data you will come across in SAP?

There are three kinds of data residing in any SAP system:

- **Table data:** It refers to the Customized information for a particular Client. This includes data like payment terms, discounts, pricing, tolerance limits, etc., which you do not normally change daily.
- **Transaction data:** It is the day-to-day recording of business information like purchase orders, sales returns, invoices, payments, collections, etc.; this includes both the system-generated (tax, discount, etc., automatically calculated by the system during document posting) and user-generated.
- **Master data:** They are the control information required to decide how transaction data gets posted into various accounts (like customers, vendors, G/L, etc.). Master data are usually shared across modules (for example, customer master records are common both to FI and SD in SAP), obviating the need for defining them in various application areas. The master data remains in the system for a fairly long period.

370. What objects comprise the 'Master Data in SAP G/L Accounting'?

The master data in SAP G/L Accounting comprises the following objects in the system:

- G/L Account Master Data
- Profit Center Master Data

- Segment

371. Explain 'G/L Account Master Data.'

The **G/L account master data** determines how to post a business transaction to a G/L account. It also determines how the system processes the posted transactions. You need to have these master data defined in the system before posting the G/L account transactions.

372. What is 'Profit Center Master Data'?

The **profit center master** data enables you to post and analyze accounting data from the point of 'SAP Profit Center Accounting.' The profit center master data is made up of several objects, including the following:

- Profit center
- Standard hierarchy (of the profit centers)
- Alternate profit center hierarchies (if required)
- Dummy profit center (for managing non-assigned postings)

373. What are the different 'Types of G/L Account Master Data'?

The following are the different types of G/L account master data:
- Balance sheet account
- Non-operative income and expense
- Primary costs (or Revenues)
- Secondary costs

374. What are 'Balance Sheet Accounts'?

The **B/S (balance sheet) accounts** are the G/L accounts to which you post your business transactions daily. At the end of the year, the system carries forward the balance in these accounts to the new fiscal year.

375. What are 'Non-operative Income and Expense Accounts'?

In any business, you may come across some expenses or income not part of your regular business activity, like interest income from investments. Such an expense or income is known as **non-operative income or expenses**. You must define separate income statement G/L accounts to post these non-operative income and expenses.

376. What do you mean by 'Primary Costs' or 'Revenue Accounts'?

The income statement G/L accounts act as the cost element for routing the **primary costs** (also known as operating expenses like manufacturing expenses, payroll expenses, expenses related to selling your company's products, and the like) or **revenues**.

377. What are 'Secondary Costs'?

Secondary costs are value flows within your company arising out of various internal activities like overhead cost allocation, settlements, etc. The income statement G/L accounts that act as the cost elements for secondary costs are known as the 'secondary cost G/L accounts.'

378. Explain the Structure of G/L Account Master Data.

The G/L account master data in SAP S/4HANA Finance is divided into three data areas (*Figure 15.2*), namely:

- **Chart of accounts area**: (valid across Company Codes) Consisting of information like G/L account number, G/L account type, account group, functional area, trading partner number, G/L account description (short & long text), P&L statement account type, etc.,

- **Company Code area**: (valid for the specific Company Code) Comprising of data including account currency, valuation group, tax category, inflation key, tolerance group, sort key, authorization group, field status variant, house bank, interest indicator, etc.,

- **CO area-specific area**: (valid for the specific controlling area) Consists of data relating to cost element category, record quantity, internal UOM, etc.

G/L Account Master Data

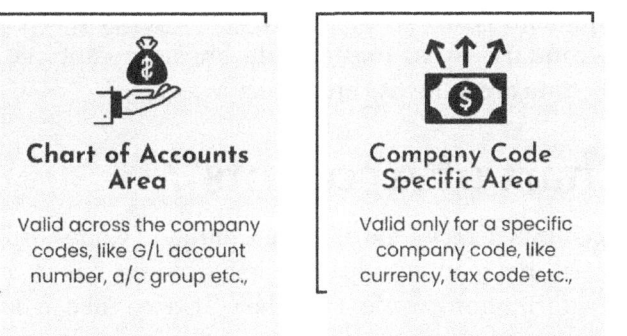
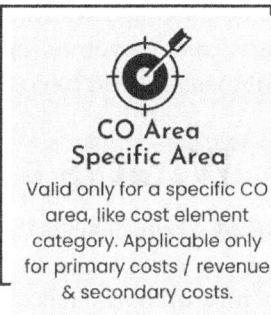

Chart of Accounts Area

Valid across the company codes, like G/L account number, a/c group etc.,

Company Code Specific Area

Valid only for a specific company code, like currency, tax code etc.,

CO Area Specific Area

Valid only for a specific CO area, like cost element category. Applicable only for primary costs / revenue & secondary costs.

Figure 15.2: G/L Account Master data areas

The compartmentalization of the G/L account master record into three distinct areas (*Figure 15.3*) enables you to use the same G/L accounts in multiple Company Codes. When you use the same chart of accounts, you just need to change the data for the fields in 'Company Code area' and 'CO area specific area.' Otherwise, if there were no such distinct data areas in a G/L account master record, you may need to create several charts of accounts in the system, as your Company Code data and CO area-specific data may differ in different Company Codes.

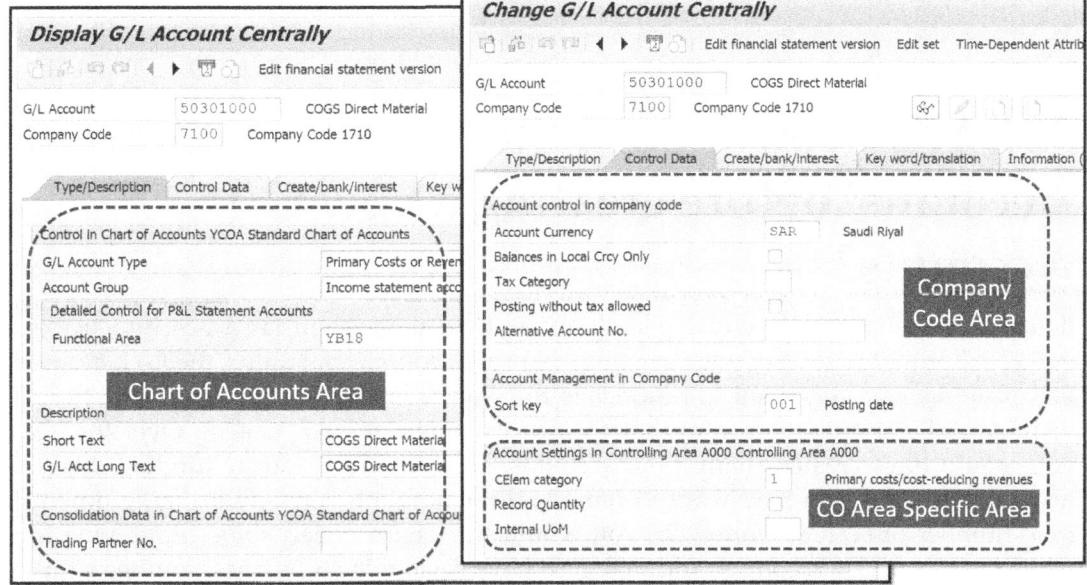

Figure 15.3: G/L Account Master Record Example: the three Data Areas

Earlier in SAP R/3, there were only two data areas for G/L account master data: the chart of accounts area and the Company Code area. This was because FI and CO were separate, and you had to create the required cost element master data (for primary and secondary costs) in the CO application component. With SAP S/4HANA Finance, as the cost element (primary costs/revenue, and secondary costs) master data are now captured in G/L account masters, you have the 3rd data area: the CO area specific area.

379. What is a 'Chart of Accounts'?

A **Chart of Accounts** lists G/L accounts used in one or more Company Codes. All the G/L accounts in a chart of accounts will have an account number, account name, and some control information. The control information decides how the G/L account can be created.

380. What is a 'Chart of Accounts List'?

The '**chart of accounts list**' contains all the charts of accounts for a particular Client. The chart of the account list comes pre-delivered with sample charts of accounts like INT, and CANA, etc. You can check if you can use any of the sample ones. If not, you can create your own charts. While defining, you will maintain attributes like name, G/L account number length, maintenance language, name of the group chart of accounts, etc.

Figure 15.4

381. Why you should 'Revise Chart of Accounts' before creating a new G/L Accounts?

Before you embark upon creating G/L accounts in the system, as a best practice, you need to thoroughly review your existing chart of accounts containing the G/L accounts. For example, you may want to rationalize the way of creating G/L accounts in the SAP S/4HANA Finance system from that of your existing non-SAP system. Over the years, you would have created many G/L accounts, some of which are redundant or not in use anymore, and you may want to remove those accounts, thereby bringing down the total number of G/L accounts. Or, you would have hard-coded some numbering logic while creating those accounts. You may also have several legal business entities all using different charts of accounts, which you want to change so that they all use the same chart in

SAP S/4HANA Finance. Or the current length of the G/L account numbers is insufficient to insert accounts in between, so you want to change the G/L account number's length considerably.

Once you have brainstormed on all the points above, you will be in a better position to structure and create only those G/L accounts that you really need in SAP G/L Accounting in SAP S/4HANA Finance.

382. What are all the major components of a 'Chart of Accounts'?

A **Chart of Accounts** is defined with the following items:

- Chart of account key
- Name
- Maintenance language
- Length of the G/L Account Number
- Controlling Integration
- Group chart of accounts (Consolidation)
- Block Indicator

383. What are the different types of 'Charts of Accounts'?

In general, you will come across the following types of charts of accounts:

- Operative or operating or standard chart of accounts
- Country or alternate chart of accounts
- Group chart of accounts or corporate chart of accounts

384. What is an 'Operating Chart of Accounts'?

This is the chart of accounts, which is used for day-to-day postings. Both FI and CO use this chart of accounts. This chart of accounts must be assigned to the Company Code. This chart of accounts is also known as the '**Operative**' or '**Standard**' chart of account.

385. How does the 'Group Chart of Accounts' differ from the 'Operating Chart of Accounts'?

The **Group Chart of Accounts**, or the **Corporate Chart of Accounts**, consolidates all Company Codes (with dissimilar Operative Charts of Accounts) under a Company. This is the 'universe' of all-inclusive G/L accounts from which the Operative Chart of Accounts is derived. This does not need to be assigned to a Company Code.

386. What is a 'Country Chart of Accounts'? Why do you need this?

The **Country Chart of Accounts**, also known as the **Alternate Chart of Accounts**, contains the G/L accounts to meet the specific statutory/legal requirements of the country where a Company Code operates. The assignment of this chart of accounts to a Company Code is also optional. It is possible that both the operative and the country chart of accounts are the same. In that case, you will not need two different account charts.

In cases where the operative and country chart of accounts are different, the link needs to be established by entering the G/L account number from the 'Country Chart of Accounts' in the G/L master record (under the Company Code section) of the 'Operative Chart of Accounts' in the field '*Alternate Account Number.*'

387. Can one 'Chart of Accounts' be assigned to several Company Codes?

Yes. You can assign a single chart of accounts to more than one Company Code. However, the reverse is not possible; that is, you will not be able to assign more than one chart of accounts to a single Company Code.

388. Explain the objects that are crucial for the creation & maintenance of G/L Accounts.

There are three objects (*Figure 15.5*) that play a crucial role in creating and maintaining G/L accounts in SAP S/4HANA Finance. They are:

- Chart of accounts list
- Chart of accounts
- Account Group

We have already seen that the **chart of accounts list** contains several charts of accounts, from which you use a chart to be used in a Company Code. We have also seen that the **chart of accounts** comprises several G/L account master records that you use in one or more Company Codes.

The '**account group**' (or 'G/L account group') controls how you create a G/L account master record in the system, what fields you define as mandatory or optional, what interval you use to number the G/L account master records, and the like. You can group the G/L account master records that use the same field status and number range under a particular account group. This way, it is easier to control the field statuses.

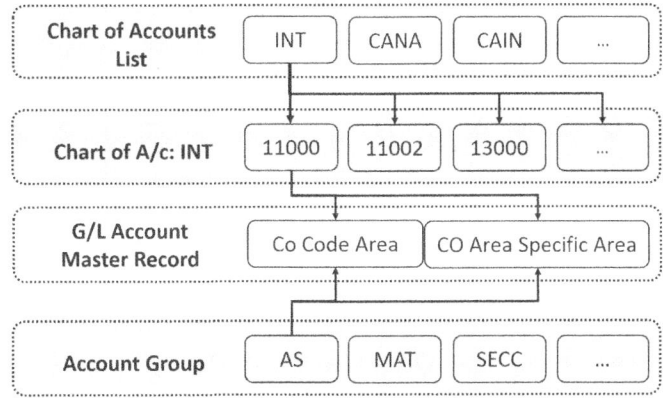

Figure 15.5: Crucial Objects in G/L Account Master Creation & Maintenance

389. What is an 'G/L Account Group'?

The **Account Group** (or **G/L Account Group**), a 4-character alphanumeric key, controls how the G/L account master records are created in the system. This helps to 'group' G/L accounts according to the '*functional areas*' to which they belong. The account group is mandatory for creating a master record. You may use the same account groups in more than one Company Code when the Company Codes use the same chart of accounts. Each G/L account is assigned to only one account group.

The account group determines the following:

- What *number interval* is to be used while creating the master record?
- What *screen layout* is to be used while creating the master record in the Company Code area?

While defining the account groups in the system, you also need to define the corresponding *field status* for each group (you may refer to *Question 153* to *Question 157* to learn more about field status). Otherwise, you will not be able to see any fields as all these would be hidden by default.

Change View "G/L Account Groups": Overview

🛠 🔍Field status   New entries 🗋 🗑 🔄 🔃 🔃 🔃 Print field status

Chrt/Ac...	Acct Group	Name	From Acct	To Account
CAIN	AS	Fixed assets accounts		99999999
CAIN	CASH	Liquid funds accounts		99999999
CAIN	GL	General G/L accounts		99999999
CAIN	MAT	Materials management accounts		99999999
CAIN	PL	Income statement accounts		99999999
CAIN	RECN	Recon.account ready for input		99999999
CAIN	SECC	Secondary Costs/Revenues		ZZZZZZZZZZ

Figure 15.6: G/L Account Group: Standard settings

SAP comes delivered with several *'account groups'* like 'AS,' 'CASH,' 'GL,' 'MAT', etc., for each of the standard charts of accounts, as shown in *Figure 15.6*. In most situations, you will not require additional groups other than the ones already available in the standard system. However, if you need to create a new one, it is easier to copy an existing one and modify it instead of creating it from scratch.

Figure 15.7

390. What is a 'Screen Layout'?

The account group determines which **screen layout** should be used while creating a G/L account master record. For each of the account groups, you can define different screen layouts, which essentially determine the *'field status'* of a field.

There are two levels of controls of field status, deciding which takes priority while defining the screen layout:

- Field status at the account group level
- Field status at the activity (create/change/display) level, i.e., at the transaction level.

The standard system comes configured with the setting 'optional field entry' for G/L account posting keys ('40' & '50'), which does not influence the field status. That is, you cannot have a G/L account-specific screen layout that is differentiated via these posting keys.

391. What is a 'Sample Account' in G/L Account processing?

The '**sample account**' is like a template from which you can transfer field values when creating new G/L account master records. Via the '*data transfer rules*' (*Figure 15.8*), you can decide which field values from the sample account can be transferred to the newly created G/L master record and whether such transferred values can be changed later once the transfer is complete. Though optional, you can use this functionality when creating Company Code data centrally in several Company Codes. Unlike other settings, SAP does not provide any sample account or document transfer rule by default in the standard system; you need to create your own.

There are multiple settings that you need to complete in Customizing before you can create the sample accounts:

- Maintain List of Rule Types (Transaction **OB15**)
- Define Data Transfer Rules (Transaction **FSK2**)
- Assign Company Code to Rule Type (Transaction **OB16**)
- Create Sample Accounts (Transaction **FSM1**)
- Define Field Groups (Transaction **OBBJ**)

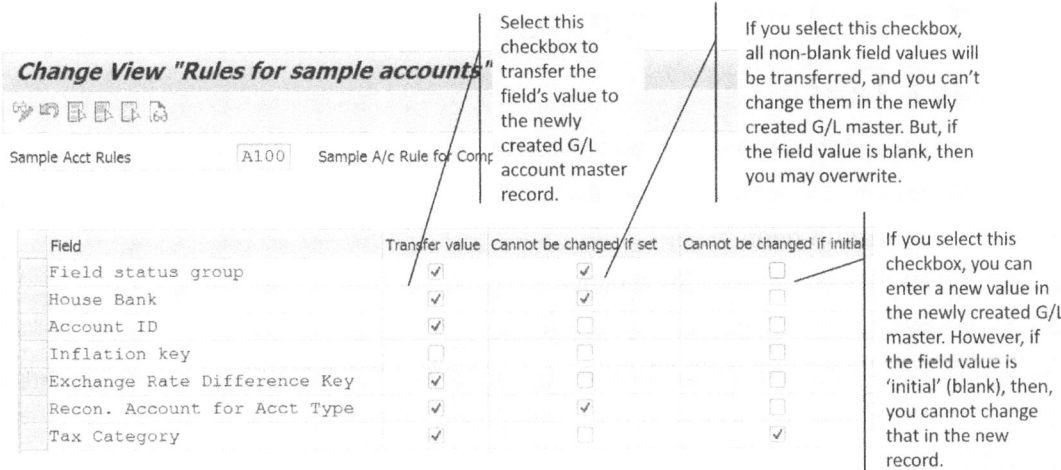

Figure 15.8: Data Transfer Rules for Sample account

392. How is 'Reference Account,' 'Sample Account,' and 'Account Group' different?

SAP provides several procedures, including the reference account, sample account, and account group, to enable you to create G/L account master records in the system.

With the **reference account** procedure, you use an existing G/L account in the system to create a new G/L account master record. While doing so, the system copies all the field values from the reference (source) to the target account. Once completed, you may change the field values in the newly created G/L account master record. The reference method for creating a new G/L account master record is optional.

With a **sample account**, you can decide (via the 'data transfer rules') which are the field values that need to be transferred to the newly created G/L account master record from the sample account, besides deciding whether the transferred values can be over-written or not. You normally use sample accounts when you want to create or change multiple G/L account master records centrally in more than one Company Code. The use of a sample account also is optional.

You use **account groups** to decide the screen layout for the newly created G/L account master record to control the field statuses. You also use the account groups to number the G/L master records from a pre-defined number range that is unique to each of the account groups. The **creation of an account group is mandatory**, without which you cannot create any G/L account master record in the system. You can create any number of account groups, but each G/L account is assigned (in the chart of accounts area) to only one account group. You can use the same account group in multiple Company Codes, provided those Company Codes work with the same chart of accounts.

393. How do you create a 'G/L Account Master Data'?

The **G/L Account Master Data** can be created by any one of the following methods:
- Manually
- Creating with reference
- Through Data Transfer Workbench
- Copying from existing G/L accounts

The **manual creation** of G/L account master records is laborious and time-consuming. You will do this only when you cannot create master records using the abovementioned methods.

You will follow the second method, **creating with reference**, when you are already in SAP and have an existing Company Code (*Reference Company Code*) from which you can copy these records to a new Company Code (*Target Company Code*). You can do this by accessing the Menu: '*SAP Customizing Implementation Guide | Financial Accounting | General Ledger Accounting | G/L Accounts | Master Data | G/L Account Creation and Processing | Create G/L Accounts with Reference.*' While doing this, you can copy the '*account assignments*' as well so that the integration of G/L with other applications is intact. SAP facilitates that you can limit the number of G/L records thus copied to the target Company Code, create new records, if necessary, and change the account number/name.

When you have G/L accounts in a non-SAP system, and you feel that these accounts will meet your requirements, you will then use SAP's 'Data Transfer Workbench' to transfer these records into SAP and change the same to suit the SAP environment. Since this will not have 'Account Assignment' logic as defined in SAP, you must carefully define these assignments.

You will resort to the last option of **copying from existing G/L accounts** only when you feel that there is a *Chart of Accounts* in the system that 100% meets your requirement. Otherwise, follow the second method described above.

394. What is the 'Collective Processing' of G/L accounts?

The **collective processing** helps you to make systematic changes to several G/L accounts in a single step. For example, you have used the *'creating with reference'* method to create G/L accounts in a new Company Code, and you want to change the account names and the 'G/L account type' (P&L or B/S). Then, you may use this *mass processing method* to achieve the same easily and quickly. You can make changes to:

- Chart of accounts data
- Company Code data
- Controlling area data
- Name / Descriptions

Use Menu Path: *SAP Customizing Implementation Guide | Financial Accounting | General Ledger Accounting | Master Data | G/L Account Creation and Processing | Change G/L Accounts Collectively*: then, select any of the options like:

- Change Chart of Accounts Data (Transaction Code **OB_GLACC11**)
- Change Company Code Data (Transaction Code **OB_GLACC12**)
- Change Account Name or Change (Transaction Code **OB_GLACC13**)
- Create Controlling Area Data (Transaction Code **OB_GLACC14**)

You can also use the SAP Easy Access Menu: *Accounting | Financial Accounting | General Ledger | Master Records | G/L Accounts | Collective Processing*: then, select the following:

- **OB_GLACC11** - Chart of Accounts Data
- **OB_GLACC12** - Company Code Data
- **OB_GLACC13** – Descriptions
- **OB_GLACC14** - Controlling Area Data

Remember that 'collective processing' only helps to edit, and you cannot use this method if you need to create new master records.

395. What is 'Individual Processing' of G/L accounts?

Unlike the 'collective processing' of G/L accounts, wherein you edit several accounts in a single step, **individual processing** helps edit or create G/L account master records one at a time. Here, you can edit (including display, change, block, unblock, and delete) or create a new G/L account in three different ways, listed as follows:

- **Centrally**: You will edit or create a G/L account master record in both the chart of accounts and Company Code areas in one go. This is also known as '**One-step' G/L creation**.

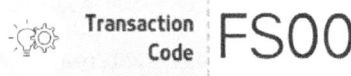

Figure 15.9

- **In the Chart of accounts area**: You first edit or create the record here before doing the same in the Company Code area.

Figure 15.10

- **In the Company Code area**: You edit or create the record here after the same has been done in the chart of accounts area.

Figure 15.11

Put together, steps 2 & 3 relate to the 'step-by-step' creation of G/L account master records.

396. Can you change an existing 'G/L Account of Type' from 'B/S' to 'P&L'?

Technically, you can change all the fields, except the account number, of a G/L account in the chart of accounts area. However, in this specific instance, when you change the 'G/L *account type'* from 'B/S' to 'P&L,' make sure that you again run the 'balance carry forward' program after saving the changes so that the system corrects the account balances suitably.

397. Why does the system not allow the changing of the 'tax category' in a G/L Account Master?

You can change the 'Company Code' related fields, like tax category, currency, etc., of the G/L accounts, provided that there has not been any posting to these accounts. However, keep the following in mind:

- If you need to denote an existing G/L account to be managed on an 'open item' basis or vice versa, make sure that the account balance is zero in either case.

- If you are trying to change an existing *'reconciliation account'* (to a regular G/L), make sure the account has not been posted.

- If you are attempting to denote an existing ordinary G/L account as a 'reconciliation account, ' ensure that the account has a zero balance.

398. What do you mean by 'balances in local currency' only?

When you create G/L account master records, it is necessary to decide whether you want the account to have the transactions updated only in local currency. Then, you will set this 'Balances in local currency only' indicator accordingly in the 'Company Code area' of the master record. You need to set this indicator for the *clearing accounts* like:

- Cash discount clearing accounts
- GR /IR clearing accounts

Note that you need to set this indicator 'on' for all the *'clearing accounts'* where you use the local currency to clear the line items in various currencies so that the transactions are posted without posting any exchange rate difference that otherwise might arise.

Example: Consider an invoice for USD 1,000, which, on that day, translates into an amount of INR 83,000 with an exchange rate of I USD = INR 83. Imagine that when the goods are received, the exchange rate is 1 USD = INR 84. Then, one of the following is applicable:

- If the indicator is set, the system ignores the exchange rate as if the line items have been maintained only in the local currency (INR), and the items are cleared.

- If the indicator is NOT set, the system makes a posting for the 'exchange rate difference' (INR 1000) before clearing the two line items.

399. What is a 'line-item' display'?

To display line items of an account, you need to set the indicator '**line item display**' to 'on' in that account's master record. This is mandatory for customer and vendor/supplier accounts. The line items can be displayed using classical display or SAP List Viewer (ALV). You can use several '*display variants*' to suit your need to display various fields when you feel that the *Standard Variant* is not meeting your requirements.

400. How does 'archiving' differ from 'deletion'?

We have already discussed (*Question 302* to *Question 313*) that **archiving** refers to deleting data from the documents from the database and storing the same in a file, which can be transferred to an 'archiving system' later. Archiving does not physically delete the documents. However, *deletion* removes the documents from the database. To proceed with archiving and deletion, you need to consider the following:

- *Block* posting to these archived master records.
- *Mark* (the master records) *for deletion* at the 'Chart of Accounts area' to delete the records from all the Company Codes. However, if you do not want to delete from all the Company Codes but only from one or more Company Codes, then do the same in the 'Company Code area' of the master record(s).
- *Archive* all the transaction figures from the relevant documents.
- Call up a special program to '*delete*' the records: The program will check whether that document could be deleted. If yes, it will proceed to 'archive' and then to 'deletion'.

401. What are the two uses of 'blocking' an account?

You may use '**blocking**' to:

- Block an account from further postings
- Block creation of the account itself (at the Company Code level or chart of accounts area)

402. Can you post an a/c document if the 'credit' is not equal to 'debit'?

In general, as we discussed earlier (*Question 246*), unless the 'debits' are equal to the 'credits' in a document, you will not be able to post the document. However, the system allows you to post some of the documents, even if this is not true:

- **Noted items**: This will contain only a debit or credit. Since accounting entries are not updated, the system will allow you to go ahead with posting these items.

403. What is a 'financial statement version'?

A hierarchical arrangement of G/L accounts, according to the legal regulations, the **financial statement version (FSV)** helps to define the *Financial Statements* (both the *Balance Sheet* and *Profit & Loss statements*). Apart from being used in generating the financial statements, you can also use the financial statement versions to generate a structured listing of account balances, as in the case of a '*trial balance.*' When you copy the settings from an existing Company Code to a new one, you will copy the financial statement version defined for the 'source' Company Code.

Transaction Code OB58

Figure 15.12

SAP comes with several versions of its financial statements (*Figure 15.13*), which you may copy and customize to suit your specific requirements.

Change View "Financial Statement Versions": Overview

New Entries   Financial Statement Items

	FS Version	Financial Statement Version Name
	BAHU	Financial Statement Hungary
	BAIN	Financial Statement Version - India
	BAJP	Financial Statement (Japan)
	BAKR	Financial Statement (Korea)
	BAKZ	Financial Statement Kazakhstan
	BALU	Financial Statement Luxembourg
	BANO	Financial Statement Norway
	BAPE	Financial Statement - Peru
	BAPL	Balance Sheet - Poland

Figure 15.13: Sample financial statement versions in the standard SAP system

You may also define a new FSV and build the financial statements from scratch. You may create the financial statements for external reporting (Company Code financial statements) and internal reporting (business area financial statements). When you create an FSV, the system automatically generates the following nodes known as 'special nodes' or 'special FS items' (*Figure 15.14*):

- Assets
- Liabilities and Equity
- Net Result: Profit
- Net Result: Loss
- P&L Result
- Financial Statement Notes
- Not Assigned

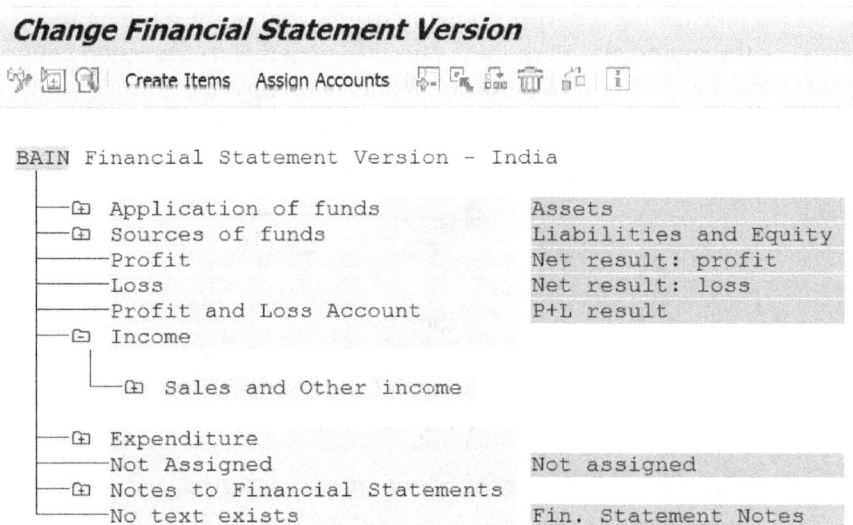

Figure 15.14: *Financial Statement Version (BAIN) – Nodes*

An FSV can have a maximum of ten hierarchy levels, each assigned to an item (*account category*). As you go down the hierarchy, you define the account categories in more detail, with the lowest level being represented by the G/L accounts. The system displays the relevant amount for each of these items (*Figure 15.15*):

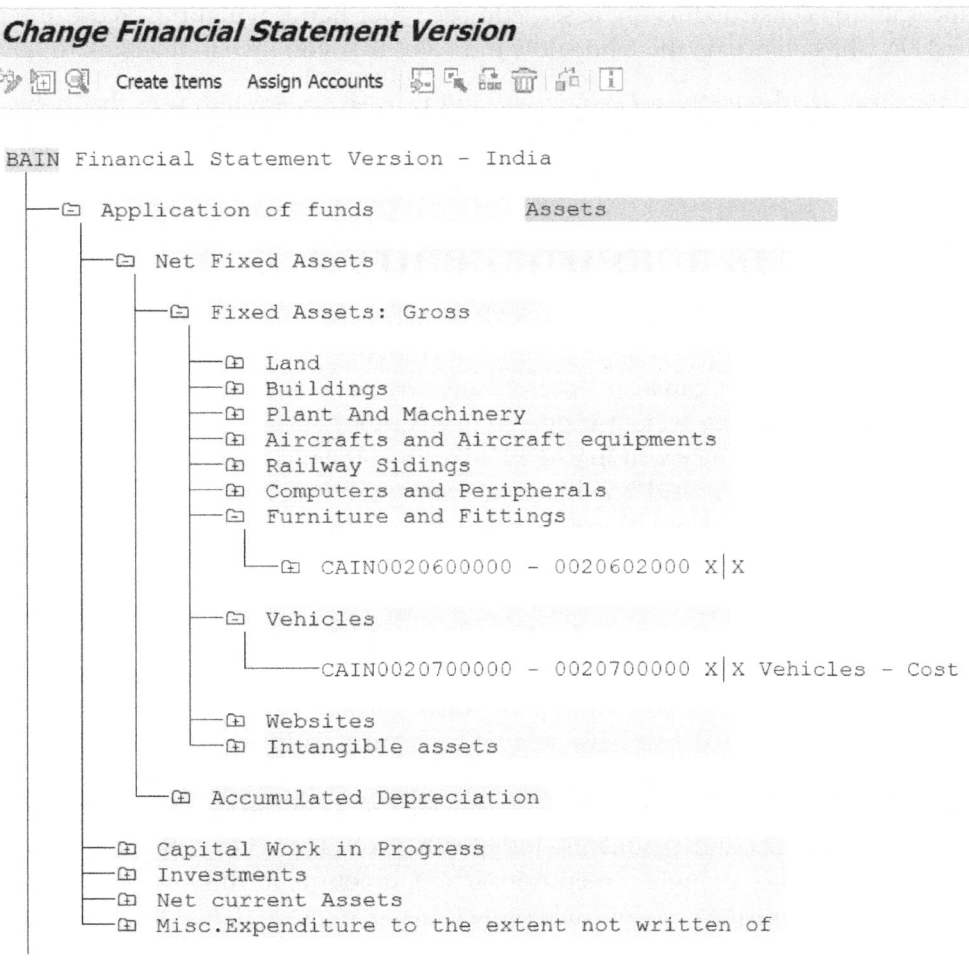

Figure 15.15: Financial Statement Version (BAIN) – Expanded view

404. How to ensure 'correct' balances in 'FSV'?

To have a balanced financial statement (*Profit & Loss* and *Balance Sheet*), you need to ensure that the accounts are correctly and completely assigned to the nodes of the FSV You may do this by resorting to the necessary assignments at the account balance level or node balance level.

At the *account balance level*, you need to ensure that the account is shown in two different nodes, but you will turn "ON" the 'debit indicator' of the account on one node and turn *ON* the 'credit indicator' on the other node. Imagine that you have a bank current account of 10001000. When you turn "ON" the debit indicator, this account shows only the debit balances and is construed as an 'asset.' On the other hand, when the credit indicator is turned *ON*, the balance on this node now indicates that you owe to the bank (overdraft).

You may also use the *node level assignment*. In this case, the system uses the 'debit/credit shift' and shows only the 'effective' balance at the node and **not** at the individual account level.

405. What is a 'journal entry'?

A record of business transactions in SAP S/4HANA Finance, the journal entry can represent special documents like sample documents, recurring entry documents, or parked documents. They can also represent any original documents like invoices, receipts, etc. A journal entry can be system-triggered in any other business application outside SAP FI or a manual journal entry within SAP FI. Like any other accounting document, a journal entry comprises a header and line items (at least two). It may contain additional ledger-specific information or information relating to document splitting, for example. When you post the journal entry, it updates the universal journal.

406. What is a 'cash journal'?

Being a sub-ledger in bank accounting, the '**cash journal**' helps you manage the cash for your Company Code. You can have several cash journals in a Company Code, and you can deploy at least one cash journal per currency. Through the cash journal, the system calculates and displays the opening and closing balances automatically, besides calculating the totals for receipts and payments. Independent of other transactions, you can enter, edit, and display, via a single screen transaction, amounts in different currencies in the cash journal and save the cash journal before transferring to SAP FI. Once transferred, the cash journal entries correspond to the FI documents. For each cash journal document, you can assign different account assignments, business areas, tax codes et

407. What is 'document splitting'?

The '**document splitting**' lets you automatically split the line items for select dimensions (say, segment, business area, etc.) to result in a zero balance. During document splitting, the system automatically creates additional line items. With document splitting, you can draw up complete financial statements at any time for dimensions like segments, profit centers, funds, receivables, business areas, etc. Through document splitting, you can also allocate additional costs when posting to CO cot objects.

To facilitate document splitting, SAP comes with two wizards: 'configuring document splitting' (*Figure 15.16*) and 'configuring document split rule' (*Figure 15.17*). When you use the wizards, you do not need to carry out the individual Customization activities listed in SAP IMG.

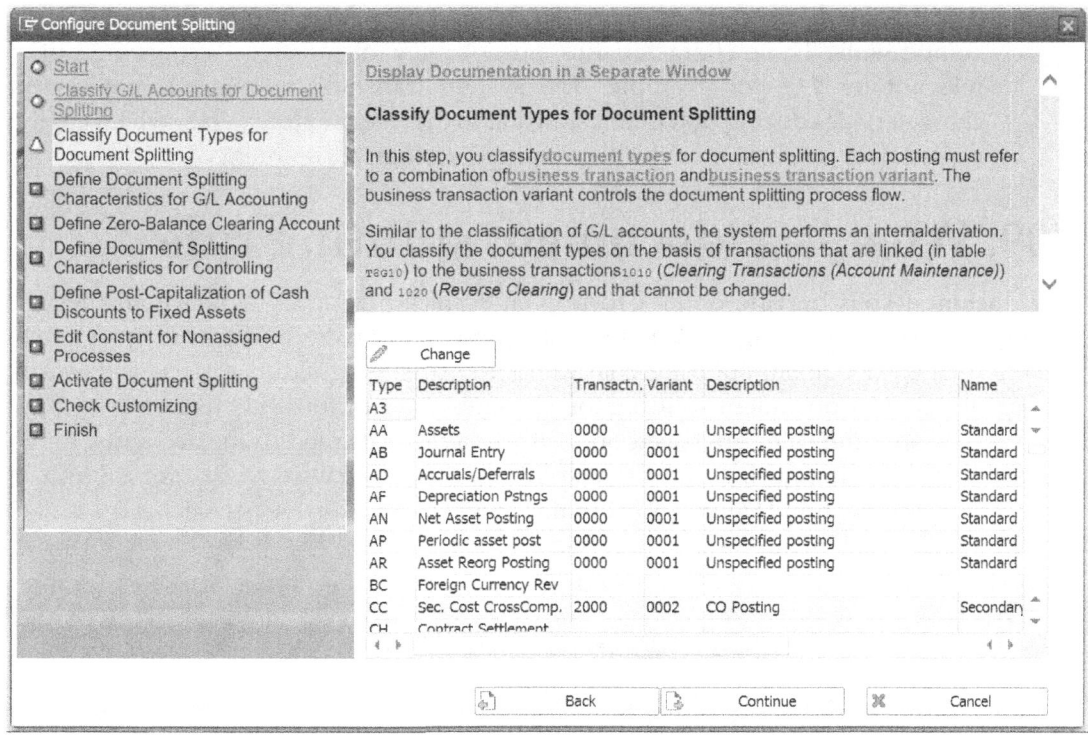

Figure 15.16: *Wizard for configuring document splitting*

408. What do you mean by 'document splitting characteristic'?

The '**document splitting characteristic**' is an account assignment object like a profit center, business area, segment, etc., for which you carry out document splitting in the system. The document splitting characteristics are classified into two categories:

- **Document splitting characteristics relevant for G/L Accounting**: Define the document splitting characteristics for G/L Accounting by specifying the fields or partner fields. You will also make the required settings for '*zero-balance*': when set, the system checks, during posting, whether the balance is zero for that characteristic. If the balance is not zero, the system creates additional clearing lines on the clearing accounts to produce a zero balance. Set this indicator if you want to produce a B/S based on a specified characteristic. You will also set if it is '*mandatory*' for a field to have value: when set, the field must contain a value after document splitting. Set this indicator for fields for which you require a complete B/S and for which inaccuracies due to non-assigned postings cannot be tolerated. When this indicator is set, the system rejects, with an error message, any posting that, after document splitting, lacks a value for the specified field.

- **Additional document splitting characteristics relevant for other application components:** These characteristics are not relevant for G/L Accounting but are relevant for CO, for example. The system transfers these document-splitting characteristics during document splitting to the relevant line items, which are then copied over to CO along with the required account assignments.

409. What is a 'document splitting rule'?

The '**document splitting rule**' defines, for a given '*business transaction*', which item categories the system splits and from which item categories it derives the account assignments for the defined document splitting characteristics. It is assigned to a '*document splitting method*' and defines document splitting for a business transaction and business transaction variant. The splitting rules are based on '*item categories*' assigned to the accounts. As you have a wizard for configuring document splitting, you also have a wizard for configuring document splitting rule (*Figure 15.17*), which means you do not need to carry out the individual Customizing tasks in SAP IMG.

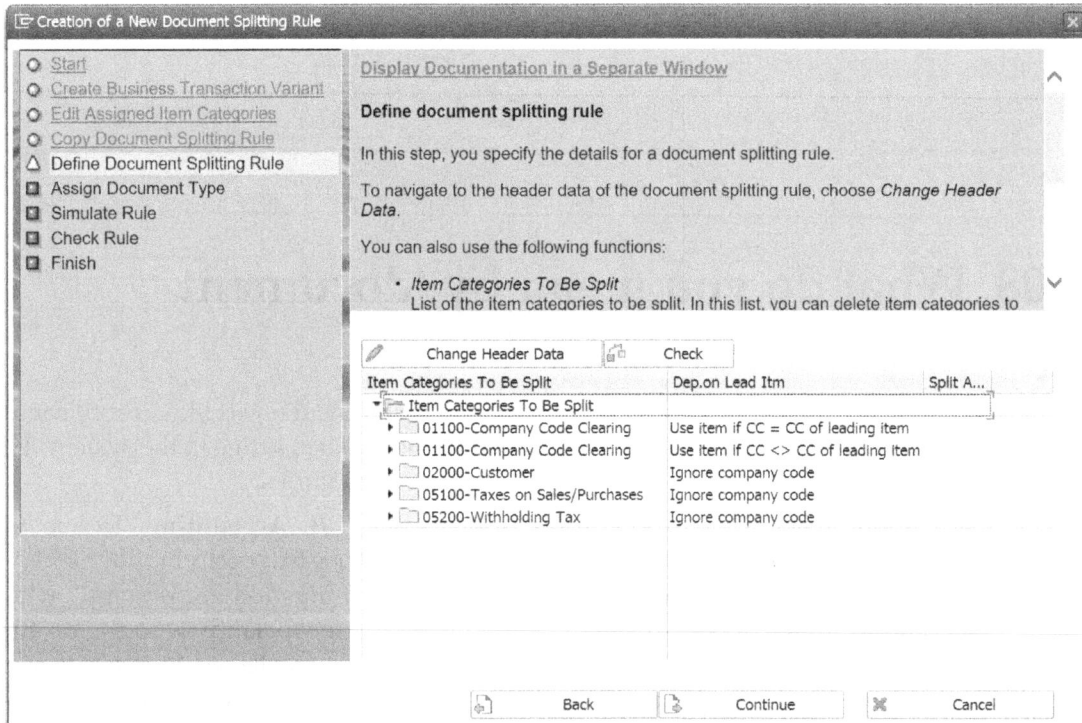

Figure 15.17: Wizard for creating Document Splitting Rule

410. What is a 'document splitting method'?

The '**document splitting method**' consists of document splitting rules for the business transaction and business transaction variant. Using the method, you define how the system splits the document. The standard SAP system contains three document splitting methods that use the business transaction variant '001' for each business transaction.

The three standard document-splitting methods are:

- 0000000012 Standard document splitting method (follow-up costs online)
- 0000000101 Document splitting method for US Fund Accounting
- 0000000111 Document splitting method for US Fund Accounting (follow-up costs online)

The default document splitting method is '0000000012'.

411. What is an 'Item Category'?

Derived from the account type, an '**item category**' enables the classification of accounts for document splitting. There may be more than one item category for the G/L accounts. A pre-requisite for document splitting in G/L Accounting, the system uses account numbers to determine the item category of line items. SAP comes delivered with several standard item categories (like 01000-B/S account, 01100-Company Code clearing, 20000-Expenses, 30000-Revenue, 40200-Exchange rate difference, etc.) that you need to use as such (*Figure 15.18*). You cannot create any additional item categories.

Item Cat.	Description	Forbidden	Required	Only Once
01000	Balance Sheet Account			
01100	Company Code Clearing			
02000	Customer		✓	
02100	Customer: Special G/L Transaction			
05100	Taxes on Sales/Purchases			
05200	Withholding Tax			
07000	Fixed Assets			
20000	Expense			
30000	Revenue			
40200	Exchange Rate Difference			
80000	Customer-Specific Item Category			

Figure 15.18: Default Item Categories for Document Splitting

412. What is 'Passive Document Splitting'?

A function of document splitting in SAP G/L Accounting, the '**passive document splitting**' comprises all document processes (like clearing) created internally by the program, and you will have no say or control in the splitting processes with your Customizing settings.

This kind of splitting creates a reference to the existing account assignments. Passive splitting covers the functions like clearing, clearing reset, reversal, and payment-relevant invoice reference.

413. What is 'Active Document Splitting'? How does it differ from 'Passive Splitting'?

Like passive document splitting, **'active document splitting'** is also a function of document splitting in SAP G/L Accounting. However, unlike passive splitting, here, in active splitting, you can control the way the documents are split via the Customizing settings in the system. This kind of splitting comprises all processes that are used to split documents without reference to any of the preceding documents. The splitting is based on the Customizing settings like document splitting methods and document splitting rules. Once configured, the active document splitting runs automatically. That is, the system splits the document line items based on the document's assignments to the business transaction and the assigned document splitting rule. Hence, you can make use of active splitting only for documents that are uniquely associated with a business transaction.

414. What is 'Enhancement Logic' in Document splitting?

The **enhancement logic** in document splitting enables you to add missing account assignments by an inheritance mechanism or a standard account assignment.

Consider that you have performed an active document splitting, but there are missing account assignments for the document splitting characteristics that you have used. In this case, you can use **'inheritance'** to complete the missing assignments. For this to take effect, you need to select the '*Inheritance*' indicator while activating document splitting (*Figure 15.19*).

Also, when the system cannot derive missing account assignments automatically during an active splitting, you can overcome that by defining a **'standard account assignment'**. You do this by selecting the '*Standard A/c Assgnmt*' indicator and entering a '*Constant*' when activating document splitting (*Figure 15.19*). By this, the system will enter the standard account assignments, defined in the constants, for the line items without any account assignment.

Figure 15.19: Activating Document Splitting with 'Inheritance' & 'Standard A/c Assignment'

415. Explain the process of 'Document Splitting'.

When you configure **document splitting** with the various settings (including document types, business transactions, business transaction variants, document splitting method, document splitting rules, item categories, and activation of document splitting together with the enhancement logic), the system proceeds to complete document splitting as follows (*Figure 15.20*):

1. When you post a document, the system determines the 'business transaction' from the 'document type' and assigns the appropriate 'item category' to the various line items of the document. While doing such an assignment, the system checks if a particular item category is allowed for that business transaction.

2. Now, the system starts with the 'passive document splitting'; besides creating a reference to the preceding documents (like clearing, invoice reference, etc.), the system applies the account assignments that you have already defined as the document splitting characteristics for SAP G/L Accounting.

3. Next, the system initiates 'active document splitting'; it applies the appropriate 'document splitting rule' based on the document classification and completes the splitting according to the specifications regarding how the document is split and what line items are to be taken into the split.

4. During the process, if the system fails to determine the account assignments in the normal course, it proceeds to decide either by 'inheritance' or 'standard A/c assignment.' This may be because the account assignment information was not available when posting.

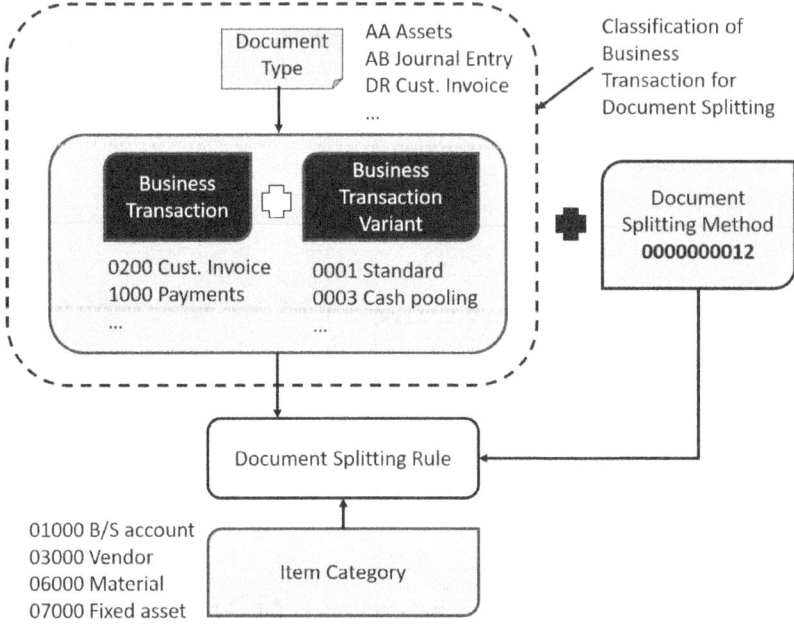

Figure 15.20: Document splitting process

5. If you have defined, in SAP G/L Accounting, that the line items for document splitting characteristics must always be assigned to an account, and when the system finds out that there has not been any such account assignment available, then it throws an error message and rejects the posting.

6. When the document does not result in a 'zero-balance' for the balancing dimensions, the system automatically creates additional clearing items to ensure that they do.

It is possible that you can 'simulate' document splitting before the actual split happens in the system. While in simulation in G/L view, you may call up the 'expert' mode and view the detailed information of the split, including the document splitting rule that the system has applied.

416. Explain 'Document Splitting' using an example.

The following figure *(Figure 15.21)* illustrates how document splitting happens in the system:

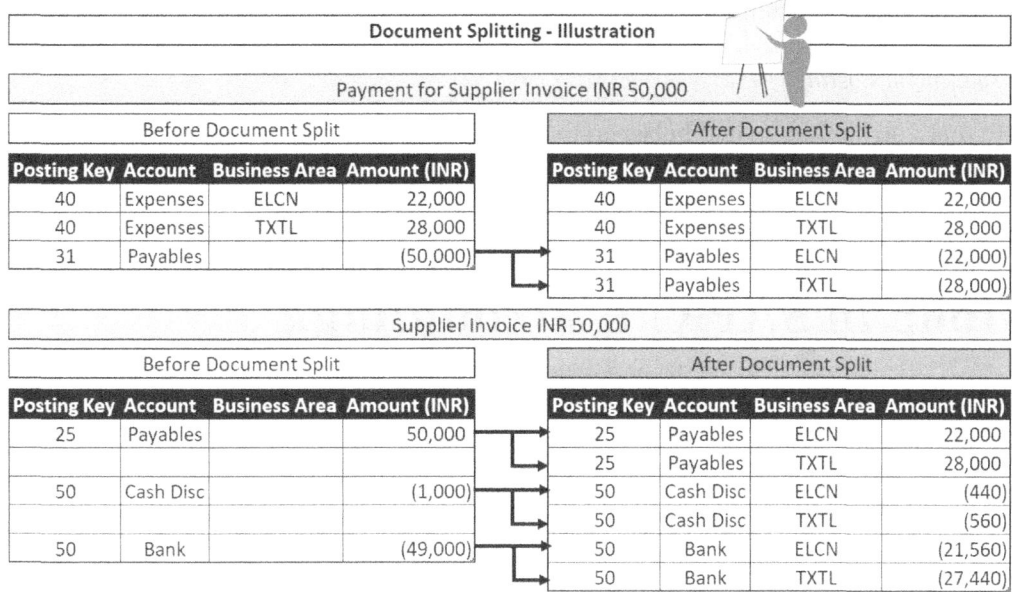

Figure 15.21: Document splitting – An illustration

The explanation is as follows:

- In the case of the payables of Rs. 50,000 (with no information on business area assignment), during document splitting, the total payable amount is split into two items: a payable of Rs. 22,000 for the business are 'ELCN' and another for Rs. 28,000 relating to the business area 'TXTL.'

- In the case of supplier invoice for Rs. 50,000, during document splitting, the system does a 3-way split as indicated below:

  o The payables of Rs. Rs. 50,000 (without a business area assignment) is split into two: a payable of Rs. 22,000 for the business area 'ELCN' and another for Rs. 28,000 for the other business area 'TXTL.'

  o The cash discount (Rs. 1,000) is split between the two business areas: Rs. 440 for 'ELCN' and Rs. 560 for 'TXTL'.

  o Similarly, the bank credit amount of Rs. 49,000 is also split: Rs. 21,560 for the 'ELCN' business area and the remaining Rs. 27,440 for 'TXTL".

417. How do you post to all Ledgers in SAP G/L Accounting?

You can post all ledgers in SAP G/L accounting via the SAP Easy Access Menu path: *SAP Menu | Accounting | Financial Accounting | General Ledger | Document Entry | Enter G/L Account Document* or Transaction Code **FB50**. This is a single-screen transaction.

You can also use the standard function via Transaction Code **F-02** or the SAP Easy Access Menu path: *SAP Menu | Accounting | Financial Accounting | General Ledger | Document Entry General Posting*.

Note that you cannot switch between the single-screen and the standard document entry function when entering a document.

418. How do you post to a specific Ledger Group in SAP G/L Accounting?

If you want to post only to the ledgers in a specific ledger group, you can achieve the same via the SAP Easy Access Menu path: *SAP Menu | Accounting | Financial Accounting | General Ledger | Document Entry | Enter G/L Account Document for Ledger Group* or Transaction Code **FB50L**. When you post, the document is posted to all the ledgers in that group; if the ledger group contains only one, the system posts only to that ledger.

Instead of single-screen transaction, you can also use the standard function via the SAP Easy Access Menu path: *SAP Menu | Accounting | Financial Accounting | General Ledger | Document Entry | Enter General Posting for Ledger Group* or Transaction Code **FB01L**.

419. What are the conditions stipulated for posting to a Ledger Group?

When you post to specific ledger groups in SAP G/L Accounting, note that you can post only in the currencies assigned to the participating ledgers or ledger group. When posting to a ledger group, you cannot make tax-relevant postings, postings directly to tax G/L accounts, and postings to G/L accounts that you maintain on an open item basis. When posting to a ledger group, the system determines the **fiscal year variant** (**FYV**) and the Company Code using the group's 'representative ledger'. It then checks to see if the posting period is open for that Company Code: if yes, it posts to all the assigned ledgers of the ledger group, using the appropriate FYV of each ledger. The system posts to all other assigned ledgers, even if the posting period is not open.

420. What do you mean by 'Document Simulation'?

After inputting the details in a document, before you post the same, you can **'simulate' the document** to see the overview of the line items that you have entered to verify if you have put in the details correctly (*Figure 15.22*). During simulation, the system displays the auto-generated line items so that you get a complete picture of the document that will be posted later. When simulated, the document undergoes all the checks required for posting. If the document does not have zero balance, when you click "Document | Simulate" from the menu bar or press F9, you may get a message: 'Posting is only possible with zero balance; correct document.' Based on the simulated view, you may then correct the line items that you have already entered, enter new line items, delete system-generated line items, and hold, park, or post the document.

You may simulate the documents in the Entry view or G/L view. The simulation in the G/L view (menu bar: "*Document | Simulate General Ledger*") is for specific ledgers: what you will first see is the simulation for the leading ledger; from there, you can simulate for a specific ledger by specifying that ledger

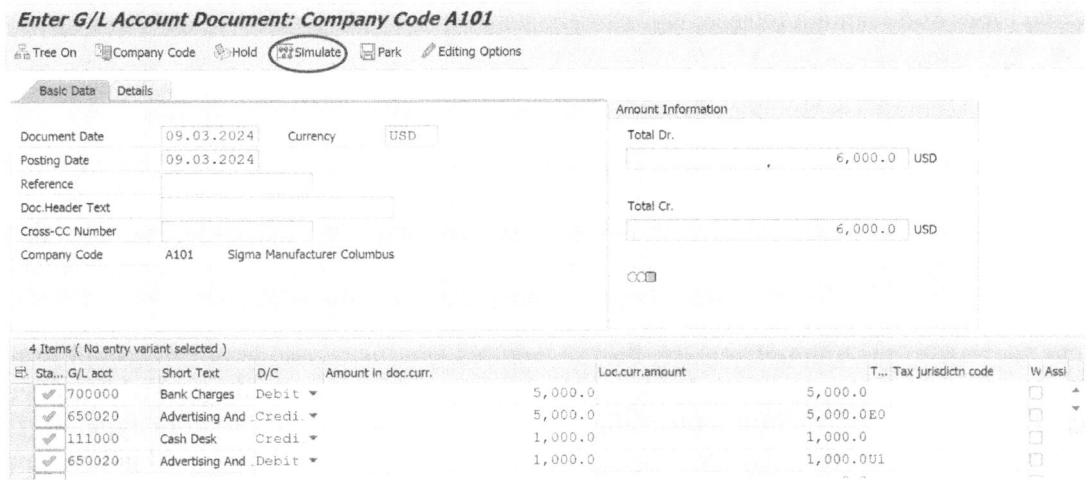

Figure 15.22: Document Simulation

421. What is 'Document Release'?

You may resort to '**document release**' when you have 'parked documents' in the system (refer to *Questions 274 & 275* for more about document parking).

For the 'release' to take effect in SAP FI, you need to make the required **workflow (WF)** configurations: follow the IMG Menu Path - *SAP Customizing Implementation Guide | Financial Accounting | Financial Accounting Global Settings | Tools | Workflow | Workflow for Document Parking*. You need to complete several Customizing steps, including 'Create Workflow Variant for Parking Documents,' 'Assign Company Code to a Workflow Variant for Parking Documents,' 'Define Release Approval Groups for Parking Documents,' 'Define Release Approval Paths for Parking Documents,' 'Assign Release Approval Paths for Parking Documents,' 'Assign Release Approval Procedure for Parking Documents,' 'Define Users with Release Authorization for Parking Documents,' 'Reset Release Approval (Customers),' 'Reset Release Approval (Vendors)' and so on.

When you make the workflow configurations, you actually define the amount from which a 'release' is required in the system, define the 'release approval procedure' within the workflow, and specify the fields, if the content of which is changed, that can result in cancellation of the release so that the system can restart the release approval process all over.

422. Explain the two 'Types of Releases' in parked documents.

In SAP S/4HANA Finance, while working with parked documents, you may come across two types of document release:

- Amount release
- Account assignment release

The system triggers *'amount release'* when the document is first parked. Based on the configurations, you can have a single-level, two-level, or three-level amount released. This determines whether the document requires a release by one person, two persons, or three persons: the higher the document amount, the higher the level of release. For each level of release, you can authorize a number of people to complete the release.

In contrast to the amount release, the *'account assignment release'* is not triggered in the system until you have entered all the data and confirmed the same in the parked document. While making the configuration settings, you would define, per account type, all the applicable organizational objects (job, organizational units, etc.) that would get assigned to this release type. For example, you may assign the persons responsible for release to cost centers; these persons must release the documents.

You can post a parked document only when both the amount released and the account assignment release are completed. Otherwise, the system returns the document to the person who entered it to make corrections and resubmit.

423. What are the 'Clearing Transactions'?

You may define a '**clearing transaction**' as requiring an item to be cleared. The clearing transactions include incoming payment, outgoing payment, and transfer posting with clearing. In a standard system, you will use incoming payment-clearing transactions to clear items against incoming customer payments. Similarly, you will use outgoing payment-clearing transactions to clear items against outgoing supplier payments.

424. What are all the options available for Clearing?

When you work with the accounts that are maintained on an open item basis, you can resort to:

- Post with clearing (automatic clearing)
- Manual clearing

It is possible to process several accounts, different account types (S, D, & K), and accounts from multiple Company Codes while carrying out the clearing. You will use the 'clearing program' for **automatic clearing**, wherein the system matches the open items, unlike **manual clearing**, wherein you determine what to match with what. When the system completes the clearing, it assigns a clearing number and date to all the items that have been cleared. This way, for example, the system marks the vendor invoices as 'paid' and indicates bank clearing account items as 'cleared.'

If you have special G/L transactions, you cannot use the clearing program to clear those items. Also, the clearing program cannot clear items that require additional postings, such as items with cash discounts that require posting of the cash discount amount.

425. What is 'Manual Clearing'?

Instead of using the payment program to automatically clear the open items, you resort to 'manual clearing,' in which you manually select the open items from an account so that they balance to zero. When cleared, the system enters a clearing document number and the clearing date (current date or manually entered date) in the document items.

You will normally undertake manual clearing when making a refund to the supplier when you have agreed to the debit memo procedure, and for bank subaccounts and clearing accounts.

426. How can you manually 'clear' the 'Open Items' and when?

In **manual clearing**, as mentioned earlier, you will manually select the open items based on, for example, the incoming payment so that the selected 'open items' are 'cleared' (knocked-off). When cleared, the system flags these line items as 'cleared,' creates a clearing document, and enters the clearing document number and clearing date in these open items. Besides the clearing document, the system may also automatically generate 'additional documents' in cases of *partial* or *residual processing* and for posting the loss/gain to the assigned G/L account.

While doing this, if there is a *payment difference*, then the system considers the following:

- If the difference is within the tolerance limit, the cash discount is adjusted, or the system automatically posts the difference to a gain/loss G/L account.

- When the payment difference exceeds the limits of defined tolerance, then the incoming amount may be processed as a *partial payment* (the original open item is not cleared, but the incoming payment is posted with reference to that invoice), or the difference is posted as the *residual item* (the original open item is cleared and a new open item created by the system for the difference amount) in the system. Refer to *Questions 294 to 297* for more details on partial/residual processing.

You may also use the SAP Easy Access Menu Path:

- *SAP Menu | Accounting | Financial Accounting | General Ledger | Document entry,* and select any of the following Transactions:

  - **F-04** - Post with Clearing

  - **F-06** - Incoming Payments

  - **F-07** - Outgoing Payments

- *SAP Menu | Accounting | Financial Accounting | Account Receivable | Document entry | Incoming payment* or Transaction Code **F-28**.

427. Explain 'Automatic Clearing'.

Instead of manually selecting the open items to be cleared, in '**automatic clearing**,' you let the system run the *clearing program,* which selects the open items to be cleared with the payment.

You can execute automatic clearing from G/L, A/P, or A/R components. For example, in SAP G/L Accounting, you will be using the SAP Easy Access Menu: *SAP Menu | Accounting | Financial Accounting | General Ledger | Periodic Processing | Automatic Clearing,* and select the appropriate task:

- Without Specification of Clearing Currency (Transaction Code **F.13**)

- With Specification of Clearing Currency (Transaction Code **F13E**)

- G/L Accounts - Specific to Ledger Groups (Transaction Code **F13L**)

- GR/IR Accounts with Extended Open Item Management (Transaction Code **FGRIR_CLEARING)**

Besides entering the parameters like Company Code, fiscal year, what accounts to be considered (G/L accounts, customers, and/vendors), etc., you can also enter specifications, according to which the system gives you a proposal list consisting of, for example, items that can be cleared, items that cannot be cleared, and errors. Once you are satisfied with the clearing item list that is output by the system, you can deselect the 'Test Run' checkbox and run the program so that the clearing is effected for the given parameters.

428. What is 'Cross-Company Code Clearing'?

Available in SAP G/L Accounting, FI-A/R, and FI-A/P application components, the 'Cross-Company Code Clearing' functionality is useful if you have centralized procurement and/or payment in your Company involving more than one Company Code. Here, for example, a designated central Company Code makes payment on behalf of all the participating Company Codes with respect to the procurement invoices of the individual Company Codes. During clearing, the system makes appropriate clearing entries (representing the A/R and A/P) between the Company Codes participating in such a cross-Company Code clearing procedure. The system creates a separate clearing document for each of the Company Codes, with a joint transaction number tying up all these individual documents together.

Besides centralized procurement and/or payment, the cross-Company Code clearing may also be useful when customers make wrong payments to a Company Code or when you operate with more than one Company Code in a group Company setup. For example, suppose that you receive a payment from a customer to Company Code A101 instead of paying to A102. In this case, via cross-Company Code clearing, you can debit the bank account in Company Code A101 and credit the customer account in Company Code A102, thereby minimizing the number of accounting entries you will otherwise have to pass. The system will create the required clearing entries automatically. When posted, the transaction results in three documents: for the paying Company Code (say, A101) in its books, for the other Company Codes (say, A102), and for the cross-Company Code transaction itself.

Also, when one of the Company Codes (of the corporate group) is the manufacturer and the other is the merchandiser, you can use cross-Company Code clearing functionality.

While making the required settings in Customizing, per each pair of Company Codes, you have to specify the posting keys and G/L (or customer or vendor) account numbers for the clearing entries (*Figure 15.23*):

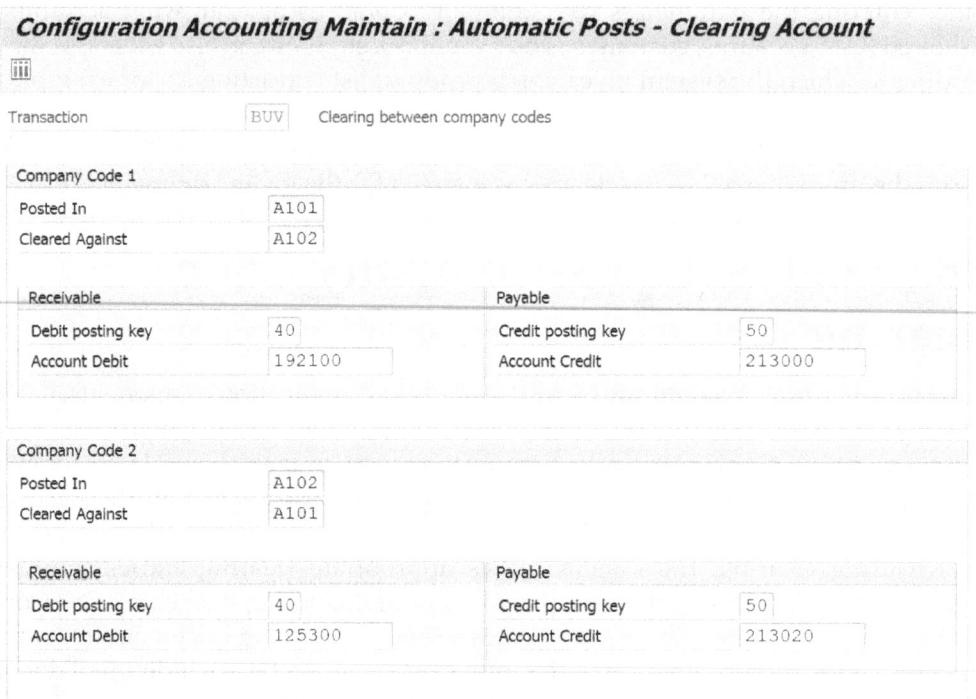

Figure 15.23: Cross-Company Code Transactions Customizing for SAP G/L Accounting

You need to maintain the cross-Company Code transaction specifications for each clearing procedure like:

- AUSGZAHL (outgoing payment)
- EINGZAHL (incoming payment)
- GUTSCHRI (credit memo)
- UMBUCHNG (transfer posting with clearing)

You may either use the IMG or Transaction Code to complete the configuration relating to cross-Company Code clearing as detailed in *Table 15.1*:

Application area	IMG customizing	Transaction Code
SAP G/L Accounting	*SAP Customizing Implementation Guide	Financial Accounting	General Ledger Accounting	Business Transactions	Prepare Cross-Company Code Transactions.*	**OBYA**
SAP FI-A/R	*SAP Customizing Implementation Guide	Financial Accounting	Accounts Receivable and Accounts Payable	Business Transactions	Outgoing Payments	Manual Outgoing Payments	Prepare Cross-Company Code Manual Payments.*	**OB60**

Application area	IMG customizing	Transaction Code
SAP FI-A/P	*SAP Customizing Implementation Guide	Financial Accounting	Accounts Receivable and Accounts Payable	Business Transactions	Incoming Payments	Manual Incoming Payments	Prepare Cross-Company Code Manual Payments.*	**OB60**

Table 15.1: IMG Path / Transaction Code for Cross-Company Code Configuration

429. What are the different postings that happen automatically during Clearing?

During clearing, the system can automatically post the following:

- Cash discount paid/received
- Entries that are required to clear the cash discount in the 'net' method of posting
- Gain/loss arising out of over/underpayments and from exchange rate differences.
- Tax: input, output, and withholding tax

430. What are 'Bank Subaccounts'? Why do you need them?

You use **'bank subaccounts'** in SAP G/L Accounting to reconcile the balance of bank G/L accounts corresponding with the balance of the accounts with your bank. This way, you can ensure that the incoming and outgoing payments are posted only to the bank G/L account(s) via these bank subaccounts (like checks payable, checks receivable, wire transfer, bank direct debit, etc.) as and when the actual debits/credits are happening in the bank accounts. The standard accounts charts come with several pre-defined bank subaccounts that you can use. Note that the bank subaccounts must be maintained on an open-item basis with the line-item display.

431. What is 'Accruals Management' under SAP G/L Accounting?

The **'accruals management'** is all about accounting for expenses in the period they are incurred, irrespective of when they are posted in the system. SAP provides different functions for calculating, checking, and posting accruals in SAP G/L Accounting and SAP S/4HANA Finance. You can use the system to calculate the accruals and then post them at the end of the month. Besides, you can use the accrual functions to consider, for example, invoice posting, to adjust the system-calculated accruals. All accruals management functions are built around the 'accrual engine.' You must make the required Customizing settings in SAP IMG for different accrual item types like manual accruals, purchase order accruals, service entry sheet accruals, etc.

432. What are the 'Periodic Processing' functions that you carry out in SAP G/L Accounting?

The following are the three '**periodic processing**' functions that you carry out at regular intervals in SAP G/L Accounting in SAP S/4HANA Finance:

- Integrated business planning
- Closing operations
- Balance interest calculation

433. Explain the 'Closing' operations that you will undertake at the year-end.

There are several processes and functions as a part of closing operations that you undertake at the end of every fiscal year in the system:

- **Check/count:** Use the program '*Reconciliation of Receivables/Payables in Group (Cross-System)*' to reconcile customer and supplier documents of the Company Codes in the group. This program reads the open items of selected Company Codes for the key date specified, helping you identify documents that cause a difference.

- **Valuate:** Complete foreign currency valuation for foreign currency B/S accounts that are not managed on an open item basis and open items that you have posted in a foreign currency and are open on the key date.

- **Regroup**: Before creating the B/S, analyze the GR/IR clearing account to carry out corrections postings, if any. Perform a 'rollup' by specifying how data from various source ledgers are rolled up into the rollup ledger. Complete the ordering of A/R and A/P according to their remaining term.

- **Allocation:** Before creating the B/S, complete allocation of amounts and quantities from sender objects to receiver objects.

- **Value adjustment:** Before creating the B/S, if there are doubtful receivables, you need to post individual value adjustments for that or write off that receivable.

- **Carry forward:** You must carry the account balances to the new fiscal year.

434. Explain the 'SAP Financial Closing Cockpit' that you can leverage for period-end closing.

The '**SAP financial closing cockpit**' (*Figure 15.24*) helps you to plan, execute, and analyze the closing operations for your Company Code in SAP. With its structured user interface, it makes closing operations simple to carry out and complete the different tasks in time. The event-controlled closing activities can be closely monitored with the process overview and many built-in analytical tools.

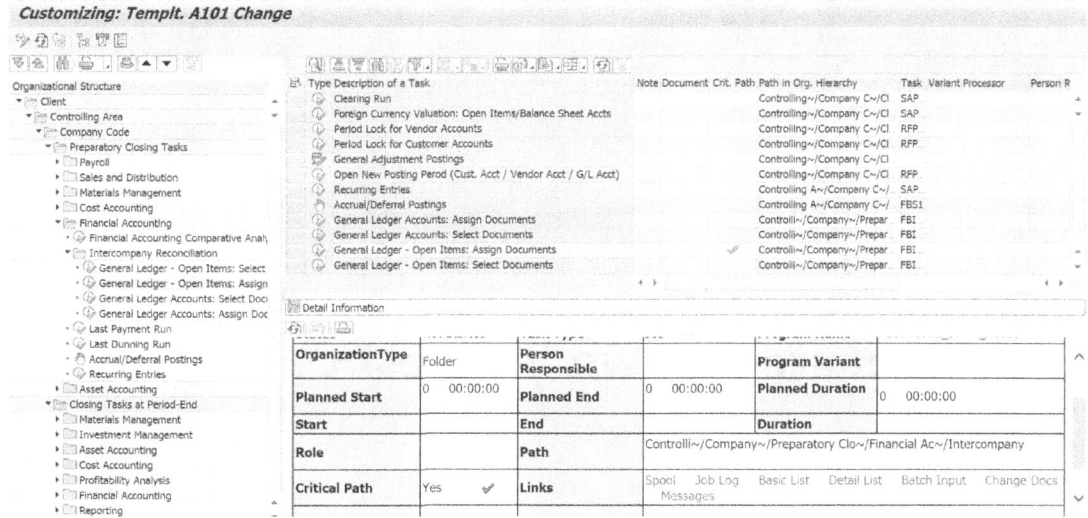

Figure 15.24: SAP Financial Closing Cockpit

Figure 15.25

435. What are all the 'Structural Objects' in the SAP Financial Closing Cockpit?

Figure 15.26 shows all the '**structural objects**' that you will notice within the 'SAP Financial Closing Cockpit' in SAP S/4HANA Finance:

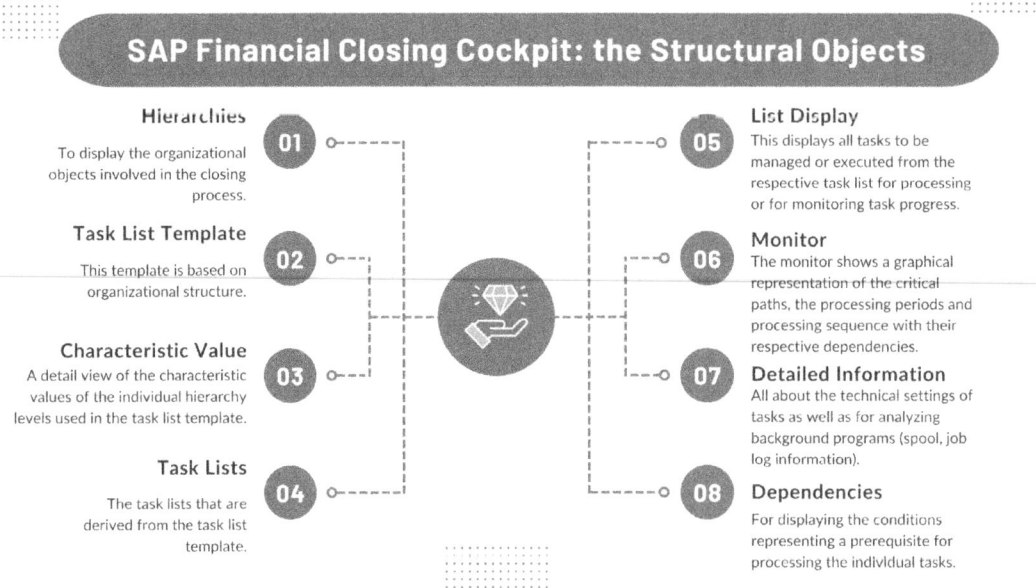

Figure 15.26: *SAP Financial Closing Cockpit: The Structural Objects*

436. What are the two 'Interest Calculation Types'?

The two 'interest calculation types' are:

- **Balance interest calculation (S)**: For calculating interest on the account balance (also known as 'interest scale').
- **Item interest calculation (P)**: This is used to calculate interest on arrears (per item) based on supplier/vendor or customer account's open items.

437. What is the use of the 'Balance Interest Calculation' functionality in SAP G/L Accounting?

With the help of '**balance interest calculation**' (aka "*bank interest calculation*") functionality, you can:

- Calculate the interest on the balance of your G/L accounts managed on an open-item basis. This is useful, for example, to check the interest calculated on your accounts by your bank.

- Calculate interest, for example, on employee loans that you have been managing in A/R and A/P.

438. List out the specifications to control 'Balance Interest Calculation.'

The following specifications control how the system calculates balance interest:

- Specifications in G/L account **master records** include interest indicator, interest calculation frequency, and details relating to the last interest calculation.

- Specifications stored in the **interest indicator**, such as the interest rate, rules for interest calculation, interest determination calendar, etc.,

- You make specifications for an **interest calculation run**, such as the selection criteria, posting control, negative interest, etc.

439. Explain the G/L fields relevant for 'Balance Interest Calculation.'

The following four fields in a G/L account master record (Company Code area) are relevant for balance interest calculation in the system (*Figure 15.27*):

- **Interest indicator:** The balance interest calculation program considers the interest indicator from the G/L account master record. If you want to include a G/L account for interest calculation, enter an interest indicator value in this field. If there is no entry in this field, then that specific account will not be included in the interest calculation run. For balance interest calculation, the interest indicator should be of type *'balance interest calculation.'*

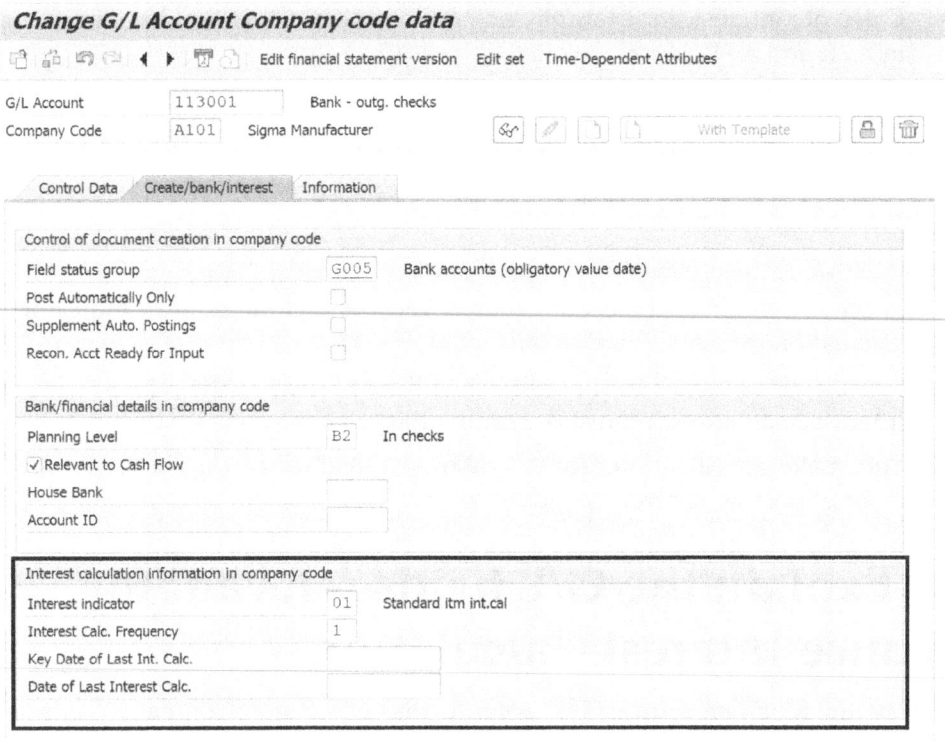

Figure 15.27: G/L Account Master Record- Fields relevant for Balance Interest Calculation

- **Interest calculation frequency (monthly, bi-monthly, quarterly, etc.)**: To arrive at the upper limit of the current interest calculation run, you will add this interest calculation frequency to the date of the last interest calculation. If you do not maintain the interest calculation frequency in the master record, the system considers the frequency specified in the interest indicator.

- **Key date of last interest calculation**: Inserted by the system automatically, this is the upper limit of the interest calculation period. The system uses the date in this field to arrive at the interest calculation period for an account. You will not normally make an entry in this field unless there is an error.

- **Date of last interest calculation**: Used only for calculating interest on account balances, the system updates this field automatically with the last date of account balance interest calculation. Not relevant for interest on arrears.

440. What is an 'Interest Indicator'?

The '**interest indicator**' controls the system's interest calculation. You define an interest indicator in Customizing and enter this in the G/L account master record if you want the system to consider that account for interest calculation. While defining an interest indicator (*Figure 15.28*), you can specify the following:

Figure 15.28: Interest indicator

- The *period determination* helps specify the 'interest calculation frequency' in months. As mentioned, the system adds this to the date of the last interest calculation to arrive at the upper limit for the interest calculation run. You can also specify this in the G/L account master record; the entry in the master record has priority if you have specified the frequency both in the master record and in the interest indicator.

- The *calendar type* (for interest determination) specifies how many days per month and how many days per year as the basis for calculation. It can be 'B' - Bank calendar (30/360), 'F' - French calendar (28...31/365), 'G' - Gregorian calendar (28...31/365), 'J' - Japanese calendar (30/365). For example, the calendar type 'B' considers 30 days per month and 360 days per year, whereas 'F' considers the actual number of days as in a calendar month and 365 days in a year.

- *Month-end indicator*, *Interest calc. numerators* (if interest is calculated using the numerators), *Interest rate rates* depend on the *total amount* and other settings can be altered by selecting the appropriate checkboxes under 'interest determination' settings.

- The *amount limit* for interest settlement. If the calculated interest is less than the amount limit entered, the system does not settle the interest amount thus calculated. This helps eliminate settlements for small interest amounts.

- *Output control* and also the *terms of payment*, if required.

441. List out the Customizing steps for Balance Interest Calculation.

The Customizing steps that are required for configuring balance interest calculation in SAP G/L Accounting are outlined in *Table 15.2*:

#	Customizing task	Details	Menu path: *SAP Customizing Implementation Guide | Financial Accounting | General Ledger Accounting | Business Transactions | Bank Account Interest Calculation*	Transaction Code
1	Define interest calculation types	Specify the interest calculation type as 'S'.	*Interest Calculation Global Settings | Define Interest Calculation Types*	**OB46**
2	Prepare account balance interest calculation	Define the interest indicator and the specifications there on.	*Interest Calculation Global Settings | Define Interest Indicator*	**OBAA**
3	Define reference interest rates	Specify the reference interest rate that the system will use in interest calculation.	*Interest Calculation | Define Reference Interest Rates*	**OBAC**
4	Define time-dependent interest terms	Specify per currency and a validity date, how the system determines the interest rate for each interest indicator.	*Interest Calculation | Time-Dependent Interest Terms*	**OB81**
5	Enter interest values	Maintain the validity date and the interest rate, per reference interest rate key that you have specified in Step 3.	*Interest Calculation | Enter Interest Values*	**OB83**

| 6 | Prepare G/L account balance interest calculation | Maintain the specifications, including G/L accounts and account symbols, for posting the balance interest calculated. | *Interest Posting | Prepare G/L Account Balance Interest Calculation* | **OBV2** |

Table 15.2: Customizing steps for Balance Interest calculation

442. How to determine the 'Interest Calculation Period'?

You can determine the 'interest calculation period' for balance interest calculation in two ways:

- **Manual determination of interest calculation period:** Manually enter the interest calculation period (from and to) in the field '*Calculation Period*' under "*Further Selections*" while maintaining the parameters for every interest calculation run via the Transaction Code **F.52**. Do not make any other entry in the G/L account master record including for the field '*Key date of last int.calc*'. As the system does not check overlapping periods, if any, ensure you do not enter any overlapping periods for which the system has already calculated the interest. This is useful when calculating interest at fixed intervals, say every 90 days.

- **Automatic determination of interest calculation period:** Automatic determination of interest calculation period will come in handy if you have a requirement to calculate interest at irregular intervals with no period overlapping. Based on the parameters that you maintain, the system automatically determines the interest calculation period, thereby identifying the accounts that are to be included in a particular interest calculation run. The parameters that you need to maintain include the following:

  o Maintain the *interest calculation period* so that the system can determine which accounts to include in the current interest calculation run. Enter the specifications using Transaction Code **F.52**.

  o Ensure that the field '*Key date of last int.calc*' in the G/L account master record has an entry. The system normally inserts this automatically after completing an interest calculation run. However, if you have errors, you may need to maintain this manually.

  o Ensure that there is an entry in the field '*Interest Calc. Frequency*' in the G/L account master record. Instead of the master record, you may also maintain this value (in the field '*Interest calc.freq.*') while defining the interest indicator. If you have maintained it in both places, then the entry in the master record has priority.

o You must also maintain a value in the field '*Settlement day*' for interest calculation. This date, together with the month of the key date of the last interest calculation frequency and the interest calculation frequency, will help the system arrive at the **upper limit** of the interest calculation period for the current interest calculation run. The system arrives at the **lower limit** by adding one day to the key date of the last interest calculation. For example, consider the following *Table 15.3*:

Parameter	Value & remarks
Key date of last interest calculation	03/18/2023
Interest calculation frequency	1 (month)
Settlement day	20
Lower limit of interest calculation period	03/19/2023 (1 day is added to the key date of last interest calculation)
Upper limit of interest calculation period	04/20/2023 (month of key date of last interest calculation 03 + interest calculation frequency 1 = upper limit in months 04; day = settlement day 20)

Table 15.3: Interest calculation parameters: an example

443. What parameters must we maintain for an 'Interest Calculation Run'?

You can start an interest calculation run via the SAP Easy Access Menu path: *SAP Menu | Accounting | Financial Accounting | General Ledger | Periodic Processing | Interest Calculation | Balances*, or Transaction Code **F.52**. On the resulting screen (*Figure 15.30*), maintain the required parameters as indicated.

Figure 15.29

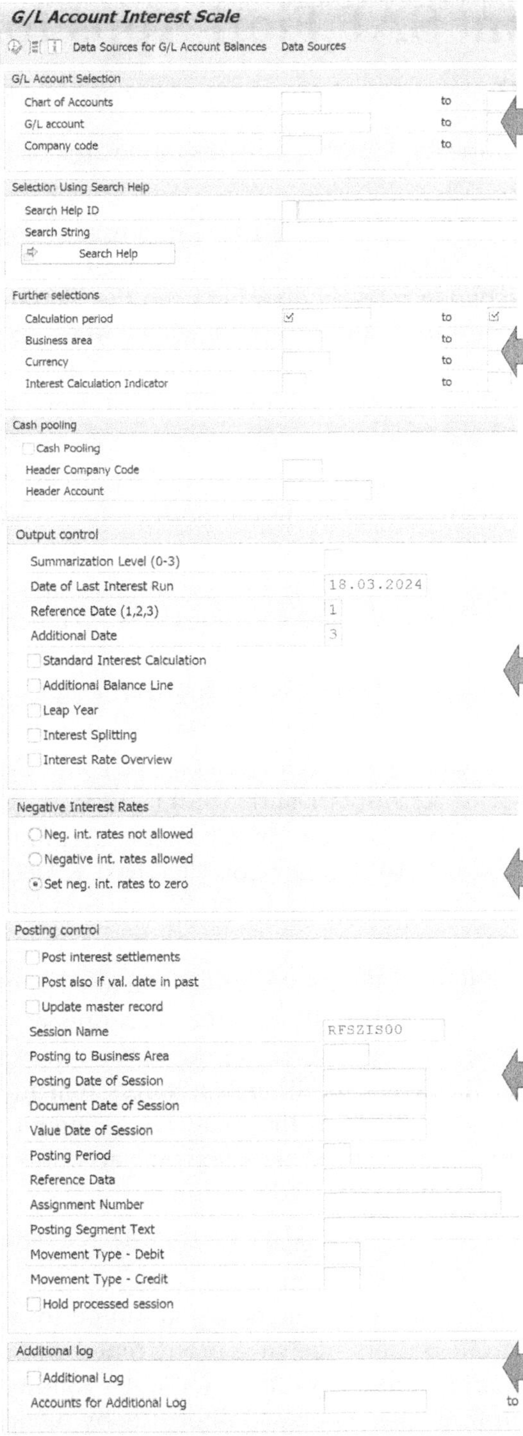

G/L Account Interest Scale

Data Sources for G/L Account Balances   Data Sources

G/L Account Selection

Chart of Accounts		to
G/L account		to
Company code		to

Use this section to limit the accounts (via 'chart of accounts', 'G/L accounts' and 'company code' selections) that you want to include in the current interest calculation run. Normally all those accounts, within the range mentioned here, that have an interest indicator in the respective master records are all included.

Selection Using Search Help

Search Help ID
Search String
⇨   Search Help

Further selections

Calculation period	☑	to	☑
Business area		to	
Currency		to	
Interest Calculation Indicator		to	

Use this to further limit the accounts. Enter the interest 'calculation period' (from & to), 'business areas', 'currency' and 'interest calculation indicator'. The system arrives at the upper limit based on the key date of last interest calculation (specified in the account master), interest calculation frequency (entered in the account master or in the interest indicator) and settlement day (maintained in the interest indicator). And this upper limit is compared with the calculation period that you maintain here, to include or exclude the accounts for the current interest run.

Cash pooling

☐ Cash Pooling
Header Company Code
Header Account

Output control

Summarization Level (0-3)	
Date of Last Interest Run	18.03.2024
Reference Date (1,2,3)	1
Additional Date	3
☐ Standard Interest Calculation	
☐ Additional Balance Line	
☐ Leap Year	
☐ Interest Splitting	
☐ Interest Rate Overview	

Enter the 'summarization level' to control the level of details of the list that will be output. Also enter the 'date of last interest run', if you have not maintained the same in the master record; the system uses this date to decide if the item should be treated as having a value in the past. Use the 'reference date' to decide which date the system considers for the interest calculation: posting date, value date or document date. Maintain other parameters as you may require like 'interest splitting', 'interest rate overview' etc.,

Negative Interest Rates

○ Neg. int. rates not allowed
○ Negative int. rates allowed
● Set neg. int. rates to zero

Decide as to how the system treats if it encounters negative interest amount in the interest calculation. Normally, you will set the indicator to 'Set neg. int. rates to zero'.

Posting control

☐ Post interest settlements	
☐ Post also if val. date in past	
☐ Update master record	
Session Name	RFSZIS00
Posting to Business Area	
Posting Date of Session	
Document Date of Session	
Value Date of Session	
Posting Period	
Reference Data	
Assignment Number	
Posting Segment Text	
Movement Type - Debit	
Movement Type - Credit	
☐ Hold processed session	

Enter the parameters for posting control: you may decide if you want to 'post interest settlements'; even if you select this but have not selected 'post also if val. date in past', then, the system does not post interest if there are values in the post. Normally, the interest posting for balance interest happens via a batch input session. Select 'update master record, when you want the system to update the master record with the interest calculation run details. Maintain other values, if required.

Additional log

☐ Additional Log		
Accounts for Additional Log		to

You may want to select 'additional log' checkbox to make the system to output a detailed log as to: why interest is not calculated on an account, why certain items are not selected, how the interest calculation period was determined per account, which items were processed as having value dates in the past etc., As this will be very extensive, try limiting the accounts for additional log.

***Figure 15.30**: Interest Calculation Run – Parameters*

444. List the important SAP Fiori Apps for SAP G/L Accounting.

The following list contains some of the important SAP Fiori Apps in the area of SAP G/L Accounting in SAP S/4HANA Finance:

- **Currency exchange rates:** Using this app, you can create new exchange rates, copy/modify/delete existing exchange rates, maintain validity periods for specific rates, view all active exchange rates, choose between the 'Standard' and 'Full Overview' display variants, use the 'Check Currency Pairs' function to check for duplicates and inconsistencies, convert amounts within the app using the 'Currency Converter' and view the exchange rate trend for a currency pair over the last seven days, 30 days, or 12 months.

- **Manage G/L account master data:** Use this app to view G/L account master data, view and edit a G/L account, mass change descriptions and other attributes of multiple accounts from Chart of Accounts View, Company Code View, and Controlling Area View, mass copy G/L accounts that are in the same chart of accounts (in Company Code View), make multiple copies of a G/L account (in Chart of Accounts View) and view where the account is used in a 'Financial Statement Version' or in the 'Automatic Account Determination' app. For each mass change action, you can select up to 5,000 G/L accounts.

This app is related to the backend transactions like **FS00** (Edit G/L Account Centrally), **FSP0** (Edit G/L Account - Chart of Accounts Data), **FSS0** (Edit G/L Account - Company Code Data), **FSP4** (Display Changes in Chart of Accounts), **FSS4** (Display Changes in Company Code), **KA01** (Create Cost Element), **KA02** (Change Cost Element), **KA03** (Display Cost Element) and **KA06** (Create Secondary Cost Element).

- **Manage chart of accounts:** Depending on the role to which you are assigned, you can perform several tasks, including display (all accounts, accounts assigned to B/S, accounts assigned to the P & L statement, accounts that are currently not assigned to the financial statement version at all, and accounts that must have a zero balance and therefore have no effect on the financial statement results), search, access (for editing account attributes) and copy (existing accounts to create new ones, and existing FSV assignments to selected accounts).

From this app, you can directly access the 'Manage G/L Account Master Data' app to display detailed information about a G/L account.

- **Manage profit centers:** Depending on the role assigned, you can perform several tasks, including searching for profit centers, viewing profit center master data, creating-edit-copy-deleting a combination of a profit center and a validity period, assigning Company Codes to profit centers, viewing all objects by navigating to the app 'Where-Used List—Profit Centers', and seeing the changes that were made to a specific profit center.

- **Automatic account determination:** This app provides you with all the settings that are needed for assigning accounts in the areas/subareas of Controlling (Cost Center Accounting), Financial Accounting (Accounts Receivable and Accounts Payable, Bank Accounting, and General Ledger Accounting), Joint Venture Accounting (JVA Cost Calculation and Other Postings), Sourcing and Procurement, Personnel Management (SAP S/4HANA for Human Resources) and Sales (Sales Billing).

- **Edit options for journal entries:** This app provides you with several editing options, as follows:

  o 'Documents in local currency' (to enter documents in local currency),

  o 'Use alternative account' (when your Company Code is assigned to a country chart of accounts),

  o 'No Company Code proposal' (for document parking and posting),

  o 'Foreign exchange rate from first line item' (to automatically correct the foreign exchange from the document header to the foreign exchange of the first line item of the document),

  o 'No copy tax code' (to deactivate the standard setting that automatically copies the last tax code used into the G/L item),

  o 'Negative posting' (for automatically created line items for simulation or posting),

  o 'Display net amounts' (instead of the standard setting that displays the gross amount first during open item processing),

  o 'Documents in Company Code' (to prevent entering cross-Company Code documents by removing the input fields from the entry screen),

  o 'Amount in local currency' (to allow inputting of only foreign currency when entering documents in foreign currency),

  o 'No special G/L transaction' (for not entering any special G/L transaction during document entry),

  o 'Display periods' (to display the posting period in the document header),

  o 'User invoice reference' (to control activation or deactivation of line items that are linked by invoice reference during open item processing),

  o 'Posting special periods' (to enable inputting the '*Period*' field with a value during document entry),

  o 'Copy payment base' (to automatically change the payment deadline baseline date for a change in the document for a change in the posting date of a parked document),

  o 'Set default currency' (to automatically display the last used document currency in the '*Currency*' field overriding the default of no currency display),

- o 'Set document type' (to enable the system to allow you to change the document type for journal entry, instead of the default that just displays the configured document type without allowing to change),

- o 'Set document date' (to allow changing of document date and posting date from the current date prompted),

- o 'Enter net amount' (when you want to enter the G/L account's amount net of tax, the system, accordingly, calculates the tax; otherwise, the system assumes that the entered amount is gross), and

- o 'Payment reference as search criterion' (for making the system select open items for clearing based on the payment reference that you have specified).

- **Upload general journal entries:** This app enables you to upload multiple general journal entries by providing a built-in template (spreadsheet or CSV file) within the app. After uploading, you can directly post those entries in all relevant ledgers for the accounts for which you are responsible. If there are errors in uploading, you can correct them, copy the batch ID of the initial upload, and repeat the upload.

- **Verify general journal entries:** This app in SAP S/4HANA Finance enables setting up a 'general journal entry verification process' with the configuration of conditions (by adjusting the default workflow) that require verification, as well as authorizations for approval. After the configuration, the business users and the account team can view and participate, in different steps in the verification process, depending upon their respective authorizations. If there is a status change to the submitted journal, the app sends notifications to the users for appropriate action, if any.

- **Clear G/L accounts - Manual clearing:** Use this app to manually clear the G/L account open items that have not been automatically cleared by the system. You can find open G/L account items using a range of search criteria, manually clear multiple open items with notes (and attachments) while posting the clearing document, simulate the resulting journal entry with an option to export the data to a spreadsheet for further analysis, and share the open item in question together with any additional information via email.

- **Manage journal entries (New version):** You can use this app to analyze the journal entries and to make adjustments via reversals if required. You may use the filtering, sorting, and grouping based on certain selection criteria, like journal entry type, user, etc., to view the journal entry information like G/L accounts posted account assignment objects, and tax (on sales or purchase). You may create new journal entries based on other journal entries. You can attach notes or information to a journal entry posted. You can simulate the posted entries in the entry view. You can use mass processing to view/reverse several journal entries in one go.

- **Display document flow:** With this app, you can view the preceding and succeeding documents just by entering a single document number. During such an action, the app displays the documents and journal entries (including the archived ones) in different document flows but on the same screen. From there, you can select the documents to access additional controls, access the journal entries, and view their accounting impact by branching out to different apps.

- **Schedule accrual jobs:** Using this app, you can schedule accrual jobs using the built-in templates for both purchase order accruals and service entry sheets. You can use the scheduling to carry out periodic accrual activities like transferring POs to the accrual engine, proposing periodic accruals, simulating the accrual posting, and finally posting the accrual entries.

- **Manage posting periods:** You can use this app to open/close posting periods. You can also use the scheduling option to open the posting periods once or multiple times to suit your business requirements. Via the app, you can view the open posting periods both from the **posting period variant** (**PPV**) view and Company Code view, view the latest open fiscal year for a Company Code, manually shift the open intervals in the system, reset all adjustment periods so that the periods for adjustments are not open anymore, and reset all CO periods to prevent any further postings from CO to FI.

- **Balance Carryforward status:** This app lets you view the carryforward run details and the current status. You can search for the details relating to a specific run date or for a specified time period.

- **Post-tax payables:** Through this app, you can pay tax by posting the balances of input and output tax accounts to a tax payable account (non-tax-relevant account). You can make postings in all the relevant ledgers. This is very useful in making manual adjustments directly to tax accounts, and you do not need to enter any tax code while doing so.

- **Reconcile GR/IR accounts:** This app helps reconcile GR/IR accounts. You can leverage this app to reduce open items, thereby increasing the accuracy of financial statements. This app enables you to spot, for example, issues with suppliers early on. Using this app, you can compile a worklist with open items that require some clarification, graphically display items to be processed using different chart types, and leverage 'smart facts' that describe business situations for an item to be clarified without you doing any analysis thereby concluding by yourself, display information from both purchasing and accounting at the same time, and continuously reduce the purchasing document items with FI open items, etc.,

- **General ledger overview:** This analytical app helps you monitor important G/L accounting indicators and enables you to access the relevant G/L apps. This app consists of several *cards*, including:

  ○ **Recognized revenue:** To display your Company's year-to-date revenue and per-month revenue for the last six months

  ○ **Recognized CoS:** To display your company's year-to-date expenses and per-month expenses for the last six months

- o **Journal entries to be verified**: To display descending-sorted journal entries that require verification

- o **G/L account balance:** To display G/L account balances that are grouped by account groups

- o **Tax reconciliation account balance:** To display the balance in various reconciliation accounts

- o **G/L item changes**: To display, by change date, the list of journal entries that were changed with the details as to who made the changes and what changes were made

- o **Days of sales outstanding (DSO)**: To display the average DSO in days and in a chart vis-à-vis actual DSO vis-à-vis possible DSO

- **G/L account changes:** This app allows you to view the changes made to G/L accounts, the user who made them, and the fields that were changed, both before and after.

- **Balance sheet/Income statement:** Use this app to display the financial statements, both the B/S and P&L statements, on the fly for your companies for various charts of accounts, including operative, global, and local charts. From the statements, you can drill down to specific G/L accounts and customer & supplier account line items. It is possible to display, via the app, full B/S or P&L statements for multiple Company Codes, or if you want, you may just display the select nodes. You can compare the items with key dates or comparison periods. You can also download the statements in PDF format.

- **Year-to-date balances:** Using this app, you can display the balances for specific dimensions of universal journal entries for a fiscal year. You can specify the start date and end date (corresponding to fiscal periods, fiscal quarters, or posting dates) within a fiscal year to generate the balances. The app, by default, displays the balances in Company Code currency for the leading ledger for the current fiscal year up to the previous fiscal period.

- **Trial balance:** Use this app to display the debit and credit balances of accounts for a given time period. You can display the balances per ledger, per Company Code or all Company Codes. When you select individual periods, the app displays the balances of the previous and following periods of the fiscal year.

- **Audit journal:** You can use this app to run various auditing reports to ensure the correctness of journals. The app facilitates viewing the compact journal, complete journal, journal entry changes, and referenced customer/vendor documents, besides enabling the check of the number of gaps in journal entries. You can filter the display by Company Code, fiscal year, and ledger in that order. You can also use the posting date range and G/L accounts (from and to) as additional filtering criteria.

CHAPTER 16

FI: Accounts Receivable & Accounts Payable – I

Introduction

The discussion on 'FI: **Accounts Receivable (A/R)** & **Accounts Payable (A/P)**' has been divided into two chapters, chapters 16 and 17. Now, in this chapter, you will learn about the overview of FI-A/R and FI-A/P, the respective customer and vendor master records (overview, creation, editing, deletion, blocking and archiving), the one-time accounts, the payment program (both manual and automatic) together with the configuration settings that are required for making use that, how the payment program selects the open items/house bank while making the payments and the details on payment run: how to create, edit and run a payment program. You will also learn about payment advice notes and SEAP direct credits.

445. Give a brief overview of Accounts Receivable & Accounts Payable in SAP.

An integral part of sales management, the **'accounts receivable'** (FI-A/R) component of SAP FI in SAP S/4HANA Finance, takes care of accounting of all your customers. Besides directly recording the receivables in *SAP G/L Accounting*, FI-A/R provides the data for effective credit management as this application is closely integrated with *SAP SD (Sales & Distribution)*. It also enables optimization in liquidity management by linking it with *SAP*

Cash Management. Through different tools, you can monitor open items, 'dun' (remind) the customers of the outstanding receivables, and use the payment program for automatic debits and customer down payments. With its variety of reports, you can analyze the receivables, create DSO reports & charts, and view due date lists and alarm reports for effectively managing the receivables. You may use the *SAP Dispute Management* component to process receivable-related disputes and use *SAP Collections Management* to collect the outstanding receivables.

As with FI-A/R, which administers accounting for all your customers, the '*accounts payable*' (FI-A/P) component of SAP FI takes care of recording and administering accounting for all your vendors (suppliers). An integral part of purchasing, it is tightly integrated with *SAP MM (Materials Management)*. As in the case of FI-A/R, the accounts payable directly update *SAP G/L Accounting* with the payable (and down payment) information, besides providing the required data from invoices and payments to the *SAP Cash Management* component for optimizing liquidity management. You will use the built-in payment program to pay vendors/suppliers via several country-specific payment methods, including **electronic data exchange** (**EDI**). You can also use the dunning program to 'dun' your vendors as well, in cases of pending payments for credit memos. You can use the various tools and reports to monitor the open items.

446. Explain the 'Key Features of Accounts Receivable.'

The '**accounts receivable**' component (FI-A/R) comprises several key features for managing your customers' accounting data.

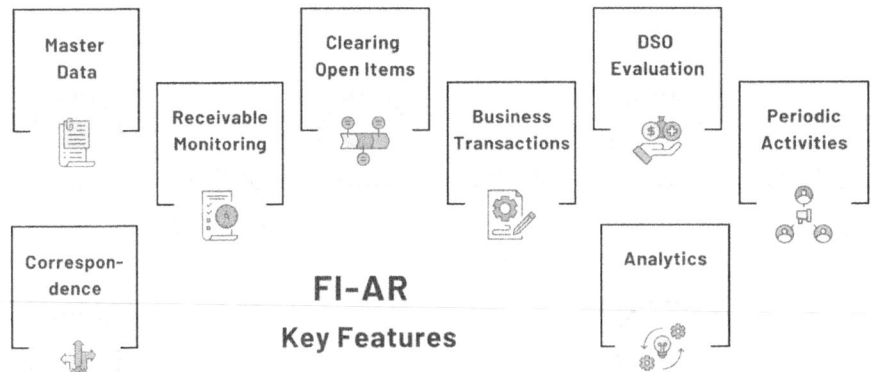

Figure 16.1: *Key features of Accounts Receivable*

Some of the key features (*Figure 16.1*) include the following:

- 'Master data' (that helps in managing and centralized storing of customers' data as business partner master records that are shared between SAP FI and SAP SD),

- 'Monitoring of receivables' (which enables processing of customer open items besides displaying customer account balances and overdue receivables),
- 'Posting of business transactions' (that enables posting of accounting data – like receivables, down payments received, bill of exchange, and the like - for customers in FI-A/R, which also gets posted in SAP G/L Accounting),
- 'Clearing of open invoices' (by posting, manually or automatically, the incoming payment towards outstanding receivable items),
- 'DSO evaluation' (to determine the customers with the highest or lowest DSO - Days of Sales Outstanding),
- 'Correspondence' (for communicating with the customers on open item lists, payment notices, account statements, etc., with the correspondence media customized for the Company Code and for the customers),
- 'Periodic activities including closing' (to carry out the periodic tasks like interest calculation dunning, automatic payment, and so on), and
- 'Analytics' (for evaluating customers' payment history, DSO, currency risk, etc.)

447. Briefly discuss the 'Key Features of Accounts Payable.'

The '**accounts payable**' component (FI-A/P) comprises several key features to manage the accounting data of your vendors (suppliers).

FI-AP: Key Features

MASTER DATA	BUSINESS TRANSACTIONS	SUPPLIER INVOICES	PAYMENT ANALYSIS	CASH DISCOUNTS
1	2	3	4	5
OVERDUE REVIEW	DPO EVALUATION	PAYMENT MANAGEMENT	PAYMENT BLOCKS	PAYMENT MEDIA
6	7	8	9	10

Figure 16.2: Accounts Payable – Key features

The important key features (*Figure 16.2*) include the following:

- 'Master data' (that helps in managing supplier's information as a business partner by storing the details in a centralized master record that is shared between SAP FI and SAP MM components),

- 'Posting business transactions' (enabling posting of accounting data for vendors in SAP FI-A/P, which also gets simultaneously updated in SAP G/L Accounting),

- 'Import of supplier invoice' (enabling importing multiple supplier invoices all at once),

- 'Analysis of payments to suppliers' (helps in viewing the overdue & future payments besides the current payment, enabling notifying the supplier when there is a negative trend in payment),

- 'Management of cash discount' (to forecast the available cash discount besides monitoring cash discount utilization),

- 'Reviewing cleared overdue items' (to get insights into the cleared overdue items),

- 'DPO evaluation' (as with DSO, DPO – Days of Purchase Outstanding – enables understanding the suppliers with the highest or lowest DPO vis-à-vis the average and minimum DPO),

- 'Management of payments' (to create, post, and reverse – if required – the payments),

- 'Management of payment blocks' (to set or remove payment blocks on vendor invoices and accounts, besides trying to find out potential irregularities or invoice fraud in association with *SAP Fraud Management* for SAP S/4HANA),

- 'Management of payment proposals' (for creating and editing payment proposals before triggering payments to the suppliers) and

- 'Management of payment media' (to manage electronic payments via EDI for quicker online payments besides the conventional modes of payment).

448. Who is a 'Customer' from the perspective of SAP FI-A/R?

A '**customer**,' from the perspective of SAP FI-A/R, is an individual, an organization, or a group from whom receivables are due for some services rendered, including delivery of goods and transfer of rights. The customer can be a goods recipient, sold-to-party, payer, consumer, bill-to-party, and the like.

449. Explain the 'Customer Master Record'.

You create a customer in the system as a *business partner*, and the details are captured in a master record. The **customer master record** comprises different data areas, including general data, Company Code data, sales & distribution data, and ETM data (*Figure 16.3*).

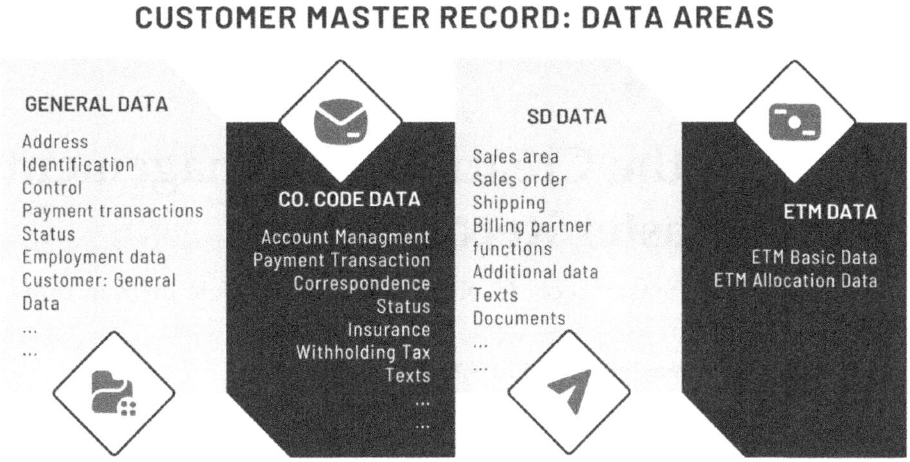

CUSTOMER MASTER RECORD: DATA AREAS

GENERAL DATA

Address
Identification
Control
Payment transactions
Status
Employment data
Customer: General
Data
...
...

CO. CODE DATA

Account Managment
Payment Transaction
Correspondence
Status
Insurance
Withholding Tax
Texts
...
...

SD DATA

Sales area
Sales order
Shipping
Billing partner
functions
Additional data
Texts
Documents
...
...

ETM DATA

ETM Basic Data
ETM Allocation Data

Figure 16.3: Customer Master Record – Data Areas

The explanation for each area is as follows:

- The **'general data'** is at the Client level and is valid across the Company Codes; for example, you can use the 'address' stored here in this 'general data' area in multiple Company Codes when the same customer is serviced by more than one Company Code. This obviates the need to maintain such data more than once.

- The **'Company Code data'** is valid only for the specific Company Code; for example, you can have different 'payment terms,' 'reconciliation account,' etc., in different Company Codes for the same customer.

- The **'sales & distribution data,'** such as sales area, sales order, billing partner functions, documents, etc., are all available for all sales areas.

- The **'ETM data'** is data relating to equipment and tools and is specific to the engineering and construction industry; to use ETM, you should have implemented SAP SD, SAP FI, SAP CO, and SAP FI-AA (Asset Accounting), as well as SAP PM (Plant Maintenance) and SAP PS (Project Systems).

450. How does the system make use of the Customer Master Record?

The **customer master record** supplies some default values, like 'payment terms', during document entry in the system. Also, it supplies some of the key dates like 'last dunning date', 'last interest calculated date', etc., while carrying out the business transactions. Through 'authorization groups' attached to the master records, the system prevents any unauthorized changes to the field contents of the master records, besides logging the changes as to 'who has changed' and 'what.' The information contained in the master records is used in the SAP SD application component for functions like sales order management, including shipping and billing. With the address data in the customer master records, you can correspond with the customers, including sending out dunning notices and payment requests.

451. Explain the Creation & Management of Customer Master Records.

You can create customer master records, edit, change, and delete them in three different ways:

- Maintaining the master record in SAP FI (FI data only)
- Maintaining the master record in SAP SD (SD data only)
- Maintaining the master record centrally (for all data areas)

It is possible that your company's SD and FI departments maintain the general data together but specify the FI and SD data individually. It is also possible that you have centralized maintenance of all the data for all the Company Codes.

Before SAP S/4HANA Finance, there were multiple transaction codes to maintain the customer master records. For example, you would have to use Transaction Code **FD01 / FD02 / FD03, VD01 / VD02 / VD03, and XD01 / XD02 / XD03** to create/edit/display a master record in the FI area, SD area, and for central maintenance, respectively. However, with the advent of SAP S/4HANA, all these have now been dovetailed into a single Transaction Code, **BP**. In fact, you use this same transaction to create /edit/display vendor master records as well, as you now create these master records, both for customer and vendor, as business partner master records.

452. Who is a 'Vendor' from the perspective of SAP FI-A/P?

A '**vendor**' (aka 'supplier'), from the perspective of SAP FI-AP, is an individual, an organization, or a group from whom you purchase materials and/or services. The vendor can be a goods supplier, alternate payer, party who presents an invoice for payment, forwarding agent, special vendor, and the like. You will create a vendor, like a customer, as a 'business partner' in the system.

453. Explain the 'Vendor Master Record'.

As in the case of a customer, you create a supplier/vendor in the system as a *business partner*, and the details are captured in the supplier/vendor master record. Similar to a customer master record, a supplier/vendor master record is made up of three data areas, namely general data, Company Code data, and purchasing organization data. You should have implemented the SAP **Materials Management** (**MM**) application component to manage purchasing-related information in a supplier/vendor master record and process purchase-related business transactions in the system. The explanations for the data areas are as follows:

- The **'general data'** is used to identify and correspond with the suppliers/vendors for whom you have created the master records. As these data (address, identification, control, status, where-used list, employment, general data, texts, etc.) are stored at the Client level, this information is available across several Company Codes.

- The **'Company Code data'** is valid only for a particular Company Code. Due to this, you can have the same supplier/vendor in multiple Company Codes with varying Company Code data with varying data on 'account management' (planning group, release group, interest indicator), 'payment transactions' (terms of payment, tolerance group, house bank, payment block), 'withholding tax' (withholding tax type, withholding tax code, exemption number), etc.

- Derived from the SAP MM application component, the **'purchasing organization data'** comprises information from the purchasing organization. The data includes information about the **request for quotation** (**RFQ**), the **purchase order** (**PO**), invoice verification, etc.

As in the case of a customer master record, you can create supplier/vendor master records, edit, change, and delete them, in three different ways:

- Maintaining the master record in SAP FI (FI data only)
- Maintaining the master record in SAP MM (Purchasing organization data only)
- Maintaining the master record centrally (for all data areas)

It is possible that your Company's MM and FI departments maintain the general data but specify the FI and MM data individually. It is also possible that you have centralized data maintenance for all the Company Codes.

Before SAP S/4HANA Finance, there were multiple Transaction Codes to maintain the supplier/vendor master records. For example, you would have to use Transaction Code **FK01/FK02/FK03, MK01/MK02/MK03,** and **XK01/XK02/XK03** to create/edit/display a master record in the FI area, MM area, and for central maintenance, respectively. However, with the advent of SAP S/4HANA, all these have now been dovetailed into a single Transaction Code, **BP**.

454. List the default types of 'Business Partners' in SAP S/4HANA Finance.

The '**business partners**' are legal or natural persons with whom you, as a company, have a business relationship. There are three types of default business partners defined in SAP S/4HANA Finance, as shown in the following figure (*Figure 16.4*):

BUSINESS PARTNER TYPES

CUSTOMER
- Internal Customers (own sites)
- External Customers

VENDOR
- Internal Vendors
- External Vendors

OTHERS

Figure 16.4: Default Business Partner types

Business partners are defined with several functions known as 'partner functions' that signify the rights and responsibilities of each partner type in accordance with a business transaction that you use in your company. It is possible that a single business partner may be associated with more than one partner function. A business partner like a 'customer' may have different partner functions like sold-to-party, ship-to-party, bill-to-party, payer, etc. Similarly, the business partner 'supplier or vendor' may have different partner functions like ordering address, goods supplier, invoice presented by, and so on. You create master records to capture the details of business partners.

455. What settings must be in place to create a Customer/Vendor Master?

Before you start creating a master record, either for a customer or a vendor, you need to make sure that you have defined the following three objects in the system:

- **Number ranges:**
  - o You maintain the required **number ranges** from which the system allocates each master record with a number, either internally (automatic numbering) or externally (manual). You need to decide beforehand the number of ranges you would require, looking at the current number of vendors (or customers) and the expected future additions. Normally, you would define several number ranges when you need several account groups.
  - o To **configure the number ranges for customer account groups**, use the menu path *SAP Customizing Implementation Guide | Financial Accounting | Accounts Receivable and Accounts Payable | Customer Accounts | Master Data | Preparations for Creating Customer Master Data.* The Transaction Codes are:
    - ▪ Create Number Ranges for Customer Accounts or Transaction Code **XDN1**.

- Assign Number Ranges to Customer Account Groups or Transaction Code **OBAR**.

o To **configure the number ranges for supplier/vendor account groups**, use the menu path *SAP Customizing Implementation Guide | Financial Accounting | Accounts Receivable and Accounts Payable | Supplier Accounts | Master Data | Preparations for Creating Supplier Master Data*. The Transaction Codes are:

- Create Number Ranges for Vendor Accounts or Transaction Code **XKN1**.

- Assign Number Ranges to Vendor Account Groups or Transaction Code **OBAS**.

- **Account group:**

  o The **account group** controls the creation of master records in the system. Each account group is associated with a number range that you have already defined in the system. Though technically, you need one account group at the minimum; you can have any number of account groups defined in the system. Your account groups may represent different types of customers (like goods recipient, sold-to-party, payer, consumer, bill-to-party, one-time customers, domestic customers, sales partner, etc.) and vendors (goods supplier, alternate payer, invoicing party, forwarding agent, special vendor, one-time vendor, domestic vendor, etc.). In general, you will create as many account groups as the number ranges. Since you use the account group to control the screen layout and the field status, you should think of having at least two different account groups: one for regular or standard accounts and the other for one-time accounts. You must specify an account group when creating a master record, and you cannot change that after the master record has been created in the system.

  o To create an account group, you can use the menu path *SAP Customizing Implementation Guide | Financial Accounting | Accounts Receivable and Accounts Payable*. The Transaction Codes are:

    - *Customer Accounts | Master Data | Preparations for Creating Customer Master Data | Define Account Groups with Screen Layout (Customers)* or Transaction Code **OBD2**.

    - *Supplier Accounts | Master Data | Preparations for Creating Supplier Master Data > Define Account Groups with Screen Layout (Vendors)* or Transaction Code **OBD3**.

- **Field status:**

  o As the **field status** decides the status of various fields on the data entry screens for creating master data, you specify the required field status (and screen layout) per account group. You may also control the field status via business transactions and Company Code.

o   To **configure field status for customer master records**, you can use the menu path *SAP Customizing Implementation Guide | Financial Accounting | Accounts Receivable and Accounts Payable | Customer Accounts | Master Data | Preparations for Creating Customer Master Data*. The Transaction Codea are:

- Define Screen Layout per Company Code (Customers) or Transaction Code **OB21**.

- Define Screen Layout per Activity (Customers) or Transaction Code **OB20**.

o   To **configure field status for supplier/vendor master records**, you can use the menu path *SAP Customizing Implementation Guide | Financial Accounting | Accounts Receivable and Accounts Payable | Supplier Accounts | Master Data | Preparations for Creating Supplier Master Data*. The Transaction Codes are:

- Define Screen Layout per Company Code (Vendors) or Transaction Code **OB24**.

- Define Screen Layout per Activity (Vendors) or Transaction Code **OB23**.

456. What is the advantage of using 'Reconciliation Accounts'?

You know that both FI-A/R and FI-A/P are subsidiary ledgers. Each subsidiary ledger will have one or more '**reconciliation accounts**' (aka 'recon accounts') in FI-G/L. You will maintain the reconciliation account while defining the customer or supplier/vendor master record. When you post to the subsidiary ledgers, the system automatically updates the G/L with the same data. Since the reconciliation ledgers ensure that the balance of G/L accounts is always zero, you will be able to bring out the B/S at any time; there is no need to transfer the totals from the subsidiary ledgers to the G/L.

Through the reconciliation accounts, you can specify the currencies that you can post to the corresponding customer or supplier/vendor accounts and configure the screens (specifying, for example, which fields are to be made hidden for data input) for posting to customer or supplier/vendor accounts.

457. List out the 'Special Fields' in the Customer/Supplier Master Record.

The following are considered to be the '**special fields**' in the customer or supplier/vendor master record:

- **Accounting clerk**: Each accounting clerk (identified using an 'ID' in Customizing) can be made responsible for certain master records of customers or suppliers/vendors. While creating a master record, if you enter the clerk's ID in the master records, then the system prints the name of the accounting clerk in all correspondence with the customer or supplier/vendor. Also, you can sort the dunning list/payment proposal list by the accounting clerk's ID.

- **Affiliated companies**: To eliminate inter-company expenses and revenues during inter-company consolidation, you need to enter the corporate-wide Company ID in the *'Trading Partner No.'* field of every customer and supplier/vendor master record that you have set up for the affiliated companies. During consolidation, the system uses this ID to process the inter-Company elimination.

- *Alternative Payee*: You can configure the system to pay a vendor/supplier other than the one to which the system posts the invoice. This vendor/supplier is known as the 'alternate payee,' and to make payment to such a vendor/supplier, you need to maintain that in the corresponding master record. While specifying the alternate payee in a supplier/vendor master record, you can do so either in the general data area and/or the Company Code data area. Then, the payee mentioned in the general data area receives the payment in all the Company Codes, and the payee specified in the Company Code area receives payment only for that Company Code.

- **Alternative payer**: Like the alternate payee, the 'alternative payer' is a customer other than the one to make payment in the normal course for the receivables. As in the case of vendor/supplier, you need to maintain this alternative payer in the respective customer master record to receive the payment. More about alternate payers in *Question 458*.

- **Clearing Between Customer and Supplier/Vendor**: If your customer is also your supplier/vendor or vice versa, then you can make the system clear the related open items between the two while running the dunning and payment programs. You can also display the supplier/vendor line items while displaying the customer line items and vice versa. For this to happen, you need to make certain specifications in the respective master records:

  o Maintain the supplier/vendor account number in the *'Supplier'* field under *Customer: General Data* in the general data area of the customer master record, and maintain the customer account number in the *'Customer'* field under *Vendor: General Data* in the general data area of vendor/supplier master record.

  o Select the *'Clearing with Vendor'* checkbox under *Customer: Payment Transactions* in the Company Code data area of the customer master record, and select *'Clearing w. customer'* checkbox under *Vendor: Payment Transactions* in Company Code data area of the vendor/supplier master record

- **Group**: When several customers/vendors belong to a group, you can use an ID (user-defined) to group them together. Later, using the ID that you have entered in the respective master records, you can evaluate them as a group.

- **Search term**: You can use the 'search term', which contains the most important part of the customer's/vendor's name, to search for a specific customer/vendor. Usually, you will formulate certain rules as to the search ID's content so that your users enter the search term uniformly; it does not matter if the search term is in upper case or lower case.

458. Explain the concept of using 'Alternative Payer'/'Alternate Payee.'

A customer who pays on behalf of another customer is known as an 'alternative payer'. Though the alternative payer pays on behalf of another customer, the system maintains all the transaction details in the account of the original customer. Designating an 'alternative payer' does not absolve the customer of his / her obligation to pay.

The 'alternative payer' can be maintained in the general data area or the Company Code area. When maintained in the Company Code area, you can use that payer only in that Company Code; if defined in the general data area, you can use the same across all Company Codes.

There are three ways of 'selecting 'the alternative payer when an invoice is processed:

- The alternative payer (say, 1000) entered in the customer master record is the one selected by the system as default.

- When there is more than one alternative payer (say, 1000, 1900, 2100, etc.) defined for a single customer in the master record (you will do this by clicking on the *'Permitted Payer'* button under 'Additional Payment Transactions Data' section of 'Customer: General Data' tab, and create more than one payer), you may select a payer (say, 2100) other than the default, 1000, while processing the invoice. Now, the system will ignore the default alternative payer (1000) from the master record. You can also add additional alternative payers in the Company Code area as well, under the section *Additional Company Code Data* on the 'Customer: Payment Transactions' tab.

- When an alternative payer already exists in the master record, then the system allows you to propose a new alternate payer, say, 3000 (other than those already defined in the master record) during document entry. The system does this by automatically selecting the *'Alt. payer(doc.)'* checkbox under *Additional Company Code Data* on the 'Customer: Payment Transactions' tab of the Company Code area data. You can maintain any new additional payer by clicking on the *'Permitted Payer'* tab in the checkbox. Now, after defining the new alternate payer, you can use it during document entry to process the invoice. In this case, this alternate payer (3000) takes precedence over the payers (1000 & 2100) in the above two scenarios.

Similar to the concept of 'alternative payer,' you have an **'alternative payee'** in the case of supplier/vendor wherein you pay this designated alternative payee in the place of the default or original supplier/vendor.

459. What is 'Dual Control' in Customer or Supplier/Vendor master records?

You can define certain important fields (for example, 'Terms of Payment', 'Payment Methods' etc.,) in customer or supplier/vendor master records as 'sensitive fields' and manage them under **dual control**. This way, you can protect the contents of these sensitive fields from any unauthorized change. In case of a change to any of these fields, the system requires a second person to authorize the changes; otherwise, the respective customer or supplier account will be blocked by the system in the payment run, for example.

460. What happens when creating a 'Customer/Supplier Master with Reference'?

You can create a new **customer or supplier/vendor master record with reference** to an existing master record in the system. You can use a master record from any of the Company Codes as a 'reference'; the transferred values from the reference record act only as defaults, which you can change before saving the new master record. While doing so, the system does not copy all data from the reference record, and the copying is subject to the following:

- The system copies data from the 'source' to the 'target' depending on what you have already created for the new master record. For example, unless you select *'Overwrite Customer General Data'* (*'Overwrite Supplier General Data'* in case of Supplier master record) on the initial pop-up screen, wherein you select the customer reference record from which to carry out the copying, the system does not over-write the already created general area data in the new master record.

- When you have created the general area data for the new customer (or supplier), the system copies only the Company Code data into the new master record unless you choose to 'overwrite' the general area data. In cases where you have not already created the general area data, the system copies only the 'Country' and 'Language' from the referenced master record.

- In general, the system copies only the data that is not customer-specific (or supplier-specific) from the reference record to the new one. For example, the system will not copy data like 'address.'

461. How do you create & link 'Head Office/ Branch Office Master Records'?

It is possible that sales accounting happens centrally at your head office, but the branch offices of your company are actually involved in sales. In this case, you need to create separate master records for the head office and branch offices. Then, to link the branch office accounts with that of the head office master record, you need to enter the head office master record number in the '*Head office*' field of the respective branch office master records under the *Customer: Account Management* tab of the Company Code area data.

In this arrangement, the system manages the sales orders in branch accounts. However, the system does not update the branch office accounts with the sales and transaction figures but does that automatically in the head office account. The head office completes outgoing payments in one go for all the linked branches. To link head office and branch office accounts, ensure that the head office account is not a one-time account and that the head office and branch office accounts belong to the same Company Code. Of course, you cannot link the branch office accounts by themselves.

Similar to the head office/branch office accounts for customers, you can create supplier accounts as well in cases where procurement is managed centrally at the company level (head office), with each branch procuring its materials.

462. Explain 'One-Time Accounts' for Customers or Suppliers.

Sometimes, you may be forced to buy from a supplier/vendor who is not your regular supplier/vendor for the simple reason that a particular material is unavailable from your regular supplier. Since such a transaction happens very rarely or only once, there is no point in creating a regular master record for such a supplier/vendor. SAP provides you with an option of creating a '**one-time account**' to cover such a scenario. Here, in this case, you create **one and only one master record** to cover all such one-time suppliers/vendors. You will not enter the name, address, bank address, etc., in the supplier/vendor master record but enter them while posting the invoice (the system will branch out to a separate master data screen wherein you can input these data). In this way, you can manage several one-time supplier/vendor accounts using a single, one-time supplier/vendor master record. This helps in preserving the disk space, besides doing away with numerous master records that you may not otherwise need. The other functions of one-time master records are as follows:

- When you create the one-time master record for one-time accounts, it will have its own account group, which suppresses fields like name, address, bank address, etc.

- The one-time master record also needs a reconciliation account to be specified in the master record. You may want to enter a different reconciliation account for the one-time master record to differentiate that from the reconciliation accounts associated with the regular supplier accounts. In cases where you have separate reconciliation accounts for domestic and overseas suppliers, then you may need one reconciliation account each to represent the one-time domestic suppliers and one-time overseas suppliers.

Similar to one-time supplier/vendor accounts, you may want to create one-time customer accounts as well to accommodate customers who do business with you only once or rarely. You will cover all such customers using a single, one-time customer master record.

463. How do you 'Block a Customer or Supplier Account'?

You may want to **block a customer account** to prevent any postings to that account in the future and/or before marking the customer account for deletion. You may be able to block a customer account either centrally for posting and order processing or just by blocking the account from posting only. You can also block a customer account for dunning and payment. Whatever the block is for, you can block the customer account in one Company Code or in all the Company Codes. When implemented and integrated with SAP SD, you can set the block indicator for posting, order processing, delivery, and invoicing. However, you need to be careful when you set the block indicator: do not set it if there are still open items in that account; otherwise, you will be unable to clear those open items once you set it. To unblock, you must remove the block indicator in the respective master records.

Similar to blocking a customer account, you **can block a supplier/vendor account** as well. When integrated with SAP MM, you can enable a purchasing block for a specific or all the purchasing organizations. The block, as in the case of a customer master record, can either be for posting and order processing or only for posting or for payments. As in the case of a customer account, once you have blocked a supplier account, you will not be able to clear if there are still open items in that account.

Table 16.1 provides you with the menu path and Transaction Codes for blocking / unblocking customer and supplier/vendor master records:

Details	SAP Easy Access Menu Path	Transaction Code
Customer Master: Block/unblock, FI area	*SAP Menu	Financial Accounting	Accounts Receivable	Master Records	Block/Unblock*	**FD05**
Customer Master: Block/unblock, centrally	*SAP Menu	Financial Accounting	Accounts Receivable	Master Records	Maintain Centrally	Block/Unblock*	**XD05**

Details	SAP Easy Access Menu Path	Transaction Code
Supplier/Vendor Master: Block/unblock, FI area	*SAP Menu	Financial Accounting	Accounts Payable	Master Records	Block/Unblock*	**FK05**
Supplier/Vendor Master: Block/unblock, centrally	*SAP Menu	Financial Accounting	Accounts Payable	Master Records	Maintain Centrally	Block/Unblock*	**XK05**

Table 16.1: *Menu Path / Transaction Codes for Blocking / Unblocking Customer / Supplier Master Records*

464. Explain 'Archiving & Deleting' a Customer or Supplier/Vendor Master Record.

You can **archive a customer or supplier/vendor master record** that you no longer actively need in the system. When you archive, the system extracts the master record from the database, deletes it, and places it in a file that you transfer to an archiving system later. However, the process is not this straightforward; for you to archive a master record, the system looks to fulfill the condition that the account does not have any transaction figures or documents in the system and the account has been 'marked for deletion.'

Before marking an account for deletion, as we have already discussed, you should block that account for further postings. However, you will block an account only when there are no open items that are pending for clearing. You can set the deletion flag centrally or for a specific Company Code. Once the deletion block is set, the system issues a warning if you try posting to that account subsequently.

Table 16.2 shows the menu path/Transaction Codes for setting the deletion indicator for customer or supplier/vendor master records:

Details	SAP Easy Access Menu Path	Transaction Code
Customer Master: Set Deletion Indicator, FI area	*SAP Menu	Financial Accounting	Accounts Receivable	Master Records	Set Deletion Indicator*	**FD06**
Customer Master: Set Deletion Indicator, centrally	*SAP Menu	Financial Accounting	Accounts Receivable	Master Records	Maintain Centrally	Set Deletion Indicator*	**XD06**

Details	SAP Easy Access Menu Path	Transaction Code
Supplier/Vendor Master: Set Deletion Indicator, FI area	*SAP Menu	Financial Accounting	Accounts Payable	Master Records	Set Deletion Indicator*	**FK06**
Supplier/Vendor Master: Set Deletion Indicator, centrally	*SAP Menu	Financial Accounting	Accounts Payable	Master Records	Maintain Centrally	Set Deletion Indicator*	**XK06**

Table 16.2: Menu Path / Transaction Codes for setting the Deletion Indicator in Customer / Supplier Master Records

465. What is 'Terms of Payment'?

Also known as 'payment terms', the **terms of payment** refer to the conditions of payment when you sell on credit to your customers. The terms of payment (or 'credit terms') outline the credit period provided (the number of days before which the customer should make the payment) and the discount, if any, for early payments.

For example, suppose that you define **terms of payment** like "*15 Days 3%, 30/2%, 60 Net*". This means that the customer has a maximum credit period of 60 days to pay for the A/R, with a 3% discount if paid within 15 days of invoicing and a 2% discount for payments before 30 days but after 15 days. If the payment is made after 30 days, then no discount will be allowed, and the customer must pay the entire receivable as mentioned in the invoice.

As with the payment terms to your credit customers, your suppliers/vendors will also provide you with the appropriate payment terms when you, as a company, buy on credit. When you pay early for the invoices raised by your supplier/vendor, you will pay after deducting the applicable discount.

SAP comes delivered with the most common payment terms in the standard system. You can use them or define your own payment terms using a payment terms identifier in Customizing: *SAP Customizing Implementation Guide | Financial Accounting | Accounts Receivable and Accounts Payable | Business Transactions | Incoming Invoices/Credit Memos > Maintain Terms of Payment.*

If the terms of payment are the same, you can use the same payment terms (*Figure 16.5*) for both customers and suppliers/vendors. Once defined, you must enter the payment terms in the customer's (or supplier/vendor) master records. The system uses the payment terms when processing the incoming /outgoing payments to arrive at the applicable discount while clearing the open items.

Change View "Terms of Payment": Details

ᵍ⁄ New Entries 🗋 🗐 ↰ ↱ 🗋 🗐

Pyt Terms	0003	Sales text	14 Days 3%, 20/2%, 30 Net	
Day Limit	0	Own Explanation		

Account type

☑ Customer

☑ Supplier

Baseline date calculation

Fixed Day

Additional Months

Pmnt block/pmnt method default

Block Key

Payment Method

Default for baseline date

○ No Default   ⦿ Posting Date

○ Document Date   ○ Entry Date

Payment terms

☐ Installment Payments   ☐ Rec. Entries: Supplement fm Master

Term	Percentage	No. of Days	/	Fixed Day	Additional Months
1.	3.000 %	14			
2.	2.000 %	20			
3.		30			

Explanations

within 14 days 3 % cash discount	within 20 days 2 % cash discount
within 30 days Due net	

☐ Hide Entry in Input Help

Figure 16.5: *Terms of Payment Customizing Screen*

Transaction Code **OBB8**

Figure 16.6

466. How do you configure 'Cash Discount Base' for Incoming Invoices?

When the discount base is 'net', the system calculates the discount net of tax from the invoice amount; that is, the system deducts the tax amount from the total invoice and applies the discount percentage on the balance amount of the invoice. Also, in this case, the system does not consider the freight charges, if any, for calculating the discount; that is, along with tax, the system reduces the freight amount also from the total invoice amount before applying the discount. When the discount base is 'gross', the discount is applied to the entire invoice amount, including the tax and freight (if any).

Figure 16.7

You can configure the cash discount base for incoming invoices in Customizing by selecting/ deselecting the 'DiscBaseNet' checkbox via the path *SAP Customizing Implementation Guide | Financial Accounting | Accounts Receivable and Accounts Payable | Business Transactions | Incoming Invoices/Credit Memos | Define Cash Discount Base for Incoming Invoices*. You can also configure this setting while maintaining the Company Code global parameters (Transaction **OBY6**) by selecting/deselecting the *'Discount base is net value'* checkbox (refer to *Question 264*).

467. Explain the purpose of SAP's 'Payment Program'.

With the '**payment program**' in SAP S/4HANA Finance, you can handle both incoming payments (from your customers) and outgoing payments (to your suppliers/vendors). The standard system consists of several common payment methods (like check, bank transfer, bill of exchange, etc.), as well as several country-specific ones. You can configure the various features of the payment program regarding payment methods, forms, data transfer media format, etc., for a particular country wherein your Company Codes operate. Using the program, you will be able to clear open items between customers and suppliers/vendors, pay and clear any type of open item, including, for example, down payments, make inter-company payments, and put in place user restrictions as to who can access the payment program in the system. The payment program is being used by various application components in SAP Financial Accounting, including FI-A/R, FI-A/P, TR (Treasury), and FI-BL (Bank Accounting).

468. What are all the 'Global Settings' for Configuring Outgoing Payments?

There are several **global settings** that you need to configure in the system for both manual and automatic outgoing payments (*Table 16.3*). These settings include the following, which you will configure via the Customizing menu path *SAP Customizing Implementation Guide | Financial Accounting | Accounts Receivable and Accounts Payable | Business Transactions | Outgoing Payments | Outgoing Payments Global Settings*:

Customizing Task	Transaction Code	Remarks
Make and check document settings		Make new settings or check the settings that you would have already made in SAP FI (Global Settings), for the various business transactions that you will be processing here.
Define accounts for cash discount taken	**OBXU**	Define the necessary G/L accounts for accounting of cash discount received. When processing the open items, the system posts the cash discount to these accounts.
Define accounts for lost cash discount	**OBXV**	Define the required cash discount expense G/L accounts to record the cash discount lost (for invoices that are posted on 'net' basis, the system credit the difference between cash discount estimated and actual cash discount claimed).
Define accounts for overpayments/ underpayments	**OBXL**	Define revenue and expense G/L accounts to post when there is a payment difference (over/under payment), when the payment difference is within the tolerance limits, in case of automatic adjustment posting, and when the payment difference cannot be adjusted with cash discount.
Define accounts for exchange rate differences	**OB09**	Define the required G/L account numbers for automatic posting of exchange rate differences realized (gain or loss) when clearing open items. For clearing open items of customers/vendors, specify the reconciliation G/L accounts of customers or suppliers/vendors in the '*Reconciliation act*' field, under *Customer: Account Management* tab, in the respective master records. You may define separate accounts for each type of currency. Do not change these accounts once you make the first valuation run; else, you cannot the reverse valuation postings.
Define account for rounding differences	**OB00**	Define the required G/L accounts (revenue/expense) for automatic posting of gain/loss arising out of currency rounding off during clearing open items.
Define accounts for payment differences with altern. currency	**OBXO**	Define G/L accounts for payment differences occurring with alternative currencies (only when you work with alternative payment currencies in manual or automatic payment transactions).
Define clearing accts for payment diff. with altern. currency	**OBXQ**	Define clearing G/L accounts for payment differences occurring with an alternative payment currency (only when you work with alternative payment currencies in manual or automatic payment transactions).
Define accounts for bank charges (vendors)	**OBXK**	Define the required G/L accounts for your bank charges accounts to which the system can post the charges amounts that you specify for a bank item when settling payments.

Customizing Task	Transaction Code	Remarks
Define posting keys for clearing	**OBXH**	Here, you can define the posting keys that the system should use to automatically create line items during clearing transactions. For each of the clearing transactions namely: AUSGZAHL (outgoing payment), EINGZAHL (incoming payment), GUTSCHRI (credit memo), JVACLEAR (JVA clearing), and UMBUCHNG (transfer posting with clearing), the standard system comes with default posting keys that we recommend to use without making changes. Note that the payment program also uses these posting keys.
Enable translation posting	**OB66**	When translation posting is enabled for your Company Code, the system posts translation gain/loss for clearing open items, in foreign currency, to the appropriate G/L accounts. The system posts the translations, if the item to be cleared has already been revalued once during foreign currency valuation. Then, the system posts the valuation difference to a separate G/L account (translation account that you define here in this task), with an offsetting entry to a clearing G/L account.
Define payment block reasons	**OB27**	Define the required payment blocking reasons with which you can differentiate why invoices are to be blocked for payment. Valid across Company Codes, you can also use these reasons to prevent items from being processed manually with the clearing procedures (incoming payment & outgoing payment).
Define default values for payment block	**OBBC**	Using this task, you may change the default blocking key value (proposed from the payment terms) when posting to customer accounts and vendor accounts.

Table 16.3: Configuring Outgoing Payments- Global Settings

469. What are the two scenarios in Manual Outgoing Payments?

SAP S/4HANA Finance supports the following two scenarios in manual outgoing payments:

- Direct payment without an invoice
- Payment of vendor open line items

470. What are the 'Pre-requisites' for using the Payment Program?

To configure the payment program to handle the payments automatically, you should have defined the following in the system:

- House banks
- Bank accounts
- Payment methods appropriate for the country
- Payment forms

471. What do you need to consider while configuring the Payment Program?

Before making the required configuration settings for the payment program in the system, you need to consider the following:

- **What is to be paid**: Determine the rules for which the payment program selects (and groups) the open items for payment.
- **Whom to be paid**: Specify the payee(s) to whom the program should make the payments. Also specify if the program should consider alternative payee, if any. To consider an alternative payee, you should have maintained that in the supplier/vendor master or the document. Refer to *Question 458* for more details on the alternative payee.
- **When to be paid**: Specify the payment deadline based on the due date of open items.
- **From where to make payment**: Determine how the program selects the appropriate house bank/bank account to make the payment. You can maintain the house bank details in the customer or supplier/vendor master record or the line items. Or you can specify that the payment program arrives at the appropriate house bank/bank account via certain rules specified beforehand.
- **How payment is made**: Determine how the program arrives at the appropriate payment method to make the payment. You can maintain the payment methods in the vendor/supplier (or customer) master records or the open items. You can also make a payment program to determine the payment method using certain rules.
- **How posting is carried out**: Specify the document type, posting key, and accounts to which the payment program for automatic posting of payments will be applied.

472. Where do you specify the 'Parameters' that control the Payment Program?

You will be able to control the payment program by specifying the different parameters in:

- Customer or supplier/vendor master records
- Payment program configuration
- Line items
- Specification for each payment run

473. How does the Payment Program process the Open Items?

The payment program **first** determines the open items to be paid and creates a payment proposal list. You can look at the proposed list and edit it, if necessary, to change the payment methods, house banks, and payment blocks. You can even cancel the payment blocks proposed.

Next, the payment program carries out the payment as per the payment proposal (edited or otherwise), including only the open items listed in the payment proposal. The program posts the payment details and provides you with the data for printing out the payment forms and payment advice. It also provides the necessary data for creating the payment data carriers for the online transmission of payment information. It also provides you with the payment summary.

Finally, the payment program uses the built-in programs to print the payment forms and advice and create the data carriers.

474. What is a 'House Bank'?

A **House bank** is the bank (or financial institution) in which your Company Code keeps its money and does the transactions. A house bank in SAP is identified by a 5-character alphanumeric code. You can have any number of house banks for your Company Code, and the details of all these house banks are maintained in the *'bank directory'* (*Figure 16.8*):

- Each 'house bank' in the system is associated with a country key (US, IN, etc.) representing the country where the bank is located and a unique country-specific code called a 'bank key'. The system uses both the *'country key'* and the *'bank key'* to identify a *'house bank'*.
- For each of the *'house banks,'* you can maintain more than one bank account; each such account is identified by an *account ID*; for example, Chek1, Check2, Pybl1, etc., Here 'Chek1' may denote Checking account 1, 'Pybl1' may denote

Payable account one and so on. You may name the accounts in such a way that they are easily comprehensible. The 'Account ID' is referenced in the *customer or supplier/vendor master record,* and the same is used in the *payment program* by the system.

- To reach this *'account ID,'* you will also specify the *'bank account number'* (the maximum length of this identifier is 18 characters). You may name this so that it is also comprehensible easily.

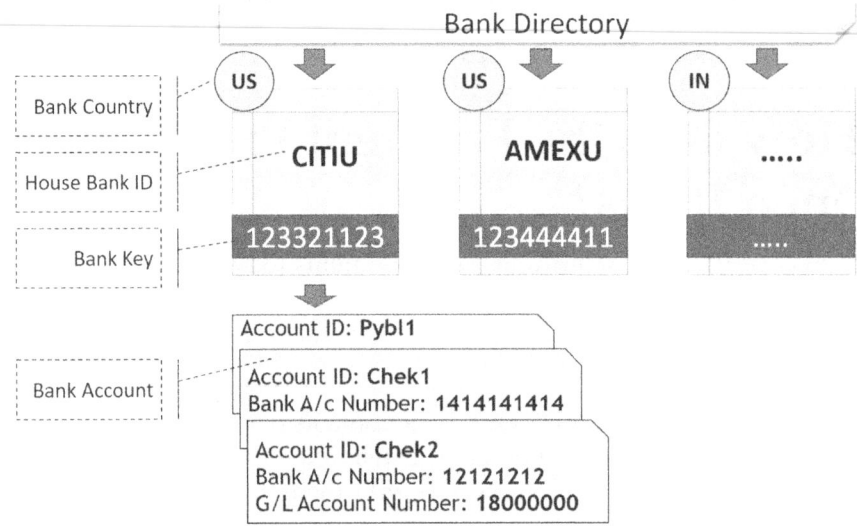

Figure 16.8: House Bank and Bank accounts

- For each *'bank account number'* so defined in the *'house bank'*, you need to create a G/L account master record, and while doing so, you will incorporate the 'house bank ID' and the 'account ID' in that G/L master record.

475. How to define 'House Bank' and 'Bank Accounts'?

You may define a **house bank** via the menu path *SAP Customizing Implementation Guide | Financial Accounting | Bank Accounting | Bank Accounts | Define House Banks.* The *'Bank key'* identifies the bank (*Figure 16.10*). Enter the bank number in the 'bank key' field for all the domestic banks; in the case of foreign banks, enter the SWIFT code. Once you have created the house bank, create the accounts with the house bank.

The house bank can contain several accounts; you need to maintain a G/L account for each of these accounts.

Figure 16.9

Figure 16.10: *House Bank and Bank Accounts creation*

You can configure bank determination for an automatic payment program using the Transaction Code **FBZP**.

476. What is a 'Bank directory' in SAP?

SAP stores the bank master data (details like bank key, bank name, bank country, bank address, and so on) in the **bank directory** (Table: BNKA). Normally, the 'bank masters' are not created in the application but in Customizing, using the IMG. Of course, you can also create the bank master on the application side in FI-TR, FI-A/R, and FI-A/P and **not** in FI-G/L. For example, in the case of FI-A/R or FI-A/P applications, you may use the SAP Easy Access menu path: *SAP Menu | Accounting | Financial Accounting | Accounts Receivable (or Accounts Payable) | Master Data | Bank | Create* or Transaction Code **FI01**, to create a bank. You may also use the menu path *SAP Menu | Accounting | Financial Accounting | Banks | Master Data | Create*.

Figure 16.11

If you are in the process of creating a master record for a vendor/supplier or customer and you enter some bank details that the system does not find in the 'Bank Directory', you can select that row of data under 'Bank details' on the Payment Transactions tab in the general data area and maintain the required bank master data by clicking on the 'Bank data' push button.

You may create the bank directory in two ways: either by creating the bank master data in the application areas of FI-TR, FI-A/P, and FI-A/R or via Customizing using SAP IMG or importing the bank details using a special program. You can display the bank directory (*Figure 16.12*) using the Transaction Code **S_P99_41000166**.

Bank Directory

Bank Directory
Ctry/Reg.: USA

C/R	Bank Key	Bank Name	Rg	Street	City	SWIFT/BIC	BG	PObk	CurAc	DlI	Bank no.	BankBranch
US	011000390	Bank 1 - SAMPLE BANK		2275 El C	Palo Alto	BOFAUS3M					011000390	
US	021000021	Bank of America NA New Y		335 Madis	NEW YORK	BOFAUS3NXXX					021000021	
US	021000022	CitiBank NA										
US	02100021	JPMC	UM	BLYD stre	New York							
US	021000322	Bank of America NA New Y		335 Madis	NEW YORK	BOFAUS3NXXX					021000322	
US	023000032	CITIBANK NA		388 Green	New York	CITIUS33					023000032	NY Branch
US	1111111111	JPMC		MRF Street	California						999999999	US Branch
US	1111122222	Yes Bank	CA	MRF	California							
US	1234567	BOA	IL	USA								
US	1234CHASE01	CHASE										
US	1234CITI	CitiBank	TX	NEWYORK	DALLAS	XXXXUS01						DALLAS
US	150350300	Bank of USA - SAMPLE BANK		530 Lytto	Palo Alto	SWFTUST0302					150350300	
US	456789	bank										
US	820800001	Bank 2 - SAMPLE BANK		400 Hamil	Palo Alto	CITIUS33MIA					820800001	
US	88888887	Credit Card Bank		2285 El C	Palo Alto	BOFAUS4M					88888887	
US	98765	ICICI	IL									
US	99999912	External Payment Bank										
US	ABNAUS33XXX	ABN AMRO BANK N.V.		335, MADI	NEW YORK	ABNAAEAAIPC					50300120	
US	CHASUS33XXX	CHASE MANHATTAN BANK, TH		4 NEW YOR	NEW YORK	CHASUS33XXX						
US	CITI00002	Citi Bank	NY	XYZ New Y	New York						23451299	Main Bran

Figure 16.12: Bank directory

477. What is an 'Intermediate Bank'?

Intermediate banks are used in SAP, in addition to the 'house bank' and partners' banks, to make or receive payments from business partners abroad. The payment processing involving an intermediate bank uses the 'bank chain', which may consist of the correspondent bank of the house bank, the recipient's bank, or the intermediary banks. The bank chain may consist of a maximum of three banks.

478. What is a 'Payment Method'?

The **payment method** represents the procedure by which you make payments either manually or via the automatic payment program. SAP S/4HANA comes with several country-specific payment methods (Figure 16.13) as standard delivery. If you need a new or additional payment method, you can, of course, define it in Customizing.

Payment Methods

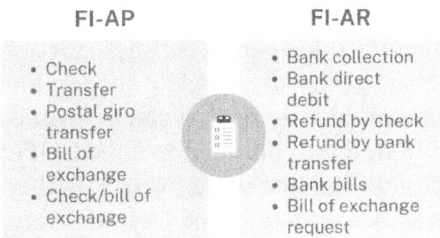

Figure 16.13: *Standard Payment Methods*

479. How do you configure the Payment Methods?

You shall maintain the payment method settings in two stages:

First, you make the required specifications for each of the payment methods for each of the countries. Per payment method and country, you will specify if the payment method is to be used for outgoing payment or incoming payment, the classification of the payment method (check, bank transfer, bill of exchange, etc.), whether the payment method can also be used for personnel payments, what are the necessary details that need to be maintained in the master record (like address, bank details, etc.), and the posting details (document type for payment, document type for clearing, etc.), the payment medium related specifications including payment medium program, name of the print data set, etc.,

Second, you make the specifications per payment method, per Company Code. Specify, among other things, the amount limits (minimum and maximum), how to group the items for payment (by payment due or separate payment for each reference), foreign payment/foreign currency payment settings, and the bank selection control settings (optimized by bank group, optimized by postal code, or not optimized). You will also maintain the specifications for payment forms and payment advice notes.

480. Explain the 'Forms' that you will be using in the Payment Program.

SAP S/4HANA Finance comes with several standard forms (in SAPScript) that you may use with the payment program. You may copy the standard forms and create your own forms that you will then use while configuring the payment method.

The program uses various print programs (some of them country-specific) to print the payment forms. As mentioned previously while discussing the configuration of payment methods, you will specify the payment program for each method while making the settings for payment methods. This specification ensures that the payment program uses the correct print program when printing the payment forms.

When you make the 'Company Code-specific settings' for a payment method, per paying Company Code, you will also specify the name of the payment form to be used. You will also be specifying how many invoice items that can be printed on the form (default is 99). If more items are to be printed, then you need to specify if extra forms can be created to accommodate the printing of all the line items. You will also mention the address details of the form's issuer that must be printed on the payment form.

The payment program provides the required data for form printout after every payment run. The program stores this data in the following structures:

- **REGUH**: There will be a REGUH record per payment. This record will consist of details like the payee, payment document number, and payment method.

- **REGUP**: Each paid item in payment will have a corresponding REGUP record with details like payment amount, cash discount, and invoice document number.

- **REGUD**: This structure consists of certain derived values that you do not find in REGUH and REGUP. These may include certain information from the business partner bank master, amounts with protective asterisk marks, etc. Once the payment transfer medium is printed, the system deletes the contents of this structure.

- **SPELL**: This structure provides the payment amount in words.

481. Explain configuring Automatic Payments.

Configuring the payment program for automatic payments (both for incoming and outgoing payments) involves completing the following tasks via the menu path: *SAP Customizing Implementation Guide | Financial Accounting | Accounts Receivable and Accounts Payable | Business Transactions | Outgoing Payments | Automatic Outgoing Payments*:

- **Set up all company codes for payment transactions:**
    - o Make the required specifications for all the Company Codes involved in the payment transactions. You need to specify the sending Company Code, the paying Company Code, whether separate payment is required per business area, whether payment method supplement is to be used, the settings for cash discount and tolerance limits for payment processing, and what types of special G/L transactions (A: down payment, F: down payment request, and H: security deposit for suppliers/vendors; A: down payment, F: down payment request, G: guarantee, H: security deposit, and P: payment request, for customers) are to be included.

o   As regards the paying Company Code, if one of your Company Codes makes the payment on behalf of other Company Codes (centralized payment), then you will enter that Company Code in the '*Paying Company Code*' field. Otherwise, the '*Sending Company Code*' and the '*Paying Company Code*' will be the same.

- **Set up paying company codes for payment transactions:**

  o   Specify the settings for the paying Company Code as to the control data (minimum amount for incoming/outgoing payment, exchange rate difference, etc.), bill of exchange data, forms and the sender details for payment advice, and EDI accompanying sheets. From this screen, you may click on the '*Company Codes*' push button to view all the Company Codes that use this paying Company Code.

  o   You can view the specifications of the paying Company Code (by clicking on the '*Paying Company Code*' push button) while you are in the first step ('*Set Up All Company Codes for Payment Transactions*') of configuring the automatic outgoing payment.

- **Set up payment methods per country for payment transactions:**

  o   Here, you need to specify (per payment method, per country) if the specific payment method is to be used for incoming or outgoing payments. You also need to maintain the settings relating to payment method classification (like bank transfer, check, bill of exchange, etc.), including setting whether the method can be used for personnel payment. Also, maintain the master record specifications (like address details, bank details, etc.) and posting-related settings (payment document type, clearing document type, etc.). Finally, enter the settings for the payment medium (payment medium program, print dataset's name, and so on). Besides these, you also need to maintain the currency details for the payment method per country; if you do not specify a currency, then you can use the payment method for payment in all the currencies.

  o   Instead of the Customizing menu path via IMG, you can also use the Transaction Code **OBZ3** to configure the settings mentioned above. However, note that the configuration interface will look different than the one via the IMG menu path.

- **Set up payment methods per company code for payment transactions:**

  o   Specify the payment methods that you want the payment program to use in each of the paying Company Codes. Besides entering the allowed payment methods per paying Company Code, you will use this configuration activity to specify the amount limits (minimum and maximum) for that payment method, the grouping criteria (for example, payment per due day, single payment for marked item and so on), the stipulations for foreign/foreign currency payments and the settings for controlling bank selection (say, no optimization, optimization by bank group or optimization by postal code).

- **Set a payment medium format per company code:**
  - o Published by your house bank or the central banking Company of a country, the payment medium format specifications control how the payments to the banks and the debit memos are to be created. Here, you will specify the payment medium format per Company Code, per payment method, and per house bank. For example, for the payment medium 'C' (check), you must use the payment medium format 'CHECK_OM.'

- **Set up bank determination for payment transactions:**
  - o Here, you will specify how the payment program selects the house bank/ bank accounts to process the payments. First, you specify which house banks will participate in the payment. Then, you rank them in the order in which you want the payment program to pick up the banks (the lower the ranking order number, the higher the priority). Second, specify the bank accounts and subaccounts for the house banks from which the payments will be processed. Third, specify the amount limits per currency for outgoing and incoming payments. Fourth, specify the days that need to be added to the posting date of the payment run to arrive at the value date at the bank; this will depend on the payment method, bank account, payment amount, and currency. Finally, specify the charges that you want the print program to print on the bill of exchange forms (this is valid only for certain countries).

- **Define value date rules:**
  - o Here, you will be configuring the rules for arriving at the value date of bank-related transactions at the house bank. Per the house bank and bank account, you need to specify the reference date (document date, posting date, or due date) to determine the value date. Then, enter the number of days that you want the payment program to add to the reference date to arrive at the value date. In arriving at the value date, you may also specify a calendar ID to take into account only the working days in arriving at the value date. You can also use the Transaction Code **OBBA** to configure the settings.

- **Assign payment method to bank transaction:**
  - o Specify the payment method for each house-bank-related transaction per house-bank and bank account combination. Ensure that the payment method you specify here has already been maintained in the respective customer or supplier/vendor master record.

- **Define payment groupings:**
  - o Configure the grouping keys that the payment program can use to group customer or supplier/vendor open items together for payment. According to the grouping key, you can specify whether it is to be used for customer-supplier/vendor accounts or both. Per the grouping key, you can select up to three fields (like BLDAT – document date, BUDAT – posting date, etc.) for grouping the payments. Since the settings are cross-Client, you can use the same grouping key across several Company Codes across Clients. After the definition, you need to enter the grouping key in the supplier/vendor master (in the *'Grouping key'* field under 'Automatic Payment Transactions' on the 'Vendor: Payment Transactions' tab in the Company Code data area) or customer master (in the *'Grouping key'* field under 'Automatic Payment Transactions' on the 'Customer: Payment Transactions' tab in the Company Code data area). During clearing, when you have maintained the grouping key in both the customer and supplier/vendor masters, the grouping key entered in the supplier/vendor master has priority. You may also use the Transaction Code **OBAP** to configure payment groupings.
  - o You can access the above Customizing tasks under the folder 'Payment Method/Bank Selection for Payment Program' under *Automatic Outgoing Payments.*

- **Prepare automatic postings for the payment program:**
  - o You will see this Customizing task under the folder 'Automatic Posting' under *Automatic Outgoing Payments.* Here, you will specify the posting keys for each of the automatic payment procedures: ZBA, payment program (bank posting); ZWE, payment program (bill of exchange/bill of exchange request); and ZWO, payment program (bank bill liability). You may not want to change the standard posting key specifications. If required, you just need to specify the special G/L indicator. Instead of the IMG menu path, you may also use the Transaction Code **OBXC**.

- **Prepare automatic posting for payment requests:**
  - o You will also see this Customizing task under the folder 'Automatic Posting' under Automatic Outgoing Payments. Configure the posting key and the special G/L indicator for automatic posting of payment requests. The standard system is pre-configured with the posting keys 09 (debit), 39 (credit), and 'P' as the special G/L indicator (for 'payment request,' which does not increase the account balance) that you do not want to tinker with. You may also use the Transaction Code **OBXP**.

- **Select search fields for payments:**
  o You will see this Customizing task under the folder 'Payment Run Display' under *Automatic Outgoing Payments*. Using this Customizing activity, you may specify the search fields (like HBKID, house bank, HKTID, account ID, RWBTR, amount paid, LIFNR, customer, KUNNR, vendor, PAYGR, grouping, and so on) that the payment program uses to find the individual payments or the line items that have been paid. You can also use these fields as the filter criteria for the display of proposals and payment runs. Look at the fields already included in the standard settings; add or change them if required. You may also use the Transaction Code **O7FC** to reach this Customizing activity.

- **Select search fields for line item display:**
  o This Customizing task is also under the folder 'Payment Run Display' under *Automatic Outgoing Payments*. It is similar to the previous Customizing task except that the system uses the fields specified here (like BELNR, document number, XBLNR, reference, BLDAT, document date, WRBTR, amount, KOART, account type, etc.) to search for the line items that have been paid. As mentioned earlier, check the standard settings and add or change them if necessary. Again, you may use the Transaction Code **O7FE**.

You may also complete the above-discussed Customizing tasks using the Transaction Code **FBZP** from a single screen (*Figure 16.14*):

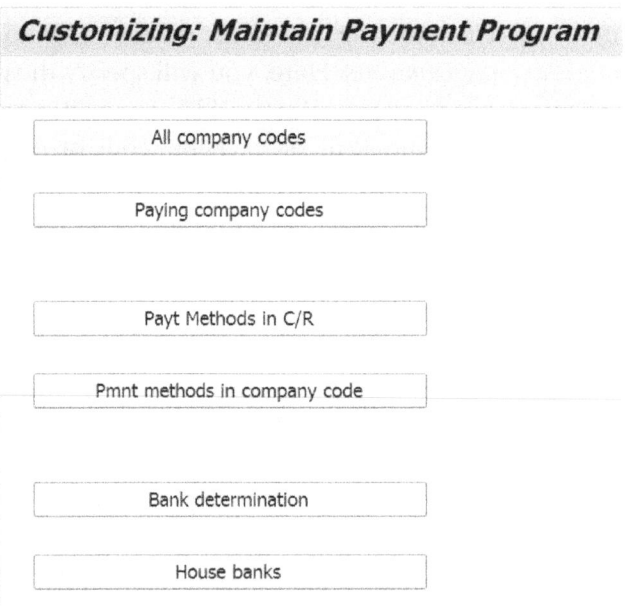

Figure 16.14: *Payment Program Configuration via Transaction Code FBZP*

482. What should you consider when you maintain Payment Methods in multiple places?

It is possible that you may maintain the payment methods in more than one place (*Figure 16.15*):

You enter the payment method in the **master records**, in supplier/vendor (or customer) in the '*Payment Methods*' field under *Automatic Payment Transactions* on the 'Vendor: Payment Transactions' (or 'Customer: Payment Transactions') tab under the Company Code data area. This enables the system to pick up the appropriate payment method during automatic payments. Though you can maintain more than one payment method in the master record (you can enter up to ten payment methods!), the order in which you maintain that is important: the payment program will try making a payment using the first method, then use the second one if the first one is not successful and so on. If you have maintained, for example, 'CDLTX' as the payment method in the master record, then the payment program will first consider making payment using the payment method 'C'; if not successful, then it will try the payment method 'D' next, and other methods in that order (L | T | X).

Besides the customer or supplier/vendor master, you can also maintain the payment methods in the **line items**. Unlike a customer or supplier/vendor master, wherein you can maintain more than one payment method, you will be able to enter only one payment method for a line item of a customer or supplier/vendor. This payment method entered in a line item should be one among the payment methods that have been maintained in such a master; you cannot enter a method that is not already available in the customer or supplier/vendor master. Now, the payment method you have entered in the line item takes precedence over the payment methods in the master record. Suppose that you have maintained 'CDLTX' as the payment method in the master record, but you enter 'T' as the payment method in a line item; then the payment program will consider the payment method 'T' in the first place, though it is not appearing in the first position of payment methods in the master record.

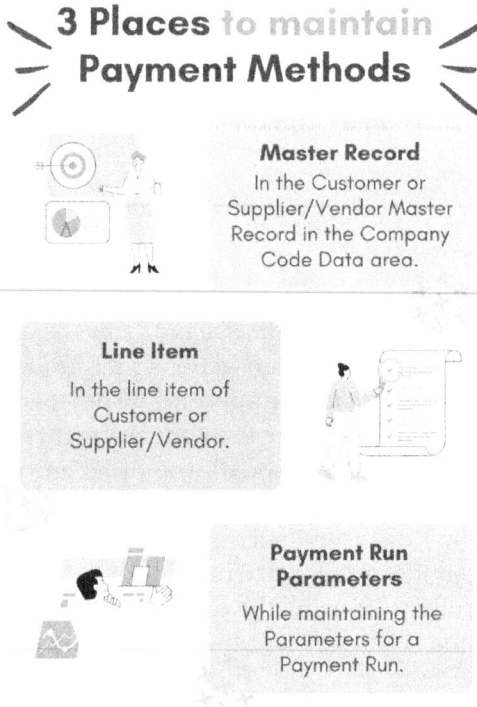

Figure 16.15: Payment Methods: Where to enter?

The third place wherein you can maintain the payment method is under 'Payments Control' on the *Parameter* tab while maintaining the **payment run parameters**. As in the case of customer or supplier/vendor master, here also in '*Pms Meths*' field, you can enter the payment methods (again, you can enter up to ten payment methods!) in the order in which they need to be considered by the payment program, and without any separators in between the payment methods. Take care not to enter any payment method that you have not already maintained either in the master record or in the line item; otherwise, the payment program will consider that a 'conflict' and will not proceed with the payments. For example, when you have entered 'CDLTX' in the master record and 'T' in the line item if you enter 'P' as a payment method in payment run parameters, then this will be considered as a 'conflict'; accordingly, the payment program will not proceed with the payment processing.

483. How does the payment program determine the correct Payment Method?

We have already discussed that you can maintain the required payment methods in three places. How does the payment program determine the correct payment method?

Consider that you have maintained payment methods in all three places: master record ('DLTXC'), line item ('T'), and payment run parameters ('TCLXD'). Here, the payment program will select the payment method 'T' and proceed even though the payment method 'D' appears in the first place in the customer or vendor/supplier master record.

Let us consider another situation where you have maintained the payment methods only in the master record ('DLTXC') and in payment run parameters ('TCLXD') but not in the line item. In this case, the payment program will check the first payment method in the master record ('D') and compare the same with the first payment method in the payment run parameters ('T'); if both are the same, then the program, uses that method for payment. Otherwise (like in our case), it goes back to the master record to check the second payment method ('L') and compares it with the second payment method in the payment run parameters ('C'). If both are the same, then the program stops the search and uses that payment method. Otherwise, it makes comparisons until it finds a payment method that is the same in both places and uses that (in our case, it will be 'X'). If the program finds no such match, it will not proceed with the payment.

484. What variants of 'ACH Payment Method' are available in SAP S/4HANA Finance?

SAP S/4HANA Finance supports three forms of **Automated Clearing House (ACH)** bank transfer as a payment method: 'ACH-CCD,' 'ACH-CTX,' and 'ACH-PPD.' The ACH payments are electronic transfers of money, carried out in batches via a clearing house but are free or with very low cost when compared to wire transfers that are initiated individually by the bank branches and are often costlier to process. The ACH equivalents in India are the **National Electronic Funds Transfer ('NEFT')** and **Real-Time Gross Settlements ('RTGS')**. While the 'NEFT' payments happen in batches every half-hour, the 'RTGS' batches happen in real-time but are meant for large payments exceeding INR 200,000. The difference between ACH-CCD, ACH-CTX, and ACH-PPD can summarized as follows:

- ACH-CCD is the widely used automated payment transfer method for corporate accounts. The 'CCD' stands for 'Cash Concentration and Disbursement' and denotes the debits and credits in corporate accounts.
- The 'CTX' in ACH-CTX stands for 'Corporate Trade Exchange.' ACH-CTX is mainly used for money transfers by corporate and government entities.
- ACH-PPD is normally used for consumer (like 'personnel') accounts, including payroll transfers. The 'PPD' here denotes 'Pre-arranged Payments and Deposits.'

485. Explain 'Classic' and 'Enhanced' Bank Account Determination.

The payment program, while determining the appropriate house bank/bank account (from the settings that you made under '*Set up Bank Determination for Payment Transactions*'), first goes through the 'classic bank account determination,' which contains only one bank account, together with the account determination, for each combination of 'house bank-payment method-currency.'

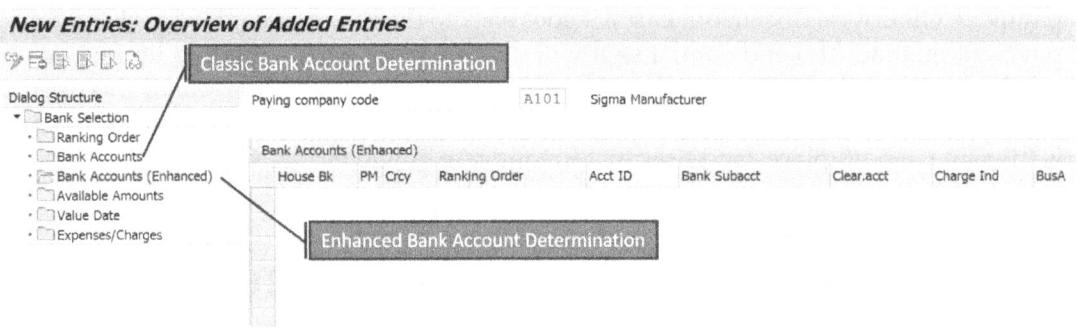

Figure 16.16: Classic & Enhanced Bank Determination Views

However, the classic maintenance of bank determination parameters may not be sufficient when you have already entered a house bank while posting an open item and you want to use more than one bank account (within a single house bank) with a ranking order. In such a case, you must define the *enhanced bank determination* parameters using the '*Bank Accounts (Enhanced)*' view (*Figure 16.16*).

486. How many 'House Banks' can you configure per Payment Method?

While configuring automatic payments with SAP S/4HANA Finance, it is possible that you can define a maximum of 9,999 house banks for a single payment method with proper ranking order.

487. How can the same House Bank be made valid for all Payment Methods?

When you make the settings under the Customizing activity '*Set up Bank Determination for Payment Transactions*', if you want a particular house bank to be picked up by the payment program for all payment methods, then you just need to leave the '*PM*' field blank. In case you want the payment program to consider the specific house bank for all payment methods and for all currencies, besides leaving the '*PM*' field blank, you should also leave the '*Crcy*' field blank (*Figure 16.17*):

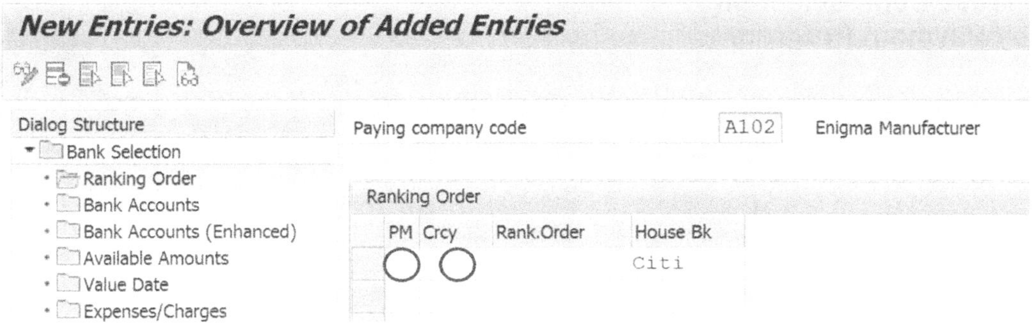

Figure 16.17: *Configuring a single House Bank for all Payment Methods & Currencies*

488. How does the Payment Program make use of 'Available Amounts' settings?

While making the settings under '*Available Amounts*,' you will specify the amount limits for both incoming and outgoing payments:

- In the case of **outgoing payments**, the payment program will check the amount that you specified under '*Available for outgoing payment*' to decide if that bank account has sufficient balance to make the outgoing payment for that specified payment method. If the balance is sufficient, then the program clears the outgoing payment. Otherwise, it will go down in the ranking order to see if the next bank account has the required account balance. This iteration continues until the payment program exhausts verifying all the bank accounts. If none of the accounts meet the account balance requirements, the payment program will not make any payment. Note that the payment program will not draw the shortfall amount from another bank account when a particular bank account's balance is not sufficient to make the payment.

- In the case **incoming payments**, it is always better to leave the '*Scheduled incoming payment*' field blank so as to receive any amount.

489. How does the Payment Program determine the correct House Bank for payments?

The payment program iterates the payment method, currency, and ranking order combinations before arriving at the appropriate house bank for the payments, as shown in *Figure 16.18*:

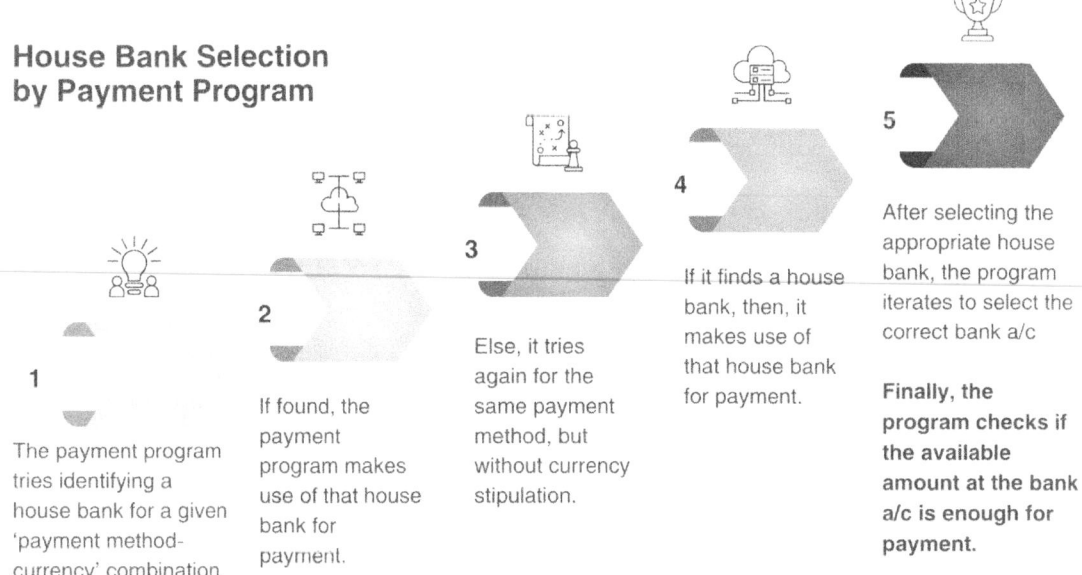

House Bank Selection by Payment Program

1 — The payment program tries identifying a house bank for a given 'payment method-currency' combination.

2 — If found, the payment program makes use of that house bank for payment.

3 — Else, it tries again for the same payment method, but without currency stipulation.

4 — If it finds a house bank, then, it makes use of that house bank for payment.

5 — After selecting the appropriate house bank, the program iterates to select the correct bank a/c

Finally, the program checks if the available amount at the bank a/c is enough for payment.

Figure 16.18: House Bank determination by the Payment Program

If the program, during the above process, finds more than one bank, then it makes use of the 'ranking order' to select the appropriate house bank with the highest-ranking order (denoted by the smallest rank number) and uses that bank. This is, of course, on the assumption that there is no bank optimization either via 'postal code' or 'bank group'; else, if there is some bank optimization, then the selection of the appropriate house bank will be based on the results of that optimization.

Suppose that the payment program does not find a house bank fulfilling all three criteria, house bank, house bank account, and available amount limit, for a given payment method; it tries to locate another house bank that fulfills all these requirements for that payment method. If it is unable to find a house bank, then it decides that the payment cannot be made using that specific payment method. Now, the program starts all over again with another payment method.

490. How does the Payment Program select the open items to pay?

The selection of open items by the payment program, for payment, depends on several factors, including whether the open item is payable or receivable:

- For all the payable items, the payment program:
  - o Selects the open items in such a way to get the maximum cash discount in the current payment run than in the subsequent run. It is possible that you can further limit this automatic selection manually by adjusting the minimum cash discount percentage.
  - o Selects all the open items that would otherwise be overdue (even after allowing the grace period) in the next payment run.
  - o Selects all the invoice-related credit memos, using a special rule, and pays them together with the corresponding invoice.
  - o Pays all other open items, that do not conform to the above criteria, in the subsequent payment runs.
- For all the receivable items, the payment program:
  - o Pays the open item as soon as possible, with the first payment run made on or after the due date of the first cash discount term, to secure the maximum possible discount.
  - o Selects the open items according to the strategy you have decided to: getting maximum cash discount or making net payments.
  - o Can make the bill of exchange payments before due date, if you have configured the payment program to take this into account.

491. What 'Cash Discount Strategies' can you set up for Automatic Payments?

While configuring automatic payments, you can follow any one of the following cash discount strategies:

- **Maximum Cash Discount**: Making early payments, to get maximum cash discount.
- **Maximum Credit Period**: Delaying payments as much as possible, even if that means foregoing cash discounts.
- Making payments in between the above two extreme scenarios.

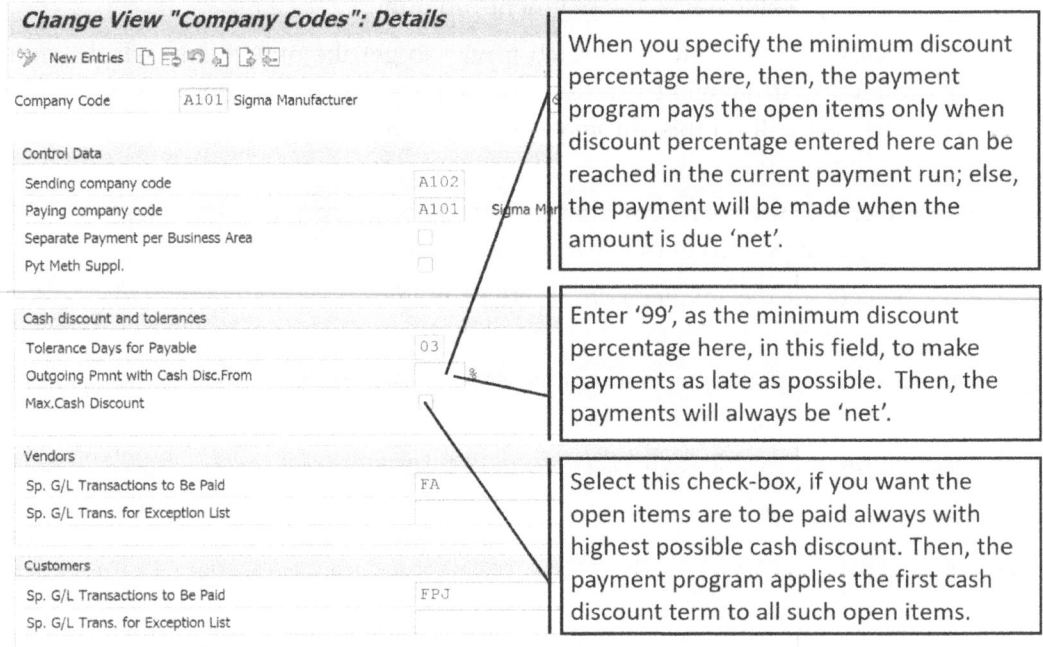

Figure 16.19: *Cash Discount Strategy configuration*

While configuring for automatic payments, make the appropriate settings under the Customizing object '*Set Up All Company Codes for Payment Transactions*' as shown in *Figure 16.19*. Select the checkbox '*Max. Cash Discount*' to fulfill the first cash discount strategy of getting maximum cash discounts. Enter '99' as the cash discount percentage in the '*Outgoing Pmnt. with Cash Disc.From*' field to delay the payments as much as possible (second cash discount strategy); the payments will become due 'net'. Adjust the cash discount percentage entered in the '*Outgoing Pmnt. with Cash Disc. From*' field to make payments between the two extremes of early and late payments (3rd cash discount strategy).

492. How do you process 'Payment Requests' using the Payment Program?

You can use the payment program to pay for the **payment requests** when they become due, as in the case of invoice payments. During the process, the payment program will check to ensure that the corresponding invoice has not been paid or is not scheduled for payment in the next payment run. If the payment program cannot process the request, then such requests will be listed in the payment proposal as an 'exception' that you can manually cancel while editing the proposal. In the case of partially paid invoices, you can make partial payment of payment requests: to do this, first, you need to 'block' the invoice in question and then make out a payment request for the partial amount.

493. How do you 'Block Open Items' for Payment?

You may **block an open item** (or all the open items of a specified account) for payment regardless of its due date.

Figure 16.20: Blocking an account (in the Master Record) for payment

- When you want to **block a particular open item** from being paid, enter a 'blocking key' in that line item. The blocking key identifies the reason for blocking, and the standard system delivers several blocking keys, together with the reason, that you can use as such; you can also create your own blocking keys.

- If you decide to **block all the open items of a specified account**, then you need to enter the appropriate blocking key in the '*Payment Block*' field under 'Automatic Payment Transactions' on the *Vendor (or Customer): Payment Transactions* tab under the Company Code data area, in the master record of the customer or supplier/ vendor master (*Figure 16.20*). When you do not enter anything in this field, then payment is free.

When the payment program creates the payment proposal list, all such blocked items are separately listed on the proposal. You may 'cancel' the blocking key while editing the proposal to enable payment. Also, it is possible to set a blocking key while editing the payment proposal to block an open item from being paid.

494. Explain the 'Payment Run' process.

When you want to start and process a payment run, you need to complete several steps as indicated in *Figure16.21*:

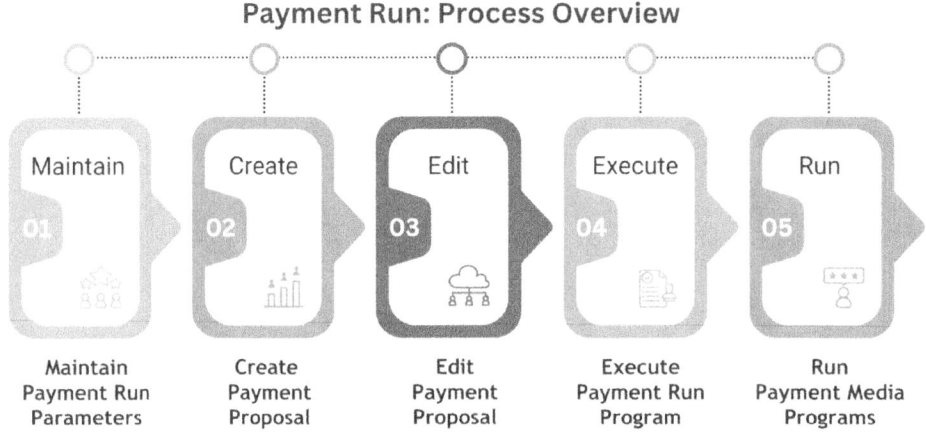

Payment Run: Process Overview

Maintain	Create	Edit	Execute	Run
01	02	03	04	05
Maintain Payment Run Parameters	Create Payment Proposal	Edit Payment Proposal	Execute Payment Run Program	Run Payment Media Programs

Figure 16.21: *Payment Run: Process Overview*

The first step starts with the appropriate planning and specifications of payment run parameters. Then, you will let the payment program come out with the payment proposal list in the next step. In the third step, you will look at the payment proposal list and edit it to make the required changes. Once you have completed editing the payment proposal, the next step is to execute the payment program to complete the payments. Here, you can combine the last step to print the payment medium together after completing the payment run, or, if you want, you can execute the payment medium programs separately as the fifth and final step. The detailed steps are as follows:

1. **Maintaining payment run parameters:**

    i. You will start the payment program using the Transaction Code **F110** or via the SAP Easy Access Menu Path: *SAP Menu | Accounting | Accounts Receivable (or Accounts Payable) | Periodic Processing | Payments*. To run the payment program periodically, use the Transaction Code **F110S** or the SAP Easy Access Menu Path: *SAP Menu | Accounting | Accounts Receivable (or Accounts Payable) | Periodic Processing | Schedule Payment Program Periodically*.

Automatic Payment Transactions: Parameters

Bills of Exchange/Payment Requests

Run Date   12.04.2024

Identification   APR24

| Status | Parameter | Free selection | Additional Log | Printout/data medium |

Posting Date   12.04.2024   Docs Entered up to   12.04.2024

     Customer Items Due By   12.04.2024

Payments Control

Company Codes	Pmt Meths	Next PstDate
A101, A102	DETPQ	12.05.2024

Accounts

Supplier	1	to	999	⇨
Customer	100	to	499	⇨

Foreign Currencies

E/R Type for Translat.

Figure 16.22: Payment Run: Parameters

Transaction Code F110

Figure 16.23

ii. When you use the Transaction Code **F110**, you will initially reach the 'Automatic Payment Transactions: Status' screen (*Figure 16.22*), in which you need to maintain the identifiers for the payment run: 'Run Date' and the 'Identification.' On the next screen, you must maintain the required parameters like the Company Codes, payment methods, the accounts (supplier and /or customer) to be included in the current run, and so on. You may also need to maintain the desired posting date, the next posting date, etc. Besides the above, you may also specify the free selections, if any, additional log requirements like (due date check, line items of the payment documents, and so on), and the variants, if any, for the printout/data medium programs.

2. **Create payment proposal:**

   i. Once you have completed specifying the parameters for the payment run, you may click on 'Schedule Proposal' to get the payment proposal list. Here, you can start the payment proposal immediately or schedule the same for a date/time in the future. The system creates the proposal (*Figure 16.24*), completes the log, and records exceptions, if any. The payment proposal list will contain all the payments and line items. At the end of the list, there will be a consolidation with the payment amounts sorted by payment methods, banks, business areas, countries, and currencies. You may print or display the same to get a complete overview of the proposal. The exception list will contain details of blocked items, special G/L transactions (if any), and the items that could not be processed for payment even though they are all due.

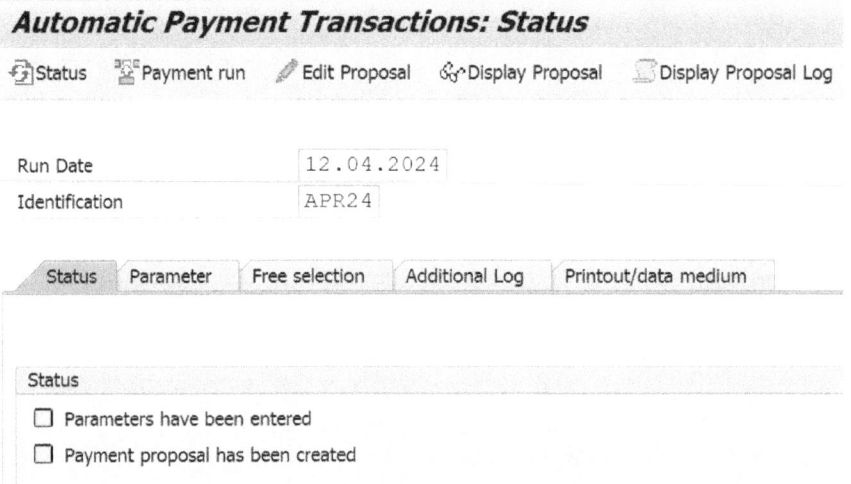

Figure 16.24: Payment Run: Status screen

3. **Edit payment proposal:**

   i. You can edit the payment proposal created by the payment program and make changes before executing the payment run for actual payments. You can make the following changes:

   * Payment
     o Payment method
     o House bank
   * Items proposed for payment
     o Block indicator (block or unblock)
     o Cash discount

ii. Besides the above, you may also assign line items to another payment. In doing all these, you may divide the payment proposal for editing between your accounting clerks. For this, after accessing the payment proposal for editing, you need to enter the accounting clerk ID that you have already maintained in the customer's master records (or supplier/vendor). All the changes you make while editing the payment proposal will affect only the specific payment proposal and not any of the source documents.

4. **Execute payment run:**

   i. After editing the payment proposal or accepting it without making any changes, you must schedule the payment run. You can schedule the job only for running the payment program or include executing the payment medium program (with the specification of variants for each payment medium program) as well. The payment program creates the payment documents and prepares the data to be used by the payment medium program(s).

5. **Execute payment medium program:**

   i. If you did not schedule the payment medium program in the previous step (Step 4) when scheduling the payment run, you can now schedule it as a separate job. While doing that, you need to specify the variant for each payment medium program. The payment medium program, per payment method, will print the payment forms or create the payment data medium.

495. What is known as 'SEPA Direct Debit'?

SEPA stands for '*Single Euro Payments Area*.' It is an initiative of the European Union, with about 40 member countries and 25+ EU member states, to create a single integrated European payments area. SEPA payments (*direct debit* and *credit transfer*) represent the cross-border cashless electronic payments within SEPA (that is, within the EU and several non-EU countries) that are as inexpensive and immediate as any local payment. It is made available for all, including the common public and businesses.

SEPA direct debits are available in two variants: 'SEPA Corde Direct Debit' and 'SEPA Business to Business Direct Debit'. SAP S/4HANA supports both, and the entire process works via *SEPA Mandates*. The SEPA mandate is an authorization for payment to be collected by you (as creditor), issued by your business partner (as debtor), in the form of a direct debit. You need to enter a SEPA Mandate for each of your bank accounts.

Figure 16.25: SEPA Mandates – Configuration

To make use of SEPA Direct Debits, you need to configure the system with various settings via the Customizing menu path: *SAP Customizing Implementation Guide | Financial Accounting | Accounts Receivable and Accounts Payable | Business Transactions | Incoming Payments | Management of SEPA Mandates* (*Figure 16.25*).

496. What are 'Payment Cards' in SAP S/4HANA Finance?

You can use '**payment cards**' for cash-free transactions, including buying from a local store using a **Point of Sale (POS)** machine or the internet. You can also use the payment cards to procure goods and services in your Company. SAP S/4HANA Finance supports a variety of payment cards, including:

o **Credit cards**: For purchase of goods and services, on credit.

o **Customer cards**: To purchase goods and services from specified merchants or groups of merchants.

o **Procurement cards**: These are cards issued to employees with a pre-defined credit limit for purchasing or procuring goods and services in a company.

Payment card processing starts in the SAP **Sales & Distribution (SD)** application component or 'SAP Retail' industry solution. The system transfers the payment card information from these applications. When transferred, the system copies the payment card information to the SAP FI document, to the A/R line items, and to the G/L line items that contain the receivables due to the payment card issuer. The payment card date is not entered or changed in the SAP FI document. Also, A/P line items are not impacted.

In addition to the settings you make in SAP SD, you need to make additional settings in SAP FI: *SAP Customizing Implementation Guide | Financial Accounting | Accounts Receivable and Accounts Payable | Business Transactions | Payments with Payment Cards* (*Figure 16.26*).

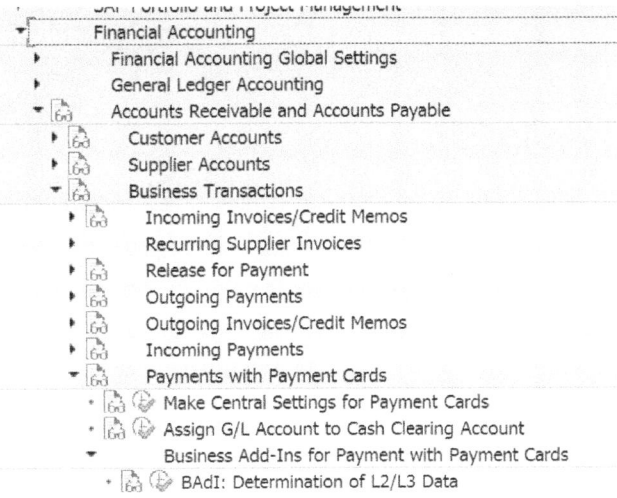

Figure 16.26: *Payments with Payment Cards – Configuration*

497. What is a 'Payment Advice Note'?

Used in incoming payments, the **payment advice note** consists of the payment details that you can use to allocate and clear an open item. The payment advice note comprises two parts: header and items. The header comprises details like payment date and payment date, among others. The item portion includes information like amount, document/reference number, billing document number, reason codes, etc. Instead of entering some selection criteria to process open items, you can simply enter the payment advice note number so that the system proposes the open items for clearing. In the process, the system also identifies the payment differences, if any, and payment on account.

With SAP S/4HANA Finance, you can create payment advice notes in multiple ways (*Figure 16.27*).

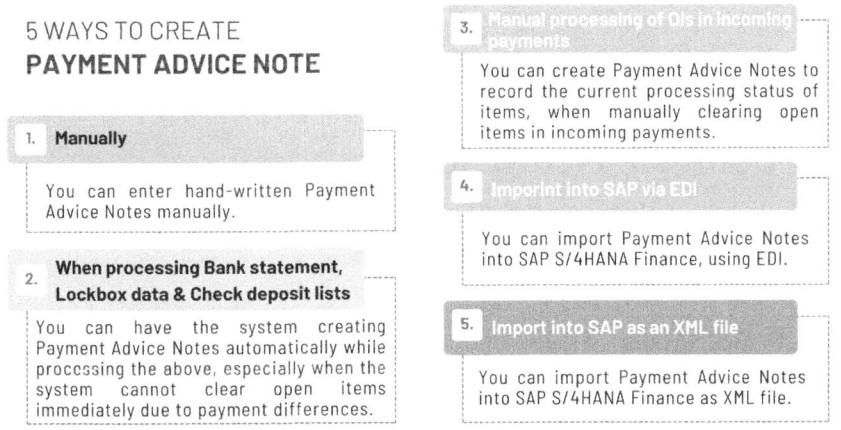

Figure 16.27: *Creating Payment Advice Notes*

Join our book's Discord space

Join the book's Discord Workspace for Latest updates, Offers, Tech happenings around the world, New Release and Sessions with the Authors:

https://discord.bpbonline.com

CHAPTER 17

FI: Accounts Receivable & Accounts Payable – II

Introduction

Continuing from the previous chapter, you will mainly learn about dunning in SAP in this chapter. You will learn about the concept of dunning, the dunning process, and the configuration that you need to make in the system to use the dunning program to dun your customers (and vendors). In the process, you will learn about the dunning key, dunning procedure, dunning level, dunning area, etc. You will also learn about the special G/L transactions, the item interest calculation, the sales and purchase cycles in SAP, the integration of FI-SD and FI-MM, and finally, about some of the important SAP Fiori apps that you will come across in FI-A/R and FI-A/P.

498. What is 'Dunning' in SAP?

The SAP System allows you to 'dun' (remind) business partners automatically. The system duns the open items from business partner accounts. The *dunning program* selects the overdue open items, determines the *dunning level* of the account in question, and creates *dunning notices* using pre-defined forms and texts. It then saves the *dunning data* so determined for the items and accounts affected, which the dunning program looks at during the next dunning. You can use the dunning program to dun both customers and suppliers/vendors. It may be necessary to dun a supplier/vendor in case of a debit balance because of a credit memo. The dunning is administered through a *dunning program*, which uses a *dunning key* (to limit the dunning level per item), dunning procedure, and dunning area (if dunning is not done at the Company Code level).

The dunning program can offset credit balances with debit and dun only for the remaining balance when your customer is also a supplier/vendor. You can use the dunning program to do a *cross-Company Code-dunning* combining business partners across several Company Codes in a single dunning. Also, you can configure the dunning program so that you dun the head office but send dunning notices to individual branches when you deal with both the head office and branch offices.

With regard to the *dunning currency*, the dunning program uses the currency (local or foreign) of the open items while dunning them. If the open items that are to be dunned have different currencies, then the dunning program uses the Company Code currency. During dunning, it displays the items in the document currency but provides the total in both the local and foreign currency.

As with the regular accounts, you can use the dunning program to dun your *one-time accounts* as well. In the process, the dunning program groups all the items of a one-time account with the same address and duns them with a single dunning notice.

Over time, you can make use of the *dunning history* to view the dunning runs that you have executed, besides examining the dunning notices (by account type, Company Code, or by customer or supplier/vendor) that you have sent through these dunning runs.

You make the settings for the dunning program when you implement the SAP S/4HANA Finance system. However, you can modify, change, or adjust these settings in the application at a later stage. In essence, you can make settings in different places:

- **In customizing**: Through the Menu Path *SAP Customizing Implementation Guide | Financial Accounting | Accounts Receivable and Accounts Payable | Business Transactions | Dunning*.

- **In the application**: Through the SAP Easy Access Menu Path *SAP Menu | Accounting | Financial Accounting | Accounts Receivable (or Accounts Payable) | Periodic Processing | Dunning*. Here, on the 'Dunning' application's initial screen, by clicking on *Environment* and then *Change Configuration* on the menu bar, you can reach the 'Dunning Procedure' configuration screen on which you can click on *Environment* to change the Company Code data, dunning areas, dunning keys, etc., as shown in *Figure 17.1*:

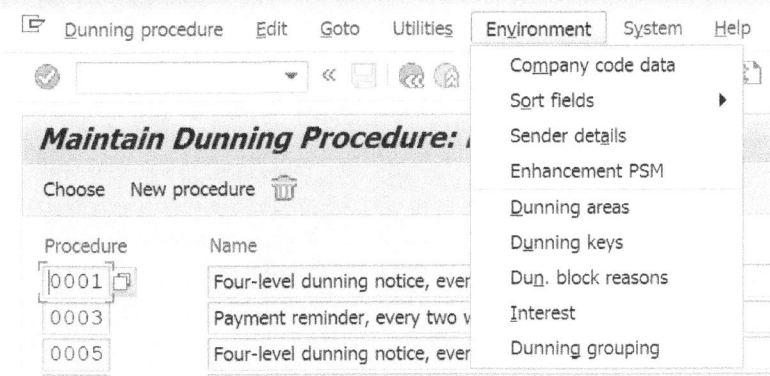

Figure 17.1: *Dunning Configuration Settings via the Dunning Application*

- **In the Application**: Through the SAP Easy Access Menu Path *SAP Menu | Accounting | Financial Accounting | Accounts Receivable (or Accounts Payable) | Master Data | Create/Change,* then, under the Company Code data under 'Correspondence,' under 'Dunning Data.'

- **In the Document**: You may enter or change the 'Dunning Block' and/or 'Dunning Key' while posting a document by reaching out to *Additional Data.*

499. What are the three 'Basic Settings' in configuring Dunning?

You need to complete the following three Customizing activities as the basic settings while configuring dunning for your Company Codes:

- Dunning Area
- Dunning Key
- Dunning Block Reasons

You can configure all three basic settings via the Customizing menu path: *SAP Customizing Implementation Guide | Financial Accounting | Accounts Receivable and Accounts Payable | Business Transactions | Dunning | Basic Settings.*

500. What is a 'Dunning Key'?

You may use a **dunning key** (Company Code independent) to limit the dunning level of an item during the dunning process. While configuring the dunning key, by selecting or de-selecting the '*Print sep*' checkbox, you can specify if you want the dunning program to print the items separately on the dunning notice for the given dunning key (*Figure 17.2*).

Change View "Dunning Keys": Overview

New Entries ▢ ⬚ ↺ ⬚ ⬚ ⬚ ⬚

Dunn.Key	Max. Leve	Print sep	Text
1	1	☐	Triggers maximum dunning level 1
2	2	☐	Triggers maximum dunning level 2
3	3	☐	Triggers maximum dunning level 3
4		☑	Tigger maximum during level 4

Figure 17.2 Dunning key

501. Explain 'Dunning Block Reasons.'

The **dunning block reasons** help you block an item or an account from getting dunned. Defined via the block keys, you will enter this dunning block key in a line item or in the master record of a business partner to prevent that item or the account from being selected for dunning. You can remove the block whenever to get the item or account dunned in the next dunning run.

502. Explain the attributes that control Dunning.

The dunning in SAP S/4HANA Finance is controlled by the following three attributes:

- Dunning Procedure
- Dunning Level
- Dunning Area

503. What is a 'Dunning Procedure'?

Using a **dunning procedure**, you can control how the system carries out dunning. SAP comes with several dunning procedures (Figure 17.4) that you can use, or you can define your own dunning procedures. You can use more than one dunning procedure: connect the dunning procedure to a customer or supplier/vendor master or to a dunning area.

You can view or create a new dunning procedure via the Customizing menu path *SAP Customizing Implementation Guide | Financial Accounting | Accounts Receivable and Accounts Payable | Business Transactions | Dunning | Dunning Procedure | Define Dunning Procedures.*

 Transaction Code FBMP

Figure 17.3

Maintain Dunning Procedure: List

Choose   New procedure 🗑

Procedure	Name
0001	Four-level dunning notice, every two weeks
0003	Payment reminder, every two weeks
0005	Four-level dunning notice, every two weeks, RE forms
0009	Weekly Dunning Notice

Figure 17.4: Standard Dunning procedures

A dunning procedure controls the following:

- Dunning interval/frequency
- Grace days/minimum days in arrear
- Number of dunning levels (at least one level)
- Items that are to be dunned
- Interest to be calculated on the overdue items
- Dunning charges
- Dunning texts via dunning forms/media to be selected for the dunning run
- Special G/L transactions that need to be included in dunning

The dunning procedure (*Figure 17.5*) is 'Company Code independent' and determines the number of **dunning levels**, the dunning interval or frequency, and the grace period for determining the line items to be dunned.

Per the dunning procedure, you can specify what charges are to be levied (in absolute terms or as a percentage) for which level of dunning and from which amount.

You can also specify what should be the **minimum amount** (minimum overdue amount) of the items that are necessary for setting the dunning level; if this amount is not reached in a dunning level, then the dunning program assigns these items to the next lowest dunning level, and the checks if a dunning notice can then be created, for those items, in this new dunning level. While configuring the 'minimum amounts' to dun, you can specify both the absolute amount and/or percentage; you can also specify the minimum amount for calculating the interest.

In the dunning procedure, you can also specify the **dunning texts** that the dunning program needs to use, per Company Code, for the customer or supplier/vendor. Here, you need to specify, per dunning level, the form to be used, the form object name (for example, F150_DUNN_01), the list name etc.,

Finally, you need to specify the **special G/L transactions** that you want to use for customers or suppliers/vendors by selecting the required special G/L indicators.

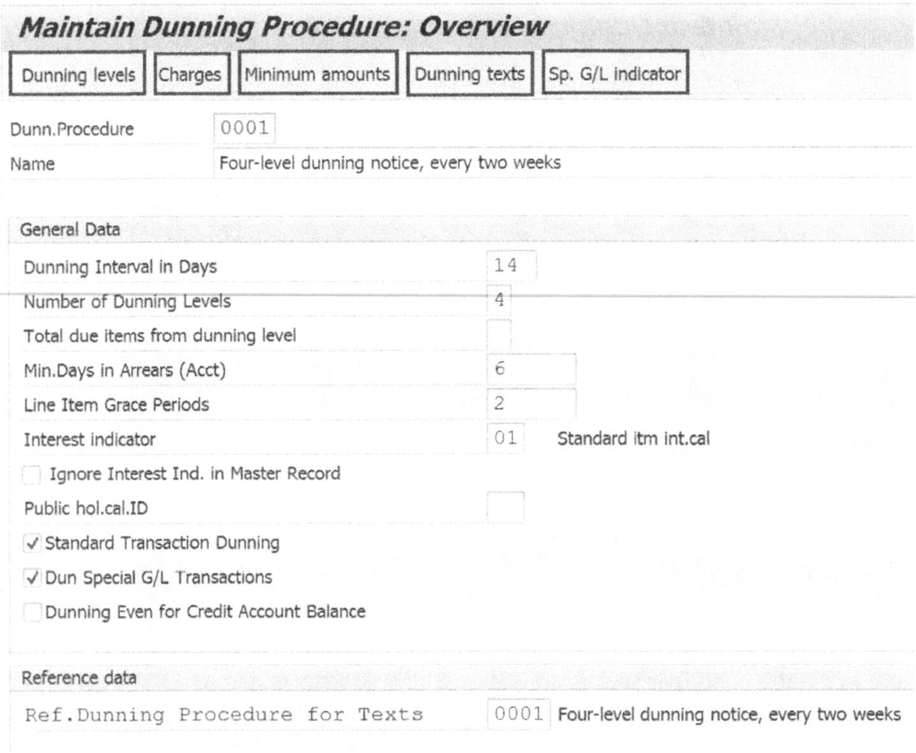

Figure 17.5: Control Information in a Dunning procedure

504. What is a 'Dunning Level'?

A processing step in a dunning procedure, the **dunning levels** control the dunning process and specify the dunning text that needs to be used for the corresponding dunning notice. The higher the dunning level, the more severe the tone of the dunning text. You may define a maximum of nine dunning levels per dunning procedure and a minimum of one.

During dunning, the system calculates the appropriate dunning level based on the number of days that an item has been overdue. It is also possible that you can configure the system in such a way that it selects the dunning level based on the dunning amount or percentage of the amount paid.

For every dunning level (*Figure 17.6*), you configure various parameters, including whether interest is to be calculated, if dunning is to be carried out always, what should be the payment deadline, and if the program needs to print all the open items on the dunning notice (normally selected for higher dunning levels so that the customer gets a clear view of the open items and the account balance). However, selecting the 'Print All Items' indicator here does not have any effect if you have already configured, in Company Code settings, that separate dunning notices need to be created per dunning level.

Figure 17.6: Dunning Level configuration

505. What differentiates one 'Dunning Level' from another?

This **dunning level** determines the 'dunning text' and a 'special dunning form' (if required). The 'dunning program' determines what 'dunning level' should be used in the 'dunning run'. The dunning level so determined is stored in the master record of the account when the 'dunning letter' is printed. The dunning level may also determine whether there will be some 'dunning charges'.

506. How many 'Dunning Levels' can be defined?

You may define up to nine dunning levels. If there is only one dunning level, then it is called the 'payment reminder.'

507. What is a 'Dunning Area'?

The **dunning area** is optional and is required only if dunning is not done at the Company Code level. The dunning area can correspond to a sales division, sales organization, etc., and these organizational units then carry out the dunning using the dunning areas defined. You may use a general dunning procedure or a specific dunning procedure while dunning via dunning areas. To make dunning via dunning areas, you need to enter the dunning area and the corresponding dunning procedure, if any, in the master record of the business partners. You can do so by clicking on the '*Dunning Area*' pushbutton (under 'Dunning Data') on the master record, in the Company Code data area, under the *Customer: Correspondence* tab (*Figure 17.7*). Note that the 'Dunning Area' pushbutton will be visible only when you have defined one or more dunning areas in the system.

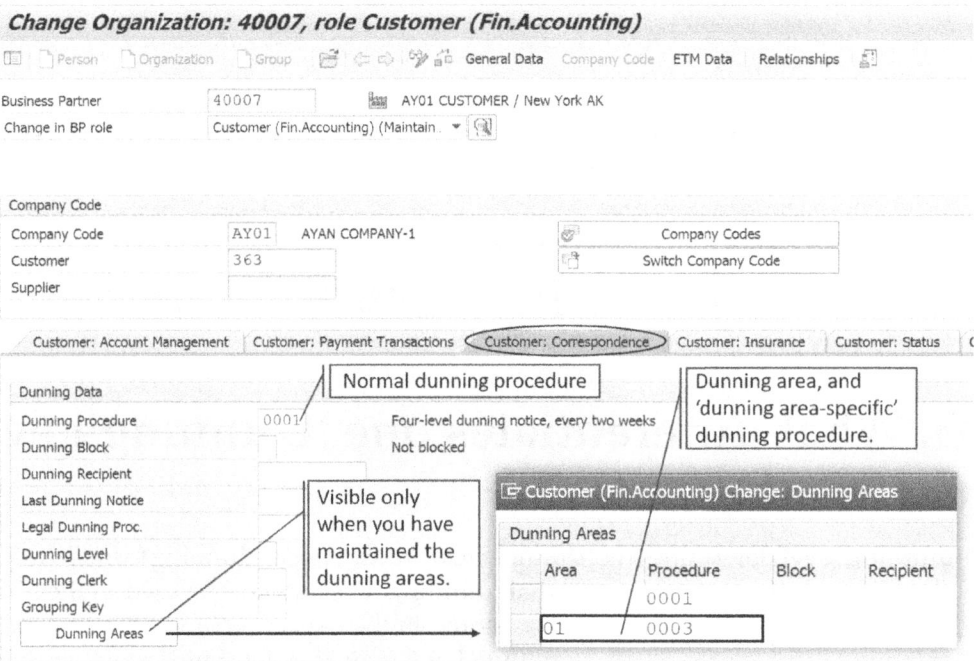

Figure 17.7: Dunning Area specifications in Business Partner's Master Record

508. Describe the 'Dunning' process.

The **dunning process** involves three major steps:
1. Maintaining the *parameters* for the *dunning run*
2. Creating/editing the *dunning proposal* generated by the system
3. Printing *dunning notices*

To start the dunning process, use the SAP Easy Access menu path: *SAP Menu | Accounting | Financial accounting | Accounts Receivable (or Accounts Payable) | Periodic processing | Dunning* or use Transaction Code F150.

Figure 17.8

The steps for the dunning process are as follows:

1. **Maintaining dunning parameter:** As the first step in dunning, you need to maintain certain parameters that identify the current *dunning run (Figure 17.9)*. Entering the date of execution (*'Run On'*) and the dunning run identifier (*'Identification'*) is the starting point, after which you will continue to maintain other parameters like:

   - *'Dunning Date'* **to be printed on the notice**: This will come in handy when you run dunning, say on Friday, but want the notice to be dated for Monday; then you should enter the Monday's date here.

   - *'Document Posted up To'*: This is the deciding date for including accounts for the current dunning run. The documents (invoices) posted after this date will not be considered for inclusion in the current run.

   - *'Company Code'*

   - *'Account Restrictions'* **(optional)**: Enter the required accounts for customers and/or suppliers/vendors when you want to restrict dunning for select accounts. When you maintain the account number of customers and your suppliers/vendors, the dunning program determines the joint balance and duns accordingly.

   a. You may also enter the specifications for *'Free Selection'* and *'Additional Log'*. Under *'Free Selection'* you may enter a maximum of eight additional selection criteria for accounts and documents, for which you can use the fields from tables like BSID, BSIK, KNA1, KNB1, KNB5, LFA1, LFB1, and LFB5.

   b. You can now save the parameters and display the log generated (to see if there were any errors), the dunning list (list of accounts and items), and some dunning statistics (blocked accounts/items, etc.).

Figure 17.9: Dunning Run: Maintaining Dunning Parameters

   c. Now, schedule the dunning run (immediately or at a later date/time). Do NOT select the '*Dunn.Print with Scheduling*' checkbox while scheduling; otherwise, the system will print the dunning notices immediately, and you will not be able to edit or delete a dunning proposal already created. When you click the '*Dispatch*' (Execute) pushbutton on the scheduling pop-up screen or press F5, the system creates the dunning proposal.

2. **Creating dunning proposal:** Once scheduled, the 'dunning program' prepares the 'dunning proposal' as described below:

  a. *Dunning Program* determines which accounts to dun:

     i. The system checks the fields '*Dunn.procedure*' and 'Last dunned' in the business partner master record to determine whether the arrears date or the date of the last dunning run falls in the past.

     ii. Check whether the account is blocked for dunning according to the '*Dunning Block*' field in the customer master record.

     iii. The dunning program processes all open items relating to the accounts thus released in (ii) above that were posted to this account on or before the date entered in the field '*Documents Posted Up To.*'

     iv. Now, the program checks all the open items in an account, as released in (iii) above, to decide:

- Is the item blocked?
- Is it overdue according to the date of issue, the base date, the payment conditions, and the number of grace days granted?

v. The program then proceeds to process all open items thus released in (iv):

- How many days the item is overdue?
- Which 'dunning level' is to be used for a particular open item?

vi. The program determines the highest 'dunning level' for the account based on (v) above. The highest 'dunning level' determined is stored in the master record of the account when you print the letters. This 'dunning level' determines the 'dunning text' and a 'special dunning form', if defined.

vii. The program then proceeds to check each account to decide if that is to be included in the current dunning run:

- Does the customer or supplier/vendor have a debit balance regarding all open overdue items selected?

  o If 'not', the account is not selected for dunning.

- If 'yes', is the total amount to be dunned and the percentage of all open items more than the 'minimum amount' and 'percentage' defined in the 'dunning procedure'?

  o If 'not', the account is not selected for dunning.

- If 'yes,' is the 'dunning level' for the account or the overdue items higher than it was for the last 'dunning run'?

  o If 'not', the account is not selected for dunning.

- If 'yes', are there new open items to dun (with a previous dunning level of 0)?

  o If 'not', the account is not selected for dunning.

- If 'yes', does the 'dunning procedure' for this level specify that dunning be repeated?

  o If 'not', the account is not selected for dunning.

- If 'yes', the program selects the account for dunning in the current run and then goes back to checking other accounts as described above.

viii. When the program completes selecting the accounts/items for the current dunning run, it creates the *dunning proposal list*.

b. Now, you can edit the *dunning proposal list*.

i. You can edit the *Dunning Proposal* to:

- Raise or lower the 'dunning level' of an item/account.

- Block an item from being dunned or remove the block.
- Block an account for the current 'dunning run' or remove the block.
- Block a document for dunning or remove the block.

ii. You can view the sample printout to ascertain how the printed notice would look like. (Maximum ten notices can be viewed on the screen).

iii. You may also display 'logs' to see the changes made in the editing earlier as a confirmation of what you wanted to change in the system-generated proposal earlier. If necessary, you can go back and change the proposal.

3. **Print dunning notices:** You can use a 'single form' or 'multiple forms,' which will have different text based on the 'dunning level.' There may also be a requirement to use a completely different form for *'legal dunning'*. Once the print option is activated, the program prints the notices, and the dunning-related information, like the 'dunning level,' 'last dunned,' etc., are updated in the customer or supplier/ vendor masters. SAP provides the option to optically 'archive' the dunning notices as the system prints them. There is also a provision to restart the printing if it is interrupted before completion.

509. How does the 'Dunning Program' determine the correct 'Dunning Level'?

The open items reach a certain dunning level when they are in arrears for a specific number of days, equal to or greater than the days in arrears specified for that specific dunning level but less than the number of days in arrears specified for the next dunning level. As we have already seen when the dunning program prints the dunning notices, the dunning level is stored in the line items.

Let us consider that you have defined the dunning levels as shown in *Figure 17.10*:

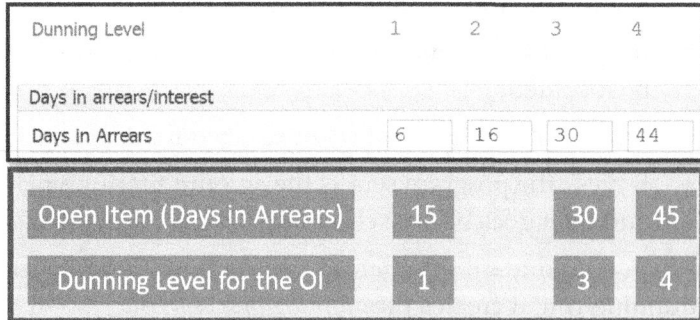

Figure 17.10: Dunning Level determination for open items

Suppose you have open items in arrears for 15 days, 30 days, and 45 days. Now what item will be assigned with which dunning level? The open item that is in arrears for 15 days will be assigned the dunning level of 1, the item with 30 days of arrears will be with the dunning level of 3, and the last item that is in arrears for 45 days will be assigned to the last dunning level of 4 (*Figure 17.10*). The system stores the highest dunning level, which is determined for the account in the corresponding master record, and this level determines the dunning text and the dunning form that will be used to print the dunning notices.

You can also configure the dunning program to dun per dunning level: in this case, the program does not use the highest dunning level to determine the dunning text/form; instead, it carries out dunning using separate notices for each dunning level.

510. How to 'Raise or Lower' the Dunning Level?

You can manually raise/lower the dunning level, or you can make the dunning program do that automatically:

- The dunning program can raise the dunning level for the line items by only one level (from the previous level) at a time, even in the case of blocked items when these items are unblocked for dunning.
- In case of manual action:
  - o You can change the dunning level (that is, raise or lower) as you want when you use the 'line item change'/'account change' function to change the dunning level.
  - o You can lower the dunning level as much as you want, but you can raise that by only one level while editing a dunning proposal. However, manually raising the level depends upon whether the dunning program has already raised that during the current dunning run; if yes, then you cannot raise the level again. In general, you will be raising a dunning level while editing a dunning proposal when you unblock a blocked item for dunning.

511. How is dunning carried out for Line Items with a Payment Method specified?

When you have customers to whom you have defined bank collection, then the system proceeds as outlined below during the dunning run:

- For line items that have a payment method specified for incoming payment:
  - o The dunning program checks if the item is blocked for payment.
    - ▪ If 'yes', the item is dunned.

- For line items that have no payment method specified for incoming payment:
  - The dunning program checks if a payment method is specified in the master record for incoming payment.
    - If 'yes', the program further checks to determine if the master record is blocked for payment.
    - If 'yes', the item is dunned.
    - If 'no' (that is, no payment method has been specified in the master record for incoming payment), then the item is dunned.

512. Can you 'dun' customers across 'Clients' in a single 'Dunning Run'?

No. All the dunning processing is carried out *per Client*. However, it is possible to dun business partners across several Company Codes within the same Client via the 'cross-Company Code-dunning'.

513. Why do you need to configure 'Minimum Amounts for the Dunning Program?

You must specify the **minimum amounts** in absolute terms and percentage rate to prevent the dunning program from dunning relatively small overdue items with high dunning levels. You can make this specification for every dunning level. The dunning program checks these minimum amounts and percentage rates for all the open items and triggers the next dunning level only when the amount to be dunned equals or exceeds these minimum specifications. If not, the program assigns the next lowest dunning level to these items and starts to check again.

514. What are all the 'Special Functions' in Dunning?

The **special functions of dunning** are outlined in *Figure 17.11:*

Special Functions in Dunning

CROSS CO. CODE DUNNING
You can dun overdue items from multiple Co. Codes in single run.

DUNNING 1-TIME A/C
You can dun one-time accounts like any other account.

DUNNING CR. MEMO
You can offset existing cr. notes with the outstanding invoices.

LEGAL DUNNING
You can initiate legal dunning proceedings.

CUTOMER / VENDOR CLEARING
You can dun a customer who is also a vendor.

OPEN ITEM GROUPING
You can group open items to dun them together.

LOCAL DUNNING
In head office - branch relationship, you can dun the branches.

ALTERNATIVE DUNNING RECIPIENT
You can send dunning notice to an alternative recipient.

Figure 17.11: Special Functions in Dunning

515. What is a 'Credit Memo'?

The **credit memo** is issued by the vendor who previously supplied you with some services or materials. The occasion is necessitated when the delivered goods are damaged or you have returned some of the goods back to the vendor. The system treats both the invoices and the credit memo similarly, except that the postings are done with the opposite sign.

If the credit memo is for the entire invoiced quantity, the system generates the credit memo automatically. On the contrary, if a credit memo relates to a portion of the invoiced quantity, you need to process the same manually in the system.

516. Explain dunning 'Credit Memos.'

It is possible that you can dun credit memos by offsetting them with the outstanding invoices in a dunning run. The process is different for customer credit memos and vendor credit memos. However, in both cases, this affects the determination of the due date and the dunning level.

In the case of **customer credit memos**, the dunning program assumes that the credit memos are always due on the baseline date (unless they are invoice-related) or they come with a specific due date. If you want the program to consider the payment terms into account, link the credit memo to an invoice or associate a due date to the credit memo. The credit memo becomes dues once the baseline date and the specific number of days entered have crossed. For all invoice-related credit memos, the dunning program ascertains the dunning level from the invoice, provided that it is included in the dunning proposal list. All other credit memos that are due are assigned with the highest dunning level determined for the account. This ensures that the credit memos are cleared with the oldest invoice.

In the case of **vendor credit memos**, both the 'vendor credit memos with specific due date' and the 'vendor credit memos without an invoice reference' are all considered the same as any customer credit memo. However, the vendor credit memos receive the same dunning level as the invoice. Hence, ensure that the dunning program also selects the vendor invoice in the dunning proposal; otherwise, these invoices will be treated as customer receivable by the dunning program.

517. How to 'Group Open Items' together for Dunning?

Normally, dunning notices are generated per business partner. However, there may be situations wherein you may have to generate a dunning notice for several open items grouped together (for example, you may want to send a dunning notice to the business partner for each of the leased properties having the same contract number). So, what you do is to define a 'grouping key.' Per grouping key, you specify a field from the line item whose contents form the main criteria for grouping. The dunning program duns all such items when it ascertains that the contents in this field are identical.

You can create the grouping keys via the Customizing menu path *SAP Customizing Implementation Guide | Financial Accounting | Accounts Receivable and Accounts Payable | Business Transactions | Dunning | Dunning Procedure | Define Dunning Groupings.*

518. Explain the 'Cross-Company Code' Dunning.

Through **Cross-Company Code Dunning**, you can combine the overdue items belonging to the same business partner(s) that exist across multiple Company Codes in a single dunning notice. This enables you to do away with the need to send separate dunning notices for the same business partner in each of the Company Codes. To carry out such a Cross-Company Code Dunning, you must assign each Company Code (aka 'reference Company Codes') to a common 'dunning Company Code' (aka 'leading Company Code') as shown in *Figure 17.12*. The dunning program makes use of the dunning procedure that is assigned to the dunning partner in the dunning Company Code. However, the program checks the dunning frequency and dunning blocks individually in each of these Company Codes and not just in the leading Company Code.

Change View "Company Code Dunning Control": Overview

CoCd	By Dun.Ar.	By Dun.Lev	Ref.CoCode	Sort. MHNK	Sort. MHND	Dun CoCd
A101	☐	☑	A101		P1	A101
A102	☐	☑	A102		P1	A101
AC01	☐	☑	AC01		P1	A101

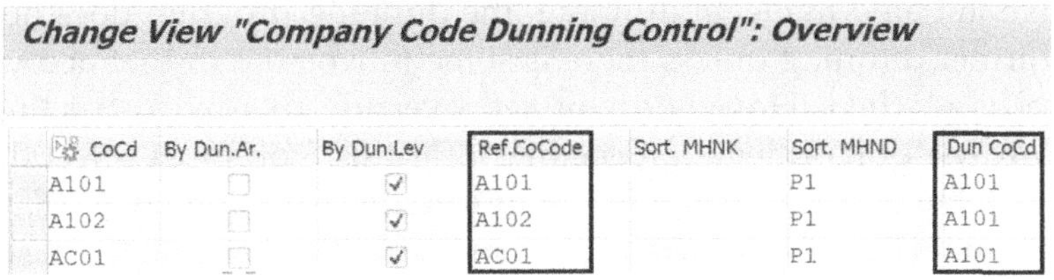

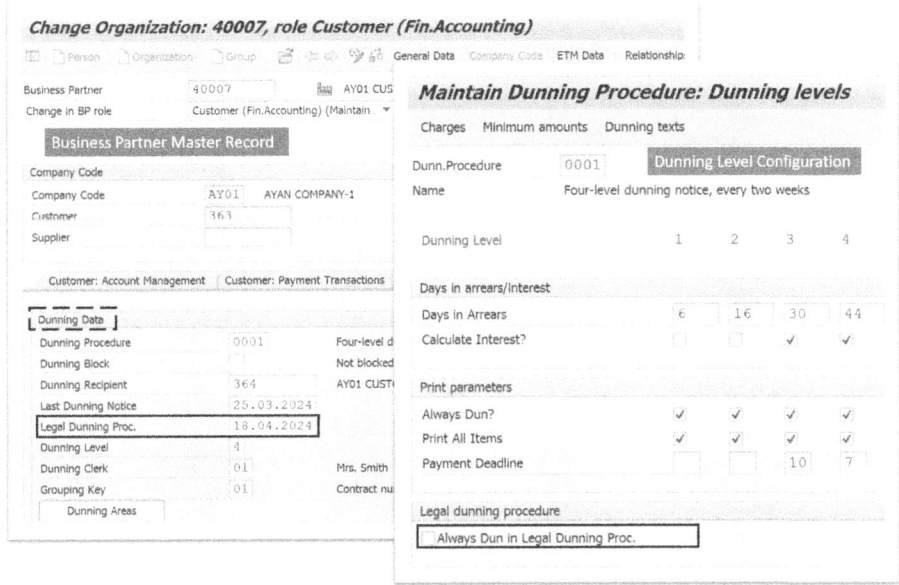

***Figure 17.12**: Cross-Company Code Dunning Configuration*

You can configure the 'dunning Company Code' and the related settings from the SAP Easy Access menu path: *SAP Menu* | *Accounting* | *Financial accounting* | *Accounts Receivable (or Accounts Payable)* | *Periodic processing* | *Dunning, click on 'Environment'* | *'Change Configuration'*. On the next screen *Display: Dunning Procedure List*, click on '*Environment*' | '*Company Code data*'. Or you can use the Transaction Code **T047**.

519. What is 'Legal Dunning'?

While dunning a business partner, you can initiate **legal dunning** proceedings as soon as the last dunning level is reached (or anytime in between for some specific reason). What you need to do is to create an 'internal dunning notice' with an appropriate dunning form and dunning text and transfer the same to your company's legal department. The legal department initiates the legal dunning proceedings by sending this notice to the business partner and stores the data sent in the '*Legal Dunning Proc.*' field in the master record of the business partner under 'Dunning Data', on the 'Customer (or Vendor): Correspondence' tab in the Company Code data area (*Figure 17.13*).

***Figure 17.13:** Legal Dunning – Details*

Once you have initiated the legal dunning, the dunning program does not consider that account for further dunning unless there is some movement in that account and the last dunning level is reached. However, you can override this by instructing the dunning program to always 'dun' in legal proceedings; for this, you must select the '*Always Dun in Legal Dunning Proc.*' checkbox while configuring the dunning levels (*Figure 17.13*). Any further movement in the account will trigger an internal message to the legal department if you have already defined the text for such message in the standard form under text element 520 ('dunning text for legal dunning proceedings') while configuring the 'Dunning texts.'

In legal dunning, the dunning program does not update the dunning level in the master record and item during the subsequent dunning runs; instead, the program updates only the date of the last dunning run in the business partner's master record.

520. What is 'Local Dunning'?

In the case of 'head office-branch office' accounting, the open items (of branches) are normally posted to the head office account, and the system will normally dun the head office on overdue receivables relating to the branch offices. However, you can make the dunning program undertake '**local dunning**' (aka '*decentralized dunning*'), in which the system sends the dunning notices directly to the branch offices instead of sending them to the head office. For this to happen, all you need to do is select the '*Local Processing*' checkbox under *Correspondence* on the 'Customer: Correspondence' tab while maintaining the Company Code data (*Figure 17.14*).

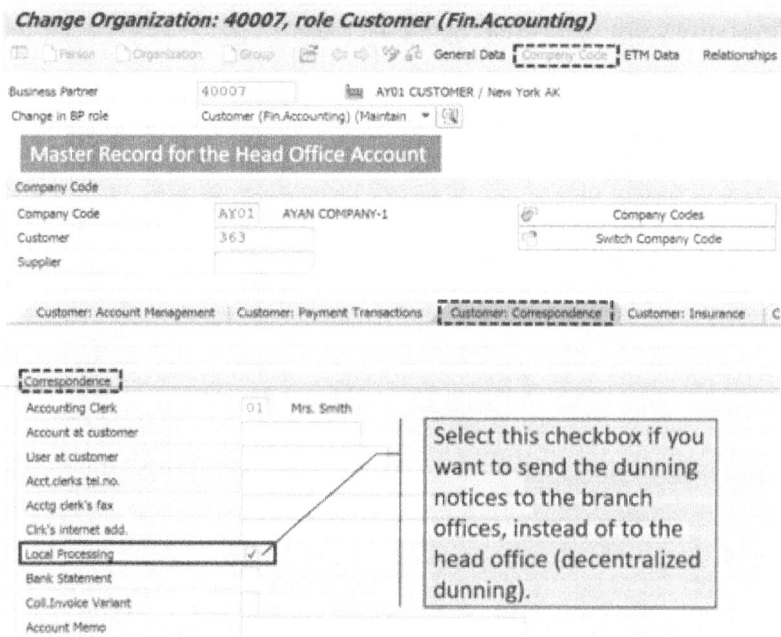

Figure 17.14: *Local Dunning Settings in Master Record*

During dunning, the program determines the branches' overdue items and uses the dunning procedure entered in the master record of the branch offices. With decentralized dunning, the program updates the master record of the branch offices (and not the head office's master record) with the dunning updates.

521. How to dun the 'One-Time Accounts'?

You can **dun the one-time accounts** as with any other regular account. You need to enter the dunning procedure and other required details in the master record of the one-time account. The dunning program determines the required master data from the open items. During dunning, the dunning program, unlike regular accounts, checks the dunning frequency not from the master record but from the individual documents, and the program groups together all the items with the same address and creates a single dunning notice. After the dunning run, the system updates the dunning level for the items and not the master record. However, the system updates the one-time master record with the last dunned date.

522. When will you use 'Alternative Dunning Recipient'?

Instead of sending the dunning notices to the customer or supplier/vendor who owes the receivables, you may be asked to send the same to a third party. This third party is known as the **alternative dunning recipient**. In this case, you must have created two master records in the system: one for the regular business partner (customer or supplier/vendor) and the other for the alternative dunning recipient. Then, you need to enter the account number of the alternative dunning recipient in the '*Dunning Recipient*' field under 'Dunning Data' on the 'Customer (or Vendor): Correspondence' tab in the Company Code data area, as shown in *Figure 17.15*:

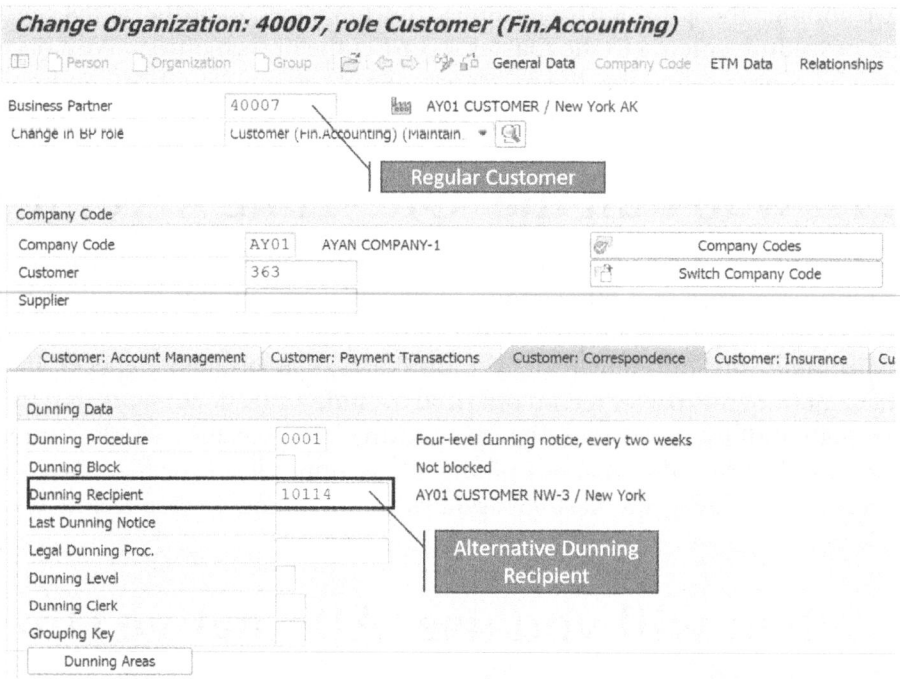

Figure 17.15: *Alternative Dunning Recipient in the Customer Master Record*

523. Explain 'Customer and Vendor Clearing in Dunning.'

It is possible that you can dun a customer who is also your vendor simultaneously and clear the items between them in the dunning run. The dunning program considers the overdue items of both the customer and the vendor/supplier and determines the joint balance in the dunning proposal. While doing so, the items will get cleared only when you have entered the same dunning procedure in the normal dunning area for both the customer and vendor. In situations like this, that is, when you 'dun' a customer who is also a vendor, the dunning program considers only the customer master record as relevant.

524. What are 'Special G/L Transactions'?

Special G/L transactions are 'special' transactions like down payments, down payment requests, guarantees, etc., in FI-A/R and FI-A/P, shown separately on the G/L and the sub-ledger. You achieved this posting by posting to alternative reconciliation accounts instead of the regular reconciliation accounts of FI-A/R and FI-A/P. The transactions to these accounts are shown separately in the balance sheet either for legal reasons, as in the case of down payments, or for control reasons, as in the case of guarantees.

When you post special G/L transactions, a separate special G/L account is created in the system for each of the special G/L transactions. Due to this, you will be able to display such special G/L transactions in the balance sheet without the need for any transfer postings. There are specific posting keys/indicators defined in the system to regulate the postings of these items. You need to specify a *special G/L indicator* (like, **F**-Down Payment Request, **A**-Down Payment, and so on) for processing such a transaction. Also, the system will use specially defined posting keys (09-customer debit, 19-customer credit, 29-vendor debit, and 39-vendor credit) to post these special G/L transactions.

SAP S/4HANA Finance comes delivered with several special G/L transactions that you can use as such (*Figure 17.16*). If you need more, you can also define new ones with the special G/L indicators and the associated posting keys.

A	Down Payment	L	Down payment offset
B	Nonrediscountable Bills of Ex.	P	Payment Request
C	Security Deposit	Q	B/e residual risk
D	Doubtful Receivables	R	Bill of Exchange Payt Request
E	Individual Value Adjustment	S	Check/Bill of Exchange
F	Down Payment Request	T	Down Payment – Other
G	Guarantees Given	U	AP sales-based rent
H	Security Deposit	V	Advance from Customer
I	Down Payments, Intang. Assets	W	Rediscountable Bills of Exch.
J	Advance Payment Request	Z	Interest Receivable
K	AP Operating Costs		

Figure 17.16: *Special G/L Transactions / Indicators*

525. What are the different 'Types of Special G/L Transactions'?

There are different **types of special G/L transactions**, which you can group under two categories: on the business side and on the technical side, as shown in *Figure 17.17*.

On the **business side,** you can differentiate the various special G/L transactions into bills of exchange, down payments, and miscellaneous. From a **technical point of view**, with regard to how the special transactions get posted with the offsetting entry, you can classify them into postings with freely definable offsetting entries (like 'down payments' and 'bills of exchange'), postings with preset offsetting entry (aka 'statistical postings'), and postings without any offsetting sentry (aka 'noted items').

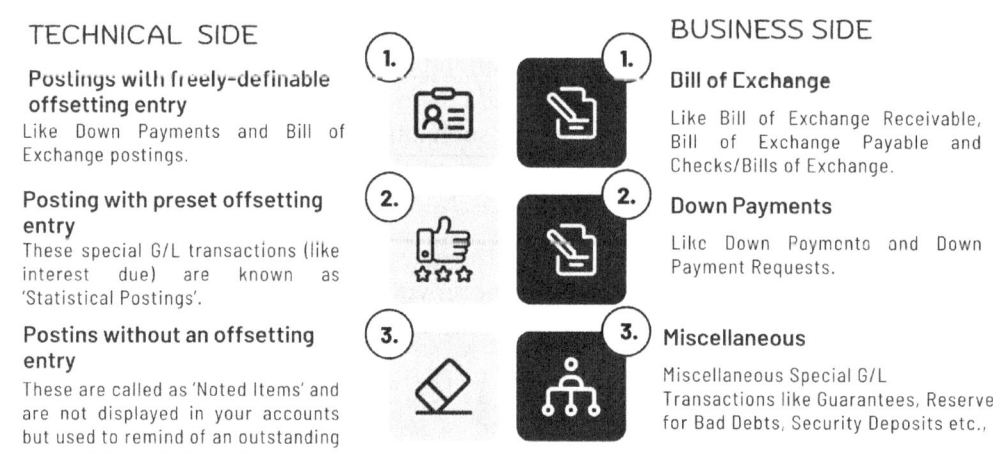

Figure 17.17: Special G/L Transaction Types

526. Explain 'Statistical Postings.'

The **statistical postings** relate to special G/L transaction postings with preset offsetting entries. Here, you post the special G/L transactions to the same offsetting account, like posting, for example, interest due 'always' to the interest revenue account. To facilitate automatic postings, during regular postings, and during clearing of open items, you just need to define the account that the system needs to use for the offsetting entry. Use the Transaction Code **F-55** for vendor/supplier and **F-38** for customer.

527. What is a 'Noted Item'?

The **noted items** are never displayed on the *financial statements* as they only remind you of a financial obligation like outstanding payments to be made or due to you, like the *'Down Payment Request.'* This kind of posting does not update any G/L account in the system but helps to keep track of such obligations for easy follow-up. This is also sometimes referred to as a *'memo entry.'* Use the Transaction Code **F-57** for vendor/supplier and **F-49** for customer.

528. Differentiate 'Free Offsetting Entry' from a 'Statistical Posting.'

Free offsetting entries are part of the regular postings and relate to the *'On-Balance Sheet Items'*. On the other hand, in a statistical posting, you will always be posted to the same offsetting entry, and these are all the *'Off-Balance Sheet Items.'*

529. What is a 'Down Payment'?

The **down payment** is the advance payment that you receive from your customers for the proposed sales of goods and services from your company. It may also be an advance payment that you send to your suppliers in anticipation of future delivery of goods and/ or services.

So, essentially, it is a financial arrangement between the company and the customer or supplier/vendor for short-term financing. The best thing in the arrangement is you or your supplier, as the manufacturer (or service provider), do not have to pay any interest on these funds. Normally, the advance is paid before the start of the service before production or just after partial completion of production.

The down payments can be of any of the following categories:
- Down payments on inventory stocks
- Down payments on intangible fixed assets
- Down payments on tangible fixed assets
- General down payments

Accounted for in FI-A/R, they are sometimes called a *customer down payments*. And, in FI-A/P, you call them 'supplier/vendor down payments'. Whether it is for the customer or vendor, you need to balance the down payments with accounts receivables or payables, as the case may be, and should show them separately on the balance sheet: the 'down payments received' on the liabilities side, and the 'down payments made' on the assets side. Once you have received the goods/services (as a customer) or when you have provided the goods/services (as a vendor), then you need to clear the down payments either manually or via the payment program. You shall process the down payments as special G/L transactions, with or without down payment requests.

530. Explain 'Down Payment Request'.

The **down payment requests** are special documents that you use as a reference for posting down payments. You need to use the down payment requests when you use the payment program to post down payments or use the dunning program to 'dun' them.

When entering a down payment request (F), you need to maintain the details required for the payment or dunning program: while entering the target special G/L transaction, enter the target as 'A' because this is required by the system to identify the correct special G/L transaction, in this case, the 'down payment.' Since you require a special G/L account to post both incoming and outgoing down payment requests, you need to have these G/L accounts maintained with a line-item display to display the overview of payments outstanding to you or to be made by you. The system does not use these to manage the transaction figures or account balances in them.

You will be able to process down payment requests using the payment and dunning programs only when you explicitly configure that: for this, you need to specify the special G/L transactions while maintaining the Company Code specifications for the payment program and while configuring the dunning procedure.

531. What are the 'Special Features' of Down Payment Requests?

The following are some of the special features of down payment requests:

- When you post a down payment request, the system creates a 'noted item' as a reference document to remind you of the down payment. Such a posting does not update the account's transaction figures.

- When posting a down payment request, the system assigns the line item to a special G/L account that you can use to display the overview of the outstanding down payments. Besides, the system also cross-references the accounts with the payment requests, with that of the down payment request's document number.

- In the case of down payment request, you need to enter one or more document items, without any offsetting entry, to the customer or supplier/vendor account. Since there is no offsetting entry, the system does not carry out the zero-balance check during document posting.

- If the down payment request document also contains tax to be posted, the system posts the tax while completing the posting of the corresponding down payment.

532. How to process 'Guarantees' in SAP S/4HANA Finance?

The **guarantees**, aka *'payment guarantees,' are* future financial obligations and can be either *'guarantees given (made)'* or *'guarantees received.'* All the guarantees that you make are shown as 'notes to the balance sheet' because of financial recourse. However, the guarantees you receive will not be shown in the notes on the balance sheet. Hence, it is good practice to record and view all the payment guarantees, both received and given.

With SAP S/4HANA, you can process both guarantees, 'given' and 'received' as special G/L transactions. To process a guarantee, you just need to enter the account assignments for posting to the customer or supplier/vendor account, and the system always posts the offsetting entry to the same special G/L, which will be a clearing account. Since these postings are 'statistical postings,' they are not displayed in the balance sheet as on-balance sheet items: you will be able to view all the guarantees that you have given in the notes to the balance sheet or in the annexure of the balance sheet or by accessing the respective customer accounts; similarly, you can view all the guarantees that you have received by accessing the respective vendor accounts besides displaying the overview of all such guarantees by accessing the special G/L account to which you have posted them.

533. Explain 'Debit-Side and Credit-Side Down Payment Chains'.

You will use **down payment chains** in long-running projects like the ones in the construction industry, which are characterized by several projects taking years to complete. During the project's lifetime, you will come across several transactions with several business partners who create several invoices, including partial ones. You must also consider the retention and additional amounts until the final invoices are submitted. During the entire course, you create several documents in the system, and you may also reverse some of the documents that you have already posted to make corrections and amendments. This is where the down payment chains help you to structure the data that is otherwise very complex, besides aiding in completing the transactions.

The **credit-side down payment chains** help you monitor the payables to the suppliers/vendors or subcontractors, besides providing you with the details of outgoing payments, both in the past and future. Likewise, the **debit-side down payment chains** enable you to monitor the receivables from your customers and the payments that you have made and are about to make. These down payment chains combine all account documents belonging to a single contract.

You must configure the required settings using the Customizing menu path *SAP Customizing Implementation Guide | Financial Accounting | Accounts Receivable and Accounts Payable | Business Transactions | Debit-Side and Credit-Side Down Payment Chains*.

534. What is 'Item Interest Calculation'?

With the **item interest calculation** feature in FI-A/R and FI-A/P components of SAP S/4HANA Finance, you can calculate interest on debit and credit items automatically. You may calculate the item interest on the following:

- **Debit items (open or cleared)**: You can calculate interest on debit items when processing individual line items or in mass processing, like when you 'dun' the business partners.
- **Credit items (such as credit memos or cash security deposits)**: You can calculate the item interest on credit items either via individual processing or mass processing.
- Installment plans
- Others

535. Explain the 'Item Interest Calculation' process.

You use **item interest calculation** on your customer and/or supplier/vendor accounts. In SAP S/4HANA Finance, you have two options to handle this interest: you run the interest calculation program, post the interest calculated as open receivable, and inform the business partner about the receivable amount due, or you calculate the potential interest due on the receivable overdue, and inform the same to the business partner without posting the interest.

The item interest calculation is almost like the account balance interest that we have already discussed in SAP General Ledger Accounting (*Question 436 to 443*). The only difference is that, instead of account balance, here, you will calculate the interest on individual items that are overdue. The process of item interest calculation is as shown in *Figure 17.18*.

During interest execution, the system selects, based on what you have defined in the interest indicator and in the interest run parameters, the items for which interest needs to be calculated. Then, the system determines how many days a particular item has been overdue, and this will be the number of days for which interest will be calculated. Now, the system checks the amounts of the selected items and compares the same with the minimum amount specifications to include or exclude the items. If the amount of the item is more than the minimum amount specified, then the system proceeds to calculate and post the interest, besides printing the interest notice on the form specified (Smart Form or PDF). The interest letter or notice to the business partners will contain the appropriate pre-defined text and an overview of interest/interest rate/line items.

While calculating the interest for all the open items (not yet cleared), the system calculates the interest from their due date for net payment up to the settlement date. In the case of cleared items (already reconciled), the system calculates the interest from their due date for net payment to the due date for net payment of the clearing document. The system excludes all the items that were cleared before the last interest calculation date for the current interest calculation run. If the system cannot calculate interest, it displays an error list.

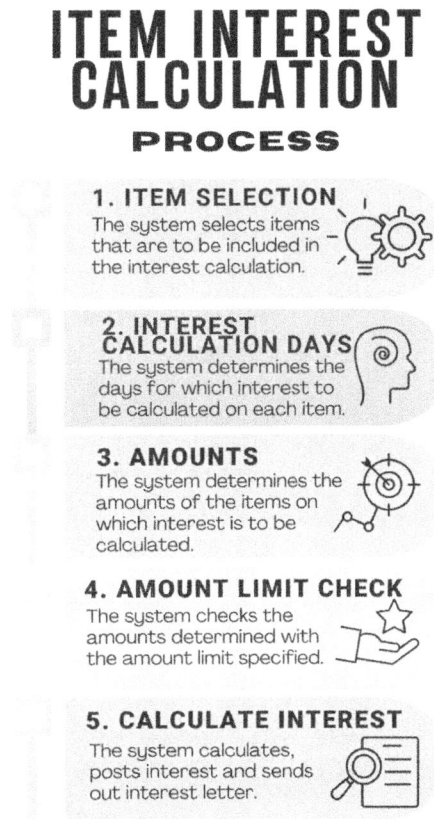

ITEM INTEREST CALCULATION
PROCESS

1. ITEM SELECTION
The system selects items that are to be included in the interest calculation.

2. INTEREST CALCULATION DAYS
The system determines the days for which interest to be calculated on each item.

3. AMOUNTS
The system determines the amounts of the items on which interest is to be calculated.

4. AMOUNT LIMIT CHECK
The system checks the amounts determined with the amount limit specified.

5. CALCULATE INTEREST
The system calculates, posts interest and sends out interest letter.

Figure 17.18: Item Interest Calculation Process

You can start the item interest calculation in FI-A/R using the SAP Easy Access menu path: *SAP Menu | Accounting | Financial Accounting | Accounts Receivable | Periodic Processing | Interest Calculation | Item Interest Calculation | Item Interest Calculation* or Transaction Code **FINT**.

Transaction Code **FINT**

Figure 17.19

On the 'Item Interest Calculation' initial screen, maintain the required parameters like a customer account range, Company Codes, interest indicator, the upper limit (date) of interest calculation, etc. If you want to include the customers who are also suppliers/vendors, then you need to select the '*Supplier Items*' checkbox. Also maintain the settings for 'Posting' (posting date, posting period, dunning block, interest block, business area, and so on), 'Form' (form-related settings for the printing of interest notices), 'Performance' (special G/L indicators, payment with a bill of exchange, etc.,) and other enhancements (for example, you may use Business Add-in (BAdI) FI_INT_CUS01). Once completed, select the 'Test Run' checkbox and execute the interest run (*Figure 17.20*).

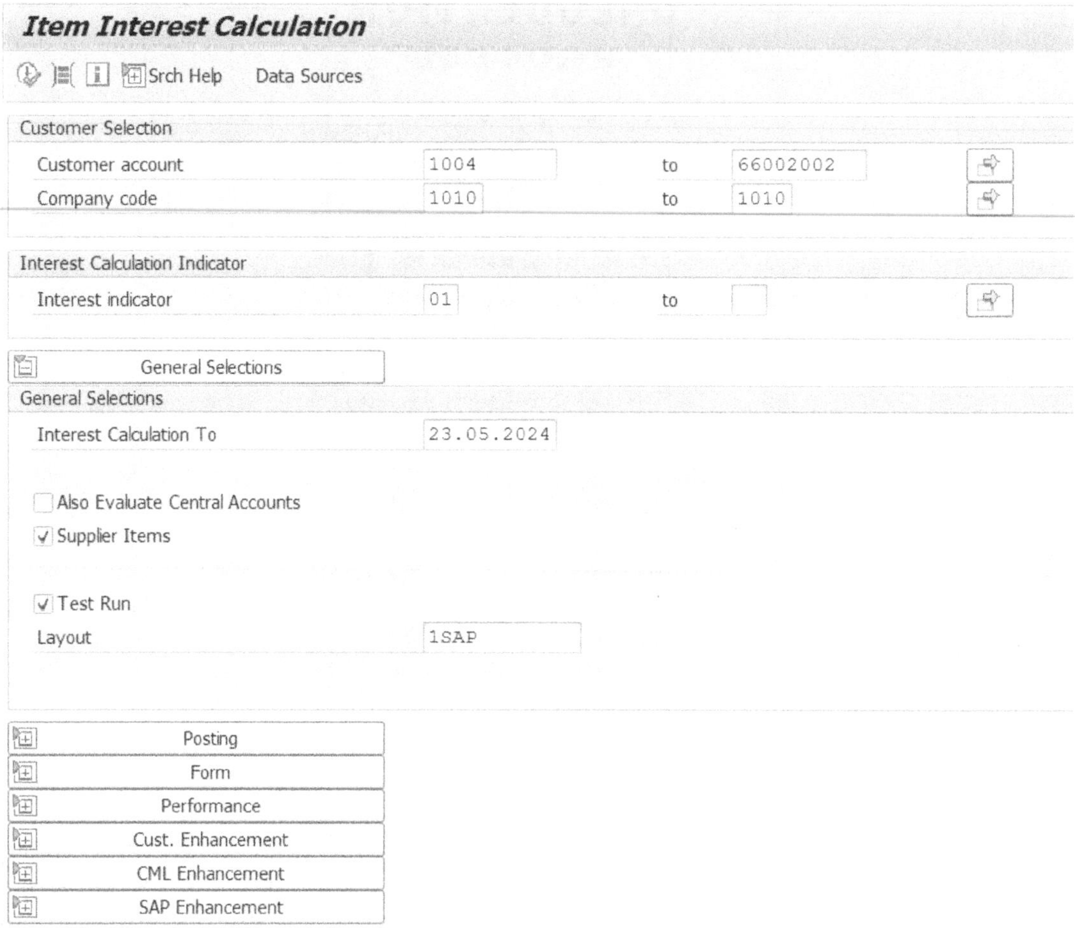

Item Interest Calculation

(✐))≡([i] [⊞]Srch Help   Data Sources

Customer Selection

Customer account	1004	to	66002002	⇨
Company code	1010	to	1010	⇨

Interest Calculation Indicator

Interest indicator	01	to		⇨

[📋]   General Selections

General Selections

Interest Calculation To	23.05.2024

☐ Also Evaluate Central Accounts
☑ Supplier Items

☑ Test Run
Layout	1SAP

[⊞]	Posting
[⊞]	Form
[⊞]	Performance
[⊞]	Cust. Enhancement
[⊞]	CML Enhancement
[⊞]	SAP Enhancement

Figure 17.20: *A/R Item Interest Calculation – Initial screen*

You may run the item interest calculation in FI-A/P using the SAP Easy Access menu path: *SAP Menu | Accounting | Financial Accounting | Accounts Payable | Periodic Processing | Interest Calculation | Item Interest Calculation | Item Interest Calculation* or Transaction Code **FINTAP**. The settings that you will maintain are like the ones that you maintain for customers. Besides selecting the supplier/vendor account range, Company Code, etc., you may need to select the 'Customer Items' checkbox to select the suppliers/vendors who are also your customers.

Transaction Code   FINTAP

Figure 17.21

536. What fields in business partners' master records are relevant for item interest?

There are four fields under *Interest Calculation* on the 'Customer: Account Management' (or 'Vendor: Account Management' in the case of supplier/vendor) tab in the Company Code data area, in business partners' master records that are relevant for item interest calculation (*Figure 17.22*):

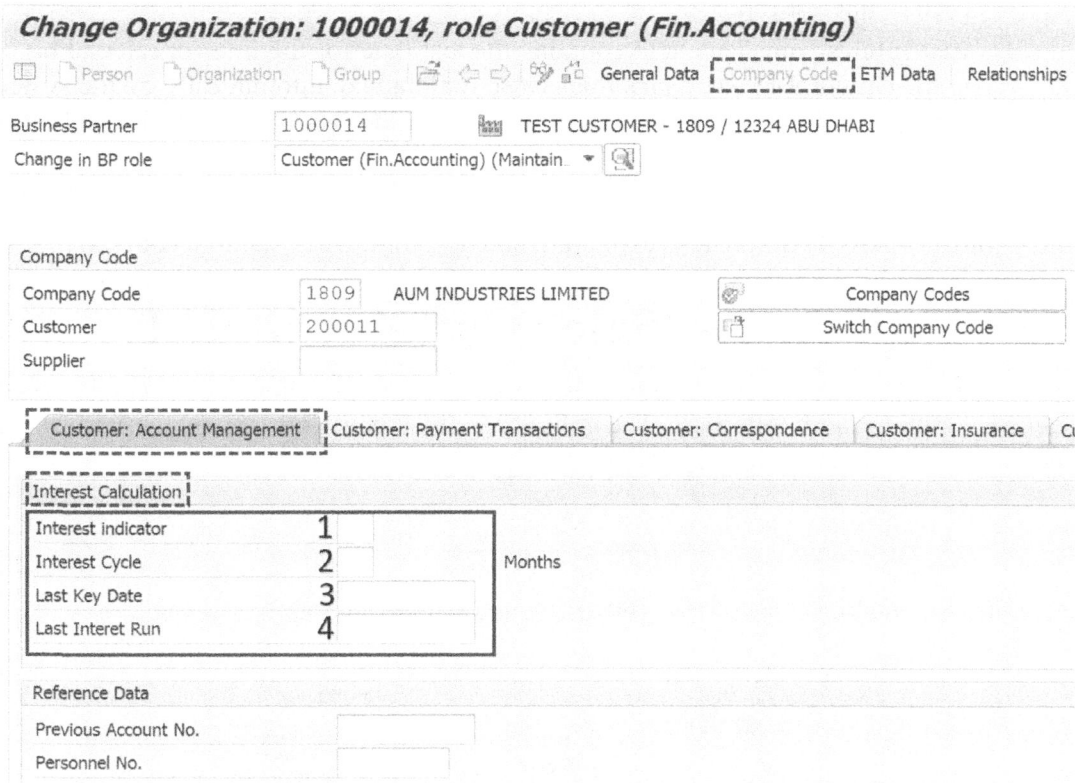

Figure 17.22: Fields Relevant for Interest Calculation in Business Partner's Master Record

1. **Interest indicator**: You need to make an entry in this field if you want the system to include the business partner's account in the automatic interest calculation.

2. **Interest cycle**: This is nothing but the interest calculation frequency in months. If you make an entry in this field, then the system makes use of that to arrive at the interest calculation upper limit by adding this frequency to the '*Last Key Date.*' The system compares the upper limit so calculated with that of the upper limit that you enter in the interest run parameters; if the calculated upper limit is after the upper limit that you have entered in the interest run parameters, then the system does not include that account for the current interest run. If you do not maintain an

entry in this field in the master record, then the system uses the interest calculation frequency that you maintain in the interest indicator.

3. **Last key date**: This is the date when the interest calculation program accessed this account last time. This is the upper limit of interest calculation of the last interest run. Normally, the system inserts the date in this field automatically by batch input. Hence, you should not manually maintain the date here unless there was an error in updating the date by the system. The system adds the '*Interest Cycle*' in months to this date to arrive at the new upper limit for interest calculation for the current interest run.

4. **Last interest run**: This field contains the last date for the interest calculation. As in the case of '*Last Key Date*,' this is also maintained automatically by the system. You should resort to manual entry only when there is an error during automatic updating.

(Since SAP SD and FI-A/R are closely integrated, the sales cycle and the account determination in SAP SD are also explained here to provide the required context).

537. Explain the 'Sales Cycle' as in SAP.

The **sales cycle** comprises all activities starting from quotation/inquiry, sales order, delivery, billing, and collection. The following are the various processes within SAP needed to complete a sales cycle (*Figure 17.23*):

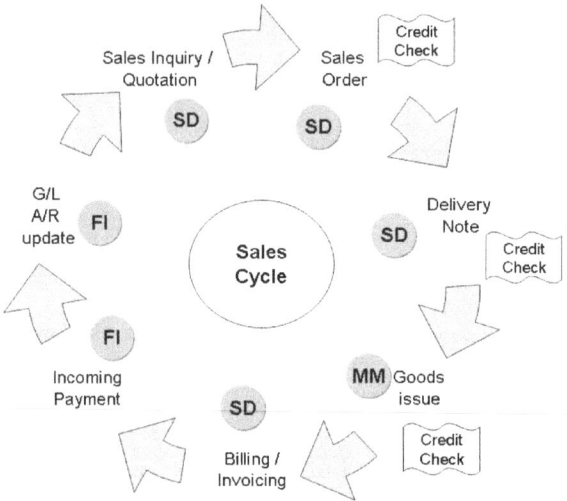

Figure 17.23: Sales Cycle

Typically, the following are the documents created during a sales cycle:

- Inquiry
- Quotation

- Sales Order
- Delivery Note
- Goods Issue
- Order Invoice
- Credit / Debit Note

538. Explain 'Automatic Account Assignment' in SD.

During goods issues in the sales cycle, the system is usually configured to update the relevant G/L accounts automatically and to create the relevant accounting documents. This customization in IMG is also called *material account assignment* and is achieved through several steps as follows:

1. Determining *'valuation level'* (Company Code or plant).
2. Activating the 'valuation grouping code' and linking it with the *'chart of accounts'* for each *'valuation area.'*
3. Linking *'valuation class'* with *'material type'* (FERT, HAWA, HALB, etc.) with *'account category reference'* (combination of valuation classes).
4. Maintaining *'account modification codes'* for *'movement types'*.
5. Linking *'account modification codes'* with *'process keys'* (*transaction/event keys*)
6. Maintaining a *G/L account* for a given combination of *'chart of accounts'* + *'valuation grouping code'* + *'account modification code'* + *'valuation classes.*

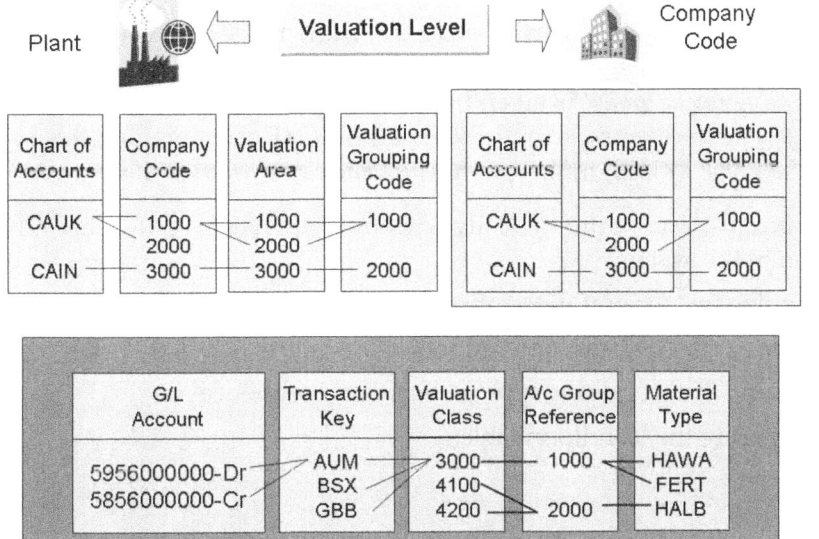

Figure 17.24: *Automatic Account Determination is Sales Cycle*

The process of automatic account determination is shown in *Figure 17.24*, which can be described as follows:

1. Depending upon the *'plant'*, entered during **goods issue (GI)**, the *'Company Code'* is determined by the system which in turn determines the relevant *'chart of accounts'*.

2. The *plant* thus entered in goods issue, determines the *'valuation class'* and then the *'valuation grouping code'*.

3. The *'valuation class'* is determined from the *'material master'*.

4. Since the *'account modification code'* is assigned to a *'process key'* which is already linked to a *'movement type,'* the *'transaction key'* (DIF, GBB, AUM, BSX, etc.) determines the *'G/L account'* as posting transactions are predefined for each *'movement type'* in 'inventory management.'

539. Explain 'Revenue Account Determination' in SD.

The billing documents created during the sales cycle result in automatic postings to G/L accounts on the FI side. In general, the **revenue account determination** is based on the following five factors:

- Chart of accounts
- Sales organization
- Account assignment group of the customer
- Account assignment group of the material
- Account key

The system determines the *'chart of accounts'* from the Company Code in the *'billing document'*, and the *'sales organization'* is determined from the corresponding *'sales order'*. The *'account assignment group'* is taken from the respective masters of customer/material. The *'account key'* helps the user to define the various G/L accounts, and this key is assigned to the *'condition type'* (KOFI) in the *'pricing procedure'* (*Figure 17.25*).

These *G/L accounts* are automatically determined when you make the following configuration in the system:

- Assigning an 'account determination procedure' to a 'billing document type'
- Assigning this 'account determination procedure' to a 'condition type'
- Assigning this 'condition type' to an 'access sequence'
- Configuring the 'condition tables'

Table	Description
1	Customer grp/Material Grp./AccKey
2	Cust. Grp/AccKey
3	Material Grp/Acc Key
4	General
5	Acc Key

Application	Condition Type	Chart of a/c	Sales Org.	AcctAsg Grp	Acc Asgmnt	A/cKey	G/L a/c
1	**Customer grp/Material Grp./AccKey: Details**						
V	KOFI	COMP	1000	1	10	ERL	5012100000
V	KOFI	COMP	1000	1	10	ERS	5012100000
V	KOFI	COMP	1000	2	10	ERL	5012200000
V	KOFI	COMP	1000	2	10	ERS	5012200000
V	KOFI	COMP	2000	1	20	ERL	5013100000
V	KOFI	COMP	2000	1	20	ERS	5013100000
V	KOFI	COMP	2000	2	20	ERL	5013200000
V	KOFI	COMP	2000	2	20	ERS	5013200000
5	**Acc Key: Details**						
V	KOFI	COMP	1000			MWS	2470000000
V	KOFI	COMP	2000			MWS	2470000000

Figure 17.25: *Revenue Account Determination: Illustration*

(Since SAP MM and FI-A/P are closely integrated, the purchase cycle, the procurement process, the integration between SAP MM and FI-A/P, invoice verification, etc., are also explained here to provide the required context).

540. Describe 'Purchase Cycle'.

The **purchase cycle** *or procurement cycle* (*Figure 17.26*) encompasses all the activities starting with purchase requisition, purchase order, goods movement, goods receipt, invoicing, invoice verification, payment to vendors, and updating vendor account balances.

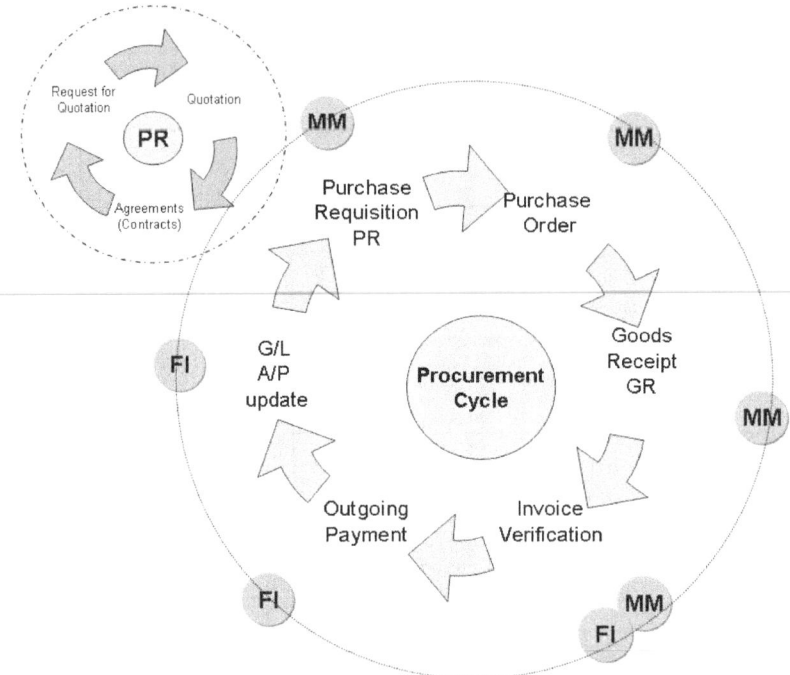

Figure 17.26: *Procurement cycle*

541. What documents result from 'Procurement Processes'?

In **Materials Management** (**MM**):

- PR: Purchase Requisition (manual or automatic using MRP)
- PO: Purchase Order

In **Financial Accounting** (**FI**):

- Invoice Verification
- Vendor Payment (manual or automatic)

Both MM and FI areas:

- Goods Receipt

You may also group these documents into Order documents, **Goods Receipt** (**GR**) documents, and **Invoice Receipt** (**IR**) documents. While GR/IR documents can be displayed both in MM and FI views, the order documents can only be viewed in the MM view.

542. What is 'Purchase Requisition'?

A **purchase requisition (PR)** is a document that outlines a company's purchasing needs of a material/service from the vendor(s). A 'PR', typically an *internal document* that can be created automatically or manually, identifies the demand for a product and authorizes the purchasing department to procure the same. The automatic creation of PR is done because of **Material Requirements Planning (MRP)**. The PR, after identifying the vendor, is processed further to result in a **Request for Quotation (RFQ)** or directly to a **Purchase Order (PO)**.

543. What is a 'Request for Quotation'?

An **RFQ**, which can be created directly or with reference to another RFQ a PR, or an Outline Agreement, is actually an invitation to vendor(s)/supplier(s) to submit a 'quotation' for supplying a material or service. The RFQ will contain the terms and conditions for supply. You may send the RFQ to a single or multiple vendors/suppliers, and you can monitor the same by sending reminders to those who have not responded to the RFQ.

544. What is an 'Outline Agreement'?

An **outline agreement** is a declaration binding both the buyer and seller. It is the buyer's intention to purchase material/service with certain terms and conditions agreed to between both parties. The essential difference between an outline agreement and a quotation is that outline agreements do not contain details like a delivery schedule or quantities. Outline agreements can be *contracts* or *scheduling agreements.*

545. What is a 'Contract'?

A **contract**, also known as a 'blanket order,' is a long-term legal agreement between the buyer and the seller for the procurement of materials or services over a period of time. The contract, created directly or with reference to a PR/RFQ or another contract, is valid for a certain period of time and clearly mentions start and end dates. There are two types of contracts: Quantity Contracts and Value Contracts.

546. What is a 'Release Order'?

A **release order** is a 'purchase order' created against a contract. The release orders usually do not contain information on quantities or delivery dates and are also called 'blanket releases' or contract releases' or 'call-offs.'

547. What is a 'Scheduling Agreement'?

A **scheduling agreement** is also a long-term agreement between the buyer and seller for the procurement of certain materials or services subject to certain terms and conditions. These agreements can be created directly or with reference to other documents like another scheduling agreement, RFQ, or PR. These agreements help in promoting **Just-In-Time** (**JIT**) deliveries, less paperwork, reduce supply lead times, and ensure low inventory for the buyer.

548. What is a 'Quotation'?

A **quotation** contains information relating to the price and other conditions for the supply of a material or a service by a vendor/supplier and is termed as the vendor's willingness to supply the same based on those conditions. You will be able to compare the data from quotations using a *'price comparison list'*, which will help in identifying the most reasonable vendor for the supply of that item(s). After you receive the quotations, you will typically enter the quotation data (pricing/delivery) in RFQ. The SAP system can easily be configured to automatically print *'rejections'* for vendors whose quotations are not selected.

549. What is a 'Purchase Order'?

A **purchase order (PO)** is a legal contract between a vendor and a buyer mentioning the material/service to be purchased/procured on certain terms and conditions. The order mentions, among other things, the quantity to be purchased, price per unit, delivery-related conditions, payment/pricing information, etc. A PO can be created directly or with reference to a PR/RFQ/contract or another PO. Remember, all items on a PO should relate to the same Company Code.

550. What is a 'PO History'?

The **purchase order history** (**'PO History'**) lists all the transactions for all the items in a PO, such as the GR/IR document numbers.

551. Will the FI document be created during the Purchase Order?

No. There will be no document created on the FI side during the creation of a PO. However, there can be a document for posting 'commitment' to a CO Cost Center. The offsetting entry is posted at the time of GR.

552. Explain FI-MM Integration.

The **FI-MM integration** is based on the following:

- **Movement type**: This is the 'classification key' indicating the type of material movement (for example, goods receipt, goods issue, physical stock transfer, and so on). The movement type (*Figure 17.27*) enables the system to find pre-defined posting rules determining how the accounts in FI (stock and consumption accounts) are to be posted and how the stock fields in the material master record are updated.

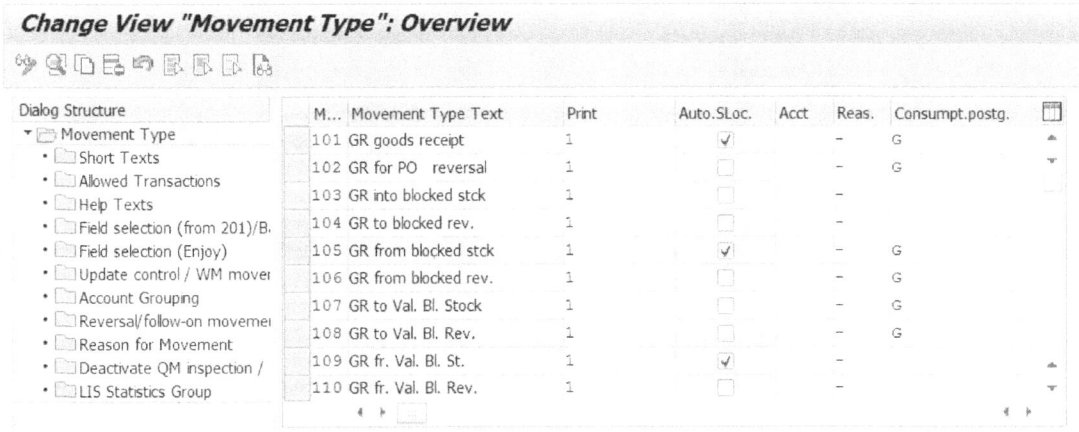

Figure 17.27: Movement types

- **Valuation class:** This refers to the assignment of material to a group of G/L accounts. Along with other factors, the valuation class (*Figure 17.28*) determines the G/L accounts that are updated because of a valuation-relevant transaction or event, such as a goods movement. The valuation class makes it possible to:

  o Post the stock values of materials of the same material type to different G/L accounts

  o Post the stock values of materials of different material types to the same G/L account

Change View "Valuation Classes": Overview

New Entries

Valuation Classes

ValCl	ARef	Description	Description
3000	0001	Raw Materials	Reference for raw materials
3001	0001	Raw materials 2	Reference for raw materials
3002	0001	Raw materials 3	Reference for raw materials
3003	0001	Raw materials 4	Reference for raw materials
3012	0001	Raw Material-Proj Stock	Reference for raw materials
3030	0002	Operating supplies	Ref. for operating supplies
3031	0002	Operating supplies 2	Ref. for operating supplies
3040	0003	Spare Parts	Ref. for spare parts
3050	0004	Packaging and empties	Reference for packaging
3100	0005	Trading goods	Reference for trading goods
3110	0005	Hardware	Reference for trading goods
3120	0005	Licenses	Reference for trading goods

Figure 17.28: *Valuation classes*

- **Transaction key:** The **transaction key** (also known as the '*Event Key or Process Key*') allows the users to differentiate between the various transactions and events (such as 'physical inventory transactions' and 'goods movements') that occur within the area of inventory management. The transaction/event type controls the filing/storage of documents and the assignment of document numbers.
- **Material type:** The **material type** groups together materials with the same basic attributes, for example, raw materials, semi-finished products, or finished products. When creating a material master record, you must assign the material to a material type (*Figure 17.29*). The material type determines:
  - o Whether the material is intended for a specific purpose, for example, as a *Configurable Material or Process Material*
  - o Whether the *material number* can be assigned internally or externally
  - o The *Number Range* from which the material number is drawn
  - o Which *screens* appear and in what sequence
  - o Which *user* department data you may enter
  - o What *Procurement Type* does the material have; that is, whether it is manufactured in-house or procured externally, or both.

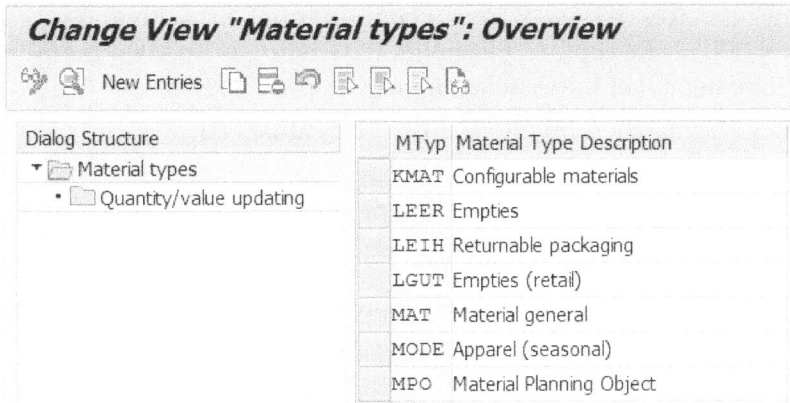

Figure 17.29: Material type

Together with the plant, the material type determines the material's inventory management requirement, which is:

- Whether changes in quantity are updated in the material master record
- Whether changes in value are also updated in the stock accounts in financial accounting

553. What happens in SAP when you post a 'Goods Receipt'?

When you post a **goods receipt** (**GR**), the stock account is debited (stock quantity increases), and the credit goes to the *GR/IR clearing account,* which is the intermediate processing account before you actually process the vendor invoice or payments to the vendor:

- **Debit**: Inventory Account
- **Credit**: GR/IR Clearing Account

During this, a material document is created, an accounting document to update the relevant G/L account is created, the PO order history is updated, and finally, the system enables you to print the GR slip.

554. Explain the conventional 'Invoice Verification' in SAP.

Conventional Invoice Verification involves:

- Validating the accuracy of the invoices (quantity, value, etc.)
- Checking for 'blocked' invoices (which varied to a greater extent from that of the PO)

- Match invoices received from vendors/suppliers with those of the Purchase Order/Goods Receipt. At this point, PO History is updated for the corresponding PO Line Item(s) of the matched invoice.
- Passing of matched invoices to the FI module. The system posts the following entries:
  - o **Debit**: GR/IR Clearing Account
  - o **Credit**: Vendor A/c (Accounts Payable open line item)
  - o **Credit**: G/L Reconciliation Account

The different scenarios in conventional invoice verification include:

- The '*GR based Invoice Verification*' indicator is **not** set in the PO detail screen:
  - o Although this setting enables you to post the invoice referenced to a PO prior to making a GR, the system will block the invoice for payment (as this kind of posting results in a *Quantity Variance* as there has not been a GR).
- '*GR based Invoice Verification*' indicator is **set** in the PO detail screen:
  - o When the PO number is referenced, the system brings up all the unmatched GR items on the selection screen. You will not be able to post the invoice for its full value unless the PO has been fully received.

555. How do you deal with the 'Tax' when you post an invoice?

When you enter an invoice, based on the configuration settings, the system checks the tax code and calculates the applicable tax or validates the *Tax Amount* entered by you:

- **Manual entry**: Input the '*tax code*' and the '*tax amount.*' The system will validate and issue a message in case it does not find the tax code or if the amount is different.
- **Automatic entry**: Leave the '*tax code*' and '*tax amount*' fields blank. Tick the '*Calculate Tax*' indicator. The system picks up the corresponding tax code and calculates the tax amount automatically.

556. What 'Variances' you will come across in Invoice Verification?

The system needs to be configured properly with *tolerances* so that you are not hampered by variances when you try invoice verification. You need to define the lower and upper limits for each combination of the Company Code and the tolerance key defined for the various variances. The system then checks these tolerance limits and issues warnings or prevents you from proceeding further when you process an invoice.

The **variances** arise because of mismatches or discrepancies between the invoice and the PO against which the invoice has been issued. Normally, you will encounter the following:

- **Price variance:** If there is a discrepancy in invoice and PO item prices.

- **Schedule variance:** If the planned delivery date is later than the invoice postings.

- **Quantity variance:** If the delivered quantity (or delivered quantity less previously invoiced quantity) is not the same as that of the invoiced quantity. When the invoiced quantity exceeds the GR, the system requires more GRs to square off the situation.

557. Explain some of the important SAP Fiori Apps for FI-A/R Manager.

Some of the important SAP Fiori apps for FI-A/R managers include:

- **Accounts Receivable Overview**: This analytical app helps in monitoring important accounts receivable indicators like 'A/R Aging Analysis,' 'A/R Breakdown,' **Days Sales Outstanding ('DSO')**, 'Cash Collection Tracker' and 'Top 10 Debtors', besides enabling access to the relevant FI-A/R apps.

- **Allowance for Doubtful Accounts**: Use this app to gain insight into doubtful accounts management regarding allowance for doubtful accounts and the adequacy of those allowance levels. You may also refer to the provisions that allow for the possible non-payment of overdue receivables. With this app, you can get a clear view of overdue receivables and their associated allowances. From there, you can drill down for details. The key features include a chart view of overdue receivables and allowances by customer, country/region, etc., details of accounts including overdue receivables and the related allowances (differentiated between manually created allowances and automatically generated allowances), and display of the allowance for each customer account, shown as a total and as a percentage of the overdue.

- **Collection Progress**: You can use this analytical app to display the 'Collection Progress' KPI. Besides viewing the overall progress in collecting payments from your customers, you can also view the collection progress for different collection specialists and collection groups. To better the app's performance, caching has been enabled: click on the 'refresh icon' on the app tile (or in the bottom-left corner of the app) for immediate refresh of the data. You may determine the frequency for cache duration in the tile configuration.

- **Customer Master FactSheets**: Use this app to display an overview of customer data in terms of Company Code data, sales area data, communication details, related documents such as sales orders or billing documents (if any), key facts (like 'City') relevant in the business context, etc. From this app, you can navigate to detailed information/apps related to the business partner master data or relevant documents.

- **Days Beyond Terms**: Through this analytical app, you can display the **'Days Beyond Terms'** (**DBT**) KPI to gain insight into the payment history of your customers and understand how effectively you collect payments from them. For example, a high DBT indicates you take too long to collect payments. You can view DBT figures in a chart or a table filtered by account group, accounting clerk, Company Code, country key, customer, calendar month/year, customer classification, currency, exchange rate type, reconciliation account, or region. You will find the 'DSO' KPI more helpful than the 'DBT' if you are a new business. As in the case of the 'Collection Progress' app, caching is enabled for this app as well.

- **Days Sales Outstanding—Detailed analysis:** Use this analytical app to analyze your Company's DSO in detail. The predefined analysis steps help you view your DSO by Company Code, due period, and customer country. You can also look at revenue and overdue receivables over time and analyze further via the filters to drill down.

- **Define Accounting Clerks**: With this app, you can define the required identification code and the user ID for your accounting clerks. Once defined, you can maintain this identification code in the Company Code data (under 'Correspondence' on the *Customer: Correspondence* tab) of the business partner's master record. You can use this code in the payment program for correspondence and reporting (for example, open item lists).

558. List some of the important SAP Fiori Apps for FI-A/R Accountants.

Some of the important SAP Fiori apps for FI-A/R accountants include:

- **Assign Open Items**: This app lets you view a customer's open items and clear them by assigning credit items to matching debit entries. Essentially, this app helps in viewing open items related to a customer, finding matching credit and debit items, assigning them to one another, and clearing such assigned items. When clearing is completed, the system displays the clearing document number. When one or more items cannot be cleared automatically, you need to note their journal entry numbers and use the 'Clear Incoming Payments app' to clear these items.

- **Bank**: Use this app to display an overview of the bank data, including 'Bank name', 'Bank key,' 'Bank country/region' and 'Key facts' (relevant to the business context) like 'Address of the bank,' 'SWIFT code' and 'Bank number.' You may use this app as a starting point to navigate to additional information relevant to your business context, like information about related business partners, related master data, or related documents. You may also navigate to apps with additional functions, such as editing or analyzing related business data.

- **Bank Statement Monitor**: Through this app, you can monitor end-of-day bank statements from individual bank accounts. Besides checking the status of these statements for a specific date, you can get an overview of the records over the last 14 days. Per bank account settings, you can identify problematic bank statements for your bank accounts and track if there is any missing statement page, any difference between the bank statement balance and the G/L account balance, or any items that are not posted. You can also switch between the single-day view and 14-day view.

- **Clear Incoming Payments**: With this app, you can manually clear a receivable payment (such as an open incoming payment for a customer invoice). Though you can clear such payments automatically, sometimes you may encounter situations, for example, the customer information is missing, and the clearing program cannot automatically find appropriate open items to match the payment. In such a case, you must intervene and manually clear this payment, by matching it to the correct open invoices and credit memos of your customer. The key features include, viewing open incoming payments, obtaining a list of open items that you can use to clear the open payments, adding/changing the discount on each invoice, creating residual items (by entering a residual amount and assigning appropriate reason code(s) and reference information about the business partner to the residual items), defining (in business configuration) whether a new item is to be posted to the business partner account, or if the difference is to be cleared, posting an incoming payment to a G/L account (if required with account assignment), posting an incoming payment 'on account' to a customer or supplier account without reference to a specific item (if clearing is not possible), getting a list of open items that is proposed based on the customer's search criteria (like invoice number, journal entry number, or payment reference), creating dispute cases for partial payments and residual items, using 'promise-to-pay' information to easily select items to be cleared, searching for open items of selected customers or of all customers by means of fuzzy logic, entering characteristics for profitability-related postings (to assign profitability segments), viewing the withholding tax that has been posted for each open item, creating notes and attachments while posting the clearing document, arranging open items using an invoice reference, simulating the resulting journal entry, clearing the open payment with the selected open items that match the payment, exporting the open items list to a spreadsheet, editing the simulated clearing document before posting it, saving your own clearing proposals, and clearing open items for down payments by selecting 'Down Payments' in the *Line Item Type* field.

559. Explain some of the important SAP Fiori Apps for FI-A/P Manager.

Some of the important SAP Fiori apps for FI-A/P managers include:

- **Accounts Payable Overview**: This analytical app helps monitor important FI-A/P indicators, as well as enabling access to the relevant accounts payable apps. You may use the filters to limit the data. The app includes indicators like:

- o 'Parked Invoices' showing average days of parked invoices,

- o 'Blocked Invoices (Chart)' showing the total amount of all blocked invoices as of today,

- o 'Cash Discount Utilization' shows the total amount of cash discount taken for the period besides the lost cash discounts,

- o 'Days Payable Outstanding Indirect' showing the average days per payable outstanding for the past 12 months,

- o 'Days Payable Outstanding Direct' showing the average days payable outstanding by month over the last 12 months calculated at the document level,

- o 'Payable Aging' displays the total overdue as of today,

- o 'Suppliers with Debit Balances' showing your debit balance as of today,

- o 'Invoices Blocked in Supplier Master Data' showing the sum of all invoices blocked in the supplier master data,

- o 'Posted Invoices in Current Period' displaying the sum of all invoices posted in the current period,

- o 'Due Invoices Free for Payment' showing the total amount of invoices due that are free for payment as of today,

- o 'Invoice Processing Statistics' showing the average time you took to process invoices for the period selected and

- o 'Posted Invoices' shows the amount or count of posted invoices in the last six fiscal periods for your selection criteria.

- **Aging Analysis**: The app enables you to view the company-wide aging information to identify negative trends in the total payable amount, the net due amount, and the overdue amount for timely intervention by your team to take appropriate actions to reverse these trends.

- **Cash Discount Forecast**: This app displays cash discounts expiring in the future and analyzes them by company, payment terms, or payment day.

- **Cash Discount Utilization**: Use this app to monitor, in real-time, the cash discount utilization in your responsibility area. By this, you can find out which Company Code or location needs to make better use of cash discounts. With this app, you can display the utilization rate of cash discounts for a past period, compare the current utilization rate versus the target utilization rate, check if the current utilization rate is critically low, deserves attention, or is acceptable, analyze cash discount utilization by different business dimensions, including company, country, supplier group, & payment terms, display the utilization rate of cash discounts by company, country, supplier group, or payment terms, and distinguish between taken cash discounts and lost cash discounts.

- **Days Payable Outstanding**: Use this app to drill down to check the top 10 suppliers with the highest or the lowest **days payable outstanding (DPO)** and view the result in a chart or a table per Company Code, supplier, country of the supplier, and timeline.

- **Display Supplier Balances**: Use this app to view supplier balances and compare sales: see debits, credits, and balances per Company Code, fiscal year, and supplier. You can further analyze the amounts by displaying all related line items. You can also compare the purchases between two fiscal years.

- **Display Supplier List**: This app allows you to view the contact details of your suppliers, create custom lists of obsolete suppliers, blocked suppliers, or suppliers based on their payment methods, and access their bank details/payment methods.

- **Future Payables**: Using this analytical app, you can analyze (by drilling down) the top 10 amounts payable and the number of open items for the relevant suppliers. In the process, you can view the future payables in a chart or a table by Company Code, supplier, country and region of the supplier, account group of the supplier, and payment blocking reason. The key features include:

  - Viewing accounts payable by due periods,

  - Viewing the top 10 amounts payable by suppliers,

  - Viewing accounts payable by Company Codes,

  - Filtering accounts payable by payment blocking reasons, and

  - Specifying the key date for data analysis.

  This app also supports caching for better performance, and as with similar apps, you can configure the cache duration while setting up the app.

- **Invoice Processing Analysis**: Through this app, you can view the total amount of posted invoices and the total number of posted line items. Specifically, you can view the total amount of invoices and the total number of line items posted in a certain month/for a certain supplier/for a certain user/in each processing status with the possible statuses being 'free for payment' (open items without payment blocks), 'cleared', 'blocked' (open items that are blocked for payment) and 'parked'.

- **Overdue Payables**: Use this app to check the overdue payable amount that you owe to your suppliers. You can filter by supplier Company Code, supplier group, supplier, and payment block. The app helps you figure out potential risks (for taking action) by monitoring overdue payments for critical suppliers.

- **Supplier Payment Analysis (Manual and Automatic Payments):** This app displays (in different colors: green for automatic payments and blue for manual payments) the consolidated data for all payment documents posted during a specific period for different dimensions (Company Code, supplier, currency, or user).

560. List some of the important SAP Fiori Apps for FI-A/P Accountants.

Some of the important SAP Fiori apps for FI-A/R accountants include:

- **Create Single Payment**: Using this app, you can make a direct payment to a supplier (by paying the supplier's line items) when no invoice exists. When making such a direct payment (without an invoice), you create the payment by specifying the supplier/bank details and the amount to be paid. The system posts the payment as a 'down payment request' and uses that document to initiate the payment run. When paying the open supplier line items, select the open items that you want to pay through the *Manage Supplier Line Items app* and create the payment to initiate the payment run. The system automatically fills the payment information and clears the open items during the payment run.

- **Display Process Flow - Accounts Payable**: This app displays the relationships between FI-A/P documents, including purchase orders, goods movements, incoming invoices, journal entries, and clearing entries.

- **Display Supplier Balances**: This app displays supplier balances and compares sales. You can view debits, credits, and balances per Company Code, fiscal year, and supplier. The app allows you to further analyze the amounts by displaying all related line items and comparing purchases between two fiscal years.

- **Display Suppliers List**: This app lets you display and download the list of suppliers. In the process, you can use the search filters to create custom lists (of suppliers) to provide to stakeholders and auditors.

- **Supplier Payment Analysis (Open Payments)**: Use the app to get an overview of the open payments (by Company Code, supplier, currency, and user) for the FI-A/P manager.

Join our book's Discord space

Join the book's Discord Workspace for Latest updates, Offers, Tech happenings around the world, New Release and Sessions with the Authors:

https://discord.bpbonline.com

CHAPTER 18

FI: Bank Accounting

Introduction

This chapter is devoted to bank accounting in SAP S/4HANA Finance. In this chapter, you will learn about the bank directory, the bank master data and the check rules associated with their creation, the house bank, the differences between SWIFT and IBAN, the different types of bank chains, the customizing settings for both manual and electronic bank statements, the concept of lockbox and its processing in SAP, the cash journal and its functionality, and the Orbian Payment System. You will also learn about some of the most important SAP Fiori apps in the application area of bank accounting.

561. Explain 'Bank Accounting' in SAP S/4HANA Finance.

Bank Accounting is a component application within SAP Financial Accounting of SAP S/4HANA Finance. It helps in handling accounting transactions with your bank(s). It is actually a sub-application (and NOT a sub-ledger as in the case of FI-A/P or FI-A/R) that you use to manage bank master data, bank chains, check and bill of exchange management, and processing of payment transactions (electronic bank statements, manual bank statement, lockbox processing, automatic payments, and payments using 'Orbian' payment system). Through this application, you will be configuring and defining all the country-specific settings required for electronic payment procedures, payment media, and payment forms.

562. Explain 'Bank Master Data'.

In SAP Bank Accounting, you centrally store the **bank master data** in the 'bank directory'. Besides the bank master data, you also maintain your bank (aka 'house bank') and your business partners' bank information (in the respective business partner's master record). While setting up the master data, you also make the required country-specific check rules to verify the correctness of bank data.

563. Explain 'Bank Directory.'

We have already discussed the **bank directory** (in *Question 476*), which contains the master data of all the banks, your bank (house bank), and your partners' banks, that you would require for payment transactions with your business partners.

There are two ways in which you can transfer the bank master data automatically into your SAP S/4HANA system:

- **Country-specific data transfer:** In the case of **country-specific data transfer**, you will use the ASCII data file you receive from your country's central banking organization. Use the Customizing menu path: *SAP Customizing Implementation Guide | Cross-Application Components | Bank Directory | Bank Directory Data Transfer | Transfer Bank Directory Data - Country/Region-Specific* or Transaction Code **BAUP**.

- **International data transfer**: For **international bank master data transfer**, you need to use the file created using the BIC Database Plus. Use the Customizing menu path: *SAP Customizing Implementation Guide | Cross-Application Components | Bank Directory | Bank Directory Data Transfer | Transfer Bank Directory Data—International* or Transaction Code **BIC2**.

You may also create the bank master data manually by using the *SAP Easy Access menu path: SAP Menu | Accounting | Financial Accounting | Banking | Master Data | Bank Master Record* or the Transaction Code **FI01**. Similarly, you can create a business partner's bank master data while maintaining the supplier/vendor or customer master records; once defined, the system adds these bank details automatically to the bank directory.

564. Explain 'House Bank'.

The system requires the details of your bank (aka '**house bank**') to process payment transactions. You need to define the house banks and maintain the details ('Bank ID') in the master records of suppliers/vendors or customers (in the Company Code data area), without which you cannot process any payment in the system. If you do not maintain the house bank information in the master records of the supplier/vendor or customer, then you need to define rules by which the payment program can determine the house bank for payment. We have already discussed the house banks in *Questions 477, 478, 489 & 490.*

565. How to define the 'Banks of your Suppliers/Vendors or Customers'?

You maintain the bank details while creating/changing the master records of your suppliers/vendors or customers. You can do so by entering the *'ID,'* country or region (*'C/R'*), *'Bank key,'* *'Bank acct,'* etc., under the 'Payment Transactions' tab in the "General Data" area of the respective master records (*Figure 18.1*). You can add as many banks as you need. The payment program uses the details that you maintain here for automatic payment transactions and to determine other information about the bank, like bank address, etc., for use in payment forms. The system establishes the link to the bank master data via the bank country (*'C/R'*) and the country-specific bank ID (*'Bank key'*)

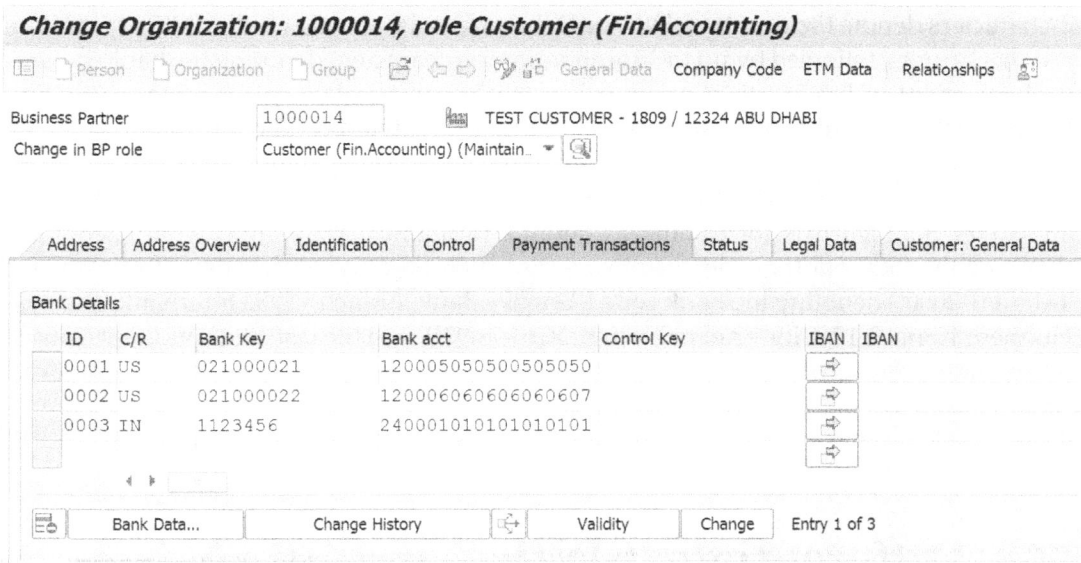

Figure 18.1: *Maintaining bank details for business partners*

566. What is a 'SWIFT' code?

The term **SWIFT** is used to route international financial transactions, and it refers to the Society for Worldwide Interbank Financial Telecommunication. The SWIFT code identifies a bank branch to which you route international money transfers electronically. The SWIFT code is generally alphanumeric, with a length of 8 or 11; for example, the SWIFT code 'DABADKKKXXX' identifies the Den Danske Bank's Copenhagen branch: the first 4-characters of the code ('DABA') denotes the bank (will always be in letters), the next 2-characters denote the country ('DK'), the next 2-characters ('KK') can either be characters or numbers or a mix, identifying the branch location and the last three optional characters ('XXX') representing the branch. Note that the SWIFT code does not have the account number reference of the beneficiary who will receive the amount. The corresponding *IBAN* for the bank branch in the above example will be 'DK0630003996056694'.

567. So, what is 'IBAN'?

Originally developed in Europe, the **'International Bank Account Number'** (**IBAN**) is the standardized numbering of individual bank accounts worldwide for simplified bank transactions. The IBAN was introduced to reduce processing mistakes during cross-border payments from one account to another and to ensure a quick and safe transfer of money globally. Almost all the banks in Europe and the rest of the world (except the USA and Canada) make use of IBAN. In the USA and Canada, though they do not use IBAN, they do recognize the numbering system for routing international bank transfers.

If you look at an IBAN (for example, 'DK0630003996056694'), you will notice that the first 2-characters denote the country ('DK' for Denmark), with the next 2-digits ('06') signifying the check digits, followed by up to 35 alphanumeric characters denoting the bank identifier (or bank code) and the account number. This alphanumeric coding is known as the **'Basic Bank Account Number'** (*BBAN*), the length of which will become the standard for that country and is decided by the country's banking association. Hence, the length of BBAN may vary from one country to the other: for example, it is 27 in France, 22 in Germany and so on. So, the IBAN for Denmark contains 18 characters: the first 2-characters ('DK') denoting the ISO country code, the next 2-digits ('06') signifying the check digits, the next 4-digits ('3000') denoting the bank code ('Danske Bank, Branch - 3952 Interbank, Address - Holmens Kanal 2-12, City – København K, Zip – 1092'), and the last 10-digits ('3996056694') representing the account number. Note that the IBAN, when transmitted electronically, cannot have any space between two characters/digits. However, it is represented in groups of 4 characters/digits (with the last group of any variable length), with a single space in between, when printed: for example, 'DK06 3000 3996 0566 94'.

568. Differentiate 'SWIFT' and 'IBAN.'

While the SWIFT code is used to identify a particular bank branch in international financial transactions, the IBAN is used to identify not only the bank branch but also the individual account that is involved in the international financial transaction.

569. Explain the 'Check Rules' you can specify for Bank Master Data.

You can specify country-specific **check rules** ('field checks') for bank master data. Once specified, these rules (*Figure 18.3*) will apply to the bank number, the bank key, and the bank account number. While creating the check rules, specify the length of the bank number and bank account number per country key. The checking rule determines if the entry is numeric or alphanumeric, the length specified is only a maximum length or must be strictly adhered to, gaps are permitted in the bank account number or bank number, and the system always carries out these formal checks. Besides these, you can also specify some further checks to avoid data entry errors: for example, postal check account numbers in Germany/Switzerland, bank account numbers in Belgium/Netherlands, and so on.

You may configure the country-specific bank master data check rules via the Customizing menu path: *SAP Customizing Implementation Guide | ABAP Platform | General settings | Set Countries | Set Country-Specific Checks* or Transaction Code **OY17**.

Figure 18.2

Change View "Field Checks for Countries/Regions": Details

Country/Reg.   US   USA

Key for the bank directory

Bank Key	4	Assign externally

Formal checks

	Length	Checking rule	
Postal code length	5		
Bank account number	12		
Bank number length	9		
Post bank acct no.	10	6	Maximum value length, numerical
Tax Number 1	11	5	Maximum value length
Tax Number 2	10	5	Maximum value length
Tax Number 3			
Tax Number 4			
Tax Number 5			
VAT registration no.			
Length of Bank Key	11		

Further checks

☑ Bank data	☑ Postal code req. entry	☐ City file active
☐ Other data	☐ P.O.box code req. entry	☐ Street postcode

Figure 18.3: Country-specific Check Rules for Bank Master Data

570. Explain 'Bank Chains'.

The '*multi-stage payment methods*' are also known as '**bank chains**' in SAP. You use bank chains to effect payments involving more than one bank; for example, a bank chain may contain the correspondence bank of your house bank, an intermediary bank, and the bank of the final recipient.

Earlier, before the introduction of bank chains, when you made a payment to your business partner who is abroad, you would specify the house bank and the partner's bank abroad. The house bank, then, will decide the intermediary bank via which the payment will be processed. However, with the advent of bank chains, you can now specify the chain with the specific intermediary bank(s) to which you want the payment to be processed. This way, you can rationalize the payment charges, as well as speed up the money transfer. You can define up to three intermediate banks in a bank chain.

The payment program uses the bank chain to process automatic payments. During a payment transaction, per payment, the payment program determines which combination of intermediary banks to use. The order of preference in such cases is based on 'scenarios' that comprise house bank, recipient's bank, currency, and payment method. The payment program determines the most optimized combination of all these. It completes the payment run based on the settings you have maintained in Customizing, master data, and payment run parameters. When editing a payment proposal, if you change an entry (say, house bank or partner's bank, currency, or payment method), the payment program re-examines the new scenario and determines the appropriate bank chain. Note that the payment program determines the appropriate bank chain only for the payment methods that call for processing via the bank chain; for all other payment methods, the program may not use the bank chain functionality.

571. What is a 'General Bank Chain'?

You can define **general bank chains** via the Customizing menu path: *SAP Customizing Implementation Guide | Financial Accounting | Bank Accounting | Bank Chains | Create General Bank Chain* or Transaction Code **FIBB**. The general bank chain is not dependent on a business partner's bank details, and you can use such a bank chain to process any of your payment transactions that do not require specifying a partner's bank.

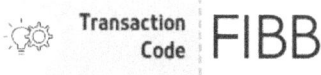 **Transaction Code** FIBB

Figure 18.4

572. Explain the 'Manual Bank Statement' functionality of FI-BL.

To configure the settings required for **manual bank statement**, use the Customizing menu path: *SAP Customizing Implementation Guide | Financial Accounting | Bank Accounting | Business Transactions | Payment Transactions | Manual Bank Statement*, and complete the tasks shown in *Table 18.1*:

Customizing Task	Transaction Code
Define Posting Keys and Posting Rules for Manual Bank Statement	OT84
Create and Assign Business Transactions	OT52
Define Variants for Manual Bank Statement	OT43

Table 18.1: *Customizing Tasks and the Transaction Codes for Configuring Manual Bank Statement*

Once configured, you can use the 'manual bank statement' functionality to manually enter the bank statements you receive periodically from your bank. There are two steps in the manual entry: first, you need to enter the account line items, and second, you post the entered line items. When you enter line items, the system ensures appropriate account determination and checks for data consistency. During posting of the line items, create a maximum of two postings per line item: a bank account posting (for example, debit bank clearing a/c and credit bank clearing a/c) and a sub-ledger posting (for example, debit bank clearing a/c and credit customer account with clearing). When you enter the data, the system automatically transfers all the payment advice created (in SAP Cash & Liquidity Management) using memo record entry.

To process the manual bank statements, use the SAP Easy Access menu path: *SAP Menu | Accounting | Financial Accounting | Banks | Input | Bank Statement | Manual Entry* or Transaction Code **FF67**. On the ensuing pop-up screen, maintain the 'Start variant' and the 'Processing Type' and then proceed to maintain the other parameters.

Transaction Code FF67

Figure 18.5

573. Explain the 'Electronic Bank Statement' functionality of FI-BL.

A part of SAP Cash Management, the **electronic bank statement (EBS)** of FI-BL helps you process incoming payments. You use this functionality in your company when you obtain bank statements from your banks in electronic format. You will receive the bank statements using software according to **Banking Communication Standards (BCS)** and import the same into SAP. The bank statement file can be in any format, like SWIFT MT940, MultiCash, and BAI. After importing the statements into SAP, you can post-process them manually (using the Transaction Code **FEBA_BANK_STATEMENT**) by posting the items that have not been processed automatically. The electronic bank statement supports the functions as outlined in *Figure 18.6*:

Post Processing

You can process in a timely and straightforward way any bank statement's item that could not be posted by the system automatically.

Bank Statement Display / Overview

You can display the information about the current bank statements in the bank statement overview, using SAP Business Client (NWBC).

Bank Statement Import

You can import bank statements electronically into SAP system, and the file format can be like SWIFT MT940, MultiCash, and BAI.

Posting & Clearing

Following the import of the Electronic Bank Statement, the SAP system searches for the information required for automatic processing: posting and clearing.

Receiving Bank Statement via EDI

The EDI import of electronic bank statements is automatic, and it allows you to process the statement information in the system.

Functional Enhancements

To optimize electronic bank statement processing, you can enhance the range of functions of the standard SAP system that are company specific.

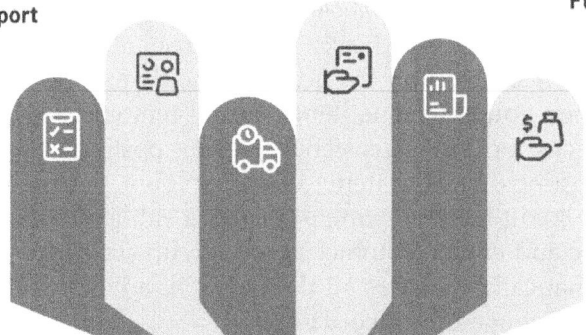

Figure 18.6: *Functions in Electronic Bank Statement*

574. Explain the Customizing for 'Electronic Bank Statement' functionality of FI-BL.

You need to complete the following six Customizing steps that form the global settings for EBS:

1. Create Account Symbols
2. Assign Accounts to Account Symbols
3. Create Keys for Posting Rules
4. Define Posting Rules

5. Create A Transaction Type
6. Assign Bank Accounts to Transaction Type

You can complete them using the menu path *'SAP Customizing Implementation Guide | Financial Accounting | Bank Accounting | Business Transactions | Payment Transactions | Electronic Bank Statement | Make Global Settings for Electronic Bank Statement'* or Transaction Code **OT83**.

Figure 18.7

575. Explain the 'Lockbox' functionality of FI-BL.

Used only in the USA, with the **'lockbox'** functionality of FI-BL, you can collect and process incoming check payments faster. Here, you create one or more lockboxes (normally a 'PO box') for your bank(s). Instead of collecting the checks (for the incoming payments) from your customers and then sending them to the bank for clearing, you just send the lockbox details to the customers and ask them to send the checks directly to the lockboxes. Now, your bank collects the checks periodically (at least once every day) directly from the lockboxes and processes the payments. The bank forwards the data relating to the payments in electronic bank statements so you can import them into the SAP system at periodic intervals. You will use a lockbox clearing account to post the payments directly to your bank G/L account. This clearing account will show a zero balance only when all the amounts have been applied to the customers' respective A/R items. When clearing the A/R open items, you will post the incoming payments to the respective bank accounts. However, when an incoming payment is insufficient to clear an open item, you may post-process the same appropriately using the Transaction Code **FLB1**. During the process, you may post a 'residual item' to the customer's account or a G/L account.

576. What is a 'Cash Journal'?

You use a 'cash journal' to manage your company's transactions. When you use the cash journal (*Figure 18.8*), the system automatically calculates and displays opening & closing balances, receipts, and payment totals.

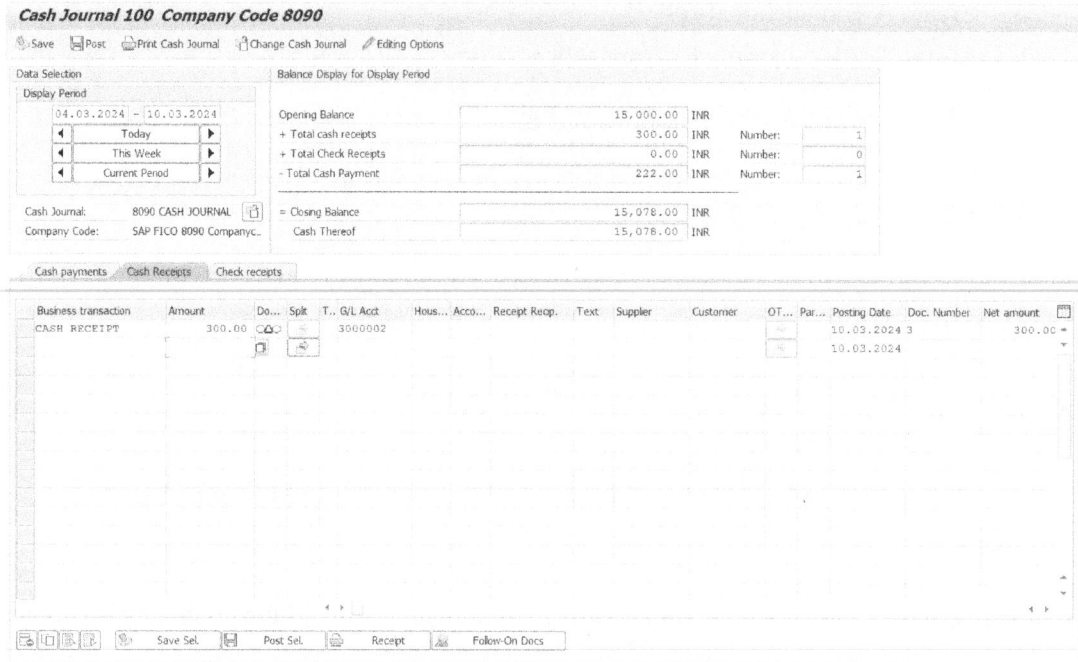

Figure 18.8: *Cash Journal*

Figure 18.9

Use Transaction Code **FBCJ** or the SAP Easy Access menu path '*SAP Menu | Accounting | Financial Accounting | Banks | Input (or Outgoings) | Kassenbuch'* to access the cash journal. It is a single-screen transaction that enables entering, displaying, and changing cash journal documents on a single screen.

Through the cash journal, you can post G/L accounts, as well as supplier/vendor and customer accounts. You can set up several cash journals for each Company Code. You can have all the cash journals with the Company Code (or local) currency, or you can have cash journals in different currencies other than the local currency. With more than one cash journal having the same currency, note that you should have different G/L accounts since you cannot post all the cash journals to a single G/L account. However, you can use a single G/L account to receive postings from more than one cash journal if the cash journals are defined for different currencies.

577. What are all the processing options in a 'Cash Journal'?

The following are some of the processing options that you can use in a cash journal:

- Entering, saving, and posting cash journal entries
- Changing the cash journal
- Defining cash journal business transactions
- Deleting cash journal entries saved
- Displaying all cash journal documents that have been deleted
- Displaying follow-on documents
- Printing receipts
- Printing the cash journal

578. What is an 'Orbian Payment System'? How can you leverage that?

A co-venture among SAP, DCE, and Citigroup, Orbian offers a new payment system known as the '**Orbian Payment System**' as an alternative to the traditional system for online payment transactions. There are two distinct parties in this payment setup: the sponsors and the banks. The 'sponsors' are primarily banks or financial institutions that offer the payment facility to the 'members', who are the end-using customers (buyers and suppliers).

The payment system is built on two tenets: the **Orbian Credit** (**OC**), which is nothing but the means of payment, and the **Primary Orbian Credit** (**PMC**), the accompanying financial instrument. In a payment transaction involving OC, both the buyers and suppliers are benefitted. As a payer (say, buyer), you do not need to pay cash; instead, you can make payments using OC with special benefits like 'target-duration based' payments (for example, payment target of 90 days). As a recipient of OC, you have the option of either converting the OC into cash at a discount well before its maturity date or just accumulating the OC for future transactions. In essence, the Orbian payment system enables the unlocking of money that would otherwise be locked up in supply chain transactions.

579. List some of the important SAP Fiori apps for Bank Accounting.

The following is a list of some of the important SAP Fiori apps in SAP Bank Accounting in SAP S/4HANA Finance:

- **Approve Bank Payments (Version 2)**: Use this SAP Fiori app to review and process the payment batches. Within a payment batch, you can view, approve, reject, or defer individual payments or the entire batch. You can search for a payment batch by batch ID, Company Code, and house bank. You will be able to edit the due dates of payment batches. You will also be able to defer the payments to a future date.

- **Bank Account Change Requests - Two-person verification**: With this transactional SAP Fiori app, you can get an overview of all the bank account change requests in the two-person verification mode awaiting approval. Using this app, you can check the changes and decide whether to approve or reject the change requests. You can compare the values 'before' and 'after' a change to understand the old values (current version) and new values (target version). When you approve a bank account change request, the app activates the new requested revision and, as a result, a new version of the bank account.

- **Bank Statement Monitor**: Use this SAP Fiori transactional app to monitor the status of end-of-day bank statements from individual bank accounts. Besides checking the receipt status of end-of-day bank statements for a specific date, you can get an overview over the last 14 days. You can identify and track any missing bank statement page, if there is a difference between the bank statement's balance and the G/L account's balance, or if there are items that have not been posted.

- **House Bank Account**: Use this SAP Fiori app to display an overview of house bank account data, including the bank account ID, description of the account, bank account number, IBAN, and other key facts relevant to the business context.

- **House Bank**: Use this app to display an overview of the house bank data, including the house bank description, country/region, city, and other relevant key facts. The app can show key facts like Company Code, Bank Key, and Bank Number. You may use this app as the starting point to navigate to more relevant information, including business partners, their master data, documents, etc. You can also branch out to other important apps.

- **Import Bank Directories**: This is not an SAP Fiori app. This app comes under SAP GUI. However, you can access this from SAP Fiori Launchpad. Through this app, you can upload the bank directory files, compare that data with existing bank data, and save the new (and changed) data in the bank master table using a global bank directory. With this app, you can compare the existing data with the data you want to upload. When comparing the data, the app adds new banks to the bank master table, updates banks with changed data, and flags banks for deletion if they are no longer valid. The app displays all the changes in an ALV list: from there, you can drill down to the old/new values of a changed bank. You will also see a summary of changes outlining the total of banks that have been added, changed, or flagged (for deletion), as well as error messages of the data that were not processed for a particular country/region.

- **Make Bank Transfers**: This is also a transactional SAP Fiori app. You can make money transfers between your bank accounts using this app. The app creates a payment request for every such transfer. Based on your company's policy, you can either create the payment request and clear the same with the transfer in a single action, or you can create, release, and make payment in a series of steps. While making the transfer, the app allows you to make transfers even in a currency that is different from that of the bank account currency; however, note that you must use only the exchange rate type 'M' for such transfers involving a different currency.

- **Manage Banks - Master data**: With this app, you can display/create master data for the banks for your company/business partners. In display, you can view the basic information relating to the banks, such as bank name, bank number, address, SWIFT code, etc. Through this app, you can create your house banks.

- **Manage In-House Bank Accounts**: With this transactional SAP Fiori app, you can create/edit/deactivate/close in-house bank accounts. While creating new bank accounts, you can save the account entry as a template to reuse later to create more accounts. You may also download the in-house bank accounts and then upload the same to the **Bank Account Management** (**BAM**) function. With this app, you can also mass-create bank accounts by uploading files.

- **Manage In-House Bank Limits**: This transactional SAP Fiori app enables you to manage account balances by setting lower limits. You can set a limit at a single account level or at the group of accounts level, with validity. You can set a positive or negative value for the account(s).

Join our book's Discord space

Join the book's Discord Workspace for Latest updates, Offers, Tech happenings around the world, New Release and Sessions with the Authors:

https://discord.bpbonline.com

CHAPTER 19

FI: Asset Accounting

Introduction

This chapter is all about Asset Accounting (FI-AA) in SAP S/4HANA Finance. Here, in this chapter, you will learn about the types of assets, representing an asset using the asset main number and asset sub-number, chart of depreciation, depreciation areas, asset class, etc. You will also learn about creating an asset master in the system, besides understanding the blocking and deleting of an asset. Then, you will learn about various asset transactions, including asset acquisition, asset transfer, asset retirement, etc. You will learn about depreciation and the various depreciation calculation methods in detail. You will also understand about asset scrapping. Finally, you will learn about the depreciation run, how to execute/restart the same, the production setup in FI-AA, the asset history sheet, the asset explorer, and the important SAP Fiori apps in FI-AA.

580. Explain 'Asset Accounting' (FI-AA).

The **Asset Accounting (FI-AA)** sub-module in SAP S/4HANA Finance manages your company's fixed assets, right from the acquisition to retirement/scrapping. All the accounting transactions relating to depreciation, insurance, etc., of assets, are taken care of through this module, and all the accounting information from this module flows to FI-G/L on a real-time basis (*Figure 19.1*).

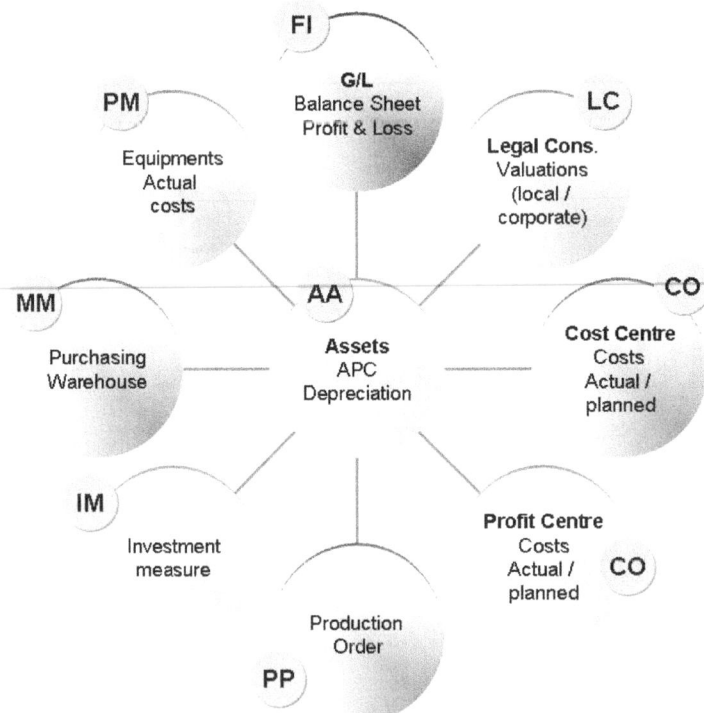

Figure 19.1: FI-AA integration with other modules

You will be able to directly post {**the goods receipt (GR)**, **invoice receipt (IR)**, or any withdrawal from a warehouse to fixed asset} from SAP MM or SAP PP to FI-AA. The integration with FI-A/R helps direct sales posting to the customer account. Similarly, integration with FI-A/P helps post an asset directly to FI-AA and the relevant vendor account in cases where the purchase is not routed through the MM module. You may capitalize the maintenance activities to an asset using settlements through the SAP PM module. FI-AA and FI-G/L have a real-time integration wherein all the transactions, like asset acquisition, retirement, transfer, etc., are recorded simultaneously in both applications. However, batch processing is required to transfer the depreciation values, interest, etc., to the FI module.

The FI-AA and CO integration helps with the following:

- Assigning an asset to any *CO Objects* like a cost center, internal order / maintenance order, or an activity type. *Internal Orders* act as a two-way link to FI-AA: they help to collect and pass on the capital expenditure to assess and collect the depreciation/interest from FI-AA to CO objects. Note that when there is a situation where the asset master record contains an internal order and a cost center, then the depreciation is always posted to the internal order and not to the cost center.

- The depreciation and the interest are passed on to the cost/profit centers.

581. What are all the kinds of 'Assets' in SAP?

An asset can be a *simple asset* or a *complex asset*. Depending on the requirement, assets are maintained with an *asset main number* and *asset sub-numbers*. A complex asset consists of many *sub-assets*, each identified using an asset sub-number. You may also use the concept of *group asset*s in SAP.

582. Explain 'Complex Asset' and 'Asset Sub-Numbers.'

A **complex asset** in SAP is made up of many master records, each of which is denoted by an asset sub-number. It is prudent to use asset sub-numbers if:

- You need to manage the 'subsequent acquisitions' separately from the initial one (for example, your initial acquisition was a PC, and you are adding a printer later).

- You want to manage the various parts of an asset separately even at the time of 'initial acquisition' (for example, the initial purchase is a PC wherein you create separate asset master records for the monitor, CPU, etc.).

- You must divide the assets based on certain technical qualities (keyboard, mouse, etc.).

When you manage a complex asset, the system enables you to evaluate the asset in all possible ways, like for a single sub-number, for all sub-numbers, and select sub-numbers.

583. What is a 'Group asset' in SAP? When will you use this?

A **group asset**, in SAP, is almost like a normal asset except that this can have several *sub-assets* denoted by *asset sub-numbers*. The concept of group asset becomes necessary when you need to carry out the depreciation at a group level for some special purposes like tax reporting. Remember that SAP's way of depreciation is always at the individual asset level. Hence, to manage at the group level, you need the group asset. Once you decide to have group assets, you must also have 'special depreciation areas' meant for group assets; you will not be able to depreciate a group asset using a normal depreciation area.

Unlike *complex assets*, you can delete a group asset only when all the associated sub-numbers have been marked for deletion.

584. What is an 'Asset Super Number' in SAP?

The concept of **asset super number** in FI-AA is used only for reporting purposes. Here, you assign several individual assets to a single asset number. By using this methodology, you can see all the associated assets with the asset super number as a single asset (for example, brakes assembly line) or as individual assets (for example, machinery and equipment in the brakes assembly line).

585. What is a 'Chart of Depreciation'? How does it differ from 'Chart of Accounts'?

The **chart of depreciation** contains a list of country-specific depreciation areas. It provides the rules for evaluating valid assets in each country or economic area/zone. SAP S/4HANA Finance comes supplied with default charts of depreciation that are based on the requirements of each country. These default charts of depreciation also serve as the 'reference charts' from which you can create a new chart of depreciation by copying one of the relevant charts of depreciation. After copying, you may delete the depreciation areas that you do not need. However, note that deletion must be made before you create any asset in that depreciation area.

You are required to assign a chart of depreciation to your Company Code. Remember that one Company Code can have **only one** chart of depreciation assigned, even though multiple Company Codes can use the same chart.

The *chart of accounts* can be global, country-specific, or industry-specific, but the *chart of depreciation* is only country-specific. These two charts are independent of each other (*Table 19.1*):

Chart of depreciation	Chart of accounts
Established by FI-AA.	Established by FI.
A chart of depreciation is a collection of country-specific depreciation areas.	The chart of accounts is a list of G/L accounts used in a Company Code. The chart of accounts contains chart of accounts area and Company Code area.
The chart of depreciation is country-specific. Usually, you may not require more than one chart of depreciation. SAP comes delivered with many country-specific charts of depreciation as 'reference charts' which can be copied to have your own chart of depreciation.	Depending upon the requirement you may have an 'operating chart of accounts', 'country chart of accounts', 'global chart of accounts' etc.

Chart of depreciation	Chart of accounts
One Company Code uses only one chart of depreciation.	One Company Code uses only one chart of accounts.
Many Company Codes, in the same country, can use the same chart of depreciation.	Several Company Codes, within the same country, can use the same chart of accounts.

Table 19.1: *Chart of Depreciation vs. Chart of Accounts*

586. How do you create an 'Asset Accounting Company Code'?

The steps involved in creating an asset accounting Company Code are as follows:

- Define the Company Code in FI configuration, and assign a chart of accounts to this Company Code.
- Assign a chart of depreciation to this Company Code in FI-AA configuration.
- Add necessary data for the Company Code for use in FI-AA.

587. What is 'Depreciation'? Explain the various types.

Depreciation is the reduction in the *book value* of an asset due to its usage over time ('decline in economic usefulness') or due to the legal framework for taxation reporting. The depreciation is usually calculated considering the *economic life* of the asset, the *expected value* of the asset at the end of its economic life (*junk/scrap value*), the *method of depreciation calculation* (straight-line method, declining balance, sum of year digits, double declining, etc.) and the defined *percentage decline* in the value of the asset every year (20%, 15% and so on).

The depreciation can either be planned or unplanned, as explained below:

- **Planned depreciation** brings down the asset's value after every planned period, say, every year, till the asset value is fully depreciated over its life period. By this, you will know the value of the asset at any point in its active life.

- On the contrary, **unplanned depreciation** is a permanent reduction of the value of the asset due to a sudden happening of an event or occurrence that is not foreseen (for example, there could be a sudden break out of a fire damaging an asset and forcing you to depreciate fully as it is no longer useful economically).

In SAP S/4HANA Finance, you will come across three types of depreciation, as shown in *Figure 19.2*:

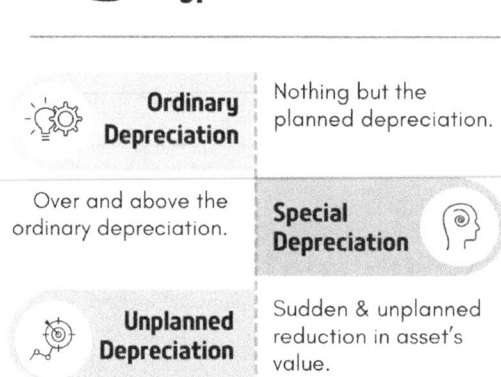

Figure 19.2: Depreciation types

Ordinary depreciation is nothing but 'planned depreciation.' The *special depreciation* is over and above the 'ordinary depreciation' and is normally used for taxation purposes. *Unplanned depreciation*, as already explained, is the result of a reduction in asset value due to the sudden occurrence of some unforeseen events.

588. Define 'Depreciation Area'.

The fixed assets are valued differently for different purposes (business, legal, etc.). SAP S/4HANA Finance manages these different valuations using *depreciation areas*. There are various depreciation areas like book depreciation, tax depreciation, depreciation for cost-accounting purposes etc.,

A **depreciation area** decides how and for what purpose an asset is evaluated. The depreciation area can be 'real' or 'derived one'. Depending on the valuation and reporting requirements, you may need to use several depreciation areas for a single asset.

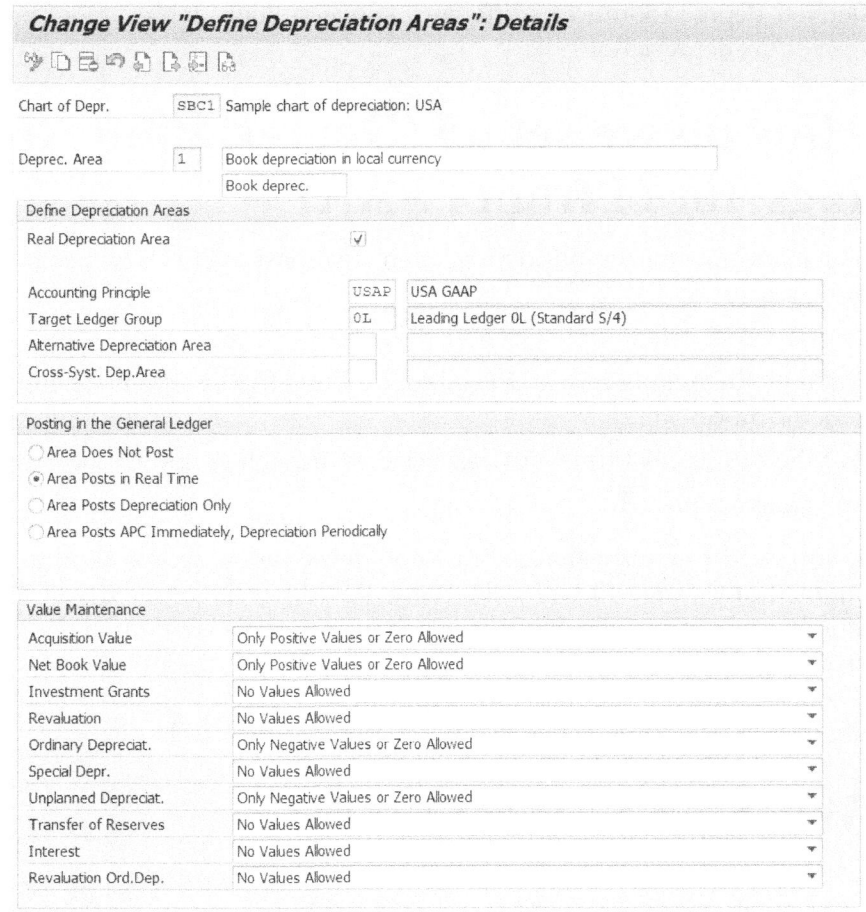

Figure 19.3: *Details of 01-Book depreciation area*

The depreciation areas are denoted by a 2-character code in the system. They contain the depreciation terms that must be entered into the asset master records or asset classes. SAP comes delivered with many depreciation areas; however, depreciation area 01—*Book Depreciation* is the major one (*Figure 19.3*).

The other depreciation areas are as follows:

- Book depreciation in group currency
- Consolidated versions in local/group currency
- Tax balance sheet depreciation
- Special tax depreciation
- Country-specific valuation (for example, net-worth tax)
- Values/depreciations that differ from depreciation area 01 (example: cost-accounting reasons)

- Derived depreciation area (difference between book depreciation and country-specific tax depreciation)

589. How do we set up 'Depreciation Areas postings' for FI from FI-AA?

You need to define how the various depreciation areas post to FI-G/L. It can be any one of the following scenarios:

- Post depreciation through 'periodic processing.'
- Post both the **Acquisition and Production Costs** (**APC**) and depreciation through periodic processing.
- Post the APC in 'real-time' but depreciation through periodic processing.
- No values are posted.

However, you need to ensure that at least one depreciation area is configured to post values automatically to the FI-G/L. Normally, this depreciation area will be 01 (book depreciation). For the rest of the depreciation areas, it may be configured that they derive their values from this area, and the difference thus calculated is automatically posted to FI-G/L. There may also be situations wherein you may define depreciation areas just for reporting purposes, and these areas need not be posted to the G/L.

590. What is an 'Asset Class?

In SAP S/4HANA Finance, the **asset class** is the basis for classifying an asset based on business and legal requirements. The standard SAP system comes with several asset classes as defaults that you can use (*Figure 19.4*), or you can create your own asset classes if required.

Change View "Asset classes": Overview

New Entries

Class	Short Text	Asset Class Description	
1000	Real Estate (Land)	Real Estate (Land)	
1100	Buildings	Buildings	
1200	Land Improvements	Land Improvements	
1500	Leasehold Improvmnts	Leasehold Improvements	
2000	Machinery Equipment	Machinery and Equipment	
3000	Fixtures Fittings	Fixtures and Fittings	
3100	Vehicles	Vehicles	
3200	Computer Hardware	Computer Hardware	
3210	Computer Software	Computer Software	
3300	Office Equipment	Office Equipment	
5000	LVA	Low-value Assets	
6000	Leasing (oper.)	Leased assets (operating lease)	
6100	Leasing (capital)	Leased assets (capital lease)	

Figure 19.4: Typical asset classes

It is essentially a grouping of assets having certain common characteristics. Each asset in the system needs to be associated with an asset class. Broadly speaking, an asset class can denote any of the following:

- Buildings
- Technical assets
- Financial assets
- Leased assets
- **Assets under Construction (AuC)**
- **Low Value Assets (LVA)**

Figure 19.5: Asset class – Control information

The asset class is the most important configuration element which decides the type of asset (like land, buildings, furniture & fixtures, equipment, AuC, leased assets, LVA, etc.), the document number range, data entry screen layout for asset master creation, G/L account assignments, depreciation areas, depreciation terms, etc. You define the asset class at the Client level, which will then be available to all the Client's Company Codes.

The asset class consists of information including 'asset type' (account determination & screen layout rule), 'number assignment' (number range & external and external sub-number), 'status of AuC,' 'lock status,' 'real estate indicator for asset class' and 'technical information' (*Figure 19.5*).

591. Why do you need 'Asset Classes'?

An **asset class** is the *link* between the asset master records and the G/L accounts. The *account determination* in the asset class enables you to post to the relevant G/L accounts. Several asset classes can use the same account determination, provided all these asset classes use the same chart of accounts and post to the same G/L accounts.

592. What is an 'Asset Class Catalog'?

An **asset class catalog** contains all the asset classes in an enterprise and hence is valid across the Client. As a result, most of the characteristics of the asset class are defined at the client level; however, there are certain characteristics (like the depreciation key, for example) that you can define in the chart of the depreciation level.

593. What is an 'Asset Value Date'?

The **asset value date** will be the depreciation start date for an asset. The system calculates the 'planned depreciation' based on this depreciation start date and the selected 'depreciation term' for that asset. Be careful with the 'posting date' and 'asset value date': both these dates need to be in the same fiscal year.

594. What is an 'Asset Master'?

An **asset master** can be created by copying an existing asset in the same Company Code or another Company Code; it can also be created from scratch when it is done for the first time. Again, while creating the master, SAP allows multiple assets to be created in one go, provided all such assets are similar (having the **same** asset class and all belonging to the **same** Company Code).

Each asset master contains the necessary information to calculate the depreciation. The information required is as follows:

- Capitalization date/acquisition period
- Depreciation areas relevant to the asset
- Depreciation key
- Useful life/Expired useful life
- Change over the year, if any
- Scrap value, if any
- Start date of (ordinary depreciation)

From release SAP R/3 4.5, the Transaction Codes for creating asset master have been changed to AS series instead of the earlier AT series (for example, create asset is by **AS01** (*AT01* earlier), change asset is **AS02** (*AT02* earlier), and so on.

595. Explain the two ways of creating 'Asset Masters.'

There are two ways in which you can create asset masters in the system:

- Copy an existing asset as a reference for creating a new one.
- Create a new asset from an existing asset class so that this asset class provides the default control parameters for the new asset.

596. Is it possible to create multiple assets in a single transaction?

Yes, you can create multiple (but *similar*) assets in one transaction. What you need to know is that all these assets should belong to the **same** asset class and the **same** Company Code. Enter the number of assets you must create in the '*Number of Similar Assets*' field (*Figure 19.6*). After creating the assets, you can change the individual descriptions/inventory numbers when you are about to save the master records. When you save the master records, the system assigns a range of asset numbers. The only drawback of using this method of creating assets in bulk is that you will not be able to create *long text* for any of these assets.

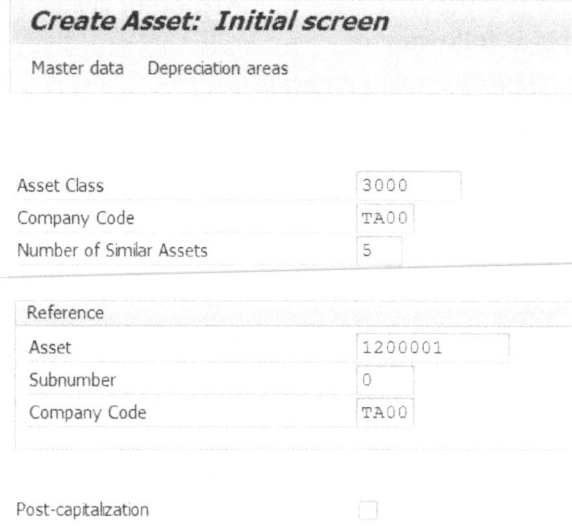

Figure 19.6: Creating multiple assets

Figure 19.7

597. What are all the 'Time Dependent Data' in the asset master?

All cost accounting assignment-related data, such as cost centers, internal orders, investment projects, etc., must be maintained as time-dependent data in asset masters. Additionally, information relating to asset shut-down and shift operation must also be maintained as time-dependent data. SAP maintains all the time-dependent data for the entire life span of the assets.

598. Explain 'Asset Acquisition'.

The **asset acquisition** can be through any one of the following routes:

- **External acquisition through purchase**: The 'external acquisition' of assets will be primarily from vendors/suppliers, either your business partners or third parties. It can also be from your affiliated companies (Transaction Code: **ABZP**). External asset acquisition can be done through different ways:

   o   The asset can be posted in the MM module.

- o The asset can be created in FI-AA by automatically clearing the offsetting entry (Transaction Code: **ABZON**). This can be achieved by either of the following methods:

    - The posting is made initially in FI-A/P and the clearing account cleared when the posting is made to the asset (FI-AA).

    - Post the asset with the automatic offsetting entry (FI-AA), then clear the clearing account through a credit posting by an incoming invoice (FI-AP).

  - o When **not** integrated with FI-A/P, you may acquire the asset in FI-AA with an automatic offsetting entry without referencing a **Purchase Requisition** (**PR**). This kind of acquisition is necessary when:

    - You have not yet received the invoice

    - When the invoice has already been posted in FI-AP

  - o When integrated with FI-A/P, acquire the asset in FI-AA using an incoming invoice but without a reference to a **Purchase Order** (**PO**).

- **In-house production/acquisition**: The 'in-house asset acquisition' is primarily the capitalization of goods/services produced by your company. The costs associated with the complete or partial production of the goods/services from within the company must be capitalized into a separate asset(s). Usually, the capitalization is done as follows:

- Create an order/project {in Investment Management (SAP IM)} to capture the production costs associated with the goods/services produced in-house.

- Settle the order/project to an AuC.

- Distribute/Settle the AuC created into a new asset(s).

You will be using *Transaction Type 110* for asset acquisition from in-house production.

- **Subsequent acquisition**: When the asset /vendor accounts are posted, the system updates the corresponding G/L accounts (FI-A/P & FI-AA) through relevant account determinations. SAP uses various 'transaction types' to distinguish the different transactions. During asset acquisition, the system makes the following entries in the asset master data:

  - o Date of initial acquisition/period & year of acquisition

  - o Capitalization date of the asset

  - o Start date for ordinary depreciation (start date is determined from the asset value date/period/year of acquisition)

  - o The vendor is automatically entered in the 'origin.'

599. What data are automatically set in the asset masters during 'Initial Acquisition'?

The following information is automatically set in the respective asset masters during initial acquisition:

- o Date of capitalization
- o Acquisition period
- o Posting date of original acquisition
- o Depreciation 'start date' (per depreciation area)

600. Why is it necessary to 'Block' an asset master record?

If you decide not to post any more acquisitions to an existing asset, you must set the block indicator in the asset master record. You can do this by selecting 'Block/Delete' under 'Asset' from the menu bar while in the 'Change Asset' transaction (*Figure 19.8*).

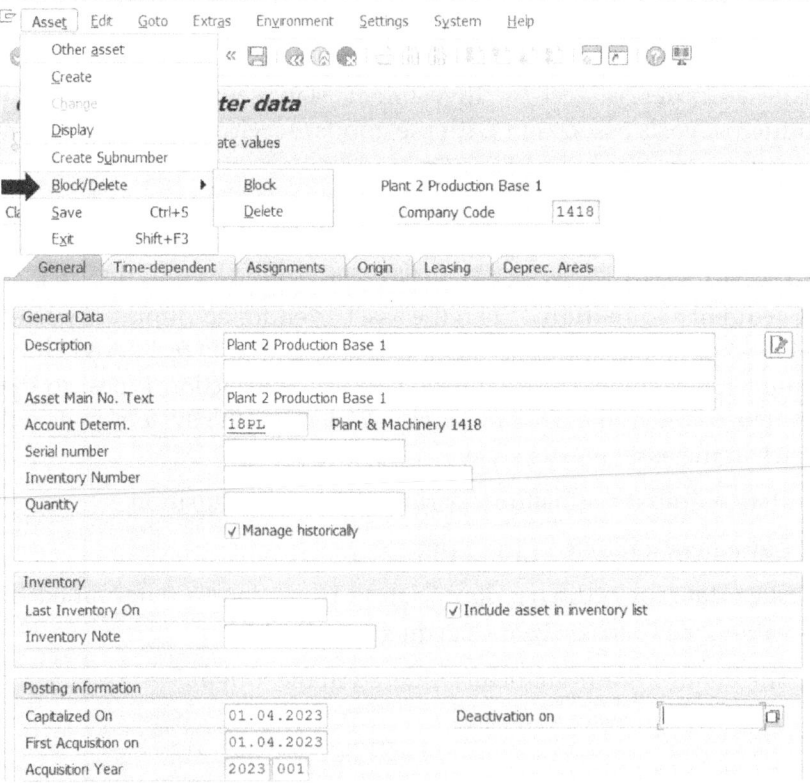

Figure 19.8: Block asset

This is usually the case with AuC, where, after the capitalization, you no longer want any further additions to the asset. The block indicator prevents only further postings but not transfers, retirements, or depreciation; even after an asset is blocked, you can continue to depreciate it as with any other asset.

601. How do you 'Delete' an asset master?

You can **delete an asset master** record from the system only when there are no transactions posted to it. The system will not allow you to delete the master record if there are transactions against the asset, even if you reverse all the previous transactions about the asset and bring down the asset value to zero. However, unlike FI-A/R, FI-A/P, or FI-G/L, where *archiving* is a prerequisite to deleting the master records, you may delete the asset master records without archiving. When deleted, the system also deletes the asset number. However, the asset should have already been 'blocked' in the system.

602. What is a '(Asset) Transaction Type' in FI-AA?

Transaction Types in FI-AA identify the nature of an asset transaction (acquisition, transfer, or retirement) to specify what is updated among the depreciation area, value field, and asset accounts in B/S.

Change View "Default transaction types for FI-AA posting..": Overview

New Entries

Default transaction types for FI-AA posting transactions

Acct. transact. ID	Description	TType	Transact. Type Text
ABAA	Unplanned depreciation	640	Unplanned depreciation on prior-year acquisitions
ABAO	Asset sale without customer	210	Retirement with revenue
ABAV	Asset retirement by scrapping	200	Retirement without revenue
ABAW	Balance sheet revaluation	800	Post revaluation gross
ABCO	adjustment posting CO	180	Down payment
ABGF	Credit memo in year after invoice	160	Credit memo in following year
ABGL	Enter credit memo in year of invoice	105	Credit memo in invoice year
ABIF	Investment support	100	Sample: D O N O T delete
ABMA	Manual depreciation	600	Manual ordinary depreciation on prior-yr acquis.
ABMR	Manual transfer of reserves	680	Transfer of reserves to prior-year acquisitions
ABNA	Post-capitalization	400	Post-capitalization
ABNE	Subsequent revenue	286	Subsequent revenue from asset retirement
ABNK	Subsequent costs	285	Subsequent costs from asset retirement
ABUB	Transfer between areas	300	Retirmt transfer of prior-yr acquis. frm cap.asset
ABUM	Transfer From	300	Retirmt transfer of prior-yr acquis. frm cap.asset
ABZE	Acquisition from in-house production	110	In-house acquisition
ABZO	Asset acquis. autom. offset. posting	100	External asset acquisition
ABZP	Acquistion from affiliated company	150	Gross interco.transf.acq. curr-yr.acq. affil.co.
ABZU	Write-up	700	Write-up ordinary and special depreciation

Figure 19.9: Transaction types

The transaction type is extensively used in most asset reports, including the asset history sheet, to display the various asset transactions differentiated by the transaction types. SAP has numerous transaction types (*Figure 19.9*) that will handle almost all your requirements. However, should there be a specific case, you may also create your own transaction type.

The following are some of the common transaction types that you will come across in FI-AA:

- **100**: Asset Acquisition – Purchase
- **110**: Asset Acquisition – In-house Production
- **200:** Asset Retirement – without revenue
- **210:** Asset Retirement – with revenue

Every transaction type is grouped into a *Transaction Type Group* (for example, 10 | Acquisition as shown in *Figure 19.10*), which characterizes the various transaction types (for example, transaction types 100 & 110) within that group. The system makes it possible to limit the transaction type groups associated with certain asset classes.

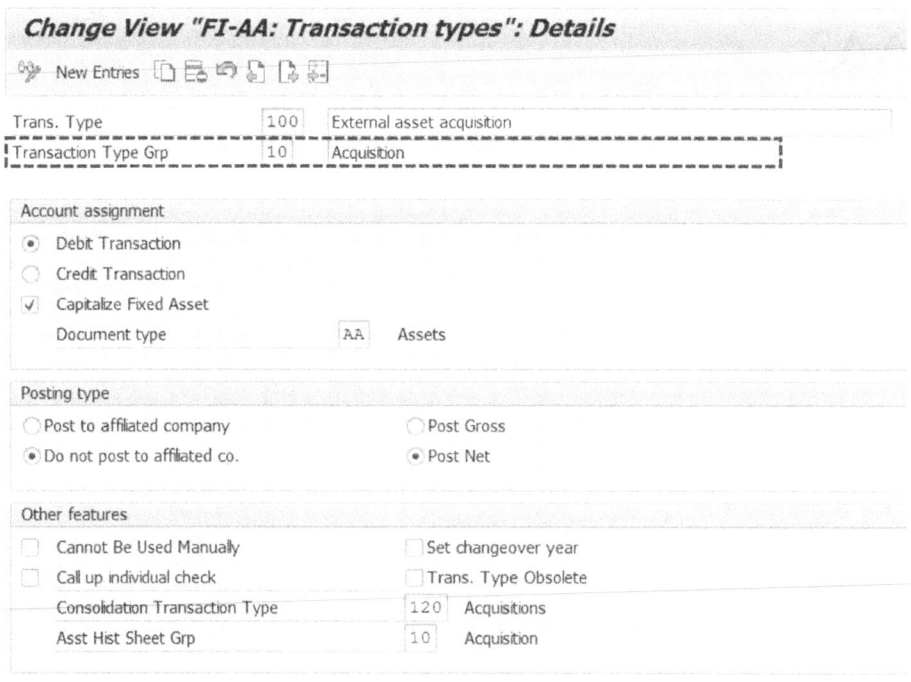

Figure 19.10: *Transaction type group*

603. Explain 'Assets under Construction' in SAP.

The goods and / or services produced in-house can be capitalized into asset(s). However, there are two distinct phases during this process:

- Construction phase (AuC)
- Utilization phase (useful or economic life phase)

It then becomes necessary to show the assets under these two phases in two different balance sheet items. The 'construction phase' is one in which you start producing or assembling the asset that is not yet ready for putting into economic utilization. SAP categorizes these kinds of assets into a special asset class called **AuC**.

The AuC is to be managed through a separate asset class with a separate asset G / L account. SAP allows posting 'down payments' to AuC. It is also possible to enter credit memos for AuC even after its complete capitalization, provided you manage this asset class, allowing *negative* **Acquisition and Production Costs** (**APC**). The SAP IM module helps to manage internal orders / projects for AuC. It is necessary that you use the *depreciation key* '0000' to ensure that you are not calculating any depreciation for AuC. However, you can continue to have special tax depreciation and investment support even for these assets.

604. How to capitalize AuC in SAP S/4HANA Finance?

An AuC can be managed in two ways, as far as the asset master is concerned:

- As a 'normal' asset.
- As an asset with 'line-item management'.

In the case of an asset with line-item management, the AuC is capitalized and transferred to the regular asset(s) by 'distribution' / 'settlement.' While doing so, the system, with the help of different *transaction types*, segregates the transactions relating to the current year from those of the previous years. The capitalization can be as follows:

- Lump sum capitalization. Use Transaction Code **AIAB**.
- With line-item settlement {for this kind of settlement, you do not need to settle all the line items and 100 % in a particular line item}. Use Transaction Code **AIBU**.

When integrated with SAP-IM, capital investments can be managed as AuC by:

- Collecting the production costs associated with an order / project
- Settling the collected costs to an AuC
- Capitalizing the AuC into new assets by distribution / settlement

605. What do you mean by 'Low Value Assets'?

SAP uses the term **low value assets (LVA)** to denote assets which will be depreciated in the year of purchase or in the period of acquisition. This categorization usually follows the statutory requirements of the country of the Company Code, wherein you define a monetary limit and consider all those assets falling below the value, say $1,000, as LVA. You have the flexibility of managing these assets either on an individual (*individual check*) basis or a collective basis (*quantity check*). SAP uses a special depreciation key called LVA, and the expected useful life of such an asset is considered to be one period (month).

606. Explain 'Asset Transfer' in SAP.

Asset transfer is of two types: inter-company asset transfer and intra-company asset transfer.

Inter-company asset transfer is between the Company Codes, resulting in the creation of a new asset in the target Company Code (the receiving one). The transaction posts the values as per the 'posting method' selected during the transfer. In doing so, the system does the following:

- Retires the asset in the source/sending Company Code by an *asset retirement*
- Posts acquisition in the new/target Company Code by an *asset acquisition* and creates the new asset in the target Company Code
- Posts inter-company profit/loss arising out of the transfer
- Updates FI-G/L automatically

Figure 19.11

An inter-company asset transfer is usually necessitated when there is a need to change the location from one company to another physically or when there is an organizational restructuring resulting in the new asset being attached to the new Company Code. You may use the standard *Transfer Variants* supplied by SAP for effecting such a transfer. The selection of a suitable transfer variant will be based on the legal relationship among the Company Codes and the methods chosen for transferring the asset values. The inter-company asset transfer can be handled individually using the normal transaction for a single asset or several assets using the *'mass transfer'*. If you need to transfer assets cross-system, use ALE functionality.

Intra-company asset transfer is the transfer of an asset within the same Company Code. This would have been necessitated by the following:

- Change in the asset class or business area, for example
- Settlement of an AuC to a new asset
- Transfer of stock materials into an asset
- Splitting an existing asset into one or more new assets.

Figure 19.12

607. What is a 'Transfer Variant'?

The **transfer variant** (*Figure 19.13*) specifies how the transferred asset will be valued at the receiving Company Code and the type of transaction (acquisition or transfer) used for the transaction. It depends on whether the Company Codes involved are legally dependent or independent.

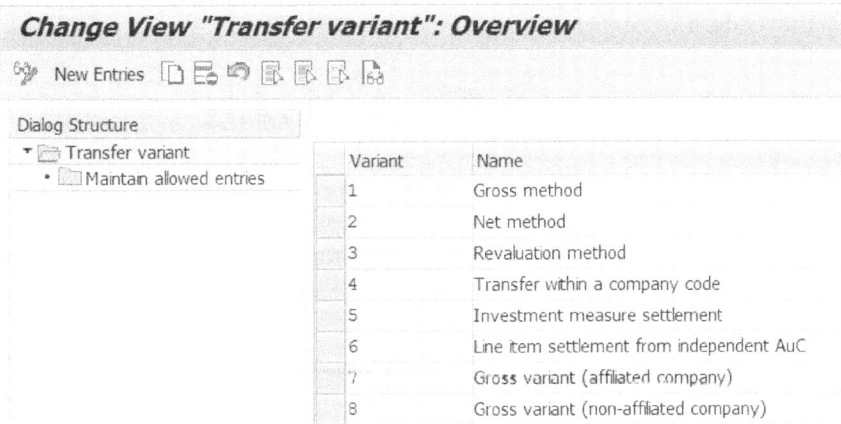

Figure 19.13: Transfer variant

608. Explain 'Asset Retirement' in FI-AA.

Asset retirement is an integral part of asset management. You may retire an asset by sale or by scrapping. In the case of sales, it can be with revenue or without revenue; again, the asset sale can be with a customer or without a customer (*Figure 19.14*).

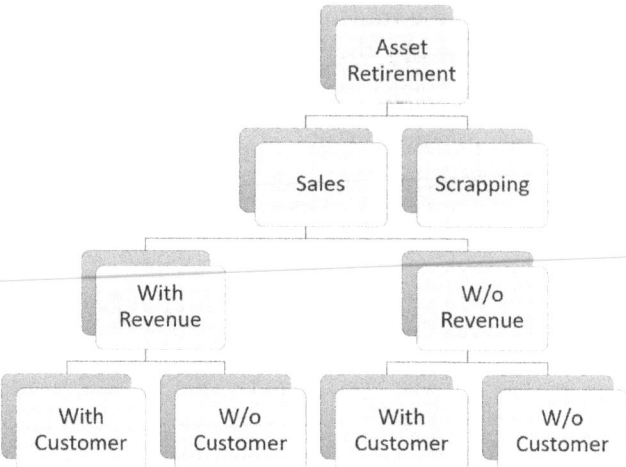

Figure 19.14: *Asset retirement*

During asset sales, the system removes the *APC* and also the corresponding *accumulated depreciation*. Then, the *profit or loss* arising out of the sale is recorded in the system. Even in the case of 'partial retirement' or 'partial sales', the system records the proportionate gain/loss arising out of the transaction. Any tax posting arising from sales is automatically created by the system.

 **Transaction Code** ABOAN

Figure 19.15

SAP provides various ways of posting asset retirement in the system, which includes the following:

- Mass retirement
- Asset retirement with revenue:
    - With customer (involving integration with FI-A/R):
        - **Debit** customer, **Credit** assets
    - Without customer
- Asset retirement without revenue:
    - With customer
        - **Debit** clearing account, **Credit** asset
        - **Debit** customer in A/R, **Credit** the clearing account
- Asset retirement using G/L document posting

609. Describe the transfer of 'Legacy Asset Data' to SAP.

One of the challenges in the implementation of FI-AA is the transfer of **legacy asset data** from your existing systems to SAP FI-AA. Though SAP provides multiple options and tools to carry out this task, you need a carefully planned strategy for completing it. You may resort to transfer the old asset values through any one of the following ways:

- Batch data inputs (large number of old assets)
- Directly updating the SAP Tables (very large number of old assets)
- Manual entry (few old assets)

Normally, you will not be resorting to a manual process as it is time-consuming and laborious; however, you may do this if you have a very limited number of assets. Otherwise, you may use either of the other two options, though batch data input with error handling would be the preferred way. You need to reconcile the data transferred if you resort to any of the two automatic ways of transferring the data. You may also use a **Business Application Programming Interface** (**BAPI**) to link and process the asset information in SAP FI-AA from non-SAP systems.

The transfer can be at the end of the last closed fiscal year or during the current fiscal year following the last closed fiscal year. You can transfer both master data and accumulated values of the last closed fiscal year. If required, you can also transfer the asset transactions, including depreciation, during the current fiscal year. It is important to note that the G/L account balances of the old assets need to be transferred separately.

610. What is an 'Asset Transfer Date'?

The **asset transfer date** refers to the 'cut-off' date for transferring old asset data from your existing system. Once established, you will not be able to create any old assets in SAP before this reference date. Any transaction happening after the transfer date but before the actual date of the asset transfer needs to be created separately in SAP after you complete the old asset transfer.

611. Describe 'Mass Change'. How to achieve this?

The **mass change** enables you to make changes (like mass retirements, changes to incomplete assets, etc.) in FI-AA to many asset master records at once. The mass change functionality is achieved through *work lists* and FI-AA standard tasks pre-defined in the system. These tasks are assigned with 'workflow objects,' which can be changed according to your requirements. The work lists are created in several ways, from asset master records, asset value displays, asset information systems, etc. To effect a mass change, you need to consider the following:

- Create a *substitution rule(s)* in which you will mention all the fields that are required to be changed. This rule will consist of an 'identifying condition' (for example, if the cost center = 1345) and a 'rule to substitute' new values (for example: replace the 'field' cost center with the 'value' '1000').

- Generate a list of such assets which need to be changed.

- Create a 'work list' to carry out the changes.

- Select the appropriate 'substitution rule' (defined earlier in point one).

- Process the 'work list'. You may also release the same to someone else in the organization so that he/she can complete the task.

- Run a 'report' to verify the changes.

612. What is a 'Periodic Processing' in FI-AA? Explain.

Periodic processing in FI-AA relates to the tasks that you need to carry out at periodic intervals to plan and post some of the transactions. The tasks include the following:

- Depreciation calculation and posting.:

  As you know, SAP allows automatic posting of values from only one depreciation area (normally, 01–book depreciation). For all other depreciation areas, including the derived ones, you need to perform the tasks periodically so that FI is updated properly.

- Planned depreciation/interest for CO primary cost planning.

- Claiming and posting of 'investment support' (either 'individually' or through 'mass change').

613. What is a 'Depreciation Key'?

Depreciation is calculated using the system's **depreciation key**. The depreciation keys are defined at the chart of depreciation level, and are uniform across all Company Codes, which are attached to a particular chart of depreciation. You define the depreciation type, ordinary or special, in the depreciation key. The depreciation key contains all the control information, per depreciation area, for the automatic calculation of planned depreciation, automatic calculation of interest, and the maximum percentages for manual depreciation. The system contains a few pre-defined depreciation keys (like 0000, LINA, DWG, DG10, etc.) with the controls already defined for calculation method and type (*Figure 19.16*). A depreciation key can contain multiple internal calculation keys. You can enter separate depreciation keys per area in the asset master record.

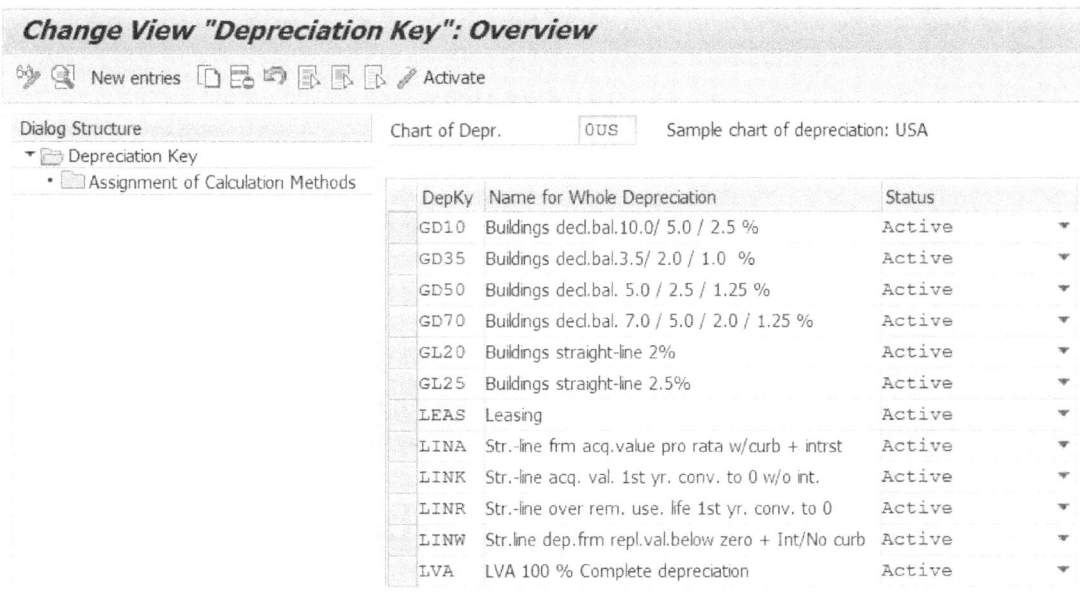

Figure 19.16: *Depreciation key*

Figure 19.17

614. What is a 'Calculation Method'?

The **calculation method** is a part of the depreciation key and is used to control the parameters of the depreciation calculation program. SAP supports the following calculation methods, all of which are dependent on the chart of depreciation except the 'base methods,' which are independent of the chart of depreciation:

- Base methods
- Declining-balance methods
- Maximum amount methods
- Multi-level methods
- Period control methods

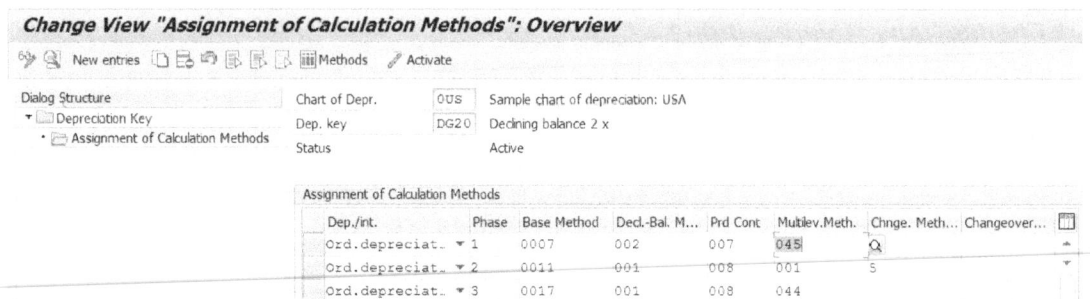

Figure 19.18: Assigning Calculation Method to Depreciation Key

While defining the depreciation key, you will also assign the required calculation methods (*Figure 19.18*) for each of the depreciation keys (Transaction Code **AFAMA**).

615. Explain the 'Based Method' of depreciation calculation.

The **base method** of depreciation calculation contains general control parameters for depreciation calculation. Since it is independent of the chart of depreciation, there are no country-specific settings.

Change View "Base Method": Overview

☼ ◷ New entries 🗋 🖺 🖆 🖺 🖺 🖺 🖧 Usage

Base Method

Base Method	Text
0001	Ordinary: sum-of-the-years-digits
0002	Ordinary: no automatic depreciation
0003	Ordinary: leasing
0004	Ordinary: decl.-balance over total life (Japan)
0005	Ordinary: percentage from useful life (reduction)
0006	Ordinary: percentage frm life (reduction, below 0)
0007	Ordinary: percentage from life (after end of life)
0008	Ordinary: percentage from life as of changeover yr
0009	Ordinary: percentage from life (curb)
0010	Ordinary: percentage from life (below zero)
0011	Ordinary: percentage from useful life
0012	Ordinary: explicit percentage
0013	Ordinary: explicit percentage (reduction)

Figure 19.19: SAP-supplied base methods of depreciation calculation

In a base method, you will specify the depreciation type, depreciation calculation method, and the end of depreciation treatment. After defining the depreciation key, you need to enter the base method. In general, the base methods (like 0001, 0002, 0003, and so on) supplied by SAP will be sufficient for any business (*Figure 19.19*). However, if you need to define your own method, you may do so via the Customizing menu: *SAP Customizing Implementation Guide | Financial Accounting | Asset Accounting | Depreciation | Valuation Methods | Depreciation Key | Calculation Methods | Define Base Methods.*

616. Define 'Declining Balance Methods'.

The **declining-balance method** (aka *diminishing-balance method*) consists of two depreciation calculation methods: the regular 'declining-balance method' and the 'sum-of-the-years-digits' method.

In the normal **declining-balance method**, the system multiplies the straight-line percentage depreciation rate (resulting from the useful life) by a given factor (*Figure 19.20*). To avoid a relatively short useful life resulting in a very large depreciation percentage rate, specify a maximum percentage rate as the upper ceiling limit in the declining-balance method. Similarly, to avoid a very long useful life resulting in a very low depreciation percentage rate, you can enter a minimum percentage rate that prevents the system from sinking the depreciation beyond the minimum level.

In the **sum-of-the-years-digits method**, you set up an arithmetic sequence based on the asset's total useful life. The depreciation *percentage* rate is proportional to the remaining useful life.

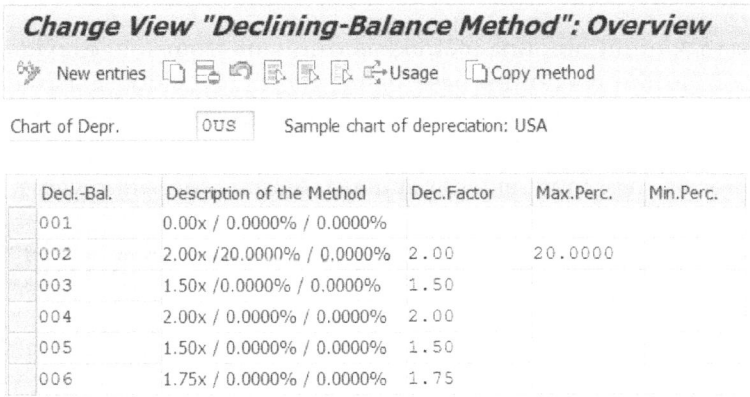

Figure 19.20: *Sample Declining-Balance Method*

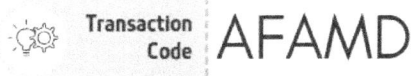

Figure 19.21

617. What is the 'Maximum Amount Method' of depreciation calculation?

The **maximum amount method** of depreciation calculation contains a maximum depreciation amount that cannot be exceeded before a specified (calendar) date. As soon as the depreciation calculated by the system reaches this maximum amount limit, the system stops calculating any further depreciation for the asset. It is possible to specify how the maximum amount applies for the time period specified: either to each individual year (in the specified time period) or to accumulated depreciation. For every maximum amount method, you need to specify the maximum amount, currency, and valid to date (*Figure 19.22*).

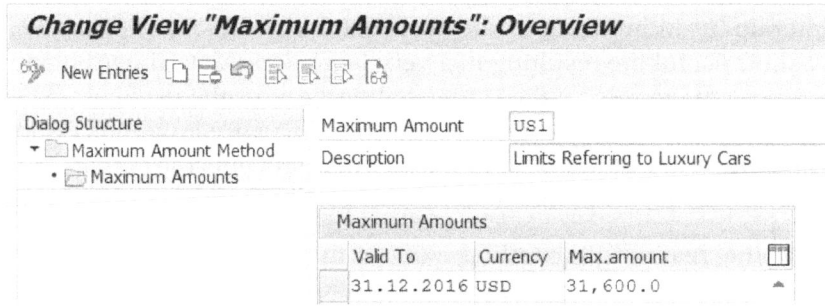

Figure 19.22: Maximum amount method configuration

Note that the maximum amount method is different from the 'maximum base value' for depreciation. In the maximum base value, the depreciation is based on a specified acquisition value (that may be less than the actual acquisition value) used from the start as the base value for depreciation. However, in the case of the maximum method, the system calculates depreciation without any dependency on the acquisition value.

618. Explain how a 'Multi-Level Method' works.

In a **multi-level calculation method**, you divide the method into multiple levels. Each level is denoted by a validity period with a specific percentage rate (*Figure 19.23*). The system, while calculating the depreciation, replaces a particular percentage rate with the next rate with the change in the level.

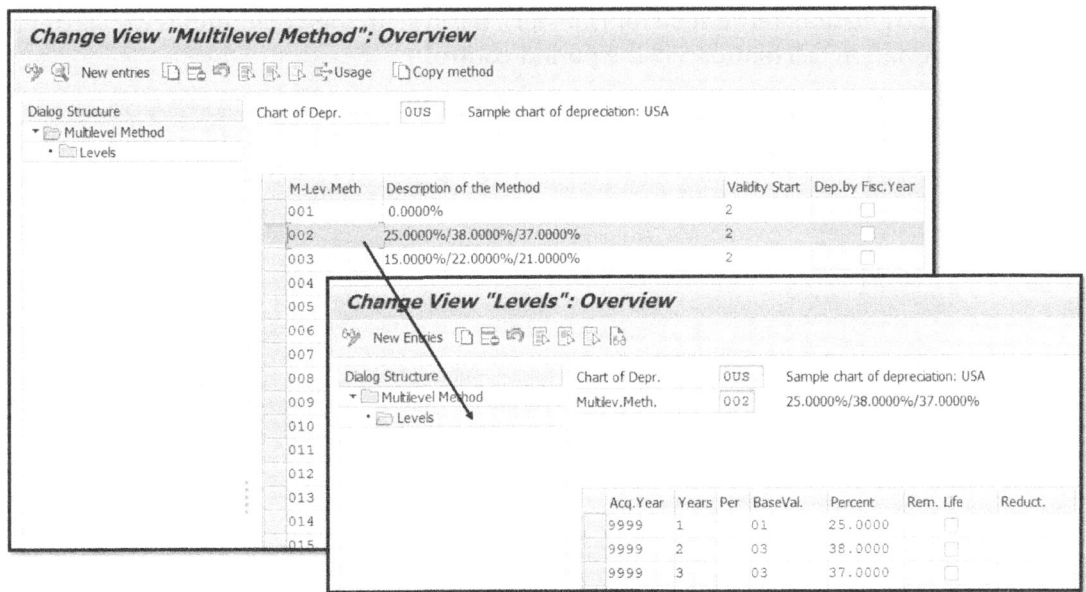

Figure 19.23: *Multi-level calculation method*

The validity period for the individual levels can begin with the capitalization date or the start date for ordinary/tax depreciation, the original acquisition date of AuC, or the changeover year. The defined time periods, denoted by a key, always have a common start date. This ensures that a key's period (from the start to end) will always overlap with the next period, having the same start date but a longer validity period. Hence, enter the validity periods (for the levels) in cumulative form. In the case of non-calendar fiscal years, you need to use a special indicator (*'Dep.by Fisc. Year'*) that allows you to specify that the periods for the levels apply to the fiscal year and not to the calendar year (*Figure 19.23*).

Figure 19.24

619. What is the 'Period Control Method' in depreciation calculation?

With the **period control method**, you can determine the start and end date of depreciation for various asset transactions like acquisitions, subsequent acquisitions (or post-capitalization), transfer postings, and retirements. For example, you can specify that the depreciation starts at the beginning of the year for all acquisitions, the asset retirements to be on the last date of a period, and so on (*Figure 19.25*). Using the value date of the asset's transaction (acquisition, retirement, or transfer), the system then determines the start/end date of depreciation calculation via the period control.

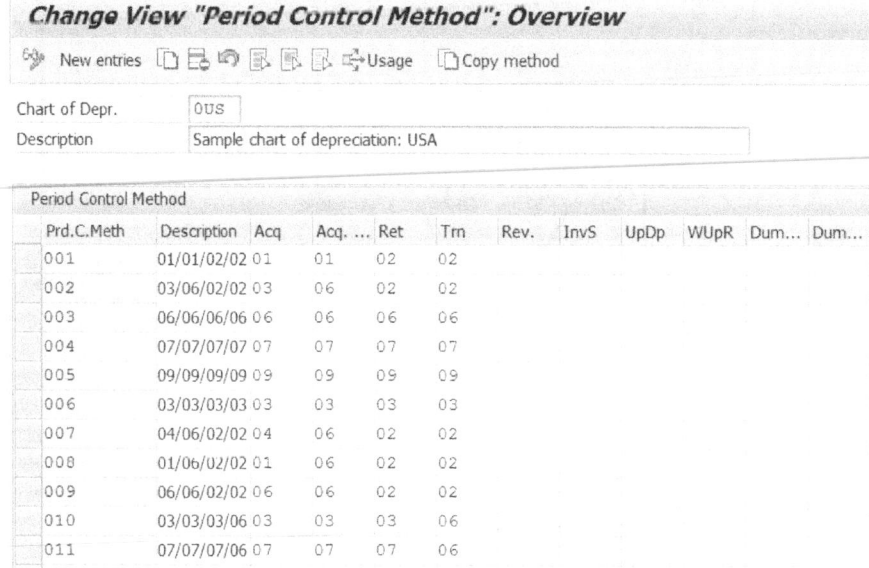

Change View "Period Control Method": Overview

⮑ New entries ⬚ ⬚ ⬚ ⬚ ⬚ ⬚ ⮕Usage ⬚ Copy method

Chart of Depr.   0US
Description   Sample chart of depreciation: USA

Period Control Method

Prd.C.Meth	Description	Acq	Acq. ...	Ret	Trn	Rev.	InvS	UpDp	WUpR	Dum...	Dum...
001	01/01/02/02	01	01	02	02						
002	03/06/02/02	03	06	02	02						
003	06/06/06/06	06	06	06	06						
004	07/07/07/07	07	07	07	07						
005	09/09/09/09	09	09	09	09						
006	03/03/03/03	03	03	03	03						
007	04/06/02/02	04	06	02	02						
008	01/06/02/02	01	06	02	02						
009	06/06/02/02	06	06	02	02						
010	03/03/03/06	03	03	03	06						
011	07/07/07/06	07	07	07	06						

Figure 19.25: Period control method

💡 Transaction Code **AFAMP**

Figure 19.26

The system automatically generates the following important standard period control rules when you first set up the asset accounting Company Code:

- At the beginning of the year
- At the end of the period (beginning in the subsequent year)
- In the first quarter
- In the following half-year
- In the following quarter/following month
- Beginning of year/middle of year/end of year
- First-year convention of a half-year
- In the middle of the period
- In the middle of the quarter
- Pro rata at the start of the period
- Pro rata at the start of the period, up to the middle of the period
- Pro rata in the middle of the period

620. What is a 'Change Over Method'?

During depreciation calculation, it may be necessary to change over to another calculation method to depreciate an asset completely over its economic period. For example, when you use the declining-balance method of calculation, the asset's **net book value** (**NBV**) can never be zero, and hence, you certainly need to change over to another method to achieve zero NBV. To make this happen, you enter a **changeover method** when assigning calculation methods to a depreciation key. The changeover method will specify when the system should change over to a different calculation method. The changeover can also specify the conditions under which the changeover takes place.

To facilitate changing from one depreciation calculation method to another, divide the depreciation into multiple phases in the depreciation key and enter the required changeover method for one or more of these phases (*Figure 19.27*). Then, the system changes to the next calculation method in the next phase as soon as the event defined for the changeover occurs.

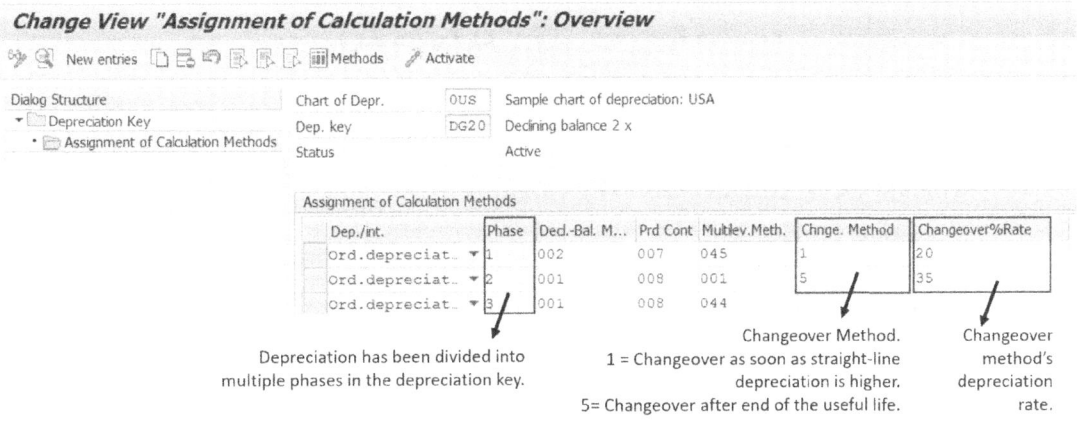

Figure 19.27: Setting up the changeover method in the depreciation key

The possible changeover options include:
- Changeover when the depreciation amount of the changeover method is higher
- Changeover when net book value percentage reached
- Changeover when net book value is less than changeover amount
- Changeover when net book value is less than the straight-line rate
- Changeover after the end of planned useful life
- Changeover in next year as soon as straight-line higher (Poland)
- User-defined changeover using a customer enhancement

621. Explain 'Scrap Value'/ 'Cutoff value'.

In your business, you may come across certain situations wherein you may not want to depreciate some of your fixed assets to their NBV but only to a certain amount, known as **scrap value** or **cutoff value**. SAP allows you to specify time-dependent scrap value for each of the depreciation areas, and you can achieve that in two ways: by entering an absolute scrap value in the asset master record and/or by specifying a scrap value in the depreciation key.

In case specifications in the depreciation key, you will first define a 'scrap value or cutoff value key' in Customizing (use the menu path: *SAP Customizing Implementation Guide | Financial Accounting | Asset Accounting | Depreciation | Valuation Methods | Further Settings | Define the Cutoff Value Key* or Transaction Code **ANHAL**), and then assign the same in the depreciation key (*Figure 19.29*). The system uses the cutoff value key only when you have not maintained any absolute scrap value for the asset in the asset master record or when negative NBV is not allowed for the asset.

Figure 19.28

Change View "Depreciation Key": Details

⚙ New entries 🗋 🖪 ↩ 🖺 🖺 🖳 ✎ Activate

Dialog Structure		
▼ ☐ Depreciation Key	Chart of Depr.	OUS
• ☐ Assignment of Calculation Methods	Description	Sample chart of depreciation: USA
	Dep. key	DG20 Declining balance 2 x
	Status	Active ▼

Maximum Amount		
Cutoff Val. Key	SCH	Scrap value 10 %

No Ordinary Dep. with Special Dep.	☐
No Interest If No Deprec. Is Planned	☐
Period control according to fiscal years	☐
Dep. to the Day	☐
No reduct. in short year	☐

Acq.Only Allowed in Capitalization Year	No
No. of Places	☐

Figure 19.29: *Cutoff value key in the depreciation key*

In an asset master, it is possible that you can maintain the scrap value either as an absolute amount or as a percentage (SAP recommends entering a percentage). If you have maintained both, then the system makes use of the percentage entered. In cases wherein you have defined a scrap value key and an absolute scrap value in the asset master, then the system ignores the cutoff value percentage of the scrap value key and makes use of the scrap value specified in the asset master.

622. What is known as 'Memo Value'?

A standard functionality in SAP is maintaining the **memo value** for each asset. During depreciation, the system decreases the annual planned depreciation in the year of the asset's acquisition by the amount of the memo value that you have defined so that the system will never depreciate the amount blow the memo value. You can define the memo value at the Company Code level or the depreciation area level.

You can maintain the memo value individually or maintain that for all assets in the same depreciation area in one go. You may use the Customizing menu path: *SAP Customizing Implementation Guide | Financial Accounting | Asset Accounting | General Valuation | Amount Specifications (Company Code/Depreciation Area) | Specify Memo Value;* on the resulting pop-up screen, double click on '*Specify Memo Value for Depreciation Areas*' (*Figure 19.31*).

Transaction Code OAYI

Figure 19.30

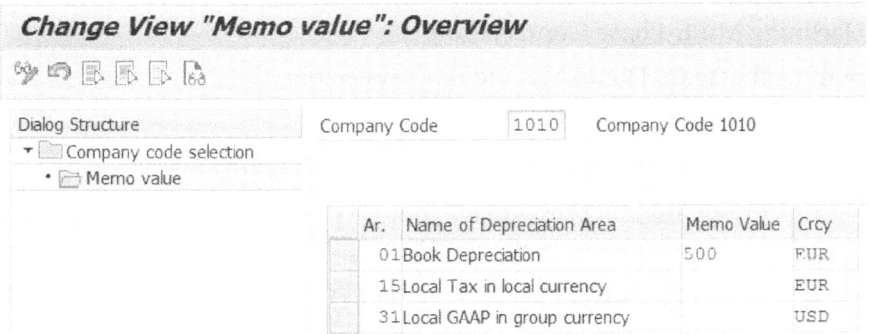

Figure 19.31: Maintaining memo value per depreciation area

While specifying the memo value, you can also exclude certain assets (say, LVA) from maintaining the memo value; you can do this by selecting the appropriate indicator in Customizing. Use the Customizing menu path: *SAP Customizing Implementation Guide | Financial Accounting | Asset Accounting | General Valuation | Amount Specifications (Company Code/Depreciation Area) | Specify Memo Value;* on the resulting pop-up screen, double click on '*Specify Asset Classes without Memo Value*' and enable the checkbox '*Do not take memo value into account*' (*Figure 19.32*).

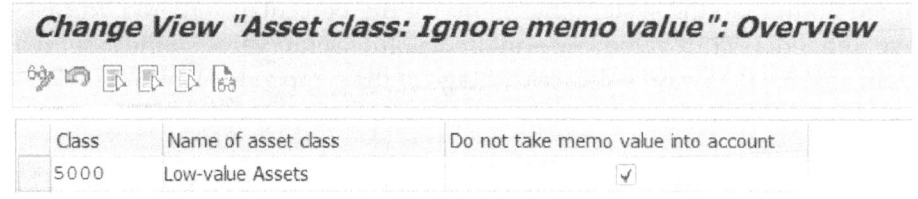

Figure 19.32: Settings for ignoring memo value

Figure 19.33

623. What are the different 'Depreciation Methods' in SAP?

SAP, with different depreciation keys, calculation methods, and the associated parameters, supports the following **depreciation methods**:

- Straight-Line Depreciation over Total Useful Life
- Straight-Line Depreciation from the Book Value over Remaining Useful Life
- Declining-Balance Method of Depreciation
- Declining Multi-Phase Depreciation
- Sum-of-the-Years-Digits Method of Depreciation
- Mean Value Method
- Depreciation for Multiple-Shift Operations and Shutdown
- Unit-of-Production Method of Depreciation

624. Explain 'Straight-Line Depreciation over Total Useful Life.'

In this method, you depreciate the asset uniformly over its expected useful life. However, note that post-capitalization and/or subsequent acquisitions will result in an increase in depreciation by the amount that would have been otherwise necessary to fully depreciate the subsequent acquisition over the original, useful life of the asset. This extends the time necessary to fully depreciate the asset till the book value becomes zero.

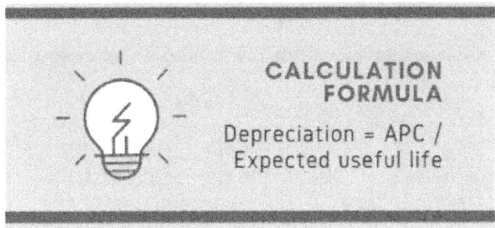

Figure 19.34:

625. Explain 'Straight-Line from the Book Value over Remaining Useful Life'

Here, the book value of the fixed asset is distributed in uniform amounts over the remaining life. Unlike the *straight-line depreciation over the total useful life*, this method ensures that post-capitalization and subsequent acquisitions do not lead to an extension of the expected useful life. As post-capitalization and/or subsequent acquisitions, after the expiration of the specified expected useful life, may result in problems when using this depreciation method, you may need to use the 'changeover method' in the depreciation key after the expiration of the expected useful life.

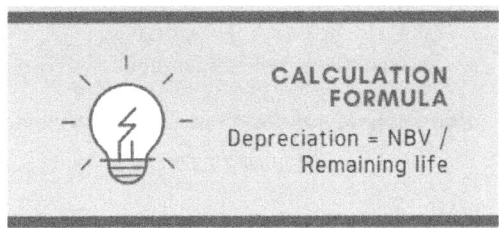

Figure 19.35:

626. Explain the 'Declining-Balance Method of Depreciation.'

Here, you depreciate the fixed asset using a progressively falling depreciation rate. First, you calculate a constant percentage rate from the expected useful life and a given multiplication factor. Next, you multiply that with the falling NBV of the fixed asset. Mathematically, the NBV will never become zero in this method. Hence, you may need to changeover to straight-line or complete depreciation when:

- Declining-balance depreciation < straight-line depreciation
- Net book value < x percent of acquisition value
- Net book value < fixed amount

- Net book value < straight-line depreciation

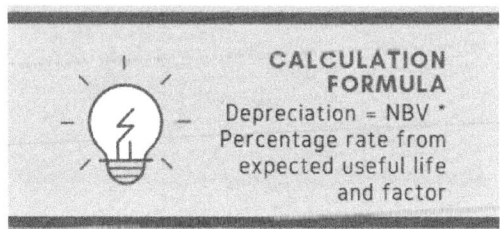

Figure 19.36:

627. Explain 'Declining Multi-Phase Depreciation.'

Here, you specify the rate of depreciation and a validity period for different phases (levels) of depreciation so that you can calculate the depreciation that changes with the defined levels over time (usually decreasing over the phases).

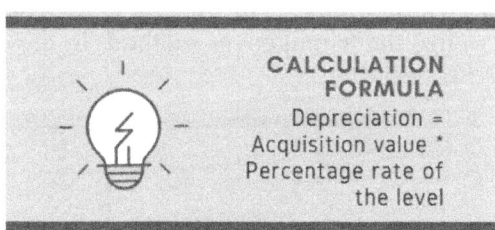

Figure 19.37:

You can define the validity period for each of the levels (by entering the validity for the individual depreciation levels as cumulative values) either on the capitalization date or on the depreciation start date. The change between the phases (of depreciation) need not have to be at the start or end of a fiscal year. In between, you can change to another rate of depreciation during the fiscal year if required.

Let us look at an example:

- APC: 10,000
- Useful life: 50
- Percentage rate year 1-10: 5.00%
- Percentage rate year 11-20: 2.50%
- Percentage rate year 21-30: 1.25%
- Depreciation level 1 = 10,000 * 15.00% = 500
- Depreciation level 2 = 10,000 * 2.50% = 250
- Depreciation level 3 = 10,000 * 1.25% = 125

628. Explain the 'Sum-of-the-Years-Digits Method of Depreciation.'

In this method, for each year of the expected useful life, the system arrives at the remaining useful life for the asset and totals that figure for each year. In each fiscal year, the system divides the remaining life by this total to calculate the depreciation percentage rate for that fiscal year. Such a calculation results in the depreciation amounts being reduced progressively by the same amount per period.

This method does not allow for depreciation after the end of the planned life, as the remaining useful life is no longer defined after the end of the planned useful life. But that does not mean that you cannot change to another method after the expiry of the expected useful life. Since acquisitions after the depreciation start year or post-capitalization generally lead to a positive NBV at the end of planned life, you cannot have such transactions using this method. So, you need to manage the subsequent acquisitions by creating asset sub-numbers. Besides, for this method, the acquisition year must be the same as the start year of depreciation.

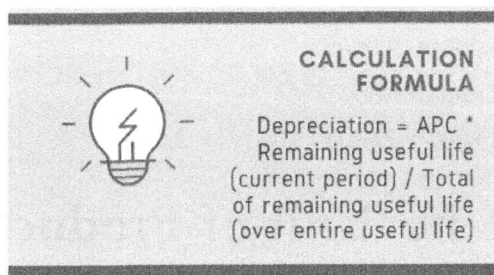

CALCULATION FORMULA

Depreciation = APC * Remaining useful life (current period) / Total of remaining useful life (over entire useful life)

Figure 19.38:

Let us look at an example:

- APC: 10,000
- Useful life: 5
- Total remaining useful life: 15 (= 5+ 4 + 3 +2 +1)
- Depreciation 1st year = 10,000 * 5 / 15 = 3,333.33
- Depreciation 2nd year = 10,000 * 4 / 15 = 2,666.67
- Depreciation 3rd year = 10,000 * 3 / 15 = 2,000.00
- Depreciation 4th year = 10,000 * 2 / 15 = 1,333.33
- Depreciation 5th year = 10,000 * 1 / 15 = 666.67

629. What is known as the 'Mean Value Method' of depreciation?

It is possible to manage the mean value of two depreciation methods in a derived depreciation area. Since the derived depreciation area links the values of the two depreciation areas, you need to identify it as a 'mean value area.' Here, instead of using the arithmetic mean, you can also use proportional values.

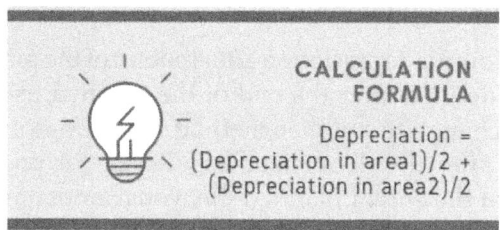

Figure 19.39:

Let us look at an example:

- Depreciation in area A: 3,000
- Depreciation in area B: 1,000
- Depreciation = (3,000 / 2) + (1,000 / 2) = 2,000

630. Explain the 'Unit-of-Production Method' of depreciation.

The **unit-of-production depreciation method** is useful for certain types of assets that require taking fluctuations in production activity into account in depreciation calculation. In this method, the system links the amount of depreciation in the given period directly to the output quantity from the asset.

The depreciation calculation depends on the depreciation method used in the base method of the depreciation key. For forecasting unit-of-production depreciation, you need to have a 'modified depreciation key' dependent on the number of units. You can achieve this by modifying one of the depreciation keys for each total output quantity. To calculate the unit-of-production depreciation, enter the probable total output quantity of the fixed asset or the remaining output. It is possible that you can change the total output quantity, or the remaining output, to the exact periods. This will make the system calculate unit-of-production depreciation based on the new total output quantity or the new remaining output, starting with the period you make the changes. You can also specify the probable output quantity for every depreciation period in fiscal years that are still open. As with any other depreciation method, the system carries out the actual posting of the unit-of-production depreciation via the periodic depreciation posting run.

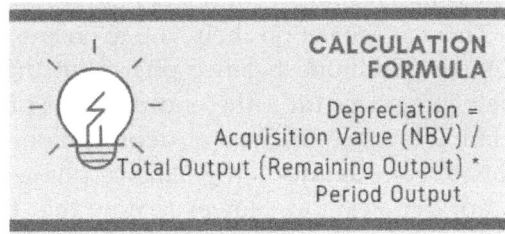

Figure 19.40:

Let us look at an example:

- APC: 50,000
- Total output: 10,000
- Period output: 100
- Depreciation = 50,000 / (10,000 * 100) = 500

631. How to handle depreciation for 'Multiple-Shift Operations'?

When you put assets into multiple shift usage, the assets need to be depreciated more than the normal depreciation. You can calculate the increased depreciation due to multiple shift operations of assets for all types except the 'unit-of-production' depreciation, which is always 100% variable. SAP takes care of multi-shift depreciation by specifying the variable depreciation portion (as a percentage rate) per depreciation area (you can have different percentages in each of the depreciation areas) in the asset master record or asset class depending upon the maintenance level that you have defined in the system, and entering a 'multiple-shift factor' in the asset master record (on the time-dependent data tab); the system multiplies the shift factor entered here by the variable portion of ordinary depreciation.

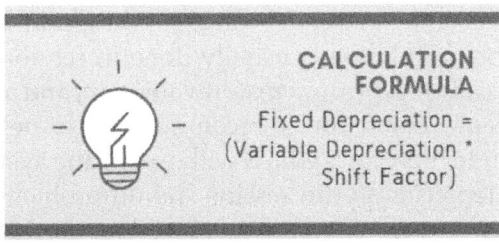

Figure 19.41:

While maintaining the depreciation key, you can specify, for multi-shift usage, whether both depreciation and the expired useful life should be increased, only depreciation should be increased, and not the expired useful life, or neither depreciation nor the expired useful life should be increased. These specifications help you to ensure, say, that the depreciation is to be increased during the declining balance phase but that the straight-line phase continues even after the changeover until the end of the expected useful life. In cases of assets using the declining-balance method of depreciation, the system will increase the depreciation amounts during the declining-balance phase based on the shift factor and the variable portion of depreciation. However, note that the system increases such depreciation only up to the maximum percentage rate that you have already specified in the depreciation key.

632. How does SAP handle depreciation during 'Asset Shutdown'?

When you shutdown an asset for a given period of time, you may be required to suspend the depreciation for that specified period. You can suspend depreciation in such cases by defining the appropriate time interval in the time-dependent data for the asset, setting the 'shutdown indicator' in the asset master record for this interval, and using a depreciation key that allows for such shutdown in the respective depreciation areas. When you make these settings, the system will not calculate depreciation during the shutdown time period. Hence, the useful life of the asset increases over this duration of time. However, when you remove the shutdown indicator in the asset master record, the system resumes depreciation automatically. Note that the shutdown does not influence the calculation of interest for the shutdown period. The system will stop charging interest only when you set the shutdown indicator in the interest calculation key, when the 'no interest if no depreciation is planned' indicator is set in the depreciation key, or when there is no planned depreciation amount for the entire fiscal year.

633. What is 'Depreciation Run' in SAP?

The **depreciation run**, an important periodic processing, takes care of calculating depreciation for the assets and posting the corresponding transactions in both FI-AA and FI-G/L. The depreciation calculation is usually done in sessions, and the *posting session* posts the different depreciation types, interest/revaluation, and also writing-off/allocating special reserves. The depreciation run is recommended to be started with a 'test run' before making it the 'production run', which will update the system. The system provides the facility to restart a depreciation run session should problems arise in the earlier run. The depreciation run needs to be completed per period. During every depreciation run, the system will create summarized posting documents per business area and account determination; no individual posting documents are created.

634. Explain the various steps in a 'Depreciation Run.'

The following are the various steps involved in a depreciation run:

1. Maintain the parameters for the depreciation run on the initial screen (*Figure 19.42*) of the Transaction **AFAB** (Company Code, accounting principle, fiscal year & posting period).

2. Enter the parameters for 'Parallel Processing'.

3. Specify the output options: if you need a total log, a detailed log, or no log output.

4. Enter the details under 'Test Run Parameters,' such as selecting the '*Test Run*' checkbox and the details of asset number and asset sub numbers. Note that it is a good practice to select the 'test run' initially, see and satisfy the outcome of the depreciation run, then remove this 'checkbox' and go for the 'productive run.'

5. Execute the test run (if the assets are less than 10,000 in number, you may then process them in the foreground; otherwise, execute the run in the background).

6. Check the results displayed.

7. Once you are convinced that the test run has gone as expected, go back to the previous screen, uncheck the 'test run' checkbox, and execute (in the background).

8. Complete the 'background print parameters', if prompted by the system. You may also decide to schedule the job immediately or later. The system uses the 'depreciation-posting program' *RABUCH00*, for updating the asset's values and generating a batch input session for updating FI-G/L. The 'posting session' posts values in various depreciation areas, interest, and revaluation, besides updating special reserves allocations and writing-off, if any. If there are more than 100,000 assets for depreciation calculation and posting, you need to use a special program *RAPOST00*.

9. Process the 'batch input session' created by the system in step 7 above. You may use the Transaction Code **SM35**. Again, you have the option of processing the session in the foreground or the background.

10. The system posts the depreciation in FI-G/L.

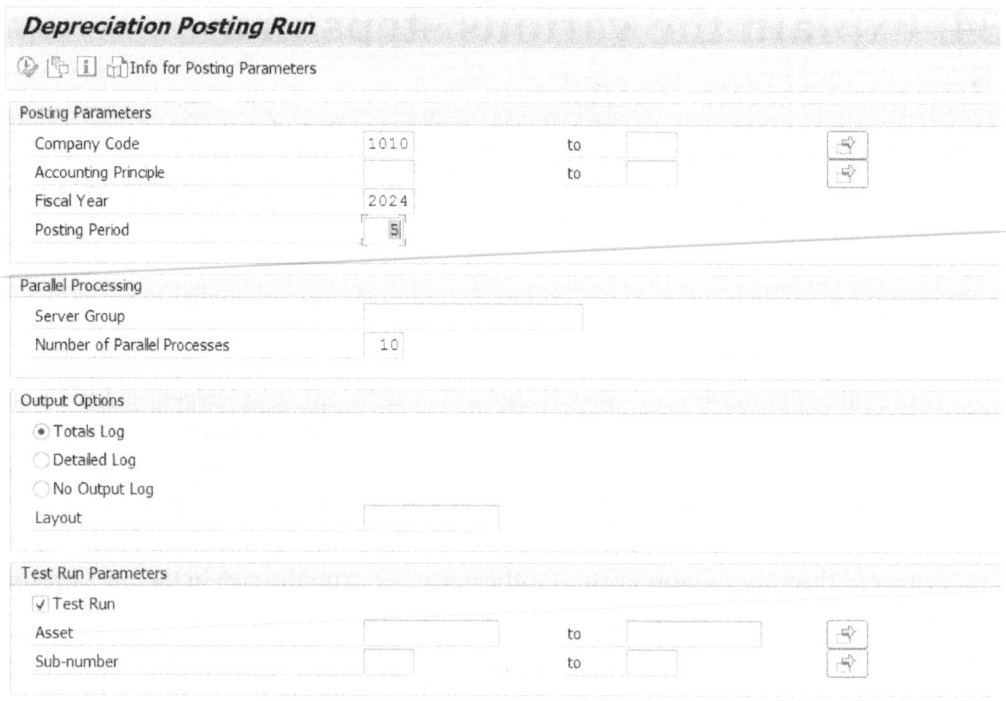

Figure 19.42: Depreciation run: Initial screen

635. How does the system calculate the 'Depreciation'?

The **system calculates the depreciation** by the following means:

1. The system takes the 'depreciation terms' from the asset master record and calculates the annual depreciation for the asset, considering the 'useful life' and the 'depreciation key'. The start date for depreciation is assumed to be the first date of acquisition of the asset.

2. The system may also calculate other values like interest, revaluation etc.,

3. As shown in point 2, the depreciation and other values are calculated for each of the depreciation areas.

636. Explain 'Derived Depreciation.'

The **derived depreciation** is a separate depreciation area that is 'derived' from two or more 'real depreciation' areas using a pre-determined rule. You may use this to calculate something like *special reserves* or to show the difference in local and group valuation etc. Since the values are derived, the system does not store any values in the database. Still, it updates the derived values whenever there are changes in the real depreciation area or its depreciation terms. You may also use the derived depreciation only for reporting purposes.

637. What is known as a 'Repeat Run' in the depreciation process?

A **repeat run** is normally used at the end of the fiscal year to carry out posting adjustments or corrections that may arise due to changes in depreciation terms or manual depreciation calculations. However, you can repeat only within the same posting period. You also can restrict the calculations to specific assets in a repeat run.

638. What is 'Restart a Depreciation Run'?

Restart depreciation run is used only when there is a problem with the previous depreciation run, resulting in the termination of that run. To make sure that all the steps in a depreciation run are completed without errors, the system logs the status at every stage of the processing and provides 'error logs' to find out the problem. This option of 'restart' is not available during the 'test run' mode.

639. What is 'Depreciation Simulation'?

Depreciation simulation refers to the 'what if' valuation of assets. This is achieved by changing and experimenting with the 'parameters' required for depreciating the assets. The simulation helps you to 'foresee' what the depreciation would be should there be changes in various 'depreciation terms.' You may simulate to see the valuation for the future fiscal years. Sort versions and options for total reports are also available in the simulation. The depreciation simulation can be applied to a single asset or your entire asset portfolio.

640. What is a 'Sort Version'?

The **sort version** defines the formation of groups and totals in an asset report. You can use all the fields of the asset master record as group and/or sort criteria to define a sort version. The sort version cannot have more than five *sort levels*.

641. Explain the 'Year Closing' in FI-AA.

The year-end is closed when you draw the final balance sheet. However, to reach this stage, you need to ensure that the depreciation is posted properly: you can achieve this by checking the 'depreciation list' and also the 'asset history sheet.' After this is done, draw a test balance sheet and profit & loss statement, and check for the correctness of the depreciation. Correct the discrepancies, if any, by adjusting postings. You may need to re-run the depreciation posting program if you change any depreciation values.

When you now run the Year-End Closing Program, the system ensures that the fiscal year has been closed for all the assets, depreciation has been fully posted, and there were no errors logged for any of the assets. If there were errors, you need to correct them before re-running the year-end program. When you reach a stage where there is no error, the system will update the last closed fiscal year for each of the depreciation areas for each asset. The system will also block any further postings in FI-AA for the closed fiscal year. If you need to re-open the closed fiscal year for any adjustments postings or otherwise, ensure that you re-run the year-end program so that the system blocks further postings.

642. Explain the 'Asset History Sheet.'

SAP comes with country-specific **asset history sheets** that meet the country's legal reporting requirements. The asset history sheet is one of the important reports that can be used either as the year-end report or an intermediate report. It is a list showing the history of fixed assets from their opening balance to the closing balance using acquisitions (including subsequent acquisitions besides the initial one), retirements, asset transfers, and accumulated depreciation.

Asset history sheets help you to freely define the report layout, headers, and most of the history sheet items. You can configure asset history sheets using the Customizing menu '*SAP Customizing Implementation Guide | Financial Accounting | Asset Accounting | Information System | Asset History Sheet*' (*Figure 19.43*).

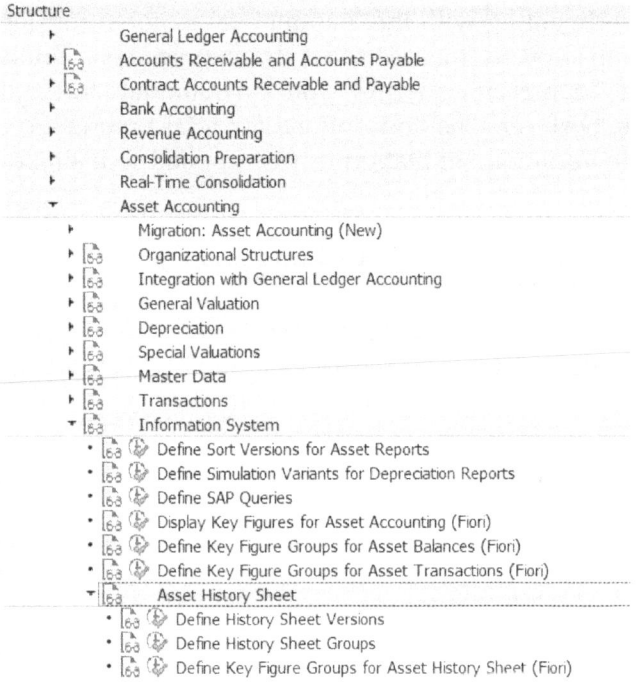

Figure 19.43: *Configuring asset history sheet*

There are several standard asset history sheet versions available as default (*Figure 19.44*) that you can use without making any changes. They include versions that display the following:

- Total depreciation
- Acquisition values
- Asset history sheet in compliance with EC directives
- Transferred reserves
- Special reserves

Choose Asset History Sheet Version

Details   New Entries

Asset hist. sheet versions

Langu...	Hist.Sht.Vers.	Asset History Sheet Name
EN	01	In compl. w/EC directive 4 (13 col.,wide version)
EN	0002	In compliance with EC directive 4 (13 col.)
EN	0003	Depreciation by depreciation type
EN	0004	Acquisition values
EN	0005	Asset Register (Italy)
EN	0006	Cost-accouting w/revaluation (derived from HGB2)
EN	0007	Transferred reserves
EN	0008	History of res.for spec.depr.
EN	0009	History version for data-collection program in EIS
EN	0010	Asset history sheet - Denmark
EN	0011	Asset history sheet - Denmark (wide version)
EN	0012	Asset history sheet - Russian Federation
EN	0013	Transfer curr-yr acq./ret. as transfer (ver. 0001)

Figure 19.44: Standard asset history sheet versions

If you need new versions, you can define them in the system (Transaction Code **OA79**). For each of these new versions, you will be able to define various columns according to your requirements, following the guidelines that column 00 represents initial values, column 99 represents final values, and columns 01 to 06 represent intermediate values (*Figure 19.45*)

Maintain Asset History Sheet Version: EN 0006

Details   Left column   Right column

Ast.Hist.Sht.Version	0006	Cost-accouting w/revaluation (derived from HGB2)
Language Key	EN	

☐ Hist.sheet complete

Hist. sheet positions

		Column 00	Column 10	Column 20	Column 30	Column 40
Line	02	APC FY start	Acquisition	Retirement	Transfer	Post-capital.
Line	04	Dep. FY start	Dep. for year	Dep.retir.	Dep.transfer	Dep.post-cap.
Line	06	Bk.val.FY strt				
Line						
Line						

Figure 19.45: Field Positions in an asset history sheet version

643. Explain 'Asset History Sheet Groups.'

The **asset history sheet groups** contain the various asset transaction types grouped. Each asset history sheet group is associated with a particular 'transaction type group' containing the respective transaction types. The standard SAP system consists of all the required asset history sheet groups for the standard versions of the asset history sheet (*Figure 19.46*). Besides the standard groups, SAP also comes with three special asset history sheet groups: YA (values at the beginning of the fiscal year), YY (values during the fiscal year), and YZ (values at the end of the fiscal year).

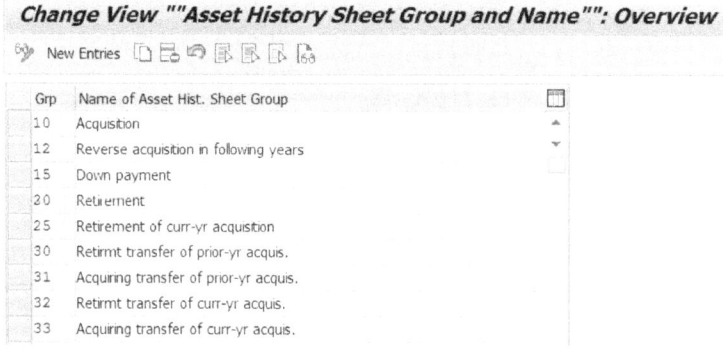

Figure 19.46: Standard asset history sheet groups

It is recommended that you use the asset history sheet groups delivered in the standard SAP system without defining your own. You should create new asset history sheet groups (Transaction Code **OAV9**) only if you want transaction types from the same transaction type group to flow into different positions of the history sheet.

644. What is an 'Asset Explorer'?

Asset Explorer is a handy and convenient single-interface transaction that helps you display asset values, depreciation details, etc., in a very user-friendly way. Gone are the days when you had to move to different pages and re-enter the same transaction many times to display the details of different assets.

Using Asset Explorer, you have the convenience of:

- Calling up various asset reports
- Currency converted views
- Displaying asset values, both planned and posted, for any number of depreciation areas from the same page but in various tab pages
- Displaying depreciation calculation function and, if necessary, recalculation of depreciation
- Distinguishing between real and derived depreciation areas with two differentiating symbols

- Jumping to the asset master, cost center master, or GLG/L account master
- Looking at the various transactions relating to an asset
- Looking up all the values for different fiscal years
- Moving from one asset number to the other effortlessly

Asset Explorer is designed for easy navigation, with the following sections (*Figure 19.47*):

- **Asset values window**: The top-left area/window is the 'asset values' window, which is in a tree-like structure expanding to various depreciation areas like 01, 03, 10, etc. By selecting any one of these depreciation areas, you will be able to view the value of an asset in the 'asset value details window.'

- **Objects related to the asset window**: This is also on the left-hand side of the display page, just below the 'asset values window.' A drill-down tree-like structure allows you to navigate between cost centers and G/L accounts relating to the asset.

- **Asset value detail window (with tab pages)**: This is the main window on the right, usually occupying most of the page area. Here, you will see information like Company Code, asset number selected, fiscal year, etc. This window comprises two completely resizable components: the top area displays the asset values, and the bottom shows the asset transactions.

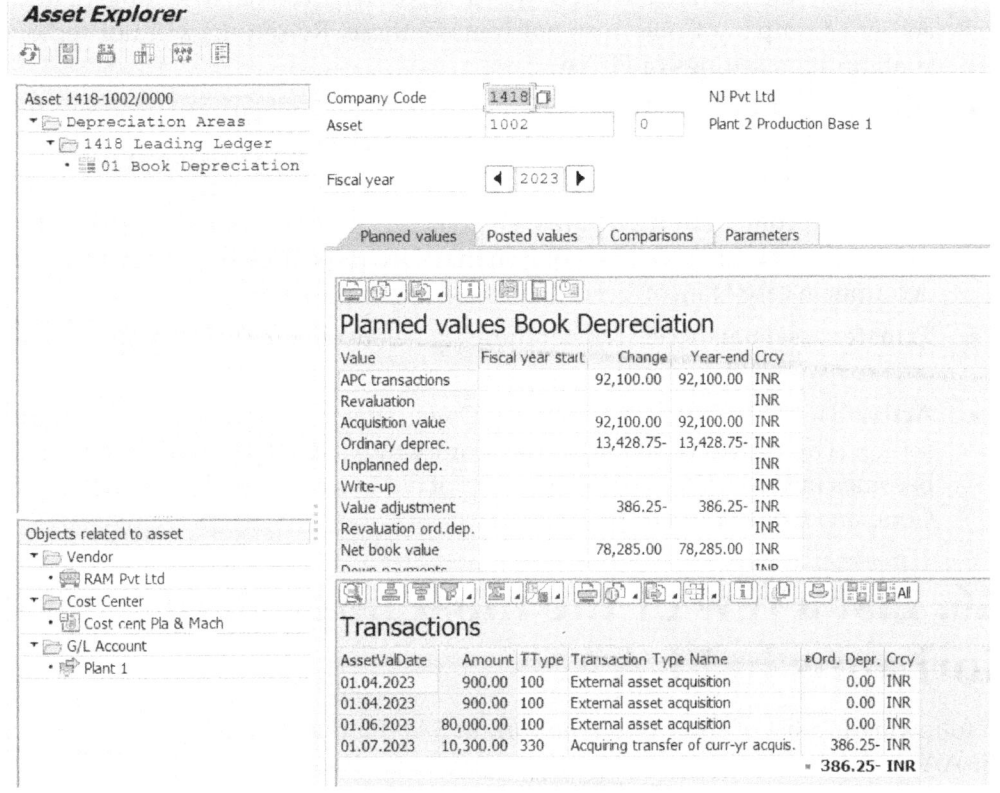

Figure 19.47: *Asset explorer*

Figure 19.48

645. Explain 'Production Set-up' in FI-AA.

The **production set-up** is a collection of logical steps in FI-AA to ensure that all the required configurations and activities are in place for making the asset accounting Company Code 'productive.' This includes the following:

- **Consistency check**: This will enable you to analyze errors, if any, in FI-AA configuration (in defining the chart of depreciation, in the assignment of Company Code to the chart of depreciation, in the definition of depreciation areas, asset classes, G/L account assignments, etc.).

- **Reset Company Code**: As you will have test data, before the Company Code becomes productive, resetting the Company Code is necessary to delete all this data. Note that this is possible only when the Company Code is in 'test' status. All the master records and values will be removed only from FI-AA. You need to remove all the FI and CO values separately, as the re-setting of the asset account Company Code does not remove these. Re-setting will not remove any configuration settings of FI-AA.

- **Reset posted depreciation**: This step is required when errors occur during a previous depreciation run. It is possible only when the asset Company Code is in the 'test' status.

- **Set/reset reconciliation accounts**: Define G/L accounts for FI-AA reconciliation if they have not been done already. You may also reset already defined reconciliation accounts in case of incorrect account assignments earlier.

- **Transfer asset balances**: Transfer the asset balances to the G/L accounts defined as *asset reconciliation accounts*.

- **Activate asset accounting Company Code**: This is the last step in the production set-up. The previous status of the Company Code (test status/transfer status) becomes invalid now. No more transfer of old asset data is allowed when the asset Company Code becomes productive.

646. List a few of the most important SAP Fiori apps in FI-AA.

The following is a list of some of the important SAP Fiori apps that you will come across in FI-AA:

- **Asset accounting overview**: This analytical SAP Fiori app is meant for the asset accountant. Using this app, you can view key information and KPIs within FI-AA. This app is the central source of information, and you can enable several 'cards' based on your requirements. For example, under 'asset balances' you can enable cards like 'asset balances' (that show the total planned asset NBV as at the end of the fiscal year/period that you have mentioned), 'asset balances - chart view' (that shows the total planned asset NBV in chart form), 'asset depreciation values' (that shows the asset depreciation values for the selected fiscal year/period), 'assets under construction' (that shows AuC in the fiscal year/period selected), 'depreciation to be posted' (that shows the value of depreciation type for the fiscal year/period) and 'origin of assets' (that shows the asset origin either by country/region or by supplier for the fiscal year/period selected). You may also enable other cards under the grouping 'Asset Transactions' and 'Other Cards.' However, be aware that when you enable many cards, you will see a noticeable drop in system performance.

- **Asset history sheet**: Using this app, you can bring up the asset history sheet. As you know, the asset history sheet displays the value changes to the fixed asset balances in a fiscal year for a given depreciation area. Using the asset history sheet values, you can document and explain the balances on fixed assets for management purposes for every accounting principle. You may use SAP's pre-configured key figure groups, such as acquisitions, retirements, transfers, and depreciation, to customize the asset history sheet layouts. If required, you can also define new key figure groups to define your layouts and report granularity. It is possible that you can exclude deactivated assets from showing up in the asset history sheet by using the 'Deactivation' option on the filter. However, note that when you use this filter, the app will not display the assets that have been deactivated before the selected fiscal year; that is, you will still see those deactivated assets if they have been deactivated in the selected fiscal year.

- **Asset master worklist**: With this SAP Fiori transactional app, you can display a worklist of assets to get a quick overview of the status of all assets in the worklist. Besides displaying the assets according to criteria like Company Code or asset class, you can refine the display list, for example, to show only the retired assets or incomplete ones. With the app, you can view the master data of any asset in the work list. You can search for a particular asset easily using the app filter bar.

- **Asset transactions**: With this SAP Fiori transactional app, you can check & evaluate daily operations in FI-AA. With the SAP **standard key figure** (**SKF**) groups, you can select asset transactions by group (like acquisitions, retirements, or transfers). The app will display all transactions for the selected key figure groups; for example, retirements will be listed with retirement revenues or costs, gains, losses, retired APC, and book value. However, when you select the 'Retirement view' in this app, you will see the results for 'Retirement Gain' and 'Retirement Loss' only if your configuration allows postings of asset retirement gain and loss to G/L.

- **Create asset**: This is not an SAP Fiori app *per se* but is an SAP GUI for HTML transactions. However, these classic transactions are available in the SAP Fiori theme, enabling a seamless user experience across the SAP Fiori launchpad that provides a harmonized UI across solutions (on-premises and cloud). Through this app, it is possible that you can create a single asset or multiple assets (of the same type). When you create multiple assets of the same type, decide if you want to copy all the fields of the first asset to the rest or if you want to overwrite certain pre-defined fields in each asset. In case of a completely new asset, enter the correct asset class besides the Company Code in the initial screen of the asset master data creation transaction. If you are adding to an already existing asset, identify the existing asset's main number and create the asset sub-number (the system will determine the correct asset class from the asset main number that you have entered).

- **Fixed asset (S/4HANA)**: This is a fact sheet in SAP Fiori apps. This object page displays contextual information about the Fixed Asset business object. From here, you can navigate to its related business objects and related transactional apps, and you can also access related transactions in ABAP back-end systems.

- **Manage Fixed Assets**: This transactional SAP Fiori app provides all the data for an asset in one place. It provides you with a graphical illustration of the asset's life cycle, allowing you to get a quick overview of the asset's status and enabling you to adjust the valuation. The key figures like APC, accumulated depreciation, NBV, etc., enable you to understand the asset's valuation from where you can find out if there were any unexpected value changes. With this app, you can also get an overview of all parallel depreciation areas in one place and a deep dive into the details of each depreciation area. You will also be able to see the related journal entries/transactions. In short, you will be in a position to see how an asset's values are evolving over a period of time. To access this app, use the 'Display Asset Maset Worklist' app. From there, select any fixed asset master data and then navigate to this 'Manage Fixed Assets' app via the link or the navigation arrow. You can also reach this app from some of the reporting apps like 'Asset History Sheet', 'Asset Balances', 'Depreciation List', 'Asset Transactions, etc.

- **Schedule asset accounting jobs**: You can use this SAP Fiori app to schedule asset accounting jobs. In doing so, you will use templates like 'Recalculate Depreciation' and 'Depreciation Posting Run'. You can use the scheduling option to schedule the job or start immediately. While scheduling, you can set up a recurring schedule, including stipulations to handle non-working days.

Index